Corrective Reading Techniques

FOR THE CLASSROOM TEACHER

Second Edition

JOAN P. GIPE
University of New Orleans

(iSP

Gorsuch Scarisbrick, Publishers
Scottsdale, Arizona

To Charlie, Daisy, and
the memory of Maisy

Editor: *John Gorsuch*
Developmental Editor: *Gay L. Orr*
Production Manager: *Carol H. Blumentritt*
Sales & Marketing: *Sandra Byrd*
Cover Design: *Nancy Paquin*
Typesetting: *Publication Services*
Printing & Binding: *BookCrafters*

Gorsuch Scarisbrick, Publishers
8233 Via Paseo del Norte, Suite F-400
Scottsdale, Arizona 85258

10 9 8 7 6 5 4 3 2 1

ISBN 0-89787-531-1

Copyright © 1987, 1991 by Gorsuch Scarisbrick, Publishers

Printed in the United States of America.

Contents

Preface

This text was written with two groups of people in mind: (1) undergraduate students enrolled in teacher education programs that include a practicum or field experience allowing each student to work with disabled readers and (2) classroom teachers who wish to expand their repertoire of techniques for working with disabled readers. My goal is to provide preservice and classroom teachers with both a guide and a resource for meeting the needs of disabled readers who are part of every classroom.

An effort is made to present techniques appropriate to, or easily modified for, any level from the primary grades through secondary school. Corrective readers can certainly be older readers having difficulty with, for example, some aspect of content area reading.

This text provides the reader with strategies for (1) recognizing a reader with problems, (2) identifying that reader's specific strengths and weaknesses, and (3) planning instruction that takes into account the basic skills needed to perform a certain reading task. A philosophy for implementing this kind of analytic approach to reading instruction is included.

The text consists of three major sections: part I, "Foundations," part II, "The Major Domains," and part III, "Other Considerations." Part I introduces the nature of corrective reading, describes the analytic approach to be taken throughout the text, and discusses formal and informal measures to assess and evaluate reading performance. Part II provides specific analytic and instructional strategies for the major reading domains of word recognition, comprehension, and study skills and strategic reading. Emphasis is given to comprehension-fostering and comprehension-monitoring instruction. The extensive coverage of instructional strategies for all the reading domains is viewed as a strength of this text. Part III discusses the special topics of linguistically variant children and reading-related factors such as physical, psychological, and environmental correlates. The section ends with suggestions for implementing an analytic approach in the classroom. This text organization corresponds especially well to a course organization that includes a practicum or clinic experience. While a theoretical basis is provided for the suggestions made throughout the text, and many citations are given, the overall flavor of the text is more applied than theoretical.

Certain format features aid learning from the text. Each chapter begins with an extended study outline, a list of learning objectives, and important vocabulary. Each chapter in parts I and II also features an overview that can be read before the chapter and again afterwards as a synthesis. These features help (1) the reader in preparing to read each chapter and again in studying for examinations and (2) the instructor in anticipating topics that need additional explanation or hands-on experience. The appendixes provide specific aids for determining readability of written material and for assessing readers' attitudes toward reading and self-concept.

Thanks to colleagues and students across the country, and the staff at Gorsuch Scarisbrick, this text has gone into a second edition. While the intended audience, major sections, order of chapters, and the focus on the analytic process have not changed, the number of detailed examples for instructional strategies has been increased. Also, the suggestions for instruction focus more on use of whole text. One chapter, chapter 10, has been renamed "Strategic Reading," as opposed to "Study Strategies," since the actual emphasis of that chapter is on strategies that readers should use while reading *any* text, not reading just for study purposes. Specific study strategies are still a part of that chapter, however.

In summary, the feedback I have received from my own students, and other instructors and students who have used the first edition, has provided the impetus for the changes reflected in this edition. I sincerely thank *all* of those people, and hope all of you will find this second edition even more helpful than the first.

PART I

Foundations

CHAPTER 1

Fundamental Aspects of Corrective Reading

Objectives

After you have read this chapter, you should be able to

1. identify dimensions of the reading process;
2. explain the importance of teachers developing a set of beliefs about reading;
3. describe the difference between a process approach and a product approach to reading instruction;
4. define corrective reading instruction;
5. explain how corrective reading is part of a developmental reading program;
6. describe characteristics of corrective readers;
7. define underachiever;
8. discuss the advantages and disadvantages of comparing reading achievement and reading potential.

Study Outline

I. Introduction

II. Dimensions of reading
   A. Reading as a language process
   B. Reading as a cognitive process
   C. Reading as a psychological or affective process
   D. Reading as a physiological process

III. Beliefs about reading
   A. Current views
   B. Personal beliefs

IV. Three major goals of every reading program
   A. Developmental reading
   B. Functional reading
   C. Recreational reading

V. What is corrective reading?
   A. Types of reading instruction
   B. The corrective reading program

VI. Who is the corrective reader?
   A. Characteristics of corrective readers
   B. Comparing achievement and potential

VII. Summary

VIII. References

Important Vocabulary and Concepts

accelerated instruction

achievement

adapted instruction

aliterates

cognition

corrective instruction

developmental instruction

developmental program

graphophonics

language

language comprehension

language production

listening comprehension

morphology

phonology

potential

pragmatics

remedial instruction

semantics

syntax

underachievers

Overview

This chapter reviews basic concepts about the reading process in general and explains the importance of developing a set of beliefs about reading in order to establish an effective reading program. The review of basic concepts of developmental reading is brief, but this does not mean that learnings from a first course in reading instruction are considered unimportant. They form the foundation for the content in this text and are essential in expanding your knowledge about teaching reading.

We begin this chapter by defining corrective reading and describing characteristics of corrective readers, which will assist you in the process of helping students in your classroom who have reading problems. The basic concept of underachievement, which is central to any discussion of readers having problems, is introduced and discussed at length. This chapter is only a beginning, however. The rest of the text, and courses in reading that you may take in the future, will give you more knowledge and insight regarding the reading process and helping students who experience breakdowns in the reading process.

Introduction

Teaching children to read is one of the most important tasks facing the elementary school teacher. Learning to read opens the door to learning almost anything. Reading provides a source of information and enjoyment, and children who have been read to before entering school are already aware of its benefits. Most children, upon entering school, look forward to learning how to read. Unfortunately, not all children are successful.

The many methods and approaches used to teach reading work with most students. But what goes wrong for the others? What does or does not happen in the process of teaching reading that hinders a child in learning to read? To answer these questions, we need to understand the reading process.

Dimensions of Reading

The reading process is complex. How it actually works is not yet clear, but some aspects that usually interact during the process can be identified.

Reading as a Language Process

Language enables individuals to communicate, that is, give and receive information, thoughts, and ideas. Before learning to read and write, children give and receive information by speaking and listening. For children to become successful readers, they must be successful language users.

Some components of language important to the reading process are phonology, syntax, morphology, and semantics. Briefly, **phonology** refers to the system of speech sounds, **syntax** to word order and the way words are combined into phrases and sentences, **morphology** to the internal structure of words and meaningful word parts (prefixes, suffixes, word endings and inflections, compound words), and **semantics** to word meanings or to understanding the concepts represented by the language (Cole & Cole, 1981).

While reading is basically an act of communication between an author and a reader, it is only one aspect of the communication process. Reading, writing, speaking, and listening are inseparable and must be seen as interrelated and developing concurrently.

Communication does not exist in a vacuum. Usually a message has both a sender and a receiver. The sender has specific intentions and produces a message that is reconstructed by the receiver. The sophisticated system through which meaning is expressed is **language.** The sender uses this system for particular functions, such as sharing a personal experience, asking a question, or complaining. The sender can also use language to persuade, inspire, comfort, or encourage others.

Sending a message is called **language production,** which can be either oral or written; receiving or decoding the message is **language comprehension.** Speaking, therefore, is the production of oral language, while listening is the comprehension of oral language. Similarly, writing and reading are the production and comprehension, respectively, of written language.

The four aspects of language can also be compared in other ways. Reading and listening share common receptive and constructive processes, while writing and speaking share common expressive processes. As Fox and Allen (1983) state:

> Writing suggests the reading of one's compositions by others and the input that reading experiences can give to written language. In addition, speaking will be drawn out with writing because it is the other expressive skill. Since oral language initially precedes written language, experiences in oral composition influence success in written composition. Listening, the remaining segment, is firmly attached to speaking and reading. . . . because the language that one hears, especially the "story language" one hears when books are read aloud or when stories are told, is another source of written expression. (p. 12)

Schallert, Kleiman, and Rubin (1977) summarize some of the differences between oral and written language. Oral and written language can differ in physical characteristics; speech transmits auditory information, while writing transmits visual information. Speech is usually temporary, while writing is more permanent. Speech has additional meaningful clues, such as intonation, stress, and rhythm, and nonverbal clues, such as gestures or eye expressions. On the other hand, listeners do not have the luxury of previewing speech for organization or main points, while good readers usually sample a text and skim, scan, skip, and reread.

A firm language base is crucial to success in reading. Children generally bring to school a wealth of language and cultural experiences upon which teachers can build literacy. Goodman (1973) demonstrated, through analyzing the oral reading behaviors of children, that children use specific language cues to predict meaning in the reading comprehension process. These he terms the *graphophonic*, *syntactic*, and *semantic* cue systems. As users of language, children bring to school expectations about language that are basic to their ability to make sense of printed text. For example, assume a child encounters the unknown word sidewalk in the sentence "The dog ran down the ____." The child may rely on one or all of the following: (1) the syntactic cue system, which indicates the unknown word is a noun; (2) the semantic cue system, which indicates the possible words that would make sense (e.g., street, alley, path, stairs, hill, sidewalk, and so on) in the context of the sentence; and (3) the graphophonic cue system, which provides sound and symbol clues, in this case, an initial sound of *s,* a final sound of *k,* and a possible long *i* because of the vowel-consonant-silent *e* pattern. Additionally, language is only really meaningful "when functioning in some environment" (Halliday, 1978, p. 28). Therefore, language users also develop a **pragmatic cue system**; that is, rules related to the use of language in context. For example, the sentence "This is bad" can be interpreted several ways depending on the context of the situation. Consider the two different meanings of the sentence if it is spoken following a mother finding a small child pulling everything out of the kitchen cabinets or by two teenagers enjoying a dance.

Engelmann (1969) describes another situation that reflects the importance of language to success in reading. If a child is able to read a sentence, for example, "The brown dog is not mine," and not understand it, this may not be a reading problem, but a language problem. For instance, for a child whose first language is Spanish, the order in which the words occur may not communicate meaning. Because language is so critical as an underlying process for success in reading, children who are linguistically variant require special attention. This topic is discussed in more depth in chapter 11, "Developing Reading of Linguistically Variant Children."

Reading as a Cognitive Process

Cognition refers to the nature of knowing and intellectual development. A child's ability to form concepts is basic to cognition. Early or prelanguage concepts are cognitive, that is, young children develop ways of organizing and understanding their experiences even before acquiring language (Bowerman, 1976). Forming concepts, then, is an attempt to classify one's experiences. When young children call all men "Daddy," they are demonstrating that they have formed a concept of "Daddy" as a man. However, they have not yet learned to distinguish that "Daddy" has the specific attribute of a man who is *their* father.

The more experience children have with their environment, and the richer that environment, the more concepts they develop. A limited conceptual development affects reading. Even if a child recognizes the words, understanding is hindered unless those words represent some familiar concepts. Active involvement with their world provides children with the necessary background for concept development and, ultimately, for literacy development. Cognitive development is crucial to reading comprehension, and is discussed in more detail in chapter 7, "Reading Comprehension: Part I."

Reading comprehension also depends on the child's ability to reason, perceive relationships among concepts, remember, and use information, that is, the child's intellectual ability. Intelligence as a reading-related factor is further discussed in chapter 12, "Reading-Related Factors."

Reading as a Psychological or Affective Process

The child's self-concept, attitudes in general, attitudes toward reading, interests and motivation for reading affect the reading process. Each of these factors is closely related to the child's experiential background in both home and community.

Psychological factors are crucial in helping students either to learn to read or to improve their reading. The desire to learn or improve reading must be present; unless success is experienced, the tendency is to avoid the reading situation. This is only human nature; all of us avoid the things we do poorly.

Developing positive self-concepts and attitudes is often the most important part of a student's reading program. This important dimension of the reading process is discussed in more detail in chapter 12, "Reading-Related Factors," and in chapter 13, "Analytic Teaching."

Reading as a Physiological Process

Anticipating the reading act in turn activates the language and cognitive processes (i.e., nonvisual information). However, for reading to proceed, printed stimuli (i.e., visual information) must also be received by the brain. These stimuli normally enter through a visual process. If a reader is blind, the stimuli may enter through a tactile process, as in using braille, or through auditory means, as in listening to a taped reading. Under normal circumstances the reader must be able to focus on the printed stimuli, move the eyes from left to right, make return sweeps, discriminate likenesses and differences, and discriminate figure-ground relationships. In addition to visual acuity, physiological factors include good health, auditory acuity, and neurological functioning. These physiological factors and other reading-related factors, such as intelligence and social-emotional and environmental factors, are discussed in chapter 12, "Reading-Related Factors."

Beliefs about Reading

Reading is a complex human endeavor. Edmund Huey (1908) believed that a complete description of the reading process would be the psychologists' greatest achievement, equivalent to explaining the intricate workings of the human mind. Gibson and Levin (1975) believe that reading is not just one process, but many, with distinctions between the beginning reader, the developing reader, and the mature reader. No matter how complex reading is, however, teachers are expected to teach children to read and must have some insight into the dimensions of reading as a process. Teachers also must develop a personal philosophy about reading.

Lamb (1980) points out that one's beliefs about reading make a significant difference in the methods and materials used to teach children to read. This is also supported by recent research on teachers' theoretical orientations toward reading (Richards, 1985). Teachers who believe that the reading process basically involves learning predetermined skills will undoubtedly stress skills. Those who believe that reading is primarily learning to process language in print will approach its teaching quite differently. The authors of reading materials often reflect their own beliefs about reading in the materials they produce. Thus a teacher's beliefs and methods may be in harmony with the materials used, but the opposite is also possible.

Current Views

The great reading debate has changed in recent years from an instructional emphasis on meaning versus an instructional emphasis on decoding during the early grades (Chall, 1967) to what some characterize as the process versus product debate (Robinson, 1977). The process side is supported by cognitive psychologists (Doctorow, Wittrock, & Marks, 1978; Rumelhart, 1980; Spiro, 1980; Spiro & Myers, 1984; Thorndyke, 1976, 1977; Wittrock, 1978), psycholinguists (Anderson, 1977; Goodman, 1968, 1973, 1979; Smith, 1988), and other educators (Clay, 1972; Rhodes & Dudley-Marling, 1988; Weaver, 1988) who are deeply concerned that instruction should focus on the cognitive and language processes. They believe a process emphasis will help students to understand what they are reading better. Generally this group of educators has responded strongly and negatively to a skills approach, which emphasizes the products of reading. Process supporters take a more holistic approach, claiming that children should be exposed to a form of reading instruction more like the process of learning to talk. They avoid fragmenting and fractionalizing reading, suggesting that children learn to read by reading prose material, without being subjected to learning unneeded and nonproven skills or bits and pieces of words (e.g., synthetic phonics), which they consider counterproductive in learning to read.

Holistic approaches (also referred to as whole language approaches) take a developmental view of children's literacy growth, and are represented in the works of Ashton-Warner (1963), Harste, Woodward, and Burke (1984), Holdaway (1979), Newman (1985), Rhodes and Dudley-Marling (1988), and Weaver (1988). The focus is on children's strengths, not their weaknesses. All learning activities are based on interest and needs and are placed in meaningful contexts. Students are encouraged to integrate new information with what they have already learned. Holistic approaches do not fragment learning, so not only are reading, writing, listening and speaking integrated, but they are integrated *across* the curriculum. In other words, learning is not subdivided into artificial subject area time periods. Such programs generally encourage students to take an active part in their own learning, with much cooperation and collaboration among students and teachers. According to Harste, Woodward, and Burke (1984) these programs are "littered with literacy," both professionally published and student-authored works.

Skills-centered approaches to teaching reading, with a focus on reading products, can be represented by the works of Collins and Cheek (1989), Harris and Smith (1980), Mangrum and Forgan (1979), Otto (1977), and Otto and Smith (1980). Skills approaches tend to reflect the behaviorist tradition, and fit well with the work done in competency-based reading programs. Such programs generally involve developing a list of skills and subskills related to reading, teaching those skills, and then assessing student mastery. The advocates of a skills-oriented reading program are particularly concerned with children who read poorly. They feel that a carefully controlled reading program, where behaviors are examined one by one, will lead more children to maturity in reading. They believe that without specific skills instruction many children may not become proficient readers.

Personal Beliefs

The focus taken in this text is a compromise between holistic and skills approaches. While I might personally espouse to a holistic philosophy, I also recognize that the majority of classrooms do *not* reflect a holistic approach, basal readers are widely used, and many classroom teachers discover there is actually a lack of institutional support for abandoning familiar ways. In short, even if teachers hold a holistic philosophy, they may find themselves "between a rock and a hard place" as so aptly stated by Mosenthal (1989, p. 628). Thus, the compromises made in this text are made in the hope that they may serve as *transitions* from a traditional skills view of corrective reading to one that represents a more strategic view of reading (i.e., the majority of the instructional strategies emphasize the development of strategies for constructing meaning as opposed to development of skills that focus on isolated words).

For me, reading is a transaction that takes place between a reader and a text in a particular situation. The reader constructs meaning by actively processing graphic, syntactic, and semantic cues representing language, and by actively using memories of past experiences to aid in building new thoughts and/or revising, reinforcing, or expanding current thoughts.

You are encouraged to formulate your own beliefs about reading, so that you can better evaluate what is suggested in this and other texts, and in materials such as basal reader manuals. Your own beliefs will help you make decisions about what to teach and how best to teach it.

Three Major Goals of Every Reading Program

When planning a reading program, a teacher must determine major long-term goals for student achievement. These goals generally fall into three categories:

1. The developmental or instructional reading program
2. The functional or content area reading program
3. The recreational or independent reading program

Developmental Reading

Good instructional programs usually have well-specified developmental goals. Major objectives in the **developmental program** focus on increasing proficiency in strategies for decoding words, expanding sight vocabulary, and comprehending what one reads. The means teachers choose to achieve these goals will reflect their individual philosophies about reading.

Functional Reading

The major goal of the functional or content area program is to help children use reading as a tool for learning. The focus is on reading to learn rather than learning to read. Functional reading refers primarily to reading in such curricular areas as mathematics, science, and social studies. Developmental programs frequently include lessons on applied skills, but these skills probably are not truly learned until they are practiced in realistic, problem-solving settings of the different content fields.

Broad objectives of the functional reading program include learning to locate information, understand special and technical vocabularies, acquire specific skills of the various content subjects, and organize and remember what has been read.

Recreational Reading

The recreational or independent reading program deals primarily with fostering positive interests, attitudes, and habits in reading. If teachers and others fail to encourage the desire to read in children and youths, many students will become **aliterates,** that is, persons who can, but choose not to, read. Building positive attitudes toward reading is of special concern when working with children who have reading problems.

Frustration, failure, and overemphasis on skills and drills may kill the desire to learn to read. When this happens, teachers' jobs become much more difficult. They must not only deal with the instructional facets of reading but also try to overcome the negative attitudes of the student.

Broad objectives of the recreational reading program include: (1) providing students with the opportunity to practice reading in a relaxed atmosphere; (2) sharing good literature with students; and (3) making provisions for students to share books with each other.

The three goals of the reading program should be maintained and balanced during the elementary school years, although emphasis may change depending on the needs of the students. Functional reading typically takes on more importance in the intermediate and upper grades after many children have learned the basics of developmental reading. Developmental and recreational reading should continue throughout a child's school years.

What Is Corrective Reading?

Types of Reading Instruction

Good instruction requires that teachers deal with the individual student's strengths and weaknesses. Otto and Smith (1980) believe that all types of reading instruction can be encompassed under the major heading "Developmental Program."

> The term *developmental program* generally has a broad meaning, whereas the meaning of developmental teaching usually is somewhat more restricted. Typically, the goal of the developmental program is achievement in the basic school subjects that approaches the limit of each pupil's capacity. Thus the developmental program subsumes the entire curriculum at all grade levels as well as specialized instructional programs designed for pupils with particular needs.[1]

---

[1] From Otto, Wayne, Richard J. Smith. *Corrective and Remedial Teaching*, Third Edition. Copyright © 1980 by Houghton Mifflin Company. Used with permission.

This idea seems appropriate inasmuch as corrective and remedial instruction are generally approached from a developmental point of view. That is, in order to help the corrective reader, an attempt is made to determine where in the developmental sequence of skills and abilities the child is experiencing difficulty.

Corrective reading instruction, then, is part of the broad, multifaceted developmental reading program. Otto and Smith (1980) define five categories for instruction within the overall developmental reading program. Briefly, the definitions are as follows:

1. **Developmental instruction** focuses on development of skills and abilities for the majority of students in the classroom making average progress.
2. **Accelerated instruction** challenges and enriches bright, motivated, and successful readers.
3. **Adapted instruction** involves adapting the pace and teacher expectations to slower learners who are achieving up to their capacity and may also involve adapting methods or materials for children with specific handicaps (e.g., omitting phonics for deaf students, including braille materials for blind students, and so on).
4. **Corrective instruction** demands immediate analysis and corrective help for students with mild or moderate gaps and deficiencies in reading development.
5. **Remedial instruction** deals with intensive case study diagnosis and special tutoring for disabled readers. These children often have nonreading problems, such as lack of motivation, poor health, and perceptual or physical defects.

The Corrective Reading Program

The purpose of the corrective reading program, then, is to provide instruction within the regular classroom setting for children who have mild or moderate reading problems or who have experienced learning gaps. Children should not need corrective instruction on a long-term, year-after-year basis. Those who do need long-term help should be considered candidates for remedial instruction.

The corrective program is conceptualized as fluid, dynamic, and short-term. Students work to overcome their reading difficulties on an individual or small-group basis centering around their needs. The same strategies and vocabulary words being taught during developmental instruction are reinforced. After a relatively brief period of appropriate teaching, reviewing, and practice, these students should achieve success.

More careful analysis may be needed for students unsuccessful after several weeks of instruction. A diagnostic work-up and intensive individual remedial instruction by qualified personnel other than the classroom teacher may be necessary. If these resources are unavailable in the school system, teachers must do the best they can for these children within the corrective program.

Materials used in a corrective reading program range from typical basal readers and workbooks to supplementary materials, additional practice sheets, games for motivation and continued practice in problem areas, or language experience stories, trade books, and children's literature. Teachers may use any instructional materials available or they may design their own, but the instructor needs to focus on specific problems identified through careful analysis. For this analysis, teachers may use standardized measures, diagnostic tests, informal measures, observations, and teacher-made materials. Assessment procedures and tools are discussed at length in chapters 3 and 4.

Many factors influence the setting of the classroom instructional program, including class size, experience and expertise of the teacher, and the availability of supplemental materials and of extra help for teachers, such as a school reading teacher, teacher aides, parents, and other paraprofessionals. The teacher's role in implementing a corrective reading program in the classroom setting is a major topic of chapter 13, "Analytic Teaching."

Who Is the Corrective Reader?

Characteristics of Corrective Readers

The classroom teacher has primary responsibility for identifying corrective readers. Initial identification may simply be based on a low reading achievement test score. For example, the vocabulary subtest score on an achievement test may be considerably lower, or higher, than the comprehension subtest score. Or a student may demonstrate consistently poor classroom performance in reading. On the basis of experience in working with corrective readers, Smith, Otto, and Hansen (1978, p. 196) offer the following general guidelines for the identification of corrective readers:[2]

1. Corrective readers are making progress in the classroom developmental program but at a slower rate than that of the majority of students.

2. The reading skills deficiencies of corrective readers can be diagnosed specifically enough to permit straightforward teaching to strengthen the weaknesses. The skill weaknesses are not masked by emotional or psychological problems. The skill area(s) in which additional instruction is needed is (are) clear.

3. The ability of corrective readers to recall and to discuss selections read to them is better than their ability to recall and discuss selections they have read to themselves. Their observed ability to learn from nonprint media is better than their ability to learn from printed material.

4. Corrective readers have some independence in reading. They are able to engage in "practice reading" without the constant and direct assistance of their teachers.

5. Corrective readers' attitudes toward improving their reading are more positive than negative. They do not require constant and sophisticated motivational appeals.

6. Their reading skills can be strengthened with additional teaching and practice exercises using supplementary instructional materials. They don't require an entirely different approach from that being used in the classroom.

The first guideline above indicates that corrective readers are underachievers. The concept of underachievement is most relevant for identifying corrective readers. **Underachievers** are not achieving in a way consistent with their potential. The key words here are "not achieving" and "potential." However, understanding the definition of an underachiever and trying to apply the definition to real students are two different things.

---

[2] From *The School Reading Program* by R. J. Smith, W. Otto, and L. Hansen, p. 196. Copyright © 1978 Houghton Mifflin Company. Used with permission.

Essentially the difficulty revolves around two issues—estimating achievement and estimating potential. In classroom situations a student's **achievement** is usually estimated by a standardized achievement test that provides an index (grade equivalent score, percentile, stanine) of how well the student is doing compared to other students. Such test results, viewed in light of other measures of reading achievement, can provide a fairly accurate estimate of a student's global achievement level, which is useful for screening purposes. One additional measure, which should be used to supplement achievement test results, is the instructional level score of an informal reading inventory discussed in chapter 4.

Estimating **potential** is more difficult for the classroom teacher. Traditionally, potential has been equated with intelligence. Intelligence quotients (IQs) between 85 and 115 are considered average with varying degrees of brightness and slowness on either side. The results of group intelligence tests are not appropriate for estimating the potential of a student suspected of having reading problems, however. Group tests usually require that students be able to read to take the test. For a poor reader, a verbal test will reflect poor reading ability, and potential will remain unknown. Thus, individual tests of intelligence are advisable. Unfortunately, the best individual intelligence tests, the *Revised Stanford-Binet Intelligence Scale,* and the *Wechsler Intelligence Scale for Children Revised* (WISC-R), can only be administered, scored, and interpreted by specially trained personnel. The teacher can refer a child to the proper people for such testing, but then must await the analysis of test results. Valuable time is lost if the teacher does indeed wait.

Some quick individual assessments of intelligence are available to the classroom teacher. Because they *are* quick and easy to administer, however, the results can *only* be used as initial indicators of a student's potential. Examples of these quick assessments are *The Slosson Intelligence Test Revised* (1990), and the *Peabody Picture Vocabulary Test Revised* (Dunn, 1981).

The teacher can estimate potential in several other ways and probably should obtain as many indications of potential as possible.

1. Success on a nonverbal task can show that a child has academic potential. If a student has been in school at least two years, a test of arithmetic computation, a nonverbal task, can be used to estimate academic potential (Wilson, 1981). Arithmetic computation scores that are noticeably better than reading achievement scores can indicate a reading problem. Caution is necessary, however, because arithmetic computation scores do not accurately indicate potential in seriously disabled readers. Nonreading problems, such as lack of motivation or other psychological reactions to previous failures, are usually involved.

2. Careful observation of a child's general responsiveness both on the playground and in the classroom gives the teacher some idea of intellectual potential (Wilson, 1981). Roswell and Natchez (1964) provide the following noticeable characteristics of reading potential:

- Ability to participate effectively in class discussions, both listening and speaking.
- Ability to achieve more successfully in arithmetic than in subjects requiring reading.
- Ability to participate effectively in peer group activities.
- Ability to demonstrate alert attitudes toward the world.
- Ability to perform satisfactorily on spelling tests. (p. 27)

Teacher observations, however, are not highly reliable indicators of potential. Bias is a frequent component, and a teacher may "observe" a characteristic based on some prior impression, such as a test score, a low achieving sibling, or even the child's name. Bond and Bruekner (1955) point out that the potentials of the aggressive, talkative, popular, well-behaved, and overage students are likely to be overestimated, while potentials of the shy, unattractive, or unpopular students are likely to be underestimated. Therefore, teacher observations should be verified through more accurate evaluations.

3. An oral vocabulary test, such as the subtest from the *Gates-McKillop-Horowitz Reading Diagnostic Tests* (1982), can also be used as an indicator. The teacher reads the items to a student. Each item consists of a stem and four possible responses. The student has to select the correct response (Zintz, 1981, p. 150):

A head is a part of a   *coat   saw   man   box.*
Gaudy means   *certainly   wealthy   beautiful   showy.*

Teachers should also observe the extent of the child's speaking vocabulary outside of the reading situation. The cautions mentioned before about teacher observations also apply here.

4. Listening comprehension tests are sometimes used as indicators of potential. In these tests, a series of graded passages are read to the student. A set of comprehension questions is prepared for each passage. The student is told to listen to the passage in order to answer some questions afterward. If the student scores 75 percent or higher for a passage, the student presumably has the potential for understanding material at that level.

Differences between a student's comprehension after reading a passage silently and after listening to a passage are sometimes used to indicate potential. If the reading comprehension score is higher than the listening comprehension score, the child's potential remains unknown. What is indicated, however, is that the child needs some training in listening skills. On the other hand, if the listening comprehension score is higher than the reading comprehension score, it is likely that the *thinking* skills needed to comprehend that level of material are developed, because reading and listening involve similar thinking skills (Sticht, et al., 1974). Thus, "a child may have excellent comprehension ability, but it may be masked because of word recognition problems" (Rubin, 1982, p. 49).

Caution, however, must once again be advised. Listening comprehension scores cannot be equated with potential. They can only serve as rough indicators of potential, and then not in all situations. For instance, Durrell (1969) found that listening comprehension of first grade students surpassed reading comprehension but reading comprehension of eighth grade students was superior to listening comprehension. Similar results were found in research by Sticht and Beck (1976), that is, listening comprehension surpasses reading comprehension until about grade seven. First graders are struggling with word recognition. Likewise, second and third graders may sometimes be unfairly labeled as underachievers if listening comprehension is found to be higher than reading comprehension. As students learn to read, which appears to take longer (grades 6–8) than the traditionally thought of primary grades (1–3), their reading comprehension skills overtake their listening comprehension skills. As stated by Sticht and James (1984), "precisely what is happening that makes this additional time necessary is not certain, though it may be that in the first three or four years of school, children learn the rudiments of reading-decoding . . . while an additional two to three years of practice is required for the automaticity of reading to equal that of auding [listening comprehension]" (p. 307).

In addition, training in listening comprehension skills often produces similar gains in reading comprehension (Kelty, 1955; Hoffman, 1978). To know when a listening comprehension test reflects the reading potential of a child therefore is difficult to say. If the teacher can reasonably expect students to have better reading skills than they do (grade 4 and up), then the listening comprehension ability apparently is a fairly accurate indication of potential. Also, if a child's reading skills build upon earlier acquired listening skills, listening comprehension can be used as an indication of early potential for the beginning reader (Sticht & James, 1984).

Comparing Achievement and Potential

The primary reason for ascertaining a student's potential is to determine if that student is an underachiever or is doing as well as can be expected (e.g., a slow learner). A student can be achieving at grade level and still be considered an underachiever. If the student demonstrates an "above grade level" potential, achievement should also be "above grade level."

The larger the difference between potential and reading achievement, the more serious the reading problem. As Wilson (1981) points out, however, the degree of difference between potential and achievement varies with the grade placement of the student. As students progress through school they are better able to compensate for some difference in potential and reading achievement. Wilson (1981) presents a standard (Table 1.1) that may be used to select a cutoff point between an acceptable difference and one too large not to interfere with a child's progress in reading.

Decisions about an individual student should be the result of several indicators of strength and weakness. The total reader must be evaluated, not just achievement test scores or measures of potential. Students with very specific deficiencies or with attitude problems may be overlooked completely if only test scores or indicators of

TABLE 1.1 Degree of Tolerable Difference Between Potential and Achievement

End of grade	Tolerable difference (in years)
1, 2, 3	0.5
4, 5, 6	1.0
7, 8, 9	1.5
10, 11, 12	2.0

Note: Tolerable difference ranges must be used as judgment points, not as absolutes.
Source: R. M. Wilson, *Diagnostic and Remedial Reading for Classroom and Clinic,* 4th ed. (Columbus, OH: Charles E. Merrill, 1981), 63. Reprinted with permission.

potential are used. Later chapters discuss many factors that should be evaluated before decisions are made.

The remainder of this text focuses on helping teachers identify readers who need help and to analyze their specific strengths and weaknesses. Topics range from the gathering of information to the implementation of corrective instruction. Many useful assessment and instructional strategies for word recognition, comprehension, and study skills are provided.

Summary

In order to provide effective reading instruction for the wide range of reading abilities in the classroom, teachers must be able to identify readers showing signs of possible reading problems. Not all students who read below grade level are in need of corrective or remedial instruction. Students reading at or near their potential are not likely to respond to special instructional efforts to push them beyond that level. Students reading below their potential because of minor problems can be helped within the classroom setting if appropriate corrective instruction is provided. Students with severe reading problems need special assistance both outside and within the classroom setting.

This chapter reviews dimensions of the reading process and discusses the importance of every teacher developing a philosophy about reading. The three major goals of any reading program are identified. Individual teachers can achieve these goals in a variety of ways, depending on individual beliefs about reading. The concept of the developmental reading program and the various types of instruction to be found within that program—developmental, accelerated, adapted, corrective, and remedial—are introduced. Characteristics of corrective readers are provided, with the concept of underachievement being treated in some detail. Within this discussion the concept of comparing achievement to potential is introduced.

References

Anderson, R. C. (1977). The notion of schemata and the educational enterprise. In R. C. Anderson, R. J. Spiro, & W. E. Montague (Eds.), *Schooling and the acquisition of knowledge.* Hillsdale, NJ: Erlbaum.

Ashton Warner, S. (1963). *Teacher.* New York: Simon & Schuster.

Bond, G. L., & Brueckner, L. J. (1955). *The diagnosis and treatment of learning difficulties.* New York: Appleton-Century-Crofts.

Bowerman, M. (1976). Semantic factors in the acquisition of rules for word use and sentence construction. In D. Morehead and A. Morehead (Eds.), *Normal and deficient child language.* Baltimore: University Park Press.

Chall, J. S. (1967). *Learning to read: The great debate.* New York: McGraw-Hill.

Clay, M. M. (1972). *Reading, the patterning of complex behavior.* Auckland, NZ: Heinemann.

Cole, M. L., & Cole, J. T. (1981). *Effective intervention with the language impaired child.* Rockville, MD: Aspen Systems.

Collins, M. C. & Cheek, E. H. (1989). *Diagnostic-prescriptive reading instruction* (3rd ed.). Dubuque, IA: Wm. C. Brown.)

Doctorow, M., Wittrock, M. C., & Marks, C. (1978). Generative processes in reading comprehension. *Journal of Educational Psychology, 70,* 109–118.

Dunn, L. M., & Dunn, L. M. (1981). *Peabody picture vocabulary test (revised).* Circle Pines, MN: American Guidance Service.

Durrell, D. D. (1969). Listening comprehension versus reading comprehension. *Journal of Reading, 12,* 455–460.

Engelmann, S. (1969). *Preventing failure in the primary grades.* Chicago: Science Research Associates.

Fox, S. E., & Allen, V. G. (1983). *The language arts: An integrated approach.* New York: Holt, Rinehart and Winston.

Gates, A. I., McKillop, A. S., & Horowitz, E. C. (1982). *Gates-McKillop-Horowitz Reading Diagnostic Tests* (2nd ed.). New York: Teachers College Press.

Gibson, E. J., & Levin, H. (1975). *The psychology of reading.* Cambridge: MIT Press.

Goodman, K. S. (1985). Behind the eye: What happens in reading. In H. Singer & R. B. Ruddell (Eds.), *Theoretical models and processes of reading.* Newark, DE: International Reading Association.

Goodman, K. S. (1979). Learning to read is natural. In L. Resnick & P. Weaver (Eds.), *Theory and practice of early reading* (Vol. 1). Hillsdale, NJ: Erlbaum.

Goodman, K. S. (1973). Theoretically based studies of patterns of miscues in oral reading performance. Washington, DC: U.S. Department of Health, Education and Welfare, Office of Education, Bureau of Research.

Goodman, K. S. (1968). *The psycholinguistic nature of the reading process.* Detroit: Wayne State University Press.

Halliday, M. A. K. (1978). *Language as a social semiotic.* Baltimore: University Park Press.

Harris, L. A., & Smith, C. B. (1980). *Reading instruction: Diagnostic teaching in the classroom.* New York: Holt, Rinehart and Winston.

Harste, J., Woodward, V. & Burke, C. (1984). *Language stories and literacy lessons.* Portsmouth, NH: Heinemann.

Hoffman, S. M. (1978). *The effect of a listening skills program on the reading comprehension of fourth grade students.* Unpublished doctoral dissertation, Walden University, Naples, FL.

Holdaway, D. (1979). *The foundations of literacy.* Sydney, Australia: Ashton Scholastic.

Huey, E. B. (1908). *The psychology and pedagogy of reading.* New York: Macmillan. (Reprint. Cambridge: MIT Press, 1968).

Kelty, A. P. (1955). An experimental study to determine the effect of listening for certain purposes upon achievement in reading for those purposes. *Abstracts of Field Studies for the Degree of Doctor of Education, 15,* 82-95. Greeley: Colorado State College of Education.

Lamb, P. M. (1980). Definitions and beliefs. In P. M. Lamb & R. D. Arnold (Eds.), *Teaching reading: Foundations and strategies.* Belmont, CA: Wadsworth.

Mangrum, C. T., & Forgan, H. W. (1979). *Developing competencies in teaching reading.* Columbus, OH: Merrill.

Mosenthal, P. B. (1989). The whole language approach: Teachers between a rock and a hard place. *The Reading Teacher, 42,* 628–629.

Newman, J. M. (Ed.). (1985). *Whole language theory in use.* Portsmouth, NH: Heinemann.

Otto, W. (1977). Orientation to remedial teaching. In W. Otto, N. A. Peters, and C. W. Peters (Eds.), *Reading problems: A multi-disciplinary perspective.* Reading, MA: Addison-Wesley.

Otto, W., & Smith, R. J. (1980). *Corrective and remedial teaching* (3rd ed.). Boston: Houghton Mifflin.

Rhodes, L. K. & Dudley-Marling, C. (1988). *Readers and writers with a difference.* Portsmouth, NH: Heinemann.

Richards, J. C. (1985). *Theoretical orientation and first and third grade teachers' reading instruction.* Unpublished doctoral dissertation, University of New Orleans.

Robinson, H. A. (1977). Reading instruction and research: A historical perspective. In H. A. Robinson (Ed.), *Reading and writing in the United States: Historical trends.* Newark, DE: International Reading Association.

Roswell, F., & Natchez, G. (1964). *Reading disability.* New York: Basic Books.

Rubin, D. (1982). *Diagnosis and correction in reading instruction.* New York: Holt, Rinehart and Winston.

Rumelhart, D. E. (1980). Schemata: The building blocks of cognition. In R. J. Spiro, B. C. Bruce, & W. F. Brewer (Eds.), *Theoretical issues in reading comprehension.* Hillsdale, NJ: Erlbaum.

Schallert, D., Kleiman, G. M., and Rubin, A. D. (1977). *Analysis of differences between written and oral language.* Technical Report No. 29, Center for the Study of Reading, Urbana: University of Illinois.

Slosson, R. L. (1990). *Slosson intelligence test revised.* East Aurora, NY: Slosson Educational Publications.

Smith, F. (1988). *Understanding reading* (4th ed.). Hillsdale, NJ: Lawrence Erlbaum Associates.

Smith, R. J., Otto, W., and Hansen, L. (1978). *The school reading program.* Boston: Houghton Mifflin.

Spiro, R. J. (1980). Constructive processes in prose comprehension and recall. In R. J. Spiro, B. C. Bruce, & W. F. Brewer (Eds.), *Theoretical issues in reading comprehension.* Hillsdale, NJ: Erlbaum.

Spiro, R. J., & Myers, A. (1984). Individual differences and underlying cognitive processes. In P. D. Pearson (Ed.), *Handbook of reading research.* New York: Longman.

Sticht, T. G., & Beck, L. J. (1976, August). Experimental literacy assessment battery (LAB) (Final Rep.: AFHRL-TR-76-51). Lowry Air Force Base, Colo.: Air Force Human Resources Laboratory, Technical Training Division.

Sticht, T. G., Beck, L. J., Haucke, R. N., Kleiman, G. M., & James, J. H. (1974). *Auding and reading: A developmental model.* Alexandria, VA: Human Resources Organization.

Sticht, T. G., & James, J. H. (1984). Listening and reading. In P. D. Pearson (Ed.), *Handbook of reading research.* New York: Longman.

Thorndyke, P. W (1977). Cognitive structures in comprehension and memory of narrative discourse. *Cognitive Psychology, 9,* 77–110.

Thorndyke, P. W. (1976). The role of inferences in discourse comprehension. *Journal of Verbal Learning and Verbal Behavior, 15,* 437–446.

Weaver, C. (1988). *Reading process and practice.* Portsmouth, NH: Heinemann.

Wilson, R. M. (1981). *Diagnostic and remedial reading for classroom and clinic* (4th ed.). Columbus, OH: Merrill.

Wittrock, M. C. (1978). Education and the cognitive processes of the brain. In J. S. Chall, & A. F. Mirsky (Eds.), *Education and the brain.* 77th Yearbook of the National Society for the Study of Education, Part II. Chicago: University of Chicago Press.

Zintz, M. V. (1981). *Corrective reading* (4th ed.). Dubuque, IA: Wm. C. Brown.

CHAPTER 2

The Analytic Process: Its Nature and Value

Objectives

After you have read this chapter, you should be able to

1. define the analytic process;
2. justify the analytic process and contrast it with assumptive teaching;
3. cite the four levels of the analytic process;
4. list the major reading domains and the areas within each;
5. describe the steps in the paradigm for the analytic process;
6. describe teacher objectives, correlated student objectives, and behavioral objectives;
7. discuss the difference between didactic and discovery teaching;
8. contrast problem-solving questions and facilitating questions.

Study Outline

Important Vocabulary and Concepts

analytic process	independent practice
assumptive teaching	inductive teaching
covert behaviors	instructional reading level
deductive teaching	overt behaviors
diagnosis	paradigm
didactic teaching	problem-solving questions
direct instruction	screening
discovery teaching	structured practice
empirical evidence	teachable units
evaluation activity	teaching hypothesis
facilitating questions	transfer of training

Overview

In this chapter the analytic process is defined and its importance to classroom teachers discussed. The analytic process is also contrasted with assumptive teaching to help teachers avoid the potential errors involved with the latter approach.

Four levels of analysis used to identify the reading strengths and needs of students are described. The effective teacher begins with an analysis of the child's general reading performance. If a deficiency is suspected, the teacher proceeds to the second level of analysis involving major domains of reading: (1) word recognition; (2) comprehension; and (3) study skills and strategic reading. If a deficiency or weakness is discovered within one or more of the domains, a third level of analysis of areas within domains is suggested. Finally, if problems within specific areas of reading are identified, the teacher uses a fourth level of assessment, searching for specific strengths and weaknesses. Instructional strategies are then based upon the analyses at levels three and four, which yield teachable units.

A basic paradigm for the analytic process is then outlined: gathering data; evaluating the data; generating possible teaching hypotheses; deciding on the best possible instructional plan to use with the child; and carrying out the instructional plan through direct instruction in order to gather further data and to reevaluate. The cyclical nature of the analytic process becomes apparent.

Translating teaching hypotheses into a set of lesson plans is then explained. This explanation includes a discussion of objectives, teaching strategies, and questioning techniques. The chapter ends with an example of a complete lesson plan.

Introduction

The analytic process can be used by any classroom teacher in any curricular area. It is not confined to reading, nor is it a reading method. Rather, the **analytic process** is defined here as a systematic way to help teachers assess and observe aspects of the reading process in their students, identify areas of strength and need for individual students, and provide instruction for specific reading deficiencies regardless of the curricular area or the teaching methods used.

Our current understanding of the reading process recognizes the importance of the reader, the text, and the context of the reading task. As Barr suggests (cited in Berglund, 1987), teachers must "look with new eyes" at students while they are reading. Rather than depend on test instruments, even informal ones such as informal reading inventories, teachers should initially gain insights into a child's reading ability by observing that child for their competence in areas such as oral reading, story retellings, written summaries, answers to key questions that reveal the important understandings in material read, and background knowledge. The analytic process described in this chapter recognizes the interactive nature of reading which, in turn, requires assessment procedures which are also interactive.

Justification for the Analytic Process

Problems Associated with Assumptive Teaching

Sometimes teachers make inappropriate assumptions about the reading status of their pupils. Herber (1970) calls the resulting instruction **assumptive teaching.** While teachers make many unfortunate specific assumptions, most fall into two major categories.

First, teachers often assume their pupils need to learn something when in fact they already have learned it. When this assumption is made, those pupils are in a "minimal growth" instructional setting. The teacher can spend a great deal of time and energy teaching something that is of little use to those receiving instruction. This type of assumptive teaching leads children to boredom, inattentiveness, and disruptive behavior.

Second, and perhaps of vital significance to all concerned with corrective reading, some teachers assume their pupils have learned something when in fact they have not. If this occurs with some regularity, reading deficits will accrue and children will slip into a "no growth" instructional setting. Teaching a lesson well will be no guarantee that pupils have learned it. Figure 2.1 lists common assumptions that teachers should try to avoid.

Assuming too much about students can lead to a mismatch between the child and the instructional program. For example, if a sixth grade teacher gives everyone in the class a sixth grade text at the beginning of the school year, the teacher has assumed that all the children are reading at about grade level and will profit from instruction at this level. This is a dangerous assumption to make. Teachers must *verify* that each student in the class can respond appropriately to the assigned reading materials.

FIGURE 2.1 Common assumptions classroom teachers should avoid. (Adapted from Delwyn G. Schubert and Theodore L. Torgerson, *Improving the Reading Program,* 5th ed. Copyright © 1981 by William C. Brown. Used with permission.)

1. Assuming a child has attained readiness for a particular learning
2. Assuming that a report card grade reflects the instructional level of a child
3. Assuming that a report card grade from one teacher means the same as that from another teacher
4. Assuming that all teachers develop independent reading habits in all pupils in the primary grades
5. Assuming that all teachers use instructional material diversified in difficulty and content in each grade
6. Assuming that disabled or problem readers are able to use material on a frustration level of difficulty
7. Assuming that group instruction is the best method to meet the reading needs of all pupils
8. Assuming that a basal reader series constitutes an entire reading program
9. Assuming that children can learn a new skill without direct instruction
10. Assuming that children who read well will read widely
11. Assuming that teacher-pupil relationships are unimportant to reading growth
12. Assuming that mastery of reading skills and mastery of reading are identical
13. Assuming that instruction for "different" children is identical to instruction for "normal" children
14. Assuming that all children have the same capacity for learning
15. Assuming that reading deficiencies are nonexistent when the class average on standardized reading tests reaches or exceeds the norm
16. Assuming that the child's reading abilities remained unchanged over the summer
17. Assuming that individual difficulties in word analysis in the intermediate grades will correct themselves
18. Assuming that all materials are adequate and appropriate as corrective materials
19. Assuming that teachers make only fortunate assumptions

Similarly, faulty assumptions about individual students can lead to inappropriate teaching. Consider the following example: a fifth grade teacher correctly determines the **instructional reading levels** (i.e., grade level of material is challenging but not frustrating for the student to read successfully with normal classroom instruction) of the students. Two boys, according to test results, are reading at third grade level. The teacher gives both of them appropriate reading materials, assuming that instruction can proceed in a manner similar to that in a typical developmental instruction program, in this case, reading and reviewing stories and exercises at the third grade level. This teacher has done well in finding each boy's proper instructional reading level, but has failed to pursue the *reasons* why each boy is not achieving satisfactorily. One boy may be reading at third grade level because he is having problems with word meanings and comprehension, while the other boy may be having problems recognizing the words. Each needs a corrective program designed to improve his particular reading problems. After a child is given appropriate materials (see appendix A for a readability method to determine difficulty levels of materials), deeper analyses of strengths and weaknesses within that level are essential to avoid inappropriate teaching assumptions.

Assumptions have features similar to hypotheses. Both terms connote the involvement of a hunch or a notion about something. They differ in that the word *assumption* implies that the hunch is accepted or taken for granted, while the word *hypothesis* always implies tentativeness and the need for verification, after which acceptance or rejection occurs.

The Analytic Process Paradigm

A loose and unstructured corrective reading program, based on unverified assumptions, often perpetuates reading problems in the classroom. Employing the analytic process alleviates many of the unfortunate results of faulty teacher assumptions. The reason is that the analytic process follows a **paradigm,** or pattern. The teacher must (1) examine reading behaviors, (2) form teaching hypotheses, (3) teach, and (4) reexamine reading behaviors. This paradigm can be expanded to allow for necessary specificity in terms of individual strengths and weaknesses. The process is basically simple, but, as you will see later in this chapter, it can become quite intricate when put to use.

Analyzing Components of the Reading Process

Reading is recognized as a total dynamic, interactive, and transactive process, and to represent its components in isolation and in static form is a distortion of the process itself. Some distortion is acceptable however, if it helps one to better understand the process. For corrective reading purposes, reading behaviors must be analyzed to attain the specificity needed to correct a problem. Additionally, the kinds of materials students read and the nature of the methods, materials, and tasks used in the classroom, as well as the social and cultural environment of the classroom, must be analyzed. Once identified, a problem is dealt with specifically and independently, but also as a part of the child's total thought processes. Corrective teaching occurs during a lesson in which the emphasis is on alleviating a problem as a part of the *child's* thought processes, whereas analysis occurs earlier as part of the *teacher's*

FIGURE **2.2** Components of the reading process.

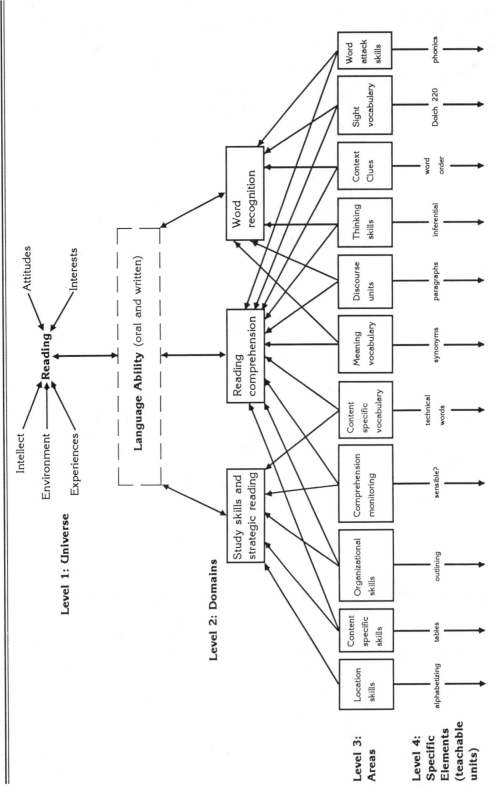

thought processes. This earlier analysis can also lead to *changes* in the teacher's methods, materials, tasks, and approach.

Figure 2.2 represents a conceptualization of the components involved in the reading process, not the process itself. The components discussed in this section are those frequently referred to in the literature, but they have been chosen arbitrarily. Little or no **empirical evidence,** evidence supported by experiment, verifies that these components do, in fact, exist, and can be broken down into smaller sets and subsets that suggest a hierarchy of specific reading tasks. Keep in mind that the following is one way, not necessarily the only way, to analyze the reading process.

First you should study the figure to see how the parts are interrelated. Analysis begins with the broadest element and, when necessary, proceeds to finer discriminations to determine more precisely the specific problem or set of problems. While it may appear that fractionated reading skills are being emphasized by even trying to deal with components of the reading process, this is not the case. Notice that the figure also demonstrates the importance of influences that are part of the whole child (e.g., environment, intellectual ability, background experiences, attitudes and interests, language ability). Valuable reading strategies which focus on the whole child can be taught directly, and an attempt is made in this text to suggest appropriate ways to teach these strategies.

Four Levels of Analysis and Correlative Diagnostic Questions

Four levels of analysis are proposed. Each level has a correlative diagnostic question, and some questions have important related subquestions. The four correlative diagnostic questions are:

Level 1: Does the child have a reading problem?
Level 2: In what domain(s) does the reading problem occur?
Level 3: In what area within the domain(s) does the problem occur?
Level 4: What specific weaknesses can be identified within the problem area? Or, is the problem related to one of the universal influences?

The questions should be asked in sequence because the answer to each question will tell the teacher whether to proceed to a deeper level of analysis. As you read the discussion, be aware that it proceeds as though the child has only one specific problem, which is unlikely. Corrective readers often have clusters of problems; furthermore, certain fundamental problems preclude analysis in other domains. For example, if a child is having a serious problem with word recognition, it is unlikely that comprehension can be adequately assessed. Some children are unable to grasp the author's message (comprehension) because they cannot read the words. Therefore, the analytical process outlined here is not as precise as it may appear at first glance.

Because the reading process is complex, teachers should always approach analysis of a reading problem with the knowledge that the resulting hypotheses may be imprecise or only partially correct. During the teaching phase, hypotheses and instructional strategies can be verified, modified, and further adapted to the needs of the corrective reader.

Although the emphasis appears to be on finding weaknesses, the analytic process will also expose strengths. Reading strengths play a crucial role in planning appropriate reading instruction and can be used to help a child overcome a specific weakness. It is most important to determine what strategies the child *does* have in order to know what the child needs help with. The strengths a child brings to reading will determine where instruction will begin. Thus, the attitude of instruction becomes one of "moving forward" as opposed to "catching up" (Jewell & Zintz, 1986). Specifics for doing this, as well as for implementing other aspects of the analytic process, are discussed in detail in later chapters.

Level 1 - Determining the presence of a reading problem

At this level of analysis only one diagnostic question is to be answered:

- Does the child have a reading problem?

A teacher may find the answer to this question several ways. The most obvious way would be to listen to the child read. Teachers are strongly advised to collect information about all their students' reading abilities, using the tradebooks, textbooks, readers, and skill development books available in the classroom. Informal reading inventories are also a common way to analyze reading behaviors.

Another indication of reading ability can be the child's score on a standardized reading achievement test, usually readily available in the child's cumulative folder. But be careful not to let one test score determine a problem. Reading achievement tests probably do a good job of identifying good readers, so by comparison teachers can identify students who possibly have problems. Teachers must be careful, however, not to assume that students who score high have the reading abilities necessary for reading tasks not represented on the test (Farr & Carey, 1986; Smith & Barrett, 1976).

The teacher may notice a discrepancy between reading achievement test scores and mathematics achievement test scores. A reading problem may be indicated if the mathematics scores are higher. The reading achievement test alone may suggest a problem if, for example, the scores on the vocabulary and comprehension subtests are at variance.

Using a child's achievement records, the teacher may expect to find one of three basic patterns:

1. From the beginning of formal reading instruction the student failed to achieve as rapidly as mental ability would warrant.
2. The student had a successful beginning, but progress gradually slowed.
3. The student had a successful beginning, but progress suddenly dropped (Kennedy, 1977).

The first pattern is an example of the controversy over comparing reading achievement with reading expectancy. It also reveals students who may be deficient in some related area.

The second pattern may not be recognized until a child has already developed a serious problem. Teachers must be alert to the proportionate gains that a student makes through the years, as in the following example: Six-year-old Jody made good progress through first grade, and her end-of-the-year test showed an average level of achievement. By the end of second grade, Jody's achievement was slightly below average. At that point the teacher could decide that a reading problem was showing up or that Jody's score just reflected the nature of tests. When the third grade test revealed that Jody was further below average, however, the teacher should have recognized the pattern and decided that Jody did have a reading problem.

The third pattern, good progress followed by a sudden drop, may have a number of causes. It may indicate an omission of instruction, an emotional factor interfering with the child's learning rate, such as a recent divorce or a death in the family, or something as simple as the child not feeling well on the day of the test. The teacher should continue with the analytic process to pinpoint learning gaps.

Level 2 - Determining the domain(s) in which the problem occurs

Once teachers have identified children with possible reading problems, they must begin to search for the precise nature of the problems. The "reading universe" can be partitioned into language ability, reading-related factors, and the three major "domains"—*word recognition, comprehension,* and *study skills and strategic reading* (often referred to as "reading to learn," or content area reading). Usually, a child exhibits weakness in one or more of these domains and demonstrates strengths in others. The three primary diagnostic questions to be answered are as follows:

- Does the child have a problem with word recognition?
- Does the child have a problem with comprehension?
- Does the child have a problem with study skills or with strategic reading?

When the answer to a question in the second level of analysis is no, analysis in that domain ends. If the answer to a question is yes, the domain is analyzed further to define the problem more precisely. If the answer to all the questions in the second level of analysis is no, the teacher needs to consider reading-related factors and may require the help of a specialist to meet the needs of the child. If the answer to several of the questions is yes, the teacher should first consider the child's language competence because this is a crucial element for success in reading (Barr, 1984).

Level 3 - Determining the areas within the domain(s)

Experts disagree about dividing the domains into smaller segments. Some label the segments differently, and others resist the separation process even for the purpose of analysis. Thus, neither empirical data nor the consensus of experts directly supports the manner in which the domains will be segmented here for analytical purposes.

Despite these differences, the domains *are* divided into smaller parts for instructional purposes. From a practical point of view, you should be aware that these areas are discussed at length in the literature, that the category labels can be found in many texts on developmental, corrective, and remedial reading, and that these smaller units are acknowledged and used in many reading systems today. Even for those with a holistic philosophy, the search for answers to why a child has a reading problem must include consideration of these areas so that appropriate instructional strategies can be developed.

Word recognition. If a child has a problem with word recognition, more specific information must be sought by asking the following diagnostic questions:

- Does the child have a problem with sight vocabulary?
- Does the child have a problem with word analysis skills?
- Does the child have a problem with context clues?

Answers to these questions tell the teacher whether to terminate these particular lines of analysis or whether to proceed to level 4. Chapter 6 details possible weaknesses in word recognition, together with suggestions for formal and informal assessment and teaching suggestions. The important point to remember here is that any area associated with word recognition can be out of balance for children. Many disabled readers have basic problems so severe that they are prohibited from reaching the heart of reading—comprehension.

Reading comprehension.   The comprehension domain is divided into smaller segments that reflect the efforts of research (Davis, 1944, 1968; Hittleman, 1983; Pennock, 1979; Spearritt, 1972; Spiro, Bruce, & Brewer, 1980). Much still needs to be learned about reading comprehension, but it is clear that comprehension is deeply intertwined with memory, thinking, and language.

When a child is reading with poor comprehension, the following diagnostic questions should be carefully considered:

- Does the child have a problem with meaning vocabulary?
- Does the child have a problem with thinking or problem-solving skills associated with comprehension, such as identifying main ideas, predicting events, or drawing conclusions?
- Does the child have a problem recognizing when he/she doesn't understand what was read?

Answers to these questions tell the teacher whether to terminate or continue the analysis in one or more of the areas listed.

Some children, especially those in the first two or three grades, appear to have trouble with comprehension when the problem actually is in the domain of word recognition. Therefore, when students of any age are having problems typically associated with first and second graders, teachers should ask the following question:

- Does this apparent comprehension problem result from difficulty in word recognition?

Similarly, especially in the upper grades, an apparent comprehension problem may in reality be a problem with study skills and/or strategic reading. If the student is experiencing difficulty reading content area material, the following question is suggested:

- Does the child's apparent comprehension problem result from a deficiency in study skills and/or strategic reading?

This question and the one preceding it probably should be considered transitional questions. They demonstrate rather clearly how reading comprehension transcends the other domains discussed.

Study skills and strategic reading.   When students have problems in the domain of study skills and strategic reading, their abilities in this domain warrant deeper analysis. The following questions are suggested:

- Does the child have a problem with locating information?
- Does the child have a problem with organizing information?
- Does the child have a problem with content-specific vocabulary?
- Does the child have a problem with content-specific skills, such as reading visual displays, formulas, or other unique symbols?

- Does the child have a problem recognizing if the text is meaningful to him or to her?

The answers to these questions tell the teacher whether to continue with analysis at level 4.

Level 4 - Determining the teachable units within each area

Within each of the areas determined at Level 3 are specific learning segments or **teachable units** that the child must learn. A teachable unit is defined as a bit of information small enough to be taught directly. For example, within the domain of study skills and strategic reading, one area is locational skills. Within this area are several units that are important and teachable. Examples include learning to locate the table of contents, identify a chapter, or contrast the functions of a table of contents, an index, and a glossary. Because the number of teachable units is too great to be dealt with in an introductory chapter, they will be discussed in the chapters dealing with the various domains.

Components Outside the Three Major Domains

Language Ability

If you again refer to figure 2.2, you see that language ability cuts across the three reading domains. This component of the reading process lies at the core of reading and is of concern when a child performs very poorly on assessment instruments or when a beginning reader has trouble with simple reading tasks. A correlative diagnostic question to be asked when a child performs so poorly is:

- Does the child have a problem with underdeveloped language skills?

Kindergarten and first grade teachers are most likely to ask this question, and its frequency generally diminishes as grade level increases. However, teachers at all levels should ask themselves if their students have the language competence needed for a particular reading task.

Reading-Related Factors

Almost all physical, psychological, and environmental problems may impede reading progress. For example, an inadequate or divergent background of experience can seriously affect comprehension, attitude toward reading, and perhaps the acquisition of word recognition strategies. Reading-related factors must be considered independent entities that may adversely affect *any* area of the school curriculum, not just reading. These factors warrant considerable study and should be pursued in advanced coursework typically found at the graduate level.

Correlative diagnostic questions associated with reading-related factors may be:

- Does this child demonstrate the influence of a factor related to reading?
- Has this child had opportunities for reading and writing for their own purposes? (In other words, is the child a "victim" of the curriculum or of poor instruction?)

Poor attitudes toward and disinterest in reading hinder reading achievement. Teachers must ask questions about children's attitudes and interests and about their own teaching and the curriculum itself, regardless of the domain in which the reading problem occurs:

- Does the child have a negative attitude toward reading?
- Does the child lack interest in reading?
- If someone asked my students "What is reading?" what would they say?
- Is my curriculum so skills-oriented that students never have the opportunity to read for their own purposes?

The answers to the correlative diagnostic questions for these additional components are not typically obtained through tests, but through observation and interviews.

Basic Steps in the Analytic Process

In the previous section, the components of the reading process were partitioned into smaller units associated with the levels of analysis. This section provides information on the basic steps involved in the analytic process. These steps can be used to answer the questions posed for any of the domains, areas, or specific tasks mentioned. The basic paradigm for the analytic process mentioned earlier in this chapter will now be expanded.

Examination of Reading Behaviors

Step 1. Gathering Information

Many sources of information about students are available to teachers. Some of these are cumulative records reflecting past achievement; test scores; grades; information gathered inside and outside the classroom, such as the previous teacher's comments; and parent comments. Assembling all the information possible about students is called **screening,** which simply means surveying a group of people in order to sort them in some way. Screening is of special interest for level 1 analysis and provides much of the information necessary to answer the question "Does the child have a reading problem?" This first step involves teacher action; the following steps represent the teacher's thought processes.

Step 2. Evaluating the Information

In this step, teachers judge the quality of information. They try to establish the students' instructional reading levels, find a pattern or set of symptoms indicative of the students' strengths and weaknesses, and prepare an appropriate instructional program. If only such information as standardized test scores are available, teachers must verify these scores through other means. Most often teachers utilize some informal, nonstandardized measures. Chapters 3 and 4 deal specifically with formal and informal measures, and later chapters provide additional suggestions for informal assessment of particular areas.

Steps 1 and 2 considered together are roughly equivalent to **diagnosis,** or identification of a reading problem from symptoms. The final outcome of step 2 can range from a more global diagnosis, as determined by the first and second levels of analysis, to identification of specific weaknesses represented by the third and fourth levels. The weaknesses or teachable units eventually identified must then be translated into teaching objectives.

Generation of Possible Teaching Hypotheses

Step 1. Determining Alternatives

Once teachers have identified students with reading problems, they need to consider how best to alleviate those problems. Many instructional strategies are available, and many of these will be detailed in the following chapters. For now, you might simply consider a **teaching hypothesis** as an instructional plan based on a student's identified educational need.

Step 2. Selecting a Tentative Hypothesis

The teacher now evaluates the alternatives generated in step 1 and decides which instructional plan seems best for the particular student. This decision may be influenced by information regarding a student's interests or self-concept. Once an instructional plan is selected, the teacher develops lessons and teaching begins.

Teaching

Step 1. Direct Instruction

Although instruction is designed for an individual, it is often carried out in a small group. Classroom teachers instruct those students having similar needs together. This is simply effective classroom management. More specific management ideas are provided in chapter 13.

Direct instruction follows either a deductive or inductive directed reading lesson format. Examples of both are detailed later in this chapter. Basically, **direct instruction** requires that the teacher be *actively* involved in the lesson by first explaining, and then by modeling.

Step 2. Structured Practice

Once the teacher has provided direct instruction, the students must be given the opportunity to practice what has been explained and modeled with the teacher still involved, that is, **structured practice.** In this way the teacher begins to determine the accuracy of the teaching hypothesis as well as the effectiveness of the lesson.

Step 3. Independent Practice

Independent practice provides an opportunity for the student to apply what has been taught without the teacher's help. This kind of practice gives further information on the accuracy of hypotheses and effectiveness of the lesson. If students seem unable or unwilling to participate in this independent practice, there are reasons: the hypothesis may be inaccurate, the lesson may not have been planned well, or the student may not have the skills to work independently. In any case, providing for independent practice gives the teacher additional information.

Step 4. Evaluation Activity

The **evaluation activity** is a direct way of assessing the effectiveness of the lesson and the accuracy of the hypothesis. These activities are usually teacher-made and relate directly to the kinds of tasks provided in the direct instruction. If the hypothesis was appropriate and learning occurred, instruction should proceed; if the hypothesis was not appropriate, alternative hypotheses should be considered.

Reexamination of Reading Behaviors

Step 1. Gathering Information

This second examination of reading behaviors differs in several ways from the first. The first time the teacher gathers information about a student it is essentially all new. This second opportunity to analyze behaviors follows an instructional sequence of events, making this analysis much more informal and dependent on the teacher's insights and observations. This analysis overlaps considerably with the previous teaching stage—as the teacher teaches, information is gathered.

Step 2. Evaluating the Information

This evaluation relates directly to the information provided by the instructional sequence. The teacher must decide whether the lesson was effective and whether the teaching hypothesis was appropriate.

Step 3. Generating Possible Teaching Hypotheses

New hypotheses are needed if the lesson is effective and the desired behaviors are learned. New hypotheses are also needed if the original one was inappropriate. In both instances, this step depends on the teacher's perceptions of the lesson and the results of the evaluation activity.

Step 4. Selecting a Teaching Hypothesis

Based on *all* of the available information, a new hypothesis is selected and a lesson planned. This takes the teacher back into the "teach" phase, and the whole cycle begins again.

From Teaching Hypotheses to Lesson Plans

Once a teaching hypothesis has been selected, the teacher designs a corresponding lesson plan or set of lesson plans. The lesson plan or plans represents the manner in which the desired reading behavior is to be achieved. Good lesson plans for corrective reading should contain three important elements: (1) specific learner objectives; (2) procedures and materials designed to help the learners achieve the objectives; and (3) activities designed to assess whether the pupils have achieved these objectives. Figure 2.3 illustrates a basic format containing the elements described. You might note the resemblance of this lesson plan format to the individual educational plans (IEPs) required by Public Law 94–142 for handicapped children. Once you are comfortable using the format presented here, preparation of an IEP is an

FIGURE **2.3** Basic format of lesson plan for corrective reading.

Lesson Plan #6

Basic data:

Child(ren)	Jane, David, Debbie
Grade	2
Teacher	Mrs. Whitaker

Date: April 3, 1991

Hypothesis: Poor word identification skills partially due to inattention to the final position in words.

Objectives

Procedures

Materials

Lesson evaluation

FIGURE 2.4 Sample IEP lesson plan form. (From D. K. Reid and W. P. Hresko, *A Cognitive Approach to Learning Disabilities*. New York: McGraw-Hill, 1981. Used with permission.)

Individualized Educational Program

Student _____
 Last   First   Middle

Address _____

Teacher _____

Date _____
        Mo Dy Yr
School _____

Short term objectives	Specific educational and/or support services	Persons responsible	Significant dates		
			Begin	End	Review
Recommendations for specific procedures or techniques, materials, and so on		Evaluation criteria for goals and objectives			

easy task. The part of an IEP that presents the teaching plan is seen in figure 2.4. Compare figures 2.3 and 2.4, and you can easily see the similarities.

Objectives

When working with corrective readers, the objectives and teaching procedures emerge from the teacher's knowledge of each child's specific strengths and weaknesses. The typical steps of a developmental lesson, such as motivation, introduction of new vocabulary, guided silent reading, oral rereading, and skill development, may or may not be the same for children in a corrective program. More often, a lesson deals with some specific reading strategy based on analysis. For example, an identified weakness in using context clues may require several weeks or months of lessons to correct. This becomes a major teaching strand with long-term goals and specific lesson plan objectives, such as learning to identify certain words in a sentence as clues to what the unknown word might be.

If more than one weakness is identified, as is likely, these weaknesses should also receive attention and be included as another important objective for corrective lessons. Similarly, the need to spend several sessions on one weakness requires the use of many materials and procedures focusing on that weakness. Teachers should try to provide variation in learning activities to achieve the lesson objectives. For example, many instructional formats are available for teaching initial consonant blends. The effective teacher takes advantage of several of these techniques, utilizing different materials and procedures until the weakness has been corrected.

Success experiences should be interspersed with corrective procedures. *Every* lesson should provide opportunities for children to do things they are able to perform well, even though the time spent this way may be minimal. This procedure helps counteract negative feelings the child may have. Thus, each lesson includes learning activities that focus on areas of strength to enhance self-concept.

Teacher Objectives and Correlated Student Learning Objectives

Teachers, especially beginning teachers, are often understandably confused about objectives because they tend to think about them from the teachers' point of view rather than from the student-learning point of view. To avoid this confusion, teachers can state objectives from both aspects. When writing teaching objectives you can begin with the words "To teach. . . ." This statement then specifies the content the teacher wants to teach. The correlated student-learning objective, which helps the teacher focus on student behavior, should be stated in behavioral terms because such objectives lend themselves to evaluation. To use the earlier example of an identified weakness in context clues, the teacher's objective might be:

To teach use of context clues to aid in decoding an unknown word.

The correlated student-learning objective might be:

Given a list of five sentences, each containing a blank followed by three word choices and two or three words in the sentence providing clues to the word that best completes the blank, the student will underline words in the sentence that help in choosing the one word to complete the sentence. The student should be able to complete 80% or four of the five sentences accurately.

Behavioral Objectives

Behavioral objectives *must* include three components: (1) the condition; (2) the behavior; and (3) the criterion. The *condition* refers to the setting, or context in which the behavior will occur. The following are examples:

> Given a 250-word section from a social studies text . . .
> Given a 10-item worksheet on sequence of events . . .
> Given a 100-word paragraph . . .
> Given a list of the 12 vocabulary words . . .
> Given Taro Yashima's book *Umbrella* . . .

The *behavior* refers to what the teacher expects the child to *do*. For best results, verbs that reflect observable behaviors need to be used. While several types of observable behaviors can be prescribed, they fall into two common categories—motoric and verbal. Note that **overt behaviors** reflect the result of mental activities. Verbs that require unobservable, or **covert,** mental activity should be avoided because they cannot be verified easily. Covert mental activities can only be assumed to have happened if the behaviors cannot be observed. Examples of motoric, verbal, and covert verbs are as follows:

Motoric:	point, circle, mark, write, underline
Verbal:	say, read orally, tell, retell, paraphrase
Covert:	know, learn, remember, decide, participate, listen

The great strength of overt verbal behaviors is their ready accessibility to the teacher in a discussion-recitation setting. Answering the teacher's questions and oral reading are common verbal reading behaviors. Probably the greatest weakness of verbal behaviors is that oral responses do not lend themselves to easy record keeping, particularly in a group or informal setting. To record overt oral behaviors accurately requires that the teacher work with students individually. This may mean working directly with a student or listening to a taped reading that the student has previously prepared. One example of recording oral behavior is use of an informal reading inventory (discussed in chapter 4). Even though the process of recording oral reading behaviors is time-consuming, the results are often highly profitable in corrective reading. Teachers are also encouraged to jot down notes as they observe students throughout the day. These informal notes can be reviewed at the end of the day.

Motoric behavioral responses, especially marking or writing, have the advantage of being relatively permanent and easily scored. Motoric responses also can be used with more than one child at a time. Record keeping is generally much less time-consuming than recording and scoring oral reading behaviors for each student. The greatest weakness of written responses is the teacher time needed to prepare appropriate written activities.

For children who have not had many opportunities to write, writing words and sentences may be a difficult task. Many poor readers write and spell at a lower developmental level than they read. This is all the more reason for poor readers to be given opportunities to write, although initially the quantity of writing and spelling required to complete an activity might be limited. Multiple choice responses which require marking, and short written answers are suggested, particularly if a written model is available for copying. If a daily writing journal is employed as an instructional strategy, children's writing abilities will likely improve more rapidly.

The teacher should also try to balance the use of verbal and motoric behavioral responses of children. Verbal behaviors can be used during the teaching phase of a lesson when the teacher judges pupil response on an informal, impressionistic basis. Motoric or writing behaviors, such as tests, workbook activities, and other independent practice activities, can be used primarily for ongoing assessment or evaluation.

The *criterion* element of a behavioral objective, the minimal standard of achievement expected of the student, serves as the basis for deciding whether the pupil has reached a performance level acceptable to the teacher or test maker. The criterion itself is a matter of subjective judgment, and often one needs to take into account the fact that certain strategies are learned over a period of time. Early in a corrective program the criterion level may be low, but as the student learns, his level is increased. For instance, the teacher plans to help Bill self-correct his miscues more often. If currently he *never* self-corrects, then initially the criterion may call for Bill to self-correct "at least once." Later, after much instruction and practice, this criterion may increase to "all miscues will be self-corrected." Examples of criteria are as follows:

with 7 out of 10 correct
with 85 percent accuracy
at least 5 times

The following are two complete examples of behavioral objectives:

1. Condition: Given a five-item worksheet on the beginning consonants *r*, *h*, and *l*
   Behavior: the student will mark the correct picture beginning with these sounds
   Criterion: with at least 80 percent accuracy (4 out of 5).
2. Condition: Given a 200-word paragraph from his story,
   Behavior: Su Lin will read out loud and show evidence of self-monitoring, by verbally correcting
   Criterion: at least half of his miscues.

Figure 2.5 illustrates both teacher and learner objectives. Note that the objectives relate directly to the hypothesis.

Procedures

The heart of every lesson resides in the teaching procedures. Teachers' roles change rather dramatically from analyzing reading behaviors and forming teaching hypotheses to the instruction function. This does not mean, however, that teachers should not use informal assessment procedures during their lessons. To the contrary, wise teachers are constantly evaluating, informally, whether students are grasping the various points of the lesson. Those teachers who are able to "reflect-in-action" can modify lessons while they are ongoing (Schön, 1987).

Planning the Steps

When planning procedures for a lesson, teachers should focus on two considerations, the steps in the lessons and the questions involved.

FIGURE 2.5 Lesson plan showing objectives that relate directly to hypothesis.

Lesson Plan #6

Basic data:

Child(ren)	Jane, David, Debbie
Grade	2
Teacher	Mrs. Whitaker

Date: April 3, 1991

Hypothesis: Poor word identification skills partially due to inattention to the final position in words.

Objectives

Teacher: To teach close examination of the final position in words.

Children: (1) Given a ten item worksheet, the students will complete the sentences by circling the missing words with at least 70% accuracy (7/10). (2) Given a copy of a short story, the students will circle words the teacher reads incorrectly with at least 75% accuracy (15/20). (3) Given the same short story, the students will orally read the story with 85% accuracy (17/20) on the words with similar final sounds. (4) While playing dominoes, the students will read the sentences correctly with four or fewer errors and match underlined words with the same final sound with two or fewer errors. (5) Given the quiz on final sounds, the students will circle words to complete the sentences with at least 80% accuracy (8/10).

Procedures

Materials

Using Sound/Symbol/Structure Clues
p. 4, worksheet; p. 5, Quiz (*Hammond Reading Skills Series*)
Teacher-written short story
Teacher-made word cards
Teacher-made Dominoes card game

Lesson evaluation

Procedural steps.   Many steps, such as changing learning activities, reviewing the lesson, and preparing for independent practice activities, are procedural in nature. These steps are needed, but they are only peripheral to the teaching function itself.

Teaching steps.   The actual steps planned to teach something new need to be considered far more carefully. Teachers have options or alternative strategies for presenting new concepts. For contrast, two are mentioned here: didactic (also called deductive) and discovery (also called inductive) teaching strategies. In **didactic,** or **deductive, teaching** new information is given to the pupil in a rather direct fashion. An example would be to "give" the child a new word and tell him to learn it.

> Teacher: Jimmy, the word is *tray—tray*. Now, you say it.

The lesson may continue with the presentation of more new words and appropriate practice activities. This strategy is direct and efficient and often works well for specific purposes. It is limited, however, in that active child involvement can be lacking and the opportunity to learn to generalize the specific word recognition process to other unknown words (**transfer of training**) is not provided for directly. To be sure, some children are capable of making their own generalizations and transferring these learnings to other tasks. Typically, however, children with reading problems have trouble transferring what they have learned from one task to another. Therefore, the discovery approach to teaching often enhances learning the process (e.g., analyzing the word) as well as the product (the word itself in this case) for these children.

In **discovery** learning, or **inductive teaching**, the children are encouraged to seek the answer for themselves. The teacher's function is to observe how the children proceed in this process and to provide reinforcement and additional clues to aid learning when they are needed. Providing clues helps prevent undue frustration in case the pupils have trouble making the "discovery." Teacher assistance is also provided to help children learn how to discover new knowledge, that is, the transfer process itself. The word *tray* can again be used as an example.

> Teacher: Jimmy, here is a new word (teacher points to the word *tray* in the sentence "The cookie *tray* fell down"). How can you figure it out?
>
> Jimmy: *(No response.)*
>
> Teacher: Look at the rest of the words in the sentence. Do they help you?
>
> Jimmy: *(No response.)*
>
> Teacher: Do you see anything or any part of this word you might already know?
>
> Jimmy: It starts the same as train.
>
> Teacher: Good! Anything else?
>
> Jimmy: No.
>
> Teacher: How about the ending?
>
> Jimmy: Well it ends like say and may.
>
> Teacher: Yes, go on.
>
> Jimmy: Tr-tr-tr-ay—tray. I think it's tray.
>
> Teacher: Very good, Jimmy. Now let's check it out in the sentence to see if it makes sense.
>
> Jimmy: "The cookie *tray* fell down." Yes, that makes sense. The new word is *tray*.
>
> Teacher: That's great Jimmy. You are becoming a good word detective. Let's

make a card for your word bank . . . great! Now on the back of the card I want you to write [or the teacher can write a dictated sentence] a new sentence using the word *tray*. Then you can practice this word later so you can read it quickly. If you have trouble remembering this word turn your card over and read your sentence for help. You might also want to add this word to your personal dictionary with a picture and your new sentence.

Notice how much more teacher time and effort are involved when the discovery approach is used. But notice also that the teacher is getting the pupil actively involved in developing a strategy for analyzing unknown words. The minimal clues given to the child and the use of ample praise for the child's efforts help reduce negative feelings of failure and frustration.

Planning the Questions

The second important consideration when planning a lesson is determining the questions that may help the children during the lesson. The teacher cannot plan the exact questions to be used but should be prepared to use certain types of questions during the lessons. Two types are discussed in this section, but you should be aware that the theme of teachers' questions will be met frequently in the remainder of this text.

Problem-solving questions.   The use of **problem-solving questions** is designed to move a child from thinking "I don't know the answer" to a more dynamic frame of mind roughly equivalent to "How can I try to solve this problem?" An example of this type of question that comes from the previous dialogue is:

"How can you figure out the word, Jimmy?"

Often a question of this type signals subtly to the pupil that the teacher is accepting lack of knowledge—that it is okay if a person does not know the word or answer. The student then focuses on the problem without feeling a sense of embarrassment or failure if a guess is wrong. The teacher thereby increases the probability that active student participation will occur without the child feeling threatened.

Facilitating questions.   Pupils frequently are not able to solve the problem on their own. Thus, a second type of question, called a **facilitating question**, is essential to encourage continued thinking. Essentially, these questions are designed to make discovery easier for the child. Examples are paraphrased from the previous dialogue:

"Do the rest of the words in the sentence help you?"
"Do you see any part of this word you might know?"

Another facilitating question encourages pupils to *focus* on a point they may have overlooked:

"How about the ending of the word?"

Other facilitating questions present clues in the form of questions:

"Do you think the new word ends like these that you already know?"
(The teacher writes or says *"say," "may."*)

Facilitating questions basically demonstrate the teacher's efforts to guide children to discovery through active participation. In the example provided, the teacher wants Jimmy to learn the word *tray,* but all that effort to teach one word is hardly justifiable. The underlying purpose for this activity is to help students learn part of the process involved in figuring out new words. The teacher and children focus on the process of analyzing a particular word with the hope that the steps in the thought processes involved are being learned and that eventually the general thinking strategy practiced here by Jimmy with the aid of his teacher will transfer to other unknown words that he will encounter when the teacher is not present.

One purpose for problem-solving and facilitative questions is to help the pupil actively seek answers to the immediate question. Far more important, facilitative questions help children develop independent thinking strategies that can be applied to many other situations.

Informal Assessment During the Lesson

This section has briefly illustrated the teaching task and discussed significant parts of the lesson plan. One important issue remains. During the lesson, while the teacher is teaching, informal assessment of whether the children are learning the lesson is extremely beneficial. The most expeditious way to do this is to ask questions during the course of the lesson that elicit oral responses. The teacher asks a question or a set of questions about each point being taught. Asking for examples or illustrations also helps informal evaluation. If the teacher is reviewing content recently taught, the lesson should be opened with general questions that start with "Who remembers . . ." or "Can someone tell us. . . ." If the students are having trouble, give clues or hints, which often can be stated as facilitating or focusing questions.

One good teaching procedure provides a brief structured practice session on the topic, but with new examples for the children to solve. Corrective readers often learn content more quickly if they can practice with the teacher and classmates. Misperceptions and incorrect learnings can be corrected immediately. A written worksheet or chalkboard work on the topics provides a common focus for the group and stimulates the evaluation activity that typically follows.

Once teachers become familiar with their students, they can use the structured practice session as a guide to whether the children are ready to take a quiz or participate in some other evaluation activity. If the children do poorly during practice, the quiz should be deferred and further instruction or a second practice period given.

A Complete Lesson

The outline below, representing the basic steps in the analytic process, should serve as a general guide and summary of this process. It is generally applicable to all of the components involved in the reading process.

1. Examine reading behaviors.
    a. Gather information.
    b. Evaluate information.
2. Generate possible teaching hypotheses.
    a. Identify several alternatives.
    b. Select a tentative hypothesis.

3. Teach (with concurrent informal evaluation).
   a. Use direct instruction.
   b. Provide structured practice with teacher.
   c. Allow independent practice.
   d. Provide evaluation activity.
4. Reexamine reading behaviors.
   a. Gather information.
   b. Evaluate information.
   c. Generate teaching hypotheses.
   d. Select a teaching hypothesis.

Note that 3d, the evaluation activity at the end of the lesson, is directly linked to 4a, gathering information. Without a lesson evaluation activity, the analytic process is incomplete. Furthermore, if a teacher never obtains written evaluations and chooses to use only observational evaluation procedures, judgment of student learning has not been adequately verified. Thus, the teacher *assumes* the lesson was learned, and that assumption is subject to the pitfalls of assumptive teaching. A written evaluation activity is not needed for every student for every lesson, however. In fact, such a rigid procedure cannot be justified for many pupils, but for children with reading problems, the risk of assuming learning has taken place is much higher. Often, these children have a history of not learning and of leading teachers to err in their judgments.

Figure 2.6 contains the procedures and evaluation sections of the earlier lesson plan (fig. 2.5) as an example of a complete plan.

Summary

In this chapter, the analytic process has been defined and explained. The analytic process is contrasted with assumptive teaching and a justification for the process is presented.

A major portion of this chapter discusses the components of the reading process. The reading universe is partitioned into the three major domains of word recognition, comprehension, study skills and strategic reading, and the additional components of language ability and reading-related factors. When necessary, each of the domains can be analyzed, and areas, such as context clues, identified. Continued analysis ultimately leads to specific teachable units within each area, for example, using word order clues. Important correlative diagnostic questions related to each level of analysis and the additional components affecting the domains, such as language ability, are presented.

Another major section of this chapter deals with moving from the formation of teaching hypotheses to writing lesson plans. Examples of teacher and behavioral objectives are provided. Procedures for lesson plans include determining the steps for deductive and inductive teaching. Problem-solving and facilitating questions, designed to promote active child involvement and transfer of thought processes, are discussed. Finally, a complete plan is presented.

FIGURE 2.6 Completed lesson plan.

Basic data:	Lesson Plan #6	Date:	April 3, 1991

Child(ren) Jane, David, Debbie
Grade 2
Teacher Mrs. Whitaker

Hypothesis: Poor word identification skills partially due to inattention to the final position in words.

Objectives

Teacher: To teach close examination of the final position in words.

Children: (1) Given a ten-item worksheet, the students will complete the sentences by circling the missing words with at least 70% accuracy (7/10). (2) Given a copy of a short story, the students will circle words the teacher reads incorrectly with at least 75% accuracy (15/20). (3) Given the same short story, the students will orally read the story with 85% accuracy (17/20) of the words with similar final sounds. (4) While playing dominoes, the students will read the sentences correctly with four or fewer errors and match underlined words with the same final sound with two or fewer errors. (5) Given the quiz on final sounds, the students will circle words to complete the sentences with at least 80% accuracy (8/10).

Procedures

Instruction

1) Discuss importance of looking at an entire word. Print on blackboard: We played in our _____. (root, roof, room). Q: What would happen if you didn't look carefully at these words? Q: What word fits? Read senseless, worng sentences, too. Repeat, including singular-plural, consonants, and blends.

Structured practice

1) Explain worksheet. Q: What parts of the words will you look at? (initial, medial, final) Ex: She drives a _____. (bun, bus, but) Complete independently. Read sentences orally. Discuss and record results.

2) Explain story. Read it orally, and check students' answers. (Story is written using words students have made mistakes on in March.)

3) Students take turns reading the story. Informally check comprehension to remind them that it is always important. Record accuracy and comprehension.

Independent practice

1) While students are not reading story, they practice reading word cards: barn-bark, loss-lost, fact-fast, and so on.

2) Explain dominoes. Students take turns placing cards with words of like endings next to each other. They must read each sentence. They miss their turn if they do not have a match. Record any errors.

Evaluation

1) Pass out quiz. Format is the same as the worksheet. Grade papers together, and discuss any mistakes. Q: What have you learned today? Q: How will this help your reading?

Materials

Using Sound/Symbol/Structure Clues p. 4, worksheet p. 5, Quiz (*Hammond Reading Skills Series*)
Teacher-written short story
Teacher-made word cards
Teacher-made dominoes card game

Lesson evaluation

(See student scores below.) Jane did not meet criterion on the worksheet, the student read story, or the reading of the sentences on the Dominoes game. David and Debbie met or exceeded the criterion on all activities except the worksheet. They all had trouble answering the comprehension questions on the story. Next time I will include words with similar endings in meaningful story length context as a review activity. They were attentive during this lesson.

Student Scores

	Worksheet	Teacher-story	Student-story	Dominoes sentences	Dominoes words	Quiz
Jane	50%	80%	75%	-5	-1	80%
David	70%	85%	90%	-4	-1	100%
Debbie	60%	80%	90%	-4	-1	90%

References

Barr, R. (1984). Beginning reading instruction: From debate to reformation. In P. D. Pearson (Ed.), *Handbook of reading research.* New York: Longman.

Berglund, R. L. (1987). Reading assessment: An interactive process. *Reading Today, 5,* 3, 21.

Davis, F. B. (1944). Fundamental factors of comprehension in reading. *Psychometrika, 9,* 185–197.

Davis, F. B. (1968). Research in comprehension in reading. *Reading Research Quarterly, 4,* 499–545.

Farr, R., & Carey, R. F. (1986). *Reading: What can be measured?* Newark, DE: International Reading Association.

Herber, H. L. (1970). *Teaching reading in content areas.* Englewood Cliffs, NJ: Prentice-Hall.

Hittleman, D. R. (1983). *Developmental reading, K-8: Teaching from a psycholinguistic perspective.* Boston: Houghton Mifflin.

Jewell, M. G., & Zintz, M. V. (1986). *Learning to read naturally.* Dubuque, IA: Kendall/Hunt.

Kennedy, E. C. (1977). *Classroom approaches to remedial reading* (2nd ed.). Itasca, IL: F. E. Peacock.

Morrison, C., & Austin, M. C. (1977). *The torch lighters revisited.* Newark, DE: International Reading Association.

Pennock, C. (Ed.). (1979). *Reading comprehension at four linguistic levels.* Newark, DE: International Reading Association.

Schön, D. A. (1987). *Educating the reflective practitioner.* San Francisco, CA: Jossey-Bass.

Shubert, D., & Torgerson, T. (1981). *Improving the reading program* (5th ed.). Dubuque, IA: Wm. C. Brown.

Smith, R. J., & Barrett, T. C. (1976). *Teaching reading in the middle grades.* Reading, MA: Addison-Wesley.

Spearritt, D. (1972). Identification of subskills of reading comprehension by maximum likelihood factor analysis. *Reading Research Quarterly, 8,* 92–111.

Spiro, R. J., Bruce, B. C., & Brewer, W. F. (1980). *Theoretical issues in reading comprehension.* Hillsdale, NJ: Erlbaum.

Chapter 3

Assessing and Evaluating Reading Performance with Formal Measures

Objectives

After you have read this chapter, you should be able to

1. describe briefly the following measurement terms: validity, reliability, and standard error of measurement;
2. list four purposes of reading tests and measures;
3. describe the differences between these scores: grade equivalent, percentile, NCE, and stanine;
4. describe the differences among the following tests: reading survey tests, diagnostic reading tests, and text-related tests;
5. identify the best types of tests to assess students at the four levels of analysis;
6. describe the difference between norm-referenced and criterion-referenced tests.

Study Outline

I. Introduction
II. Basic concepts in assessment and evaluation
    A. Definitions
        1. Percentile scores
        2. Standard scores
        3. Stanine scores
        4. NCE scores
        5. Grade-equivalent scores
    B. Basic measurement concepts
        1. Validity
            a) Content validity
            b) Construct validity
        2. Reliability

3. Standard error of measurement
    C. Types of tests
        1. Formal test
        2. Informal test
        3. Oral reading test
        4. Silent reading test
        5. Survey test
        6. Diagnostic test
        7. Criterion-referenced test
        8. Text-related test
        9. Individual test
        10. Group test
    D. Purposes of testing in reading

III. Formal reading tests
  A. Standardized reading survey tests
   1. The *Gates-MacGinitie Reading Tests*
   2. The *Nelson Reading Skills Test*
  B. Standardized diagnostic reading tests

   1. Individually administered diagnostic tests
   2. Group-administered diagnostic tests
  C. Criterion-referenced tests
IV. Summary
V. References

Important Vocabulary and Concepts

assessment
at-level testing
construct validity
content validity
correlation coefficients
criterion-referenced tests
end-of-unit tests
evaluation
formal tests
grade equivalent scores
mastery tests
NCE scores
norm-referenced tests

norms
objective-based tests
out-of-level testing
percentile scores
reliability
standard deviation
standard error of measurement
standard scores
standardized tests
stanine scores
text-related tests
validity

Overview

Knowledge of the analytic process alone is not sufficient for effective corrective reading instruction. Along with many other relevant facts, teachers must know (1) the variety of tools used to assess reading performance; (2) when, where, and with whom the tools can be used; and (3) what the strengths and weaknesses of the tools are. Chapters 3 and 4 are designed to prepare teachers to understand the assessment process and to identify the instruments and procedures that can be used to aid them in this process.

In the first section of chapter 3, concepts relevant to measurement, assessment, and analysis of reading problems are discussed. Explanations are given of the different types of scores used in tests and their strengths and weaknesses. The purposes of testing are included as well as a brief discussion of different kinds of tests.

The second major section of this chapter contains a discussion of formal reading tests. Standardized reading survey tests and standardized diagnostic reading tests are discussed at length, and some examples are provided for your consideration.

Introduction

At the time of this writing, the nature of reading assessment and evaluation is itself in the midst of reevaluation and change. Because the nature of the reading process has been more clearly defined as a constructive process between the reader, the text, and the context of the reading, instructional practices are changing. Instructional practices, in turn, should determine testing practices. However, such is not yet the case. As summarized by Glazer, Searfoss, and Gentile (1988, p. 7), "our pedagogy has expanded to reflect current research about learning literacy skills. Our tests and testing environments, however, have changed little."

Fortunately, models that represent a more natural approach to assessment are being developed. These naturalistic approaches, or "realistic evaluation" (Glazer, Searfoss, & Gentile, 1988) procedures are more appropriately discussed in chapter 4, Assessing and Evaluating Reading Performance with Informal Measures.

Unfortunately, until more naturalistic forms of reading assessment are fully accepted, there remains a need for classroom teachers to know something about formal test measures. These types of measures, while perhaps less meaningful to the teacher in terms of instructional planning, *are* being administered in schools and are likely to be around for some time to come. Therefore, this chapter is viewed as informative of the basic concepts related to formal measures enabling teachers to better decide for themselves how valuable a particular test score may or may not be. Also, the information found here should help teachers better discuss standardized test results with the parents of their students.

A review of the basic concepts of assessment and evaluation includes definitions, measurement concepts, a brief discussion of different kinds of tests, and, more specific to the goal of this text, purposes of testing in reading. After this review, the chapter proceeds with a discussion of formal reading tests.

Assessment and Evaluation: Basic Concepts

Definitions

Both assessment and evaluation are critical to reading analysis. Many educators use the terms interchangeably; this practice may be a mistake. **Assessment** usually refers to the process of gathering data about a learner's strengths and weaknesses, while **evaluation** refers to the process of judging achievement or growth, or to decision making. Thus, evaluation implies the need to use assessment techniques to obtain information for making judgments or decisions.

In schools, reading achievement is most frequently evaluated through the use of standardized achievement tests. **Standardized tests** are thus called because they have been administered in the same way to a large group of students (who represent students for whom the test was designed) in order to establish a reference or norm group. The scores of these students then become the **norms** and can be used for comparison with the scores of other students taking the test. Thus the term **norm-referenced** is also used to describe a standardized test. Part of the standardization procedure involves preparing a standard set of directions for administration that includes directions to students and time allotment for completing subtests. This standard set of directions is another reason these tests are called standardized, and because the directions for administration must be strictly adhered to, the tests have also become known as **formal tests.**

Several other terms associated with standardized testing will be used throughout the remainder of this chapter. Those related to interpreting standardized test scores will be defined here. Other important terms are defined in the next section. Because a standardized test is norm-referenced, norm tables are included in the test's manual to tell you how the raw scores are converted into normed scores. These normed scores include percentile scores, standard scores such as stanines and normal curve equivalent scores, and grade equivalent scores. Each will be defined here. For help in seeing how some of these scores relate to the normal curve, refer to figure 3.1.

Percentile Scores

Percentile scores, converted from raw scores, compare students to others of the same grade or age. Children who receive a percentile score of 63 have done as well as or better than 63 percent of the norm group. Percentile scores can range from 1 to 99 (fig. 3.1). Interpretation of percentile scores is limited, however, to comparing the child to those in the norm groups or to those in the same classroom or school. For example, if Georgia's raw score of 17 converts to the twelfth percentile, the proper interpretation is that Georgia has done as well as or better than 12 percent of a large sample of children who took this test. The teacher may also compare Georgia to her classmates who took the same test. This information helps the teacher fit Georgia into a small group for instructional reading purposes but is not at all helpful for deeper level analytic purposes. Therefore, for corrective reading purposes, the teacher must turn to other means of assessing reading behaviors to help identify Georgia's specific reading strengths and weaknesses.

Standard Scores

Standard scores are derived from the raw scores in such a way as to obtain uniformly spaced scores. Standard scores indicate an individual's distance from the average, or mean, score in terms of the variability of the distribution of all scores. Variability is indicated by a number called the **standard deviation.** (The higher the standard deviation, the more variability in the scores.) Standard scores allow comparisons to be made on different tests and subtests. Some standardized achievement tests convert raw scores to an average standard score of 50 with a standard deviation of 10 (see T-scores, fig. 3. 1). For example, if Jerry made a raw score of 52 on a math test and 42 on a reading test, the scores cannot be directly compared because they do not reflect anything about the total distribution of scores for all the students taking the test. By converting the raw scores to standard scores, Jerry's scores can be considered in relation to an average score of 50 and a standard deviation of 10. Jerry's scores convert to a standard score of 80 on the math test and 48 on the reading test. Jerry therefore did much better on the math test than on the reading test, but the raw scores did not indicate such a large difference. Jerry also scored well above average on the math test. The average is 50; thus 80 is 30 points or 3 (30 ÷ 10) standard deviations above the mean. On the other hand, Jerry did just about average on the reading test.

FIGURE 3.1 Normal curve showing relationship of standard deviations and percentile, standard, and stanine scores. (Adapted from Harold G. Seashore, *Test Service Bulletin*, No. 54, January 1956. Courtesy of the Psychological Corporation, San Antonio, TX.)

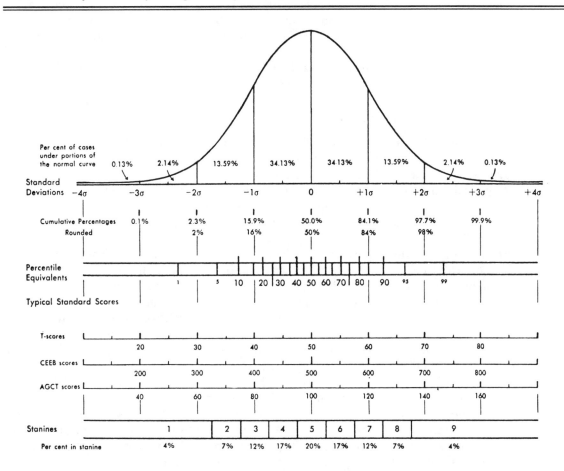

NOTE: This chart cannot be used to equate scores on one test to scores on another test. For example, both 600 on the CEEB and 120 on the AGCT are one standard deviation above their respective means, but they do not represent "equal" standings because the scores were obtained from different groups.

Stanine Scores

Stanine scores are standard scores for which the raw scores have been converted into nine equally spaced parts, with a stanine of 1 being low and 9 being high. A stanine of 5 is considered average, and the standard deviation is about 2 (fig. 3.1).

Stanine scores are interpreted similarly to percentiles, with the major difference being the number and size of units involved; there are 99 percentile units and only 9 stanines. For interpretation purposes, stanines 1, 2, and 3 reflect poor performance, stanines 4, 5, and 6 reflect average performance, and stanines 7, 8, and 9 reflect good performance on a test.

NCE Scores

Another kind of standard score based on a normal curve, the **normal curve equivalent** (NCE), is a norm that has recently come into use. NCE scores range from 1 to 99 and the mean is 50, and in these ways they are similar to percentile scores. The points in between are different from percentiles, however. Percentile scores tend to pile up around the mean and spread farther apart upon approaching the extremes; NCE scores are in equal units. Table 3.1 defines the relationships among stanines, percentiles, and NCE scores, while figure 3.2 shows this relationship.

Grade Equivalent Scores

Grade equivalent scores are usually given in terms of years and tenths of years. For example, if the average raw score of beginning fourth grade children in the norm group is 33, then 33 is assigned the grade equivalent of 4.1 (fourth grade, first month). Any child who scores 33 raw score points receives a grade equivalent score of 4.1.

Grade equivalent scores appear easy for teachers to interpret because the reference point is a grade in school, but interpretation actually has some serious limitations. The farther away a pupil's score is from the average, the greater the chances are that the "grade" equivalent will be misinterpreted. Grade equivalent scores for average children are probably quite accurate, but low or high scores are susceptible to error of interpretation. This is particularly important for teachers of students who are reading poorly to remember. To continue with the example of the fourth grader, if Georgia scores 17 raw score points (a fairly low score), which converts to a grade equivalent score of 2.1 from the norm table found in the test manual, the teacher should *not* conclude that Georgia is reading in a manner similar to a beginning second grade child. All that can be said is that Georgia is reading poorly compared to her fourth grade classmates and that she made the same raw score as the average of second graders in the first month of second grade.

Grade equivalent scores do *not* indicate grade placement for a student. For example, Tommy, a third grader, takes the test containing second, third, and fourth grade material and receives a grade equivalent score of 5.3. This does *not* mean that Tommy is able to do fifth grade, third month material because he was never tested

TABLE 3.1 Relationships Among Stanines, Percentiles, and NCE Scores

Stanines	NCE	Percentiles	Percent per stanine	
9	86–99	97–99	Highest 4%	Above
8	77–85	90–96	Next highest 7%	average
7	66–76	78–89	Next 12%	23%
6	56–65	61–77	Above middle 17%	Average
5	45–55	41–60	Middle 20%	54%
4	35–44	24–40	Below middle 17%	
3	24–34	12–23	Next 12%	Below
2	15–23	5–11	Next lowest 7%	average
1	1–14	1–4	Lowest 4%	23%

From Bjorn Karlsen, "Reading: Assessment and Diagnosis of Reading Abilities." Chap. 6 in *Teaching Reading: Foundations and Strategies,* 2d ed., by Pose Lamb and Richard Arnold. © 1980 by Wadsworth, Inc. Reprinted by permission of Wadsworth Publishing Company, Belmont, CA 94002.

Figure 3.2 Relationship of NCEs, percentiles, and stanines to the normal curve.

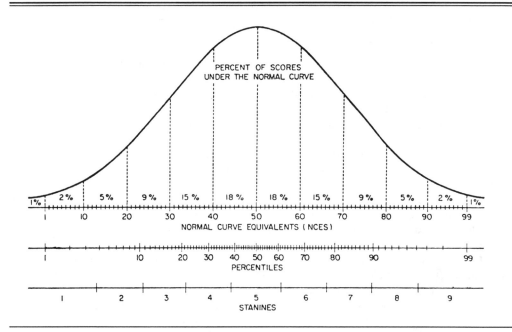

on fifth grade material. It only means that Tommy can perform second, third, and fourth grade tasks in the test as well as average students in the third month of fifth grade can perform these (below grade level) tasks.

Grade equivalent scores have been so seriously misinterpreted that the International Reading Association has passed a resolution calling upon publishers to eliminate grade equivalents from their tests. This resolution can be read in its entirety in figure 3.3. Percentile scores, stanines, or NCEs are recommended for comparing a student's performance to that of the norm group.

Basic Measurement Concepts

Successful assessment and evaluation in reading depend considerably on the tools teachers use. These tools can be called tests in the broadest sense of that term, but tests can range from informal observations of pupils to the highly structured standardized achievement tests. Some concepts are basic to all of these measurement systems, regardless of how they are constructed or used. Among the more important concepts are validity, reliability, and standard error of measurement.

Validity

The most important of all measurement characteristics is **validity.** A test is valid if, in fact, *it measures what it claims to measure and does the task for which it is intended.* The critical question for the teacher to ask is: Does this test measure what I have been teaching?

Test content that matches the instructional objectives is said to have **content validity.** If the match is poor, the test is an invalid measure of those particular

FIGURE 3.3 International Reading Association resolution regarding the misuse of grade equivalent scores. (Reprinted with permission of the International Reading Association.)

Misuse of grade equivalents

WHEREAS, standardized, norm-referenced tests can provide information useful to teachers, students, and parents, if the results of such tests are used properly, and

WHEREAS, proper use of any standardized test depends on a thorough understanding of the test's purpose, the way it was developed, and any limitations it has, and

WHEREAS, failure to fully understand these factors can lead to serious misuse of test results, and

WHEREAS, one of the most serious misuses of tests is the reliance on a grade equivalent as an indicator of absolute performance, when a grade equivalent should be interpreted as an indicator of a test-taker's performance in relation to the performance of other test-takers used to norm the test, and

WHEREAS, in reading education, the misuse of grade equivalents has led to such mistaken assumptions as: (1) a grade equivalent of 5.0, on a reading test means that the test-taker will be able to read fifth grade material, and (2) a grade equivalent of 10.0 by a fourth grade student means that student reads like a tenth grader even though the test may include only sixth grade material as its top level of difficulty, and

WHEREAS, the misuse of grade equivalents promotes misunderstanding of a student's reading ability and leads to underreliance on other norm-referenced scores which are much less susceptible to misinterpretation and misunderstanding, be it

RESOLVED, that the International Reading Association strongly advocates that those who administer standardized reading tests abandon the practice of using grade equivalents to report performance of either individuals or groups of test-takers and be it further

RESOLVED, that the president or executive director of the Association write to test publishers urging them to eliminate grade equivalents from their tests.

Resolution passed by the Delegates Assembly of the International Reading Association, April 1981

---

instructional objectives. For example, a teacher has been concentrating on teaching reading comprehension for the past three months and now wants to test the pupils. A test measuring reading comprehension would be valid; one measuring phonic knowledge would be invalid because the test would not measure what had been taught. The phonics test is not a bad test in and of itself; rather, it is inappropriate for the purpose intended. Kavale (1979) suggests that teachers determine content validity by actually taking the test.

Teachers are unlikely to make an error in situations where the validity issue is so clearly apparent as in the example above, but occasionally the matter is more subtle. Consider, for instance, a test called "Vocabulary Knowledge" being used when the match between the test and the lessons taught is a matter of approach. If the teacher has used a modified cloze procedure approach and the test measures vocabulary from a synonym matching approach, the test would not be highly valid because it does not assess vocabulary as it was taught. Teachers and school administrators must be jointly responsible for choosing appropriate tests.

Another type of validity is called **construct validity.** This refers to *what degree a test measures a certain ability or trait.* For example, an intelligence test is said to have construct validity to the extent that it actually measures intelligence. Because most traits cannot be measured directly, tests having construct validity measure behaviors believed to reflect the trait. The titles of some tests *imply* construct validity without providing empirical information in the test manual to support the existence of the validity (Sax, 1980). Such a practice is misleading to teachers and to others who may not be knowledgeable about measurement concepts. A test on reading comprehension, for example, should provide evidence that the test, in fact, measures reading comprehension.

Many tests designed to measure word recognition skills have been questioned on the basis of their construct validity. If a syllabication subtest asks students to identify how many syllables exist in various words, and the words are spoken by the examiner, the construct validity of the test can be questioned. In the real reading situation the students *see* and do not *hear* the words that they must syllabicate. Thus the question is whether the behaviors measured by oral presentation measure the same trait required during the process of silent reading.

Construct validity is typically supported by **correlation coefficients** which indicate how strongly two variables are related. To be of most value for assessment, the subtests involved must be relatively independent, as reflected by low correlation coefficients ranging from 0.00 to 0.70 (Karlsen, 1980). A high correlation (0.70 to 1.00) indicates a strong relationship between the subtests; in this case, the subtests are too interrelated to measure the different aptitudes they purport to measure.

Statistical procedures are available to determine test validity, but they are not directly related to the major purposes of this book. They are vital, however, for teachers who are asked to evaluate and select standardized tests for their school or school district. Both George Spache (1976) and Kenneth Kavale (1979) devote an entire chapter to important issues relevant to selecting standardized tests in reading. These readings are highly recommended for those who select and use such instruments.

Reliability

The consistency or dependability of a test and its measurements denotes its **reliability.** If a teacher gives the same test to a student more than once (test-retest) and the scores on each test are nearly the same, the test is considered reliable because it yields essentially the same score each time it is given.

Reliability is also expressed through a correlation coefficient. The higher the correlation coefficient, the more dependable are the scores obtained from the test. A coefficient of .90 or above is considered very reliable; if it is below .80, the teacher should be cautious in making decisions about the individual students. Reliability can be estimated in a number of statistical ways, and each has a different name. Test manuals indicate the type of reliability by using terms such as "split-half reliability," "parallel forms reliability," and "Kuder-Richardson reliability." In any case, a high correlation coefficient is desirable.

No test of reading is perfectly consistent. Some common conditions affecting reliability are: (1) objectivity in scoring; (2) needed variability among scores of students being tested; (3) number of items on the test; (4) difficulty level; and (5) standardization of test administration and interpretation (Sax, 1980).

Objectivity in scoring is critical. If different teachers independently score the same test but arrive at different scores, reliability cannot be very high. Multiple choice tests are relatively free from problems of this type compared to more subjective measures, such as essay tests.

Reliability also depends on the variability of the students taking the tests. If everyone taking the test functions at the same level and gets the same score, reliability of that test is zero, because student variability is lacking.

The easiest and most efficient way to improve reliability is to increase the number of items on the test, provided that the added items consistently measure what the original items measure. This explains, in part, why some tests are so long. In instances of behavioral observation, the teacher must increase the number of times the student is observed performing a specific task.

Difficulty level also affects reliability. A very easy or very hard test does not measure individual differences because all student responses tend to be the same (Sax, 1980). Clearly such a test cannot be used for analytic purposes.

Standardization of test administration and interpretation provides more reliable scores. Tests that lack such clear guidelines result in scores that are highly dependent on the person giving the test.

Standard Error of Measurement

When a score is obtained for a child the teacher should ask how much confidence can be placed in it as the child's "true" score. Many test manuals describe a statistic known as the **standard error of measurement** (SE$_{meas}$ or SEM). This statistic indicates how much an individual's score can be expected to vary each time the test is taken. Edward Fry (1980), in a review of the Metropolitan Achievement Test, clearly explains the SEM:

> Now we all know that every test has a certain amount of slop in it. Statisticians call this slop the Standard Error of Measurement. It means how much an individual's score is likely to jump around on repeated testings. You see the problem is, "if a student scores high one day, and lower the next day, on the same test, which score is correct?" Well, theoretically if you retook the test many times and there was no practice effect, you could average the scores and get a "true score," which is the score you really want. But you can't give the test a lot of times in the real world; so you give it just once and estimate how far away you could be from the true score. This distance is called the Standard Error of Measurement (SEM), and good statisticians that they are, the authors of the Metropolitan have given us the SEM for this test. Let's apply it to Janie Guesser's score. The SEM is 17 Standard Score points. This means that two-thirds of the time, Janie, or anyone else who got a raw score of 40, would have a true standard score between 733 and 697 [699]. You add and subtract the SEM from the obtained score to get the band of probability [confidence interval].
>
> That might sound a little technical, but you can read it slowly in any measurement textbook. However, let's make it a little more meaningful. An upper level Standard Score of 733 gives her a grade equivalent score of 6.7 and a percentile of 69. The lower level Standard Score of 697 [699] will give a grade equivalent score of 4.8 and a percentile of 48. This means that Janie, or any student getting 40 items right, has a true grade score between 4.8 and 6.7 for two out of three testings. In one out of three testings the true score would fall either above or below that band.
>
> Hence when we test a student who is in the middle of the range for the intermediate level of the Metropolitan Reading Test, we know only that the true score lies in a band almost two years wide.
>
> Test scores aren't quite as accurate as some people think.[1] (pp. 199–200).

---

[1] From Edward Fry, "Test Review: Metropolitan Achievement Tests," *Reading Teacher,* November 1980, pp. 199–200. Reprinted with permission of the author and the International Reading Association.

Ideally, we would like to use a test with a high reliability and a small SEM. The concept of the SEM is not restricted to formal tests, however. Informal tests, criterion-referenced tests, and text-related tests, which will be defined a little later, also have a potentially large SEM because they have not been given to large groups of students with the intention of modifying the test to lower the SEM. Thus, the very nature of an informal test suggests that considerable potential error will be associated with the scores. Using just one test score then, whether from a formal or informal test, is not a good idea. Before making a decision about a student's ability, the teacher must consider a variety of information (e.g., test score plus informal observation plus workbook page).

Types of Tests

Reading tests are categorized in several ways:

1. Formal (standardized or norm-referenced) or informal (nonstandardized)
2. Oral or silent
3. Survey, diagnostic, criterion-referenced, or text-related

These tests can be administered to an individual or a group and are designed specifically for each.

Formal Test

A formal test, which is the same as a standardized or norm-referenced test, has been tried out on a large number of people to establish a norm group. Individual performances can then be compared to that of the norm group.

Informal Test

An informal test is not standardized and a norm group has not been established. Many teacher-made assessments are considered informal tests regardless of their length. Any time a teacher collects information about some aspect of a student's ability, an informal assessment is being made. An informal test, however, is only as good as the person who devises or uses it. Chapter 4 deals more specifically with the topic of informal assessment, which includes such instruments as informal reading inventories, teacher-made tests such as cloze passages, or phonics surveys.

Oral Reading Test

An oral reading test requires the child to read aloud, which is the overt behavior being assessed. Oral reading provides a rich source of behavioral responses that are most often used to analyze two types of reading behaviors: fluency and word identification skills. More recently, oral reading responses have also been analyzed for evidence of the thought processes involved in mature reading (more on this in chapter 4).

Silent Reading Test

A silent reading test requires the students to read to themselves and give responses to questions on the material. These responses can be given orally or in writing, depending on whether the test is an individual or a group test.

The major advantage of silent reading tests is that they lend themselves to group assessment procedures, which are much less time-consuming than working with individual students. Another advantage is that many group silent reading tests are norm-referenced, allowing the teacher an opportunity to interpret a student's score in relationship to other students in the same age or grade level. Also, students' answers to the questions asked at the end of a silent reading selection may tell the teacher whether the author's message has been understood.

Survey Test

A survey test, also called an achievement test, is designed to sample broad knowledge or proficiency in a given area. Scores reflect overall reading achievement. Because these tests are generally standardized, the group who takes the test can be compared to the norm group and general areas of strengths and weaknesses indicated. Most reading achievement tests provide scores for the two subtests of vocabulary and comprehension plus a total reading score. Unfortunately, there are no standardized reading achievement tests that assess the strategies a reader uses.

Diagnostic Test

The diagnostic test attempts to measure discrete reading skills. Such tests usually provide several subtest scores of reading skill development. The subtest scores are analyzed to determine areas of strength and weakness.

Criterion-Referenced Test

A **criterion-referenced test** measures how well an individual performs a specific task. Usually a level of performance is specified, thus the term *criterion*. For example, the content of a criterion-referenced test may be final consonant sounds. In order to say that Jimmy knows final consonant sounds, he may have to respond correctly to 90 percent or more of the test items. Jimmy's performance is not compared to group performance. Teachers set the criterion level to coincide with their expectations for a particular individual.

Text-Related Test

In addition to core materials found in most classrooms (e.g., basal readers, workbooks, and teacher's manuals), most publishers provide ancillary materials, including tests, to help assess student learning. These tests measure acquisition of skills emphasized in a reader or text at a particular level. Such tests have the advantage of content validity, because they are intended to measure the content learned from the reading materials just completed. While carefully constructed, they usually have not been as carefully normed as previously mentioned formal tests. They also measure a smaller number of skills and objectives. Good students may not have a chance to show what they can do; they often "top the test" (i.e., obtain very high scores). The tests do, however, indicate students who need corrective and remedial work. Thus, they can have considerable analytic value for corrective reading.

Many basal systems contain **end-of-unit tests** in the teacher's manual or in the student workbooks. These tests should not be overlooked by teachers because they provide useful information regarding student accomplishment of relatively small learning segments. Corrective procedures are often recommended for children who do not do well on these tests.

Individual Test

An individual test is designed to be given to one person at a time. The efficiency is low because fewer students can be tested in a given amount of time. However, some reading strategies can only be assessed through an individual test. The ability to monitor and self-correct oral reading miscues is one example. Other advantages of individual tests include the flexibility to modify or clarify directions for some students and the opportunity to observe other behaviors, in addition to reading, during testing.

Group Test

A group test is given to several students at the same time. These tests solve the problem of inefficiency with individual tests. Group tests come with specific directions (both oral and written in some cases) and written materials (usually an answer sheet or test booklet).

In summary then, many kinds of tests are available. However, each of the classifications just defined does not necessarily indicate a distinct type of test. One test may fall under more than one classification. For example, standardized achievement tests are not only formal tests but are considered to be group tests and survey tests as well. Likewise, a diagnostic test may be an individual or a group test or an oral reading test. This overlap in classifications is demonstrated in this and the next chapter.

Purposes of Testing in Reading

Testing has many different purposes and many tests are available, so care must be taken to choose a test appropriate for a specific purpose. As Kavale says, "If the uses for the test results are not known in advance, the best test to use is none at all" (p. 9).

Test selection should be based on answers to the questions *what, who, by whom, for what* (Merwin, 1973). Kavale provides some examples of how these questions might be answered. For instance, a test is needed to:

1. assess reading achievement *(what)* of a fourth grade student *(who)* by the teacher *(by whom)* to help determine the student's instructional reading level *(for what)*.
2. assess word attack skills *(what)* of a third-grade child *(who)* by the teacher *(by whom)* to determine if a phonics program is needed *(for what)*.
3. assess gain in reading achievement *(what)* of a group of fourth graders *(who)* by a curriculum supervisor *(by whom)* to determine the effectiveness of a new set of instructional materials *(for what)*. (p. 10)

Using Merwin's guidelines, the answer to the *for what* question represents the specific purpose for testing, but the other questions are equally important to the selection of a test.

Because of the great number of purposes for testing in reading, all cannot be listed; however, some examples are relevant for classroom teachers:

1. Organizing the class into reading, skill, or interest groups
2. Assessing reading levels of individual students
3. Identifying specific reading difficulties, such as word attack skills, inferential comprehension, or vocabulary development
4. Evaluating individuals or small groups

Formal Reading Tests

Once a purpose for testing has been established, a test must be selected. Just because a test is published or its title indicates it may be appropriate does not mean you have found a quality test. The best procedure to determine the quality of a particular test is to examine the instrument itself (include the test's technical manual) and consult a professional review of the test. The American Psychological Association (1974) sets standards for test publishers, which can be of help to concerned test users. If a test manual does not contain data considered essential by the American Psychological Association, the test under consideration should be seriously questioned before it is used.

Important information about tests can be found in several different publications. The *Ninth Mental Measurements Yearbook* (Mitchell, 1985), a two-volume work, contains much information about tests, such as what they purport to measure, basic statistical data, and reviews of the tests by scholars. An important monograph by O. K. Buros, entitled *Reading Tests and Reviews* (1979), consolidates into one volume much of the information found in the yearbook. It should be considered an essential reference for evaluating reading tests that were published through the mid to late 1970s. The International Reading Association (IRA) publishes reviews several times a year in *The Reading Teacher* and *Journal of Reading*. IRA has also published L. M. Schell's *Diagnostic and Criterion-Referenced Reading Tests: Review and Evaluation* (1981), which reviews twelve tests considered important enough to be reviewed by reading professionals.

Along with the tests themselves, publishers provide examiner manuals and several additional aids, such as scoring keys and record sheets. Test technical manuals or examiner manuals contain vital information that must be studied before giving the test. A good test manual contains directions for test administration and scoring and information to aid effective interpretation of the scores. Additional information of a statistical and technical nature, such as validity and reliability coefficients and the SEM, are usually found in the technical manual.

Teachers must carefully follow directions when administering standardized tests. Tests are designed so that every pupil will get, as nearly as possible, the same chance when taking the test. If teachers do not follow standardized directions, scores cannot be used reliably and validly. Directions should never be rushed or examples omitted. On the other hand, teachers should never give more information to pupils than is specified in the test manual. Deviations from the directions or test time will put the pupils in a setting different from the norm group, and norms for the test will not be appropriate. It is imperative, therefore, that teachers follow instructions precisely or note any deviations from the standardized procedures.

A good testing environment is important because classroom conditions affect the reliability of test results. The classroom should be well lighted, ventilated, and free from undue noise or interruptions. A sufficient number of tests, answer sheets, and marking pencils should be readily available. Pupils unaccustomed to taking tests should be briefed beforehand regarding such test-taking behaviors as no talking, no helping, and no drinks of water. Younger elementary students may benefit from a practice session, using practice booklets, which are often available. At times teachers have difficulty maintaining the neutral role needed during the testing period, but the temptation to help students must be resisted. The roles of teacher and tester are *not* the same.

Standardized Reading Survey Tests

Standardized tests most widely used in schools today are achievement test batteries such as the *California Achievement Tests, Iowa Tests of Basic Skills, Metropolitan Achievement Tests,* and *Stanford Achievement Tests.* These batteries typically yield two or three reading scores plus scores for other subject areas, such as arithmetic and social studies. Common areas assessed in reading are vocabulary, comprehension, total reading (often a combination of the vocabulary and comprehension scores), and less frequently, measures of study skills and rate of reading.

These tests can be helpful to classroom teachers in two important ways. First, they allow teachers to compare students within their classroom to determine their relative standing (rank order), which should aid in the placement process involved in grouping for reading instruction. Second, they allow teachers a chance to observe strengths and weaknesses of individual children, relative to the norm group, in the curricular areas being tested. For example, a child may demonstrate strengths in arithmetic computation and weaknesses in the subtests of the reading survey test. This can be a clue that the student has a reading problem.

Survey reading tests are similar to the reading subtests on achievement test batteries. When reading is the focus of testing, a survey test saves time because other content areas are not included. These tests help in placement and in determining whether a student has a reading problem. Survey tests are particularly helpful for inexperienced teachers who may not yet know what to expect from children at a particular developmental age or grade level. Teachers should be aware, however, that scores from these tests probably reflect maximum performance on the part of many students. Children usually try hard to do their best on tests of this type, and their scores tend to reflect a level of concentration and performance not typical in day-to-day reading activities.

While survey reading tests help teachers with level 1 analysis, identifying those students with possible reading problems, and perhaps with level 2 analysis, identifying the major domain in which reading problems are occurring, the tests are not designed to do more than this. Other tests and procedures are more helpful for analyzing reading behaviors at levels 2, 3 (areas of weakness), and 4 (teachable units), and they can supplement data received on survey tests. Also consider that there are students who are effective readers but never do well on standardized tests.

Most recent survey reading tests, including the two discussed in this section, are designed to be administered in one of two ways. The first, called **at-level testing,** uses a single level of the test for a specified grade level. For example, Level A of the test is to be used for first and second grades, Level B for third and fourth grades, and Level C for fifth and sixth grades. A third-grade teacher would administer the Level B test to all students in the class.

The second option, called **out-of-level testing**, allows the teacher to select the level of the test that best reflects the average achievement of the class. For example, a teacher of students whose average achievement is atypically low or high could select a level better suited to the examinees, thus increasing reliability. If out-of-level testing is desired, be sure to check the teacher's manual of the test being used for further information.

The *Gates-MacGinitie Reading Tests,* (1989) Level 1, can be used as an example for children in first grade. Other levels of the *Gates-MacGinitie Reading Tests* are available for grade levels up through high school (Level PRE = pre-reading; Level R = beginning; Levels 1, 2, 3, 4, 5/6, 7/8, 9/10, and 11/12). The *Nelson Reading Skills Test, Level A* (1977), has been chosen as an example for children in third or fourth grade. Other levels are also available (Level B = grade 5–6; Level C = 7–9).

The Gates-MacGinitie Reading Tests

Level 1 of the *Gates-MacGinitie Reading Tests* is designed to assess reading progress for students in first grade. It consists of two subtests, vocabulary and comprehension, with an optional decoding subtest for levels A and B. On the vocabulary subtest, the child is asked to choose the word, from four choices, that best represents a picture. Items are arranged in increasing difficulty. The score is the number correct.

The comprehension subtest also contains items arranged in increasing difficulty. The students are asked to read one to four sentences per item and then to mark, from among four pictures, the one that best represents ("goes with") the story. The score is the number correct. Correct raw scores can be converted to standard scores, percentiles, and grade equivalent scores for interpretation purposes.

The Nelson Reading Skills Test

The *Nelson Reading Skills Test, Level A,* is designed to be used with pupils in grades 3 and 4. As with the previous test, two subtests assess vocabulary and comprehension. However, level A only has three optional subtests: sound-symbol correspondence, root words, and syllabication.

To test knowledge of vocabulary, students are asked to select a synonym for a given word from among four possible choices. In contrast to level A of the Gates-MacGinitie test, level A of the Nelson test expects children to read stimulus words to complete the sentence; the test for first graders uses pictures. This change, observed in many reading tests, represents the shift away from the use of pictures in tests as children mature in reading development.

The vocabulary subtest contains items arranged in increasing difficulty. Because the test is designed to survey more than one grade level, a spread of items in terms of difficulty is needed. Younger children are not expected to complete the more difficult items, and the teacher needs to prepare them for this outcome. A brief discussion before testing will help avoid possible frustration.

The comprehension subtest also contains paragraphs of increasing difficulty. Students are asked to read each paragraph and answer questions cast in a multiple choice format. The score is the number of items correct.

Raw scores for both subtests are totaled, converted to stanines and percentiles, and entered into the test booklet. The teacher has available at least three scores for the student: vocabulary, paragraph reading, and total reading. Optional subtests will give additional scores for each.

Both the Gates-MacGinitie and Nelson reading tests survey student's knowledge of vocabulary and their general understanding of sentences and paragraphs. Clearly these tests are designed to assess the domain of reading comprehension (fig. 2.2). As is typical of many survey tests, they do not reveal performance in other reading domains, except through inference or administration of the optional decoding subtests.

If a child, Tony, performs poorly on a survey reading test, a possible hypothesis resulting from this performance is that Tony *may* have a reading problem. This hypothesis should be considered tentative because scores on a survey reading test may reflect either a reading problem or a more fundamental problem. If Tony is doing his best but his academic aptitude limits him, he should be considered a slow learner and instruction adapted accordingly. If Tony has the potential to do better than his performance indicates, however, he has a reading problem that needs to be specifically identified.

Standardized Diagnostic Reading Tests

The major purpose of standardized diagnostic reading tests is to help teachers identify the strengths and weaknesses of students. A graphic profile is used to compare subtest scores for individuals and to determine level of ability in the reading areas (fig. 3.4). Because diagnostic assessment is directed at identifying more specific strengths and weaknesses, the total test score represents a composite performance and is much less meaningful than the profile. Reviewing the profiles of several children aids appropriate grouping for instruction.

Individually Administered Diagnostic Tests

Several diagnostic reading tests are designed for individual testing. For best results, teachers need special training in administering, scoring, and interpreting these tests. This is not a realistic expectation for many classroom teachers. The tests are also time-consuming to administer, score, and interpret, so they cannot usually be justified for classroom purposes. Individual diagnostic tests should be used only by teachers and other specialists who have the necessary training, experience, and time to justify their use. They are mentioned here for those who wish to pursue this topic independently. The following are four widely used, individually administered, standardized, diagnostic tests:

1. *Gates-McKillop Reading Diagnostic Tests* recently revised to *Gates-McKillop-Horowitz Reading Diagnostic Tests* (1981)
2. *Durrell Analysis of Reading Difficulty* (1980)
3. *Spache Diagnostic Reading Scales* (1981)
4. *Woodcock Reading Mastery Tests* (1973)

All four of these tests are reviewed by Schell (1981).

Figure 3.4 Graphic profile for comparing subtest scores.

Teacher _____ Date _____

Pupil's name	Auditory discrimination	Phonic analysis	Structural analysis	Auditory vocabulary	Literal comprehension	Inferential comprehension	Total comprehension	Comments

Group-Administered Diagnostic Tests

Several diagnostic reading tests are available to classroom teachers. Three commonly used group diagnostic tests are the *Silent Reading Diagnostic Test,* the *Stanford Diagnostic Reading Tests* and the *Diagnostic Reading Tests.* Several others are also available. These tests take up to three hours longer to administer than survey tests, but they can be given to groups of students, usually the suspected poor readers in a classroom; this makes them efficient for classroom assessment. If a reading specialist is available to the teacher, such a test can be administered easily.

A major advantage of these tests is that they help teachers analyze reading behaviors and plan instruction for corrective readers. A second important advantage is that they are normed and provide inexperienced teachers with a standard. They give teachers an excellent "second opinion" to compare with their personal analysis of a child's reading abilities. Group diagnostic reading tests are recommended for gathering additional information about a child's reading, especially if the teacher has doubts about a student's performance among or within domains.

On the negative side, the teacher needs some training and skill to administer, score, and interpret the tests. The skills required are considerably less, however, than those for individually administered tests. Another disadvantage is that the subtests of these instruments may be more highly correlated than is desirable. This means that the tests are not measuring the independent subskills as well as they should.

The Stanford Diagnostic Reading Tests will be discussed here because these tests are well constructed, have been positively reviewed in Buros (1979) and Schell (1981), and have been designed to provide particularly accurate assessment of low-achieving students. Furthermore, with the exception of study skills and strategic reading, the tests assess the major reading domains conceptualized in chapter 2. You should also be aware, however, that the tests do have weaknesses and critics (e.g., Durkin, 1980).

The four levels of the *Stanford Diagnostic Reading Test* (SDRT) cover grades 1 through 12 and community colleges, with two parallel forms at each level (Schell, 1981). They are designated by color: (1) Red Level for grades 1 and 2; (2) Green Level for grades 3 and 4; (3) Brown Level for grades 5 through 8; and (4) Blue Level for grades 9 through 12. All forms have out-of-level norms.

Four components of reading are assessed: decoding, vocabulary, comprehension, and rate. The red level is used in grades 1 and 2 and also for older students reading at these lower levels.[2] The red level measures auditory discrimination, phonic analysis, auditory vocabulary, word recognition, and comprehension of short sentences and paragraphs. The green level is used in grades 3 and 4 and with low achievers in grade 5. The green level measures auditory discrimination, phonic and structural analysis, auditory vocabulary, and literal and inferential comprehension. The brown level is used in grades 5 through 8 and with low-achieving high school students. The brown level measures phonic and structural analysis, auditory vocabulary, literal and inferential comprehension of textual, functional, and recreational reading material, and reading rate. The blue level is used from the end of eighth grade through the community college level with students considered relatively poor readers. The blue

---

[2] *The Test of Early Reading Ability-2* (TERA-2) by Reid, Hresko, and Hammill, 1989, is a standardized *individually* administered test best used to measure reading behaviors of five- to six-year-olds, high functioning four-year-olds, and low functioning seven-year-olds.

level measures phonic and structural analysis, knowledge of the meanings of words and parts of words, such as affixes and roots, reading rate to include skimming and scanning, and literal and inferential comprehension of textual, functional, and recreational reading material.

While several of these skills subtests are administered for all four levels, the specific skills are measured differently. For example, the phonic analysis subtest for the red level measures the reader's ability to discriminate among consonant sounds represented by single consonant letters, consonant clusters, and digraphs in the initial and final positions, while the same subtest for the brown level measures whether the reader can recognize the same consonant sounds represented by the same spelling or two different spellings (e.g., face and rain; foam and graph; pie and reply; sugar and nation). The changes in what is measured from level to level are intended to reflect the developmental characteristics of the reading process.

The test materials for the SDRT include test booklets, answer folders, *Directions for Administering*, a *Norms Booklet*, a *Manual for Interpreting*, a *Handbook of Instructional Techniques and Materials*, and a *Multilevel Norms Booklet*. Both hand- and machine-scorable answer folders are provided. If a teacher administers all the subtests of the SDRT, class summary and instructional group placement information can be generated by using The Psychological Corporation's Scoring Service. Of course, such information is most useful if the SDRT is administered as early as possible in the fall of the school year.

The last two sections of this chapter have presented information on standardized survey reading tests and standardized diagnostic reading tests. These tests are widely used for assessing reading achievement and reading problems, and the results can be helpful to teachers. They give teachers important working hypotheses to verify in the context of "real" reading during classroom instruction time. Many questions regarding specific reading problems cannot be answered from the tests, however, so teachers must be aware of ways that other instruments may assist with deeper level analysis.

Criterion-Referenced Tests

Criterion-referenced tests are relatively new as formal tests in the field of reading. They are usually linked to teaching objectives, which explains why they are sometimes called **objective-based tests.** They are also sometimes called **mastery tests** because children are said to have mastered a skill when they attain the specified criterion. Teachers have actually been using the concept of a criterion-referenced test for years. Anytime they develop a test to measure some specific objective and use a specific grade for passing, they are using a criterion-referenced test.

The assumption underlying criterion-referenced tests and the manner in which they are constructed are rather different from norm-referenced tests. Criterion-referenced tests focus on whether a child (or group of children) has learned a particular set of reading skills. This is different from the norm-referenced test that compares children to a norm group on general ability in the major reading domains. Table 3.2 compares and contrasts norm-referenced and criterion-referenced tests.

For criterion-referenced or mastery tests, interpretation of the results appears quite simple and straightforward in that 80 percent indicates passing or mastery of a skill and less than 80 percent indicates failure or nonmastery of that skill. The decision-making process is simplified for teachers. Using the score as a basis, they decide whether a student has learned the skill; if mastery is attained, the decision

TABLE 3.2 Comparison of Norm- and Criterion-Referenced Tests

Norm-referenced	Criterion-referenced
1. Norm-referenced tests assess the student's knowledge about the particular subject or content being tested.	1. Criterion-referenced tests assess the student's ability to perform a specific task.
2. Norm-referenced tests compare a student's performance with that of the norm group. (During the last phase of test construction, a final draft form is given to a large number of students who are representative of the students for whom the test was designed. This is the *norm group*.)	2. Criterion-referenced tests determine whether students possess the skills needed to move to the next level of learning.
3. Norm-referenced tests can be used annually as pretests and posttests to determine student gain while comparing these gains to those of the norm group.	3. Criterion-referenced tests can be used as pretests and posttests to determine which skills need to be taught and which skills have been mastered.
4. Norm-referenced tests contain items that are considered to be precise, valid, and reliable in order to discriminate among the weakest and best students.	4. Criterion-referenced tests contain items that determine whether the student is able to use the learned skill in particular situations.
5. Norm-referenced tests have a high degree of validity.	5. Criterion-referenced tests have only content validity; the items assess the ability needed to perform a given behavior.
6. Norm-referenced tests have a high degree of reliability. They consistently measure the same behavior with each administration of the test. This factor is *essential* for norm-referenced tests.	6. Criterion-referenced tests are not concerned with statistical calculations of reliability. If students are retested, they should not make the same score.
7. Interpretation of the student's score on norm-referenced tests depends on the scores obtained by the norm group.	7. Interpretation of the student's score on criterion-referenced tests depends upon whether the student is able to perform a specific task.
8. Norm-referenced test scores yield global measurements of general abilities.	8. Criterion-referenced test scores yield exact measures of ability to achieve specific objectives.
9. Norm-referenced test scores are interpreted in terms of norms that have been statistically listed in the test manual by the author or the publisher.	9. Criterion-referenced test scores are interpreted in terms of a score that is considered acceptable by the teacher, and by examining specific items that were correct or incorrect.
10. Norm-referenced test items are written to create variability among the individual scores in a particular group.	10. Criterion-referenced test items are designed to assess ability to perform a specific task as stated by a behavioral objective.

Adapted by permission of the publisher, F. E. Peacock, Publishers, Inc., Itasca, 111. From Eddie Kennedy, *Classroom Approaches to Remedial Reading*, 1977, pp. 82–83.

would be to move on to another skill or to a higher level of difficulty for the skill under consideration. If the student has not mastered the skill, the teacher decides either to reteach or to review the particular skill involved.

Several problems arise with criterion-referenced tests. Of great concern to some reading educators is the lack of empirical data or research evidence to substantiate the existence of specific reading skills (Farr & Carey, 1986; Goodman, 1969). They claim that even if the skills exist, the order in which they should be learned is unknown and arbitrary.

Teachers also should be aware that some children learn their reading skills well but still cannot read adequately, if at all. Likewise, some children read adequately but still fail reading skills tests (Jackson, 1981; McNeil, 1974). A pure skills approach to teaching reading can lead to problem readers just as a no-skills approach can. This probably reflects inappropriate *use* of tests for planning instruction rather than inappropriate tests themselves. As with norm-referenced tests, teachers must interpret results of criterion-referenced tests as working hypotheses that need to be verified in the context of "real" reading.

Criterion-referenced tests are being used more frequently in schools today. State-wide testing programs use tests based on objectives to determine if students have achieved a minimum level of competency with regard to specific objectives.

Many criterion-referenced tests have become available recently. Following are some of the more widely used:

- *Brigance Diagnostic Inventories*
- *The Fountain Valley Teacher Support System in Reading*
- *Individualized Criterion-Referenced Tests*
- *The Prescriptive Reading Inventory (PRI)*
- *Wisconsin Tests of Reading Skill Development*

The number of objectives covered, the number of items per objective, and the criteria for mastery vary greatly from test to test. Careful scrutiny of a criterion-referenced test is thus extremely important to ensure that the objectives covered by the test are those of the reading program. Edward Robbins (1981), in a review of the *Prescriptive Reading Inventory,* discusses a number of factors to consider in deciding if the objectives of the criterion-referenced test match the objectives of the reading program. These factors include checking to see: (1) if the testing context is consistent with the instructional context; (2) how closely the distribution of skills in the test matches that in the school's reading program; (3) if the specific skill activity is assessed in such a way that performance is attributable to knowing the skill; and (4) how well the placement of skills in the various levels of the test correspond to the school's reading program. Anyone anticipating using a criterion-referenced test would be wise to consult Robbins' review.

Summary

The early part of this chapter defines terms and identifies different kinds of tests. Several important measurement concepts, such as construct validity and standard error of measurement, are discussed.

The second part of the chapter discusses administering, scoring, and interpreting standardized tests. Particular attention is given to published diagnostic reading tests that should appeal to classroom teachers interested in helping corrective readers. To help these readers, reading analysis must proceed to deeper levels than possible with more widely used achievement batteries and reading survey tests. Criterion-referenced tests are also explained and contrasted with norm-referenced tests.

References

American Psychological Association. (1974). *Standards for educational psychological tests.* Washington, DC: American Psychological Association.

Buros, O. K. (Ed.). (1979). *Reading tests and reviews* (2nd ed.). Highland Park, NJ: The Gryphon Press.

Delegates Assembly. (1981, April). *Misuse of grade equivalents resolution.* Newark, DE: International Reading Association.

Durkin, D. (1980). *Teaching young children to read.* Boston: Allyn and Bacon.

Durrell, D. D., & Catterson, J. H. (1980). *Durrell analysis of reading difficulty.* New York: The Psychological Corporation.

Farr, R., & Carey, R. F. (1986). *Reading: What can be measured?* (2nd ed.). Newark, DE: International Reading Association.

Fry, E. (1980). Test review: Metropolitan Achievement Tests. *The Reading Teacher, 34,* 196–201.

Glazer, S. M., Searfoss, L. W., & Gentile, L. M. (1988). *Reexamining reading diagnosis: New trends and procedures.* Newark, DE: International Reading Association.

Goodman, K. S. (1969). Analysis of reading miscues: Applied psycholinguistics. *Reading Research Quarterly, 5,* 9–30.

Hanna, G., Schell, L. M., & Schreiner, R. (1977). *The Nelson reading skills test.* Boston: Houghton Mifflin.

Jackson, L. A. (1981). Whose skills system? Mine or Penny's? *The Reading Teacher, 35,* 260–262.

Karlson, B., & Gardner, E. F. (1986). *Stanford diagnostic reading tests.* New York: Harcourt Brace Jovanovich. (Order through The Psychological Corporation.)

Kavale, K. (1979). Selecting and evaluating reading tests. In R. Schreiner (Ed.), *Reading tests and teachers: A practical guide* (pp. 9–34). Newark, DE: International Reading Association.

MacGinitie, W. H., & MacGinitie, R. K. (1989). *Gates-MacGinitie reading tests,* 3rd edition, Chicago: Riverside.

McNeil, J. D. (1974). False prerequisites in the teaching of reading. *Journal of Reading Behavior, 6,* 421–427.

Merwin, J. C. (1973). Educational measurement of what characteristic, of whom (or what), by whom, and why. *Journal of Educational Measurement, 10,* 1–6.

Mitchell, J. V. (Ed.). (1985). *The ninth mental measurements yearbook* (Two volumes). Lincoln, NE: University of Nebraska Press.

Reid, D. K., Hresko, W. P., & Hammill, D. D. (1989). *The Test of Early Reading Ability-2.* Austin, TX: PRO-ED.

Robbins, E. L. (1981). Prescriptive reading inventory: Levels A and B. In L. M. Schell (Ed.), *Diagnostic and criterion-referenced reading tests: Review and evaluation.* (pp. 70–76). Newark, DE: International Reading Association.

Sax, G. (1980). *Principles of educational and psychological measurement and evaluation* (2nd ed.). Belmont, CA: Wadsworth.

Schell, L. M. (Ed.). (1981). *Diagnostic and criterion-referenced reading tests: Review and evaluation.* Newark, DE: International Reading Association.

Spache, G. D. (1981). *Diagnostic reading scales (DRS-81).* Monterey, CA: CTB/Mc-Graw-Hill.

Spache, G. D. (1976). *Investigating the issues of reading disabilities.* Boston: Allyn and Bacon.

CHAPTER 4

Assessing and Evaluating Reading Performance with Informal Measures

Objectives

After you have read this chapter, you should be able to

1. compare and contrast the following informal measures: informal reading inventories, cloze procedure, checklists and rating scales, observations and interviews, and work samples;

2. administer and interpret an informal reading inventory;

3. identify and describe which of the above measures can be used at analytical levels 3 and 4.

Study Outline

I. Introduction

II. Major informal reading measures
   A. Informal reading inventories (IRIs)
      1. Three reading levels
         a) Independent reading level
         b) Instructional reading level
         c) Frustration reading level
      2. Constructing and administering IRIs
      3. Scoring IRIs
      4. Interpreting IRIs
         a) Establishing reading levels

   b) Analyzing results of the IRI
      5. Listening capacity
   B. Cloze procedure (maze procedure)
   C. Assessment by observation and conferences
      1. Observation
      2. Conferences
   D. Checklists and rating scales
   E. Interest and attitude surveys
   F. Work samples
   G. Oral and written language samples

III. Summary

IV. References

Important Vocabulary and Concepts

cloze procedure   maze technique
emergent literacy   miscue
frustration reading level   miscue analysis
independent reading level   passage dependent
informal reading inventory   protocol
instructional reading level   qualitative   analysis
listening capacity   quantitative analysis

Overview

While measures discussed in the preceding chapter are helpful tools for the analysis of reading behaviors, they really only serve to supplement or support information obtained by informal measures. The deeper the level of analysis required, the more the need for direct, individual, and frequent observation of behaviors. This chapter discusses some of the more important informal procedures you may use in the analytic process, such as informal reading inventories. Four important measurements that can be obtained from informal reading inventories are described in this presentation. The cloze and maze techniques as well as other informal measures are also examined.

Teachers must often rely on their own assessment measures and procedures to help them identify, particularly at the level 4 analysis, specific learning segments or units that are *teachable*. Observations, conferences, checklists, rating scales, interviews, and work samples are examples of this kind of measure. Suggestions for constructing, administering, and interpreting these measures are presented.

Introduction

For many years some educators have believed that standardized measures in reading do not give teachers sufficient information for instructional decision making. Informal reading measures, on the other hand, usually contain more error than formal measures, and you may wonder why anyone would advocate their use. The main justification for using informal tests and measures is that they supply useful information for direct teaching applications. Because many informal measures involve the actual materials and tasks used in the classroom, the teacher often obtains a more realistic view of how the reader functions within the instructional setting.

Informal reading tests are frequently used to assess small segments of learning, such as a unit on real life versus fantasy or long *a* represented by *ai* or *ay*. Thus the frequency of testing is increased. If standardized reading tests were given as often, the process would be extremely time-consuming, subtracting substantially from available teaching time, already at a premium in the classroom. Furthermore, the cost would be prohibitive. Also, the information yielded by many standardized tests is not the type that teachers want most—information that tells whether specific learnings have occurred or what specific learning segments should be taught next.

A number of informal tests and measures that help teachers assess and evaluate students' reading behaviors will be explained in this chapter. No one informal technique is sufficient, nor should the results of standardized, diagnostic, or criterion-referenced tests be overlooked. Both types of tests and measures provide information for analyzing students' reading behaviors and for planning instruction.

Major Informal Reading Measures

Informal Reading Inventories

The informal reading inventory is probably the most widely known informal reading measure. The four major purposes for using this measure are: (1) to help the teacher decide whether a child has a reading problem; (2) to aid the teacher regarding the appropriate text or reader for each child in the class; (3) to aid the teacher in identifying three different reading levels—the independent reading level, the instructional reading level, and the frustration reading level; and (4) to aid the teacher in learning more about each pupil's reading strengths and weaknesses.

An **informal reading inventory** (IRI) consists of a series of graded paragraphs that students read and answer questions about. Inventories can be (1) published instruments, in which passages and questions are carefully constructed to reflect reading grade levels accurately; (2) teacher-made, with passages selected from the reading materials used in the school; or (3) constructed by a publisher to accompany a particular basal reader series. Lists of words graded by difficulty often are used as quick screening devices to determine a starting point for paragraph reading. Paragraphs are then read orally, silently, or both, depending on the teacher's purpose. Word recognition errors are recorded for the oral selections, while comprehension is checked for the paragraphs read orally or silently. Rate of reading is obtained by recording the time spent reading the paragraphs.

An advantage of a well-constructed teacher-made IRI is that its content is generally quite valid, that is, it tests pupils on reading materials used in their school. Some educators (e.g., Harris and Sipay, 1980) indicate that results from IRIs are more accurate than results of standardized tests for placement purposes. It is claimed that results from standardized tests tend to overestimate students' reading levels. Typically, studies suggest that children are able to read materials one-half to one year above the suggested placement from results of IRIs (Farr & Carey, 1986). Differences of opinion exist on this issue (Spache, 1976), and the controversy has yet to be resolved.

Probably the greatest disadvantage of many IRIs is that they assess reading comprehension—the heart of reading—using as few as five test items per level. The reliability of test results can be seriously questioned when so few items are used. The questions are not always well written, nor do they necessarily discriminate between good and poor readers (Davis, 1978). Most inventories also claim to provide information on comprehension subskills (e.g., determining main ideas, recalling details, identifying cause and effect, inferring word meanings from context), however, research shows they do not and should not be used for this purpose (Duffelmeyer & Duffelmeyer, 1989; Duffelmeyer, Robinson, & Squier, 1989; Schell & Hanna, 1981). Furthermore, comprehension is frequently assessed on oral reading of the paragraphs. This is of particular concern with poor readers and readers in the primary grades, who may expend their cognitive abilities trying to do well reading aloud, thereby diverting some attention from fully understanding the message of the author.

IRIs are time-consuming to administer and interpret, especially if administered to an individual to record oral reading ability. Average administration time per child is thirty minutes. Interpretation time can be at least as much and probably more. However, as will be discussed later, every child does not need to be tested with an IRI.

Many publishers of basal reading series include IRIs in their supplementary materials. These IRIs are constructed specifically to be used with their reading series. Using publisher-constructed IRIs seems to be a good alternative to developing your own, particularly in view of the trend to include stories in basal readers with readability levels that are not controlled as carefully as in the past. One potential problem with using basal reader IRIs is that a student can test out of a basal reader level, not because of ability to read and comprehend the material, but because the particular basal story was read the preceding year or term when the student may have been inappropriately placed.

Today, many teachers are choosing to use published IRIs because of the time required to construct an IRI. Examples of some published inventories are the *Analytical Reading Inventory* (Woods & Moe, 1989), the *Basic Reading Inventory* (Johns, 1991), the *Ekwall Reading Inventory* (Ekwall, 1986), and the *Informal Reading Inventory* (Burns & Roe, 1989). These published IRIs may or may not be better than teacher-made IRIs. The important measurement concepts of reliability and validity must be considered. Unfortunately, as pointed out by Pikulski and Shanahan (1982), IRIs may be far from reliable. The *Ekwall Reading Inventory,* the only one addressing the subject of reliability, reports correlation coefficients of .82 between Forms A and B and .79 between Forms C and D. For individual assessment, a more acceptable reliability coefficient is .90.

The question of validity is also critical. Does the IRI measure what it is intended to measure? To answer this question, you must recall the four major purposes for administering an IRI and remember that the issue of validity differs somewhat for each one. For example, if the purpose is to aid the teacher in placing a child in an appropriate reader, then a basal series publisher-constructed or teacher-made IRI based on the reading series being used may be more valid because the passages are taken from the materials being used.

Another validity issue is related to the purpose of identifying the three reading levels. For some time, writers and users of informal reading inventories have chosen to use the arbitrary criteria set up by Betts (1946) to distinguish the independent (99% word recognition, 90% comprehension), instructional (95% word recognition, 75% comprehension), and frustration (90% or less word recognition, 50% or less comprehension) reading levels discussed in the next section. These criteria were based on data obtained from 41 fourth grade students who read the passages silently before reading them aloud. Not until 1970, when William Powell adjusted these criteria to be dependent on the grade level of the child being tested, were the Betts criteria challenged. Powell (1970) found that children who could comprehend material reasonably well (70–75%) achieved average word recognition scores ranging from 83% to 94% across grades 1 through 6. Older readers were even more accurate in word recognition. Unfortunately, too little research evidence is available either to support Betts's criteria (Roberts, 1976) or to define appropriate criteria for establishing the three reading levels. Published IRIs are consistent in using the Betts criteria, with only a few exceptions. Of the inventories listed above, two suggest different criteria: the *Ekwall Reading Inventory* and the *Informal Reading Inventory* (Burns & Roe).

While it is quite apparent that IRIs have limitations, it is important to remember that IRIs are *informal* measures and should be used flexibly. Published IRIs provide what sound like rigid procedures for administration, however, teachers using published IRIs must understand their purpose(s) for using the IRI, employ good judgment, and rely on their knowledge of the reading process. For example, a study by Cardarelli (1988) points out that by allowing students to look back at a passage to answer the comprehension questions over half increased their scores sufficiently to change frustration reading levels to instructional reading levels. This procedure makes good sense if a teacher normally allows students to look back in their textbooks for answers to questions rather than insisting that the students answer the questions from memory as directed in most IRI manuals.

In any event, teachers simply must use other informal assessment procedures to supplement results of IRIs on comprehension. For instance, the child being tested should be encouraged to recall as much about the passage as possible *before* questions are asked. This procedure is called "retelling the story," and is adapted from a published instrument called the *Reading Miscue Inventory* (Goodman and Burke, 1972). General comprehension questions can be asked if the child does not respond freely. For example:

Tell me about . . .
Who was in the story?
What happened?
Where did this happen?
How did it happen?
Why do you think the story was written?

Teachers may choose to record the child's free retelling by making check marks on a previously prepared outline of the story that identifies major points from the passage related to characters, events, plot, and theme (fig. 4.1). If these items are not mentioned, questions, also prepared in advance, are used to help elicit desired information (Bowman, 1981; Spiegel & Whaley, 1980; Stein & Glenn, 1979). Nevertheless, questions about retellings should not supply information or insights the reader did not provide in the retelling. Most questions should be of the WH- variety and refer to information already given by the reader. These questions, when asked following a story, should by keyed toward the elements of a story. For example, as modified from Weaver, 1988, pp. 334–335):

Characters:
What else can you tell me about (name of character[s] provided in the retelling)?
Who else was in the story besides (the characters mentioned)?

Events:
What else happened?
What happened after (event provided in the retelling)?
Where (or when) did (event mentioned in the retelling) happen?
How did (event mentioned in the retelling) happen?

Plot:
Why do you think (action[s] mentioned in the retelling) happened?
What was (character mentioned in retelling) main problem?

FIGURE 4.1 List of major points to be used to record a child's free recall for the Aesop fable "The Lion and the Mouse."

Main Points for Retelling

___ sleeping lion
___ lion awakened by mouse who ran across his paw and up his nose
___ lion wanted to kill mouse
___ mouse promised that someday he could help the lion if he would let him go
___ lion let mouse go
___ later, lion was caught in a hunter's net made of rope
___ lion roared loudly
___ mouse recognized the lion's roar
___ mouse helped the lion by chewing through the rope of the net
___ lion was freed by the mouse
___ Moral: Even small acts of kindness are important

Theme:
How did you feel when (event mentioned in the retelling) happened?
What do you think the author might have been trying to tell us in the story?

Setting:
Where/when did the story take place?
How was (character or event mentioned in the retelling) important to the story?

These questions can easily be modified for retellings of an expository passage. For example:

• What else can you tell me about (topic of passage mentioned in retelling)?
• What else was this passage about besides (the topic mentioned)?
• What other information did the author provide about (topic, or important concept briefly mentioned in the retelling)?
• What happened after (event mentioned in retelling)?
• What do you think the authors are trying to tell us in this section?
• How was (event or fact mentioned in the retelling) important to this passage?
• How do you think you might use this information?
• How is this information like anything you read about before?

For both narrative and expository passages, you also should ask questions related to the reading event. As found in Weaver (1988, p. 335), these questions are from the *Reading Miscue Inventory: Alternative Procedures* (Goodman, Watson, & Burke, 1987):

Is there anything you'd like to ask me about this story [passage]?

Were there any (concepts, ideas, sentences, words) that gave you trouble? What were they?

Why did you leave this word out?

FIGURE 4.2 Free recall processing checklist. (From Judith Irwin, *Teaching Reading Comprehension Processes,* © 1986 pp. 170–71. Reprinted by permission of Prentice-Hall, Inc., Englewood Cliffs, NJ.)

Answer each of these questions according to the following scale:

5 Yes, very well
4 Yes, more than adequately
3 Yes, adequately
2 No, not too well
1 No, poorly
NA Not applicable or can't tell

1. ___ Did the student recall a sufficient number of ideas?
2. ___ Did the student recall the ideas accurately?
3. ___ Did the student select the most important details to recall?
4. ___ Did the student understand explicit pronouns and connectives?
5. ___ Did the student infer important implicitly stated information?
6. ___ Did the student include the explicitly stated main points?
7. ___ Did the student create any new summarizing statements?
8. ___ Did the student use the organizational pattern used by the author?
9. ___ Did the student elaborate appropriately?
10. ___ Did the student know how to adjust strategies to the purpose given?

What effective comprehension processes were evident in the student's recall?

What comprehension processes were not evident, or seemed to be causing problems?

To what extent was the student's performance as just described affected by each of the following?

1. Limited prior knowledge or vocabulary
2. Limited motivation or interest
3. Cultural differences
4. Decoding problems
5. Difficulties in the text
6. The social context
7. Discomfort with the task
8. Other environmental influences

Do you know what this word means, now?

Were there times when you weren't understanding the story? Show me where. Tell me about those times.

Remember when you said the kid was a "typeical baby"? What is a "typeical baby"? (Ask about key words that were mispronounced or otherwise miscued, to see if the reader got the concept despite the miscue.) (p. 48)

Story retellings reveal the reader's ability to remember facts, make inferences, and recall sequence (Morrow, 1985). To evaluate retellings a holistic scoring system is recommended. Irwin (1989) provides such a system which is reproduced in figure 4.2. To assess silent reading for groups or students in the upper grades, a written retelling is possible (Smith & Jackson, 1985).

The "think-aloud" procedure (Brown, 1985; Kavale & Schreiner, 1981; Olshavsky, 1977) addresses the criticism that questions do not assess the *process* of comprehension. This procedure requires readers to verbalize their thoughts while reading. These verbalizations provide insights into the ways individual readers derive meaning from text.

Three Reading Levels

Three important levels relevant to classroom teaching can be estimated from administering and interpreting IRIs. The first level is called the **independent reading level,** which refers to the difficulty level at which a child reads without teacher help. Children should be reading library books and other materials for pleasure at this level, with little or no difficulty recognizing words or comprehending. Children learn to read for fun and enjoyment when they read easy materials. At this level they develop favorable attitudes toward and positive interests in reading.

At the **instructional reading level** children read with some direction and supervision. Students are usually placed in basal readers written at their instructional reading level, but most other materials pupils read should *not* be this difficult unless a teacher or someone else is available to help them. Without help, tension and other unfortunate outcomes may result (Arnold & Sherry, 1975).

The **frustration reading level** is one at which reading deteriorates and students cannot continue reading because the material is too hard even with instruction and guidance. Physical behaviors frequently associated with frustration include frowning, crying, squirming, whispering, or rebelliousness. Teachers should steer children away from reading materials at this level.

Constructing and Administering IRIs

The informal reading inventory is ideally based on reading materials regularly used in the school, including content area textbooks. The selections, chosen from as many books as possible in the series, might range from 50 words at the primer level to 100 to 150 words in grades 1 through 3, to 200 to 250 words or so beyond grade 3. Stories should be well formed and cohesive enough to allow development of comprehension questions. These questions should be **passage dependent**, that is, answerable upon reading the passage, and balanced between literal and inferential comprehension. For help in writing questions, Johnson and Kress (1965), Pearson and Johnson (1978), and Valmont (1972) are recommended readings. Longer selections and more comprehension questions increase the reliability of the results, an important consideration, particularly when assessing a poor reader.

In order to assess free recall, a list of the main points of each selection will need to be prepared (refer to fig. 4.1). The selections, list of free recall main points, and questions are typed on separate sheets of paper and duplicated. These pages become the **protocol,** or record sheet, that the teacher uses for testing purposes. If the entire set of graded readers or textbooks is difficult to obtain, the teacher may, with permission from the publisher, reproduce the pages from the texts and bind them together in a notebook. A sample of about twenty words introduced in each reader can be placed in list format to be used for "quick" screening purposes.

Once the protocols and the child's notebook are prepared, the IRI is given. With a published inventory, begin by asking the child to read the word lists, starting with the lowest level list available. If the first list is read with at least 80 percent accuracy, the next level can be tried. If reading with less than 80 percent accuracy, the child begins with the easiest passage. The child continues to read the word lists until the 80 percent criterion is *not* met. At this point the child is asked to read the selection corresponding to the highest level word list where he or she scored 100 percent. Beginning at an easier level helps to ensure that the first selection will be read successfully. When using a published inventory, the criteria for determining starting points may vary. You should carefully read the directions for administration found at the beginning of the inventory being used.

The child reads selections of increasing difficulty while the teacher codes behaviors in oral reading and comprehension. A tape recording allows the performance to be reviewed to verify the scoring estimated during the testing session. Reading continues until the child reaches the criteria associated with the frustration level. At this point, in addition to *not* achieving a minimum level of word recognition and/or comprehension, the child usually exhibits other symptoms, such as squirming in the chair or facial contortions. Figure 4.3 provides an example of a coded IRI passage.

Scoring IRIs

IRIs are rather easy to score for placement purposes. One scoring system for oral reading accuracy is suggested by Harris and Sipay (1990, pp. 227–228).[1]

The following should be counted as one error each:

1. Any word used that deviates from the text and disrupts the meaning.
2. Any word pronounced by the teacher after the child has hesitated about five seconds.

The following should be counted as only one error, regardless of the number of times the error is made:

1. Repeated substitutions (one word substituted for another such as *when* for *then*).
2. Repetitions (individual words or groups of words that are said more than once). There is disagreement on counting repetitions as errors. For example, Spache (1976) counts two or more words repeated as a repetition error, Ekwall (1974, 1986) thinks *all* repetitions should be counted as errors, and Taylor, Harris, and Pearson (1988) do *not* count repetitions as errors at all. Generally I agree with *not* counting repetitions as errors. They usually occur for a reason and demonstrate that the reader is concerned with maintaining understanding of material read. However, if there are a great number of repetitions this may indicate the material is too difficult.
3. Repeated errors on the same word, even though the errors themselves may be different.

The following should *not* be counted as errors:

1. Errors that reflect cultural or regional dialects
2. Spontaneous self-corrections
3. Hesitations
4. Ignoring or misinterpreting punctuation marks

The total errors are counted and converted to a percentage score based on the number of words pronounced correctly and the total number of words in the selection.

In addition to recording oral reading behaviors, retellings, and responses to comprehension questions asked after each selection are also recorded. Sometimes these

---

[1] Adapted from *How to Increase Reading Ability* by Albert J. Harris and Edward R. Sipay. 9th ed. Copyright © 1940, 1949, 1956, 1961, 1968, 1970, 1975, 1980, and 1990 by Longman, Inc. Reprinted by permission of Longman, Inc., New York.

FIGURE 4.3 Example of a coded IRI passage. (From M. L. Woods and A. J. Moe, *Analytical Reading Inventory,* 4th ed. Columbus, OH: Charles E. Merrill, 1989. Used with permission.)

Primer (50 words 8 sent.)

Examiner's Introduction
(Student Booklet page 117):

Please read this story about a child who imagines some unusual things.

Look! It is me!

I can run as fast as a train!

UP
I can jump over a (big) tall tree!

train
I can ride my bike as fast as a running goat!

the   *A*
I can see ˄ very little things far away.

I can put on a good show!

Yes, I am something!

Comprehension Questions
and Possible Answers

(mi) 1. What is this story about?   *I can do things*
         (The special kid, Super kid, etc.)

(f)   2. What does the child mean by saying, "I can run
         as fast as a train"? (can run very fast)
                              he rides his bike fast

(f)   3. How high can this child jump?
         (over a big tall tree)   *up a lot*

(f)   4. How fast can the child ride the bike?
         (as fast as a running goat)   *as fast as a train*

(t)   5. What is meant by the word over?
         (above)   *like on top of something*

(f)   6. What kind of things can the child see far away?
         (very little things)   *little things*

Symbol Key
˄ insertion
𝑂 omission
A teacher pronounced
𝑁 reversal
ᴟᴟ repetition
UP substitution
over

Miscue Count:

𝑂 __//ı__ ı S __//__ A __ı__ REP __ı__ REV __ı__

Scoring Guide	
Word Rec.	Comp.
IND 0–1	IND 0
INST 2–3	INST 1–2
FRUST 5+	FRUST 3+

responses can be scored as the child answers the questions. More often, however, judgment about performance can only be made in relation to what the child read and how the child has responded. Therefore, it is best to analyze these responses carefully at a later time.

Interpreting IRIs

Establishing reading levels.   Once the teacher has obtained scores on (1) oral reading behaviors and (2) comprehension of silent or oral reading or both for the selections read, the scores are assembled in a table such as that in figure 4.4 to aid interpretation of results. All published inventories provide a similar table, usually called a summary sheet. When interpreting results of an IRI, remember that these inventories are subject to error of measurement. Thus, the criteria for establishing the independent, instructional, and frustration reading levels must be interpreted judiciously. The teacher surveys the assembled scores and makes judgments about the estimated reading levels based on the progression of scores as well as the scores themselves. Results of research by Powell and Dunkeld (1971) and Cooper (1952) indicate that the student's grade level should also be a consideration (see Table 4.1). As indicated earlier, there is not absolute agreement on the criteria to be used to determine reading levels.

Almost always, interpretation requires some estimating and interpolating. In interpreting Sandra's scores (fig. 4.4), chances are good that Sandra's independent reading level is third grade and that the 80 percent comprehension score obtained at the 2^2 reader level for oral reading reflects error of measurement. The instructional reading level is probably fourth grade, the higher of the two sets of scores yielding that outcome especially in light of the silent reading comprehension score. Notice also that the 94 and 93 percent accuracy scores are slightly below the Betts criterion of 95 percent, but are acceptable for the instructional level according to both the Powell and the Cooper criteria.

Once reading levels have been estimated, the teacher verifies these tentative working hypotheses (i.e., independent reading level equals beginning third grade, instructional reading level, fourth grade, frustration reading level, fifth grade). This is accomplished by placing Sandra in fourth grade level materials to see if she can deal effectively with the texts and accompanying lessons. Verification of placement in materials is critical to effective analysis and instructional planning. Without verification, all the analytic effort may be for naught.

Work by Beck (1981), Berliner (1981), Gambrell, Wilson, and Gantt (1981), and Jorgenson (1977) suggests that student achievement in reading, especially for developing readers, is positively affected if a large portion of instructional time is spent with relatively easy material (error rates of 2 to 5 percent), with regular exposure to more difficult material. Beck (1981) explains that in this way the reader is allowed "to develop fluent and automatic responses in less difficult text while encountering a challenge to develop new knowledge and strategies in more difficult text."

The best advice might be to be conservative. If reading levels are unclear or other characteristics about a student deserve consideration (e.g., immature personality, general academic incompetence, poor work habits, or disruptive home background), the student should be placed in the easier material under consideration (Haller & Waterman, 1985).

FIGURE 4.4 Sample table to aid interpretation of scores for reading accuracy and comprehension.

Summary of Results of Informal Reading Inventory

Name: _____Sandra_____   Grade: _____Beginning 4th_____

Level of Text	Oral Reading		Silent Reading	Reading Level
	Percent Accuracy	Percent Comprehension	Percent Comprehension	
2^1	99	100	100	Independent
2^2	97	80	90	Instructional
3^1	98	100	100	Independent
3^2	94	80	100	Instructional
4	93	80	90	Instructional
5	88	50	70	Frustration

Estimated independent reading level: $\underline{3^1}$
Estimated instructional reading level: $\underline{4^*}$
Estimated frustration reading level: $\underline{5}$

* or 3^2–4, if a range is desired.

Analyzing results of the IRI. If you choose to administer an IRI and consider the testing complete once the reading levels are established, you will be overlooking a wealth of information. Oral reading behaviors and comprehension performance can be analyzed further. Borrowing heavily from the *Reading Miscue Inventory* developed by Goodman and Burke (1972), recorded oral reading behaviors can be thought of as miscues. A **miscue** is defined as an observed response that differs from the expected

TABLE 4.1 Powell and Cooper Criteria for Determining Informal Reading Inventory Instructional Reading Levels

Powell Criteria for Instructional Level

Grades 1–2	88–97.9% word recognition 70–89% comprehension
Grades 3–5	92–97.9% word recognition 70–89% comprehension
Grades 6 +	94.4–97.9% word recognition 70–89% comprehension

Cooper Criteria for Instructional Level

Grades 2–3	95–98% word recognition 70% minimum comprehension
Intermediate grades	91–96% word recognition 60% minimum comprehension

response, that is, the reader does not say exactly what is written. With this inventory, Goodman and Burke introduced the notion of **qualitative analysis**; rather than simply count errors (**quantitative analysis**), the examiner attempts to analyze the reader's strategies. Miscue analysis will be discussed in more detail below.

The rationale for analyzing miscues is that not all unexpected responses are equally serious. For example, if the child inserts *very* before the word *happy* in the sentence "Tom was not happy," the meaning of the sentence has not been seriously altered. The teacher may overlook miscues if meaning is not changed. This kind of qualitative analysis often reveals that children are extracting meaning from what they read despite apparent word recognition errors. This is especially important for children from dialectically different cultures. If nothing else, the qualitative analysis makes the teacher aware of the language functioning of the child who speaks a dialect. At its best, the qualitative analysis makes the teacher aware of the child's reading strategies.

A detailed **miscue analysis** is not necessary for every reader, not even for every problem reader. A thorough miscue analysis may only be done for readers who demonstrate especially perplexing reading miscues. For such cases the teacher is referred to Goodman and Burke's *Reading Miscue Inventory* (1972).

To determine the instructional needs of most students, a simple form of miscue analysis is extremely useful. A partial analysis that looks at the use of graphophonic, syntactic, and semantic cues and asks whether the reader views reading as a meaning-getting process provides valuable information about strengths and weaknesses. This underlying philosophy of determining whether the reader is reading for meaning and what strategies the reader is using is essential in miscue analysis.

A brief set of questions can be asked about miscues to provide insight into the reader's use of language cues and reading strategies. These questions should (1) emphasize that reading for meaning is more important than exact reproduction of the surface structure; (2) aid the teacher in identifying both a reader's strengths and weaknesses; and (3) acknowledge the importance of self-corrections of miscues that do not fit the context. Figure 4.5 shows the results of such an analysis.

In a much abbreviated version of miscue analysis, a teacher may simply ask whether the miscue changed meaning (unacceptable), whether it was acceptable in context, or whether it was corrected. A simple form also may be used for periodic assessments of oral reading behaviors (fig. 4.6). With this form, the teacher can compare the responses to these questions. If "Yes" is checked for question 3 and "No" or "Sometimes" for question 1, the student may be relying too heavily on graphophonic cues. Instruction in the use of syntactic and semantic context clues would be in order. On the other hand, if "Yes" is checked for question 1 and "No" or "Sometimes" is checked for question 3, the student may be relying too heavily on context clues. Instruction in phonics or structural analysis would be advisable. This instruction might include such questions as "Do you see any part of the word that you know?" (e.g., *run* in *running*), or "What word do you know that starts with _____, and would make sense?"

As discussed earlier, free recalls could precede asking the comprehension questions provided in published IRIs. As the miscue analysis and evaluation of comprehension performance are being conducted, factual summary statements for observed reading behaviors and strategies can be made. Instructional goals will become more evident from examination of these summary statements. Examples of summary statements can be found in figure 4.7. Summary statements can be written for each level

FIGURE 4.5 Example of miscue and comprehension qualitative analyses based on a fifth grader's oral reading of passages from the Woods and Moe Analytical Reading Inventory.

Miscue Analysis Chart

Student: Jason

Level of Passage	Miscue in Context	Acceptable — Syntax	Acceptable — Semantics	Unacceptable	Self-Correction of Unacceptable Miscues	Graphic Similarity — Initial	Graphic Similarity — Medial	Graphic Similarity — Final	Unknown Words
3	Suddenly he dashed home and soon returned with a bucket of yellow (paint) one of black, and several brushes.			✓					
3	I thought you might want to paint your clubhouse yellow and black stripes.			✓	✓				
4	The pony's condition was growing worse as his breathing grew louder and harder.	✓	✓			✓	✓	✓	
4	At night Jody brought a blanket from the house so he could sleep near Gabilan.	✓		✓		✓		✓	
4	Looking up he saw buzzards the birds of death, flying overhead.	✓		✓		✓		✓	
4	A blizzard was perching on his dying pony's head.	✓	✓	✓		✓	✓	✓	
	Column Total	5	2	5	1/5	5	2	4	0
	Total No. of Miscues Analyzed	7	7	7		7	7	7	7
	Percentage	71%	29%	71%	20%	71%	29%	57%	0%

(continued)

FIGURE 4.5 Example of miscue and comprehension qualitative analyses based on a fifth grader's oral reading of passages from the Woods and Moe *Analytical Reading Inventory*. (*continued*)

Comprehension Analysis Chart

	LOWER LEVEL				HIGHER LEVEL		
Level of Passage		Oral	Silent	Level of Passage		Oral	Silent
2	No. Correct	3		2	No. Correct	3	
	Total Possible	3			Total Possible	3	
	Percentage	100%			Percentage	100%	
3	No. Correct	4		3	No. Correct	3	
	Total Possible	4			Total Possible	4	
	Percentage	100%			Percentage	75%	
4	No. Correct	3		4	No. Correct	3	
	Total Possible	4			Total Possible	4	
	Percentage	75%			Percentage	75%	
5	No. Correct	2		5	No. Correct	2	
	Total Possible	4			Total Possible	4	
	Percentage	50%			Percentage	50%	
	No. Correct	*Listening*			No. Correct		
	Total Possible				Total Possible		
	Percentage				Percentage		
6	No. Correct		1	6	No. Correct		2
	Total Possible		4		Total Possible		4
	Percentage		25%		Percentage		50%
5	No. Correct		4	5	No. Correct		3
	Total Possible		4		Total Possible		4
	Percentage		100%		Percentage		75%
	No. Correct				No. Possible		
	Total Possible				Total Possible		
	Percentage				Percentage		
Total No. Correct		12		Total No. Correct		11	
Total No. Questions		15		Total No. Questions		15	
Total Percentage		80%		Total Percentage		73%	

FIGURE 4.6 Form for assessing oral reading behavior.

	Yes	No	Sometimes
1. Do the reader's miscues make sense in context?			
2. Does the reader correct unacceptable miscues?			
3. Does the reader pay too much attention to graphophonic cues and not enough to syntactic or semantic cues?*			

*A miscue may be graphically similar in the initial, medial, or final position (or some combination) and be unacceptable in terms of meaning. For example, a reader paying more attention to graphophonic cues than semantic or syntactic cues might substitute *his* for *this* in the sentence "This time it was ready."

of material, the type of material (i.e., narrative or expository), listening comprehension, and for any other relevant observations such as written language samples and oral language samples (discussed later in this chapter) (Rhodes & Dudley–Marling, 1988).

Listening Capacity

Another piece of information that can sometimes be estimated by an IRI is **listening capacity**, also called the listening comprehension level. This is the highest level at which the child can understand 75 percent of the material read aloud by the teacher. The teacher reads and asks questions about a selection beginning at the next level after the frustration reading level. This score is sometimes used as an indication of a child's ability to understand oral language.

Listening comprehension is sometimes considered an estimate of reading expectancy, that is, if the child were able to read the material, the listening comprehension level, or listening capacity, represents the level at which it could be understood. As Spache (1976) states, "there is a definite relationship between listening comprehension and verbal intelligence" (p. 63). He reports a correlation of .75 between listening comprehension as tested by the *Spache Diagnostic Reading Scales* and the *Wechsler Intelligence Scale for Children* (WISC) verbal IQ test. As noted in chapter 1, however, listening comprehension is probably *not* a valid indicator of reading potential for primary grade children. For other students, if the listening comprehension level is higher than the instructional reading level, the child may be reading below what can be expected.

Cloze Procedure

Another informal measure that is used for initially determining or verifying the instructional reading level is the **cloze procedure**. This requires a child to fill in blanks for words that have been systematically deleted from the written selection. In the most common form of cloze test, every fifth word is deleted. These tests are typically administered to groups of students, which may be considered an advantage over informal reading inventories.

Cloze tests are relatively easy and inexpensive to construct, administer, and interpret. The following steps are suggested in preparing a cloze test passage.

1. Select a passage containing 250 to 300 words (Bormuth, 1975). Be sure the passage does not depend on information presented earlier in the text (i.e., a passage with many pronouns). The passage should be representative of the content of the book.

FIGURE 4.7 Summary statements based on the miscue and comprehension analysis charts for Jason.

Summary Statements

Name: Jason   **Date:**   December
Age: 10   **Level of Material:**   3–6
Grade: 5   **Type of Material:**   Narrative

1. The majority of Jason's miscues (71%) are unacceptable; that is, they change meaning.
2. Jason only self-corrected 20% (1 out of 5) of his miscues.
3. The majority of Jason's miscues (71%) are acceptable syntactically; that is, they maintain the same part of speech as the original text.
4. Jason is aware of context clues, but does not use these clues consistently.
5. Jason's substitutions are usually graphophonically similar to the initial and final position of the word in text.
6. Jason's substitutions involve words of more than one syllable (4 out of 5).
7. Jason's substitutions involve words that may not be in his meaning vocabulary.
8. Jason's oral reading comprehension is consistent for both lower and higher levels of questions.
9. Jason's oral reading comprehension level is consistent with his word recognition abilities.
10. Jason's listening comprehension is approximately one year higher than his oral reading comprehension.

2. Keep the first sentence intact.
3. Beginning with the second sentence, delete words at a consistent interval (e.g., every fifth, seventh, or tenth word) for a total of fifty deletions (Bormuth, 1975). Replace the deleted words with blanks of equal length. Duplicate the desired number of copies.
4. If the blanks are numbered, prepare an answer sheet with corresponding numbers for students to record their responses.
5. If desired, students can write their responses directly on the blanks.

Administration of the cloze test is fairly straightforward. Students who have never experienced a cloze test should be given some practice with the procedure first. This practice test should use easy material for the students to read and contain at least ten deletions (Pikulski and Tobin, 1982).

Instructions for the cloze test must direct the students to read through the entire passage before trying to fill in the blanks. Students should also be told that only one word goes in each blank and that misspellings are not counted as errors. Although the test is untimed, the teacher may want to set a reasonable time limit.

Scoring a cloze test is an often misunderstood procedure. Only exact words should be considered acceptable for a correct response. This decision is not arbitrary; it is based on considerable research (Gallant, 1964; Henk & Selders, 1984; McKenna, 1976; Miller and Coleman, 1967; Ruddell, 1964; Taylor, 1953) in which exact word replacement scores were compared to synonym replacement scores. The synonym scores were higher than the exact word scores but the two scores were highly correlated (.95 and above). Because students essentially ranked the same using either technique, giving credit for synonyms has no advantage when the purpose of the test is to estimate students' instructional levels. Preparing a list of acceptable synonyms as part of cloze test preparation would simply not be worth the time or effort (Pikulski and Tobin, 1982).

In addition to yielding slightly higher scores, synonym replacements would invalidate the scoring guidelines. Criterion scores have been established for determining independent, instructional, and frustration reading levels using exact word replacement scores. Thus, to allow synonyms would yield an inflated score and the available criteria could not be used appropriately. Pikulski and Tobin (1982) have synthesized the research on criterion scores and suggest the following guidelines:

> Independent level: Students who obtain cloze scores of at least 50 percent should be able to read the material with relative ease. No teacher guidance should be necessary. Consequently, this material should be appropriate for homework assignments and other types of independent projects.
>
> Instructional level: Students scoring between 30 and 50 percent should be able to use the material for instructional purposes. However, some guidance will be necessary to help them master the demands of the material.
>
> Frustration level: Students having less than 30 percent will usually find the material much too challenging. Since there is almost no potential for success, the material should be definitely avoided. (pp. 53, 54)

The disadvantage of the cloze procedure is that its effectiveness as an assessment tool is not clearly established. Carefully constructed cloze tests could potentially provide helpful information regarding a reader's use of syntactic and semantic cues, however for teachers to observe the reading process in action they still must listen to children read. Cloze passages can also be constructed from children's written stories or other familiar materials and used instructionally to show children how to use the syntactic, semantic, and graphophonic cue systems. When used for instructional purposes, cloze passage construction can be modified in many ways to suit specific purposes. Cloze as an instructional tool is discussed in more detail in chapter 6.

A popular variation of the cloze procedure is the **maze technique.** Instead of deleting words from a passage, the maze procedure gives the reader a number of words from which to choose. While this format may have more appeal for the test taker, construction of the test is more time-consuming and more prone to error than the cloze procedure. Guthrie, Siefert, Burnham, and Caplan (1974) suggest the following guidelines for constructing a maze test.

1. Select a representative passage of about 120 words.
2. Beginning with the second sentence, replace words at constant intervals (e.g., every fifth or tenth word) with three word choices. These should include the correct word itself, a word that is the same part of speech as the correct word, and a word that is a different part of speech.
3. Vary the position of the correct word.
4. Duplicate copies.

As of yet, little research has been done on the maze technique, and criterion scores should be considered tentative. Guthrie et. al. (1974) suggest that 85 percent or higher accuracy reflects an independent level, 60 to 75 percent, an instructional level, and below 50 percent, the frustration level. More research is needed on the maze technique before its use as a placement tool is recommended.

Assessment by Observation and Conferences

Observation

A large amount of information about a child's ability to read can be learned through observation of reading behavior. A decision should never be made on the basis of one observation, however. Teachers who try to organize the instructional setting specifically to improve and enhance behavioral observation increase the reliability of those observations. For example, the more opportunities students have to show the teacher that they know the initial consonant blend *st* or that they can use word order clues to predict the next word in a sentence, the more reliable is the information. "More opportunities" is analogous to "more items" on a test, one way test makers achieve reliability.

Observing children is a skill that teachers develop over time through practice. Rhodes and Dudley-Marling (1988, pp. 37–38) provide some excellent guidelines for observing children's literacy development.[2] They are as follows:

1. Reading and writing should be observed over a period of time in a number of different contexts. For example, contexts for silent reading might include teacher-initiated versus student-initiated reading, reading different types of material (content-area reading, novels, comics, etc.), and reading for different purposes.

2. The setting, as well as students' reading and writing behaviors, must be thoroughly considered. By *setting* we mean information about the physical setting, who initiated the activity, the teacher's instructions (if any), and the teacher's approach to teaching reading and writing.

   Students' previous instruction is also an important part of the setting. For example, students' oral sharing of what they've read may be limited to rote recall because this was what previous teachers expected. In some cases even the principal's behavior (perhaps following the dictum that only "basic skills" be taught) may be relevant. Any information that can contribute to an understanding of students' reading and writing development should be considered.

3. Teachers should also consider their own behavior as part of students' instructional setting. Teachers may find that their feedback to students' miscues may encourage the belief that reading is a matter of getting the words right. Or teachers may find that students' discussion of their reading and writing is more thoughtful when teachers increase their "wait time" (the amount of time teachers give students to respond to their prompts or questions).

4. Observations should be regularly summarized and recorded. If someone not acquainted with the child or the setting read the record of the observations would they have a clear picture of what went on? Even if the observations aren't going to be shared with anyone else, they can still be confusing to the teacher who wrote them several weeks or months later if the record of the observation is not sufficiently explicit. Teachers will learn how explicit to make observational records by rereading past records and finding out what is confusing and what they would like to have remembered more about. . . .

5. In many cases it's helpful if observations are supplemented with pictures, audiotapes, or videotapes. Teachers may, for example, tape their students' oral reading and listen to

---

[2] Reproduced with permission from Lynn K. Rhodes and Curt Dudley-Marling: *Readers and Writers with a Difference* (Portsmouth, N.H., Heinemann Educational Books, 1988).

the tape in the car on the way home. Audio- and videotapes and pictures will also be especially helpful for sharing information about students' reading and writing with parents.

6. Observations of students don't have to be unobtrusive. It's fine if students are aware that they are being observed, especially if observation is a routine practice in the classroom. It's helpful to let students know that they are being observed and why ("I just want to see what you do while you're writing"). Observation will affect students' performance only if students are rarely observed in their classrooms.

7. There are times when it's useful to ask students questions to clarify what has been observed. While observing a student's restlessness during silent reading, for example, a teacher might ask, "What's the problem? You seem restless about something."

8. Observation need not be excessively time-consuming. In some cases it may be necessary to sit back and watch students as they read and write, but these observations needn't take more than several minutes. In general, the richest source of information will be close attention to students as they respond to instruction and as they read and write.

As with miscue analysis, through observation teachers are looking for the strategies a child uses that are both appropriate and inappropriate. Those that are inappropriate become areas of instructional focus, while appropriate strategies are encouraged and built upon.

Obtaining feedback, or an overt response, from *each* child is critical and can be accomplished in several ways. Careful planning includes every-pupil response techniques (Cunningham, 1982; Hopkins, 1979), written work, and perhaps some taped readings. When reviewing these overt responses teachers must keep in mind why they initiated the behavior or what it is they are looking for. This is a good reason for developing checklists or rating scales as a way of organizing information (see figure 4.8). Observations are discussed in more detail in chapter 13, "Analytic Teaching."

Conferences

Even teachers who carefully plan opportunities for observation will have unanswered questions about the progress of some students. Thus the teacher must structure short periods of time to focus more directly on behavioral responses of individual students. These periods are often called teacher-student conferences.

The teacher arranges a conference any time during the day when five to twenty minutes can be spared for an individual child. A variety of assessment procedures (IRIs, a written lesson, teacher-made exercises) can be used to gather information, but usually the teacher is interested in finding answers to the specific question that motivated the conference. For instance, if the child has made inconsistent responses (e.g., sometimes recognizing the *st* blend and sometimes not) during the instructional period or on written work, the teacher will want to know whether the child actually knows the *st* blend.

Conferences between the student and the teacher may reveal many potential problems. If these are uncovered early and corrected promptly, the effectiveness of a corrective reading program will be enhanced. Many children, good and poor students alike, falter from time to time in their learning. Brief conferences pay great dividends because they identify reading weaknesses before they become serious reading problems.

Figure 4.8 Checklist for appraising early reading development.

Student_____ Teacher_____
Age_____ Grade_____ Date_____
School_____

Characteristics	**Yes**	**No**

Cognition
1. Understands grade level material read aloud   — —
2. Remembers new words used in class   — —
3. Remembers content of stories discussed in class   — —

Language
1. Speaks in complete sentences   — —
2. Speaking vocabulary is adequate   — —
3. Speaking vocabulary is advanced   — —
4. Speech is normal   — —
5. Hearing is normal   — —

General Reading
1. When being read to the child:
    a. sometimes finishes the sentence (anticipates what is next)   — —
    b. sometimes follows along with finger   — —
    c. pays attention   — —
2. Recognizes signs (e.g., stop signs), labels ("Wheaties"), or logos (e.g., "McDonald's")   — —
3. Recognizes his/her name   — —
4. Recognizes letters in (*state what context*)   — —
5. Recognizes words in (*state what context*)   — —
6. Remembers words taught as whole words   — —
7. Attempts to blend sound units   — —
8. Can guess new words from context   — —
9. Skips words when reading in order to use context   — —
10. Skips unknown words totally in order to maintain comprehension   — —
11. Reads fluently   — —
12. Seldom reverses letters/words   — —
13. Observes punctuation in oral reading   — —
14. During silent reading, child seldom finger points   — —
15. During silent reading, child seldom subvocalizes   — —
16. Recalls facts of material read   — —
17. Can summarize main points of material read   — —
18. Can locate answers to questions   — —
19. Comprehends narrative material   — —
20. Comprehends expository material   — —
21. Adjusts reading speed depending on reading purpose, or difficulty of material   — —

(continued)

FIGURE 4.8 Checklist for appraising early reading development *(continued)*

Characteristics	Yes	No
Motivation		
1. Enjoys being read to	—	—
2. Knows that books have a top and bottom, and turns pages front to back	—	—
3. Talks about books he/she listened to or read	—	—
4. Looks at books on his/her own	—	—
5. Has a favorite book(s)	—	—

Additional Comments and Observations:

Checklists and Rating Scales

While observation provides much information about reading behavior, teachers cannot possibly remember all the behavior of 25 to 30 pupils in a class, even if notebooks are used. A system must be organized to aid interpretation of what has been observed. Such record-keeping systems are available in the form of checklists and rating scales.

Checklists and rating scales evolve around the important sets of behaviors being considered. Common areas in reading are readiness, word recognition, comprehension, and oral and silent reading. Other relevant nonreading areas are intelligence, emotional stability, vision, and hearing. Teachers may make their own checklists, but many good checklists and rating scales are already available. You may be wise to choose one already designed by specialists and scholars in reading and add to or modify your collection as needed.

Checklists and rating scales are scored differently. A checklist asks the teacher to judge on a yes-no basis whether the behavior exists. A rating scale, on the other hand, asks the teacher to judge the *degree* to which the behavior exists. A five-point scale is common, with ratings similar to the following:

1 = not present
2 = rarely present
3 = sometimes present
4 = often present
5 = always present

Checklists and rating scales provide a structured approach to observation (fig. 4.8). Most published informal reading inventories have behavioral checklists, which are helpful and can influence teacher judgment on determining reading levels.

A checklist can also be used to summarize the performance of several students instead of one child. This procedure is useful because teachers are usually working with groups of students functioning at different levels. The checklist in figure 4.9 can be used to record the progress of students using a particular set of reading materials or receiving instruction at a level different from other classmates.

Checklists and rating scales are a good source of information that is helpful for corrective instruction. Successful use of such informal procedures, however, largely depends on the experience and expertise of the user (Shertzer & Linden, 1979). Inexperienced teachers often feel insecure making judgments about reading behavior. The wise teacher, when in doubt, will verify the information on a checklist by comparison with a variety of measures. Verification in real reading situations is highly recommended.

Interest and Attitude Surveys

Interests and attitudes are important student characteristics that are neither easily nor quickly determined by observation. Asking requires the least time and effort. Teachers can gather the information in casual conversations with students, or more efficiently, through the use of interest and attitude surveys. These surveys can be conducted as interviews or in written format, or some combination of these.

Interest and attitude surveys suggest instructional strategies that may be useful in working with the student. If interests are known, the teacher uses materials that deal with those interests. If the student has a negative attitude, expected with students having reading problems, the teacher makes special efforts to motivate the child and improve attitudes toward reading.

The importance of gathering and using information on interests and attitudes will be discussed further in chapter 13. Obtaining information on interests consists of asking a series of questions regarding what students like to do, whether they have pets or hobbies, what television programs they watch, and so forth. An example of an interest inventory is presented in figure 4.10.

Attitude surveys also ask questions, but of a different nature. Usually students respond yes or no, or indicate some degree of feeling (e.g., strongly agree, agree, don't know, disagree, strongly disagree).

Attitude surveys should also address students' perceptions of reading as a process and of perceptions of themselves as readers. For example, an interview format can be used to provide teachers with some relevant information about students' perceptions of themselves as readers and writers. The interview might include some of the following key questions:

- Do you like to read (or write)?
- What is your favorite book (or who is your favorite author)?
- When do you read (or write)?
- Do you think you are a good reader (writer)? Why or why not?
- Who is the best reader (writer) you know? Why?
- When you get to a word you do not know, what do you do?
- If someone asked you for help figuring out a word they did not know, how would you help them?
- When you do not understand what you read, what do you do?
- Would you rather read (write) or ride a bike?
- Would you rather read (write) or watch TV?
- Would you rather read a story or write a story?
- Would you rather read (write) or sleep?
- Would you rather read (write) or draw?
- Would you rather read (write) or do arithmetic homework?
- Would you rather read (write) or help do the dishes?

FIGURE 4.9 Checklist of recording oral reading characteristics for a group of students.

Date: Name	Harry	Susie	Leroy	Mark	Daisy	Kenya
Comprehension						
Recalls Facts						
Makes Inferences						
Word Recognition/Decoding						
Has Adequate Sight Vocabulary						
Infrequently Needs Words Pronounced						
Mispronounces Few Words						
Infrequently Omits Words						
Does Not Insert Words						
Uses Context Adequately						
Is Not Bound Solely By Context						
Knows High-Utility Words						
Analyzes Words Visually						
Knows Symbol-Sound Associations						
Can Blend Sounds						
Fluency						
Has Few or No Hesitations						
Has Few of No Repetitions						
Phrases Appropriately						
Does Not Read Word-By-Word						
Pays Attention to Punctuation						
Reads at an Appropriate Rate						
Seldom Loses Place						
Demonstrates Proper Use of Voice						
Demonstrates Proper Enunciation						
Demonstrates Proper Expression						
Uses Proper Volume						
Observations						
Seldom Shows Signs of Tension						
Finger Points Infrequently						
Holds Book At Appropriate Distance						
Concentrates on Task At Hand						

Comments:

FIGURE 4.10 Sample interest inventory.

Inventory of Pupil Interests and Activities

Name_____ Age_____ Grade_____
School_____ Date_____ Examiner_____

1. What is your favorite TV show?
2. Who is your favorite TV character?
3. If you could make up a TV show, what would it be about?
4. Do you have a favorite movie?
5. Do you have any pets?
6. What is your favorite animal?
7. If you could be any living thing, what would you be?
8. Where have you traveled? Name three places.
9. Name all the different types of transportation you have experienced (train, bus, auto, boat, wagon, airplane, jet, truck, buggy, subway, bicycle, ship).
10. If you received two airplane tickets to anywhere in the world, where would you go?
11. If you have a time machine for anytime in the past or future, where would you go and when?
12. What is your favorite subject?
13. What is the latest book you read? Did you enjoy it? Why or why not?
14. What kind of books do you read at home?
15. If it was a rainy day at home, what would you do?
    If it was a sunny day at home, what would you do?
16. What is your favorite sport?
17. What is your favorite hobby?
18. If I gave you $100 to buy whatever you wanted, what would you do with the money?

- When you write, what kinds of problems do you have? What do you do about them?
- Do you ever make changes in what you write? What kind of changes?

Open-ended statements are also used to assess attitudes. For example, the student is asked to complete the following sentences:

Reading is _____.
I think reading _____.
Most books _____.
My parents _____.
Teachers _____.

The entire Incomplete Sentence Projective Test may be found in Appendix B. Figure 4.11 contains representative items from an attitude survey appropriate for primary grades.

Many interest and attitude surveys are available for use or modification by teachers. Some of these are listed here.

Askov, E. N. (1973). *Primary pupil reading attitude inventory.* Dubuque, IA: Kendall/Hunt.

Harris, L. A., & Smith, C. B. (1980). *Reading instruction* (3rd ed., p. 428). New York: Holt, Rinehart and Winston.

Lapp, D., & Flood, J. (1983). *Teaching reading to every child* (2nd ed., pp. 363–365). New York: Macmillan.

McKenna, M. C. & Kear, D. J. (1990). Measuring attitude toward reading: A new tool for teachers. *The Reading Teacher, 43,* 626–639.

Strickler, D., & Eller, W. (1980). Attitudes and interests. In P. Lamb and R. Arnold (Eds.), *Teaching reading* (p. 386). Belmont, CA: Wadsworth.

Tullock-Rhody, R., & Alexander, J. E. (1980). A scale for assessing attitudes toward reading in secondary schools. *Journal of Reading, 23,* 609–614.

Work Samples

Teachers have many options for assessing reading and writing development on a regular basis. Each time a student is asked to complete a written assignment, worksheet, or workbook page, the teacher has the opportunity to determine which students need additional instruction. By carefully selecting work samples, the teacher has the means to assess students' needs on a continuing basis. The importance of these materials will become apparent in the following chapters.

Oral and Written Language Samples

Analysis of a reading problem cannot ignore the child's other language skills because reading is a language process. The mental processes involved in the production skills of speaking and writing are similar to those involved in the receptive skills of listening and reading (Loban, 1976; Pickert & Chase, 1978; Shanahan, 1980; Stotsky, 1975; Zeman, 1969), and develop in parallel, interactive ways (Teale & Sulzby, 1986). Marie Clay, an educator interested in better descriptions of young children's reading and writing behaviors for the purpose of early detection of reading difficulties, researched five-year-old children entering school in New Zealand (Clay, 1967). She found that these young children showed visual sensitivity to letters and words, knew to move from left-to-right, from top-to-bottom, and from front-to-back when looking at books, and were able to match spoken word and written word units. Such competence makes it apparent that children's literacy development does not begin when they enter school, rather these competencies have been *emerging* since birth outside of school situations. Thus, the term **emergent literacy** (Clay, 1966) is used to describe the transformation that occurs when children, having been in the presence of print, actively attempt to discover how oral and written language are related.

One good way to sample children's oral and written language is to ask them to draw, talk, and then write about what they have produced. After the drawing and writing are complete, ask the child to read what was written. If a child seems reluctant, the teacher might invite the child to draw a picture of his/her family and write something about each member. Wordless picture books are also a good source for oral language samples as well as written samples. Oral language samples can be tape-recorded for later transcription and written samples collected and dated, with teacher notations, to document growth.

Sulzby (1985) has developed a 7-point scale for assessing various levels of sophistication in children's attempts at rereading their own written language. For example, a score of 2 is given to the behavior of the child producing random marks on paper but refusing to reread them; a score of 4 is given for a child attempting to reread

FIGURE 4.11 Primary grades attitude survey.

(Teacher: Before administering this survey, be sure children can distinguish the three faces as feeling happy, don't care, and feeling sad, respectively. You might want to ask a few practice questions, such as "How do you feel about Christmas?" or "How do you feel about going to bed early?" Feel free to add items to the survey. For group administration, students can either color in or mark the face that represents the way they feel about each question. Individuals can either point to or hold up individual face cards to indicate their feelings.)

1. How do you feel when your teacher reads a story to you?

2. How do you feel about reading out loud in class?

3. How do you feel about going to the library?

4. How do you feel when you come to a new word in your book?

5. How do you feel about your reading group?

6. How do you feel about getting a book for a present?

7. How do you feel when you read at home?

8. How do you feel when you read to your Mom, Dad, or a friend?

9. How do you feel about reading a story before bedtime?

10. How do you feel when you don't understand what you read?

what was written, but not keeping eyes on the print; and a score of 7 is given when the child's eyes are following the print and there is a match between voice and print. This type of assessment not only can inform the teacher about a child's understanding of literacy concepts, but can also promote children's literacy development by drawing their attention to the distinctions between oral and written language.

Writing also plays an important role in learning our alphabetic system—graphic symbols representing oral language. Writing forces children to attend to the visual features of print, which in turn helps children become aware of letter-sound patterns and their relation to words. As children hear and see stories read over and over, learn letter names, print or spell words, and try to read and write new words, they will learn, naturally, the written English alphabetic system. Of course, children's progress can be enhanced with encouragement, modeling, and instruction geared toward their current level of understanding about print. An analysis of children's invented spellings reveals development of such phonic skills as segmentation (breaking words into parts), blending (putting sounds together to form words), and letter-sound correspondences. (See Appendix C for stages of spelling development and a spelling test that can be used to sample children's ideas about spelling.)

In addition to analyzing spelling, a more holistic analysis of written language samples of students can reveal their knowledge of writing and the writing process. Examination of writing samples should be made with the intention of providing feedback for students that will help them become more skillful writers. A system that looks at the qualities of good writing as well as the process of writing might serve a teacher's needs best. Appendix D provides a holistic scoring system for the qualities of good writing and a behavioral checklist for the process of writing.

Children build their own rules for oral grammar and written language based on their observations and explorations with print (Noyce & Christie, 1989). By listening to children speak and by examining their writing samples, we gain insight into what children have already learned about oral and written language.

Summary

A variety of informal measures have been presented. Informal assessment procedures are valuable to the teacher for gathering additional information and verifying tentative teaching hypotheses in the analytic process. A balance of both formal and informal measures is most effective in learning students' reading needs, however. The following chapter will explain how you can achieve this balance.

References

Arnold, R. D., & Sherry, N. (1975). A comparison of reading levels of disabled readers with assigned textbooks. *Reading Improvement, 12,* 207–211.

Beck, I. L. (1981). Reading problems and instructional practices. In G. E. Mackinnon & T. G. Waller (Eds.), *Reading research: Advances in theory and practice* (Vol. 2). New York: Academic Press.

Berliner, D. C. (1981). Academic learning time and reading achievement. In J. T. Guthrie (Ed.), *Comprehension and teaching: Research reviews.* Newark, DE: International Reading Association.

Betts, E. (1946). *Foundations of reading instruction.* New York: American Book.

Bormuth, J. R. (1975). The cloze procedure: Literacy in the classroom. In W. D. Page (Ed.), *Help for the reading teacher: New directions in research.* Urbana, IL: ERIC Clearinghouse on Reading and Communication Skills.

Bowman, M. (1981). *The effects of story structure questioning upon reading comprehension.* Paper presented at the American Educational Research Association Conference, Los Angeles.

Brown, C. S. (1985). *Assessing perceptions of language and learning: Alternative diagnostic approaches.* Paper presented at the International Reading Association Convention, New Orleans.

Burns, P. C., & Roe, B. D. (1989). *Informal reading inventory: Preprimer through twelfth grade.* Boston: Houghton Mifflin.

Cardarelli, A. F. (1988). The influence of reinspection on students' IRI results. *The Reading Teacher, 41,* 664–667.

Clay, M. M. (1966). *Emergent reading behavior.* Unpublished doctoral dissertation. University of Auckland, New Zealand.

Clay, M. M. (1967). The reading behavior of five-year-old children: A research report. *New Zealand Journal of Educational Studies, 2,* 11–31.

Cooper, L. J. (1952). *The effect of adjustment of basal reading materials on achievement.* Unpublished doctoral dissertation, Boston University.

Cunningham, P. (1982). Every-pupil response techniques. *Effective use of learning time: Research, tips, and materials.* Microworkshop 13 presented at the Annual Meeting of the International Reading Association, Chicago.

Davis, C. (1978). The effectiveness of informal assessment questions constructed by secondary teachers. In P. D. Pearson and J. Hansen (Eds.), *Reading: Disciplined inquiry in process and practice.* Twenty-seventh Yearbook of the National Reading Conference, Clemson, SC.

Duffelmeyer, F. A., & Duffelmeyer, B. B. (1989). Are IRI passages suitable for assessing main idea comprehension? *The Reading Teacher, 42,* 358–363.

Duffelmeyer, F. S., Robinson, S. S., & Squier, S. E. (1989). Vocabulary questions on informal reading inventories. *The Reading Teacher, 43,* 142–148.

Ekwall, E. E. (1986). *Ekwall reading inventory.* Boston: Allyn and Bacon.

Ekwall, E. E. (1974). Should repetitions be counted as errors? *The Reading Teacher, 27,* 365–367.

Farr, R., & Carey, R. F. (1986). *Reading: What can be measured?* Newark, DE: International Reading Association.

Gallant, R. (1964). *An investigation of the use of cloze tests as a measure of readability of materials for the primary grades.* Unpublished doctoral dissertation, Indiana University, Bloomington.

Gambrell, L. B., Wilson, R. M., & Gantt, W. N. (1981). Classroom observations of task-attending behaviors of good and poor readers. *Journal of Educational Research, 24,* 400–404.

Goodman, Y., & Burke, C. (1972). *Reading miscue inventory manual: Procedure for diagnosis and evaluation.* New York: Macmillan.

Goodman, Y. M., Watson, D. J., & Burke, C. L. (1987). *Reading miscue inventory: Alternative procedures.* New York, NY: Richard C. Owen.

Guthrie, J. T., Seifert, M., Burnham, N. A., & Caplan, R. I. (1974). The maze technique to assess, monitor reading comprehension. *The Reading Teacher, 28,* 161–168.

Haller, E. J., & Waterman, M. (1985). The criteria of reading group assignments. *The Reading Teacher, 38,* 772–781.

Harris, A., & Sipay, E. (1990). *How to increase reading ability* (9th ed.). New York: Longman.

Henk, W. A., & Selders, M. L. (1984). A test of synonymic scoring of cloze passages. *The Reading Teacher, 38,* 282–287.

Hood, J. (1975–1976). Qualitative analysis of oral reading errors: The inter-judge reliability of scores. *Reading Research Quarterly, 11,* 577–598.

Hopkins, C. J. (1979). Using every-pupil response techniques in reading instruction. *The Reading Teacher, 33,* 173–175.

Johns, J. L. (1991). *Basic reading inventory.* Dubuque, IA: Kendall/Hunt.

Johnson, M. S., & Kress, R. A. (1965). *Informal reading inventories.* Newark, DE: International Reading Association.

Jorgenson, G. W. (1977). Relationship of classroom behavior to the accuracy of the match between material difficulty and student ability. *Journal of Educational Psychology, 69,* 24–32.

Kavale, K., & Schreiner, R. (1979). The reading processes of above average readers: A comparison of the use of reasoning strategies in responding to standardized comprehension measures. *Reading Research Quarterly, 15,* 102–128.

Loban, W. (1976). *Language development: Kindergarten through grade twelve.* Urbana, IL: National Council of Teachers of English.

Mason, J. M. (Ed.). (1989). *Reading and writing connections.* Boston: Allyn and Bacon.

McKenna, M. C. (1976). Synonymic versus verbatim scoring of the cloze procedure. *Journal of Reading, 20,* 141–143.

Miller, G. R., & Coleman, E. B. (1967). A set of 36 prose passages calibrated for complexity. *Journal of Verbal Learning and Verbal Behavior, 6,* 851–854.

Morrow, L. M. (1985a). Reading and retelling stories: Strategies for emergent readers. *The Reading Teacher, 38,* 870–875.

Morrow, L. M. (1985b). *Story retelling: A diagnostic approach for evaluating story structure, language and comprehension.* Paper presented at the International Reading Association Convention, New Orleans.

Mosenthal, P. (1978). The new and given in children's comprehension of presuppositive negatives in two modes of processing. *Journal of Reading Behavior, 10,* 267–278.

Noyce, R. M., & Christie, J. F. (1989). *Integrating reading and writing instruction in grades K–8.* Boston: Allyn and Bacon.

Olshavsky, J. E. (1977). Reading as problem solving: An investigation of strategies. *Reading Research Quarterly, 12,* 654–674.

Pearson, P. D., & Johnson, D. D. (1978). *Teaching reading comprehension.* New York: Holt, Rinehart and Winston.

Pickert, S. M., & Chase, M. L. (1978). Story retelling: An informal technique for evaluating children's language. *The Reading Teacher, 31,* 528–531.

Pikulski, J. J., & Shanahan, T. (Ed.). (1982). *Approaches to the informal evaluation of reading.* Newark, DE: International Reading Association.

Pikulski, J. J., & Tobin, A. W. (1982). The cloze procedure as an informal assessment technique. In J. J. Pikulski & T. Shanahan (Eds.), *Approaches to the informal evaluation of reading.* Newark, DE: International Reading Association.

Powell, W. R. (1970). Reappraising the criteria for interpreting informal inventories. In D. DeBoer (Ed.), *Reading diagnosis and evaluation.* Newark, DE: International Reading Association.

Powell, W., & Dunkeld, C. (1971). Validity of the IRI reading levels. *Elementary English, 48,* 637–642.

Rhodes, L. K., & Dudley-Marling, C. (1988). *Readers and writers with a difference: A holistic approach to teaching learning disabled and remedial students.* Portsmouth, NH: Heinemann.

Roberts, T. (1976). "Frustration level" reading in the infant school. *Educational Research, 19,* 41–44.

Ruddell, R. B. (1964). A study of the cloze comprehension technique in relation to structurally controlled reading material. In J. A. Figurel (Ed.), *Improvement of reading through classroom practice.* Newark, DE: International Reading Association.

Schell, L. M., & Hanna, G. S. (1981). Can informal reading inventories reveal strengths and weaknesses in comprehension subskills? *The Reading Teacher, 35,* 263–268.

Shanahan, T. (1980). The impact of writing instruction on learning to read. *Reading World, 19,* 357–368.

Shertzer, B., & Linden, J. (1979). *Fundamentals of individual appraisal.* Boston: Houghton Mifflin.

Smith, S. P., & Jackson, F. H. (1985). Assessing reading/learning skills with written retellings. *Journal of Reading, 28,* 622–630.

Spache, G. (1976). *Diagnosing and correcting reading disabilities.* Boston: Allyn and Bacon.

Spiegel, D. L., & Whaley, J. (1980). *Elevating comprehension skills by sensitizing students to structural aspects of narratives.* Paper presented at the National Reading Conference, San Diego, CA.

Stein, N., & Glenn, C. (1979). An analysis of story comprehension in elementary school children. In R. Freedle (Ed.), *New directions in discourse processes* (Vol. 2). Norwood, NJ: Ablex.

Stotsky, S. (1975). Sentence combining as a curriculum activity: Its effect on written language development and reading comprehension. *Research in the Teaching of English, 9,* 30–71.

Sulzby, E. (1985). Kindergartners as writers and readers. In M. Farr (Ed.), *Advances in writing research: vol. 1. Children's early writing development* (pp. 127–199). Norwood, NJ: Ablex.

Taylor, W. L. (1953). Cloze procedure: A new tool for measuring readability. *Journalism Quarterly, 30,* 415–433.

Teale, W. H., & Sulzby, E. (1986). *Emergent literacy: Writing and reading.* Norwood, NJ: Ablex.

Valmont, W. (1972). Creating questions for informal reading inventories. *The Reading Teacher, 25,* 509–512.

Weaver, C. (1988). *Reading process and practice: From socio-psycholinguistics to whole language.* Portsmouth, NH: Heinemann.

Wixson, K. L. (1979). Miscue analysis: A critical review. *Journal of Reading Behavior, 11,* 163–175.

Woods, M. L., & Moe, A. J. (1989). *Analytical reading inventory.* Columbus, OH: Merrill.

Zeman, W. S. (1969). Reading comprehension and writing of second and third graders. *The Reading Teacher, 23,* 144–150.

CHAPTER 5

Implementing the Analytic Process

Objectives

After you have read this chapter, you should be able to

1. compile a list of formal and informal sources of information to be used in assessing reading problems at the first three of the four analytical levels;

2. outline a procedure for implementing the analytic process.

Study Outline

Important Vocabulary and Concepts

cumulative records   profile analysis

Overview

This chapter helps you relate the formal measures described in chapter 3 and the informal measures discussed in chapter 4 to the four levels of analysis presented in chapter 2. As you read this chapter, you will find that the analytic process can be somewhat ambiguous and that it should be viewed as a process of successive steps taken to converge on specific information the child needs to learn.

Introduction

Many different types of formal and informal measures have been presented thus far, and their uses, strengths, and weaknesses have been examined. You are now aware that a wide variety of tools is available for use in analyzing reading problems and that not one tool, or even a few, will suffice to identify strengths and weaknesses of all poor readers. A set of tools, both formal and informal, is needed to analyze reading behaviors adequately and reach the level of specificity needed for corrective instruction.

In the final analysis, teachers must verify their hypotheses and instructional plans in the context of actual reading, that is, during the teaching phase. The hypotheses are modified and adjusted as needed, based on a child's performance.

Because so many assessment options are available for analysis, you may feel more confused than enlightened. This chapter is designed to help you select appropriate informal and formal measures for the various levels of analysis. Suggested tools and strategies for use at levels 1 and 2 and, to a lesser extent, level 3 will be explored. Tools and strategies for level 4, specific strengths and weaknesses, will be examined more fully in the content-relevant chapters that follow.

Sources of Information

In gathering information about a child's reading ability, teachers should consider any available source and use its data for tentative teaching hypotheses. These hypotheses then need to be verified by observing a child read in real life situations. Available information can also be considered as an indicator of the need for further analysis.

Cumulative Records

Records of previous performance are usually entered and organized in a **cumulative record**, which often accompanies a child throughout the entire school career. Test scores, as well as final grades from previous school years, make up a major part of the cumulative record. Additional valuable data may include results of intelligence tests, relevant medical observations of the school nurse, comments from other school specialists and former teachers. This information is helpful to the present teacher if the data are interpreted judiciously.

Discussion with Others

Much can be learned about children from others. Parents, principals, special reading and speech teachers, and other adults provide a rich source of information. If a child is known to have reading problems, the present teacher will certainly hear about it early in the school year. Former teachers are especially helpful in alerting the child's current teacher. Naturally, information from others is subject to varying interpretations, but the information should not be ignored.

The Child

Teachers may overlook the information a child can provide. Sometimes youngsters, in their own words, give the teacher valuable insights regarding their reading abilities and problems. This is particularly helpful when a child transfers from a different school system without cumulative records. A child's self-perceptions may be incorrect, however, so the teacher should probably use the information to form tentative working hypotheses. These are then verified in the instructional setting or in another assessment setting.

Work Samples

The child's day-to-day oral and written work provides much readily accessible information. This work is done under less stressful conditions than achievement testing and may reveal abilities more accurately, especially in a child with problems who is anxious about tests. The teacher simply collects occasional samples of the child's work to include in a folder where they are dated and kept in chronological order.

Test Scores

Test scores included in a cumulative record also help the teacher know more about the child. Information of this nature is sometimes kept in school files to avoid possible problems with rights of privacy, and teachers must handle the information professionally and with confidentiality.

Guidelines for Analytic Strategies

Before beginning this section, you should be aware that the material presented is *suggestive* in terms of approaching the analysis of possible corrective readers. Much of the discussion is based on previous experiences that have been successful. The strategies should not be interpreted as rigid formulas but rather as guidelines to help answer the important correlative diagnostic questions presented earlier. Many tests and assessment devices are designed with different perspectives, and error of measurement varies from one instrument to another. The analytic process should be viewed as one of convergence on a problem from a number of perspectives. Ambiguities arise because the convergence is often imperfect and, at times, even contradictory. Ultimately, the teacher must make educated guesses, or hypotheses, regarding the questions being asked. These hypotheses then become the basis for an instructional plan, which in turn allows the teacher to verify hypotheses in the corrective reading phase.

Strategies to Determine the Presence of a Reading Problem

During orientation week of a new school year, teachers begin to think about their new class, tentatively classifying the pupils according to ability and achievement. The teacher sifts through cumulative records trying to find starting points. Clues to problem readers often can be found, including informal discussion from previous teachers. During this time, the classroom reading program begins to take on its rudimentary form. The teacher is thinking about matching students to appropriate reading materials. For most students this process is referred to as placement, but the teacher must be more thorough for children with suspected reading problems. This related process is analysis at the first level, that is, determining the existence of a reading problem.

The process for level 1 was discussed in detail in chapter 2. Usually the assessment devices include intelligence tests and standardized achievement tests, both of which may have been administered previously. If so, the teacher can examine each child's achievement in relation to their potential (chapter 1), before ever meeting the children. If a child is achieving below reading expectancy, a reading problem may be suspected. Comparisons of subtest scores on achievement test batteries may indicate discrepancies in areas that the teacher will want to follow up. Once the teacher actually meets the students, informal measures such as informal reading inventories (IRIs) or cloze passages can be used to determine general reading achievement and, in the case of the IRI, listening capacity. Observation and work samples are most valuable.

Strategies to Determine Domains Where Problems Exist

Analysis at the second level involves study between domains. Comparative achievement data are needed for each of the three domains: word recognition, comprehension, and study skills and strategic reading. Text-related tests are a readily available source for such data. Achievement test scores are often found in cumulative folders. The teacher learns the previous grade's scores and, at the same time, the growth a child has made over the years. Work samples appropriately designed also provide information on strengths and weaknesses.

By comparing already available achievement test scores, text-related test scores, and representative classroom work samples for each of the three domains, initial analysis of problem areas can be made. Questionable or inconsistent results can be supplemented by administering a standardized tool, such as the *Stanford Diagnostic Reading Test* (SDRT) or, more probably, by informal procedures, such as an IRI. The SDRT is one of the few standardized tests that assesses most of the domains of concern. It is also relatively valid, reliable, comparatively inexpensive, and efficient because it can be given as a group test. IRIs assess word recognition and comprehension, but other informal procedures are necessary to assess study skills and strategic reading.

Strategies to Determine Strengths and Weaknesses within Each Domain

The analytic process at the third level looks for major areas of strength and weakness within each domain. As mentioned earlier, opinions differ as to what these major areas are. Thus, teachers must be aware of how the areas are labeled and defined in the particular reading programs used in their school system. The suggestions that follow may not conform entirely to any particular labeling system, but should at least present the basic concepts of many reading programs used today. The three domains will be discussed separately.

Analyzing Word Recognition

For the purposes of this book, the major areas within the domain of word recognition are as follows:

- Context clues, which include three subareas: (1) expectancy clues, (2) picture clues, and (3) meaning clues
- Sight vocabulary
- Visual analysis, including the ability to identify unknown word parts visually
- Word analysis skills, including knowledge of word parts associated with phonics and structural analysis
- Blending and synthesizing, or the ability to reassemble word parts into a meaningful whole

No single, standardized test assesses achievement in the five major areas listed above. The *Silent Reading Diagnostic Test* (SRDT) (Bond, Balow, & Hoyt, 1972) tests most of the areas, with the exception of expectancy and picture clues and sight vocabulary, and may be the best published test for this domain. Another possibility is to use subtests of other published tests, but it is most likely that informal assessment will be needed, particularly for picture and expectancy clues.

Analysis within this domain may include a **profile analysis**, a graph of test scores in comparable units (e.g., stanines or NCEs) of the pupil's relative strengths and weaknesses in the areas tested. Ideally, a student's work reflects a relatively even, or flat, profile. The overall profile should be compared to the child's general level of achievement in word recognition. Such a profile can be obtained from the SRDT.

As an example, Sammy, a fifth-grade student of average ability, is identified as having a reading problem (level 1 analysis) and is subsequently administered the *Stanford Diagnostic Reading Test* (SDRT). A between-domain analysis reveals problems with word recognition (level 2 analysis). His score is in the second stanine, or below average. The teacher then may choose to (1) use informal assessment procedures (e.g., work samples, IRI), or (2) employ parts of the *Silent Reading Diagnostic Test* (SRDT), or (3) use parts of both informal and formal assessments to assess Sammy's level of development in the major areas (level 3 analysis). The informal profile analysis, obtained from the scores of either or both informal and formal tests, is compared to Sammy's general achievement in word recognition, in this case, below average or stanine 2. Areas found to be two stanines above this level of stanine 2 would be considered relative strengths for Sammy, while those below would be considered weaknesses. The teacher is now in a position to say what Sammy's relative strengths and weaknesses are in the areas involved in word recognition and to compare and contrast these with his average performance on daily word recognition tasks. A level 4 analysis must be conducted, however, to determine more precisely what Sammy needs to learn to improve the subarea or areas of concern. To illustrate, instructional needs at level 3 are somewhat vague.

- Sammy needs instruction in use of context clues.
- Sammy needs instruction in sight vocabulary.
- Sammy needs instruction in auditory blending.

The teacher feels much more secure about teaching hypotheses from level 3 analysis than those from level 2. Compare the specificity of the above three instructional needs to the level 2 conclusion:

- Sammy needs instruction in word recognition.

Level 3 hypotheses are much more helpful. However, analysis at level 4 yields hypotheses that are sufficiently specific to provide the teacher with *teachable* learning segments. No published standardized tests are available for level 4 analysis, with the possible exception of certain criterion-referenced tests, but many checklists and other informal procedures, such as work samples, help the teacher ascertain the specific needs of children in terms of units of instruction. Many assessment strategies are covered rather completely in the domain-specific chapters that follow.

The better the teacher understands the reading process, the more adept he/she will be at ascertaining children's specific instructional needs. For analysis in the domain of word recognition, it is important to provide students with whole text whenever possible so they have all of the cue systems (graphophonic, syntactic, semantic) available to them.

Analyzing Reading Comprehension

Word meaning is generally agreed to be a major component of reading comprehension. Assessment procedures include formal test scores from (1) vocabulary subtests on reading survey or diagnostic tests or (2) informal procedures to be discussed in chapter 7. Other important areas include understanding sentences, paragraphs, and larger selections. At this time, standardized tests assess understanding the content of sentences and paragraphs, but few are available for assessing understanding of whole text. The *Iowa Silent Reading Test* and the *SRA Reading Record* compare comprehension of words, sentences, and paragraphs. Teachers would be wise to use informal procedures such as those suggested in chapters 7 and 8.

Analyzing Study Skills and Strategic Reading

The domain of study skills and strategic reading involves many content areas. It is difficult to find a single test that adequately assesses all the areas and specific learnings possible. Some standardized tests can be considered for level three analysis:

- *California Test of Basic Skills*
- *Iowa Tests of Basic Skills*
- *Iowa Silent Reading Tests*
- *SRA Achievement Series*

Informal procedures are probably best to assess study skills and strategic reading at analytical levels 3 and 4. A good starting point is to use informal tests based on texts being used in the content areas. Areas of particular concern are (1) content-specific vocabulary and concepts; (2) special symbols such as those in mathematics or science; (3) visual displays, including maps, graphs, charts, and other graphic materials; (4) special organizational schemes and locational skills associated with the particular content area; and (5) knowledge and use of study strategies. Suggestions for informal assessment procedures are detailed in chapters 9 and 10 on study skills and strategic reading.

An Example

The foregoing detailed explanation of a possible analytic strategy may leave you with the impression that the analytic process demands test after test. Actually, testing is a relatively *minor* aspect of analysis. The example below will demonstrate the analytic process as it might be implemented by a classroom teacher.[1] (More thorough discussion will be found in chapter 13.)

The School

An upper socioeconomic, suburban, public elementary school has twenty-eight children in the third grade.

The Teacher

Miss Smith, a dedicated teacher who has helped to make the classroom an inviting, exciting place, has been teaching for three years.

Miss Smith has assembled many library books at different grade levels and has created an attractive area for individual silent reading. She displays children's work, including art projects, language experience stories, and children's creative books. Learning centers are neat, orderly, and interesting. Miss Smith believes in basal reading instruction supplemented with additional phonics lessons, independent reading, and varied language experience activities.

Miss Smith sincerely likes children. She is energetic, empathic, open to new ideas, and confident in her professional ability to make sound educational decisions.

Miss Smith conducts daily morning meetings and encourages children to discuss problems, pleasures, and reading goals.

During the first week of school, Miss Smith actively observed all of the children in her classroom during free time, reading groups, lunch, whole group instruction, art, music, independent reading, and morning meetings.

Miss Smith placed each student's name on an individual page of a large notebook. She noted peer interaction, student language ability, student ability to complete assignments, and student feelings of self-esteem. Miss Smith also made tentative notes concerning each child's apparent listening abilities and reading strengths.

Also during the first week of school, Miss Smith asked for her students' help. She told her students that she would plan with each child the reading strategies or skills needed for each student to experience as much success as possible. Miss Smith discussed the reasons for flexible reading groups and student conferences.

Jane

During the first week of school Miss Smith wrote her initial ideas about students in her notebook. One of Miss Smith's students was Jane.

---

[1] The author wishes to thank Dr. Janet C. Richards for this hypothetical example.

Jane (birthdate)
1. Quiet
2. Cooperative
3. Polite
4. Appears to have adequate speaking vocabulary
5. Appears interested
6. Appears healthy

Miss Smith observed Jane further and added notebook comments.

7. Does not volunteer to read aloud
8. Follows along carefully when others read
9. Does not volunteer to answer questions
10. Appears anxious

Miss Smith began to formulate some questions about Jane. She asked:

- Why does Jane display apparent passive behavior?
- Does Jane lack self-confidence and self-esteem?
- Is the reading material too difficult for Jane?
- What strategies might help Jane?

Miss Smith decided to look at Jane's cumulative folder and then made additional notebook comments.

11. Youngest of three siblings
12. Above average grades in first and second grades
13. Average and slightly below average standardized test scores
14. Many absences in first and second grade because of illness

Miss Smith decided to have a student conference with Jane. Because Miss Smith was an active, empathic listener and conducted the meeting in a nonjudgmental manner, Jane felt comfortable in sharing her thoughts. After the conference Miss Smith wrote:

15. Brother and sister both high achievers
16. Believes that she is not as "smart" as her siblings

Miss Smith decided to evaluate Jane's reading ability through testing. She wanted some answers to these questions:

- Is Jane reading to her fullest potential?
- What is Jane's instructional reading level? independent reading level? listening comprehension level?
- Is Jane's apparent passivity due to poor self-esteem because of inadequate reading ability?
- Is Jane a corrective reader possibly because of missing reading instruction due to illness?

Miss Smith decided to test Jane using an informal reading inventory. She gave the test while the class was actively involved in learning center activities. Afterward, she recorded the results in her notebook.

17. Adequate sight vocabulary commensurate with third grade
18. Reading independent level: second grade
19. Reading instructional level: third grade
20. Listening comprehension level: fifth grade

Miss Smith now knew that Jane probably had the potential to read with understanding at a higher level but needed to read independently at the second grade level. Jane probably would benefit from instruction in a reading group composed of children with average reading ability.

Miss Smith decided to test Jane further in order to pinpoint specific reading skill gaps and strengths. On the informal reading inventory, Jane demonstrated adequate sight vocabulary knowledge and comprehension ability. Therefore, Miss Smith decided to obtain a writing sample for documentation of Jane's understanding of written language. After examining Jane's writing, Miss Smith again wrote in her notebook.

21. Needs more writing opportunities
22. Needs help with consonant blends and medial vowel sounds
23. Needs to experience success

After analyzing Jane's reading and writing behaviors, test results, and affective dimensional behaviors, Miss Smith decided that Jane probably had far greater reading potential than she demonstrated. Miss Smith wrote:

24. Gaps in reading/writing instruction (some letter-sound correspondences), possibly because of first and second grade absences
25. Lack of motivation, possibly because of low self-esteem and inadequate reading skills
26. Possible feelings of inadequacy because of achieving siblings

Miss Smith decided to plan a program of reading instruction together with Jane. After the planning conference, she wrote the following for Jane.

Reading instructional plan:

1. Ad hoc grouping dealing with phonic analysis and decoding skills
2. Reciprocal peer tutoring (Jane will assist a less able student, and a more able student will assist Jane)
3. Physical examination, including visual and auditory testing
4. Child-parent-teacher conference

Miss Smith will continue to observe Jane's reading progress. Further considerations may include the following:

1. Determination of Jane's ability to stay on task
2. Teacher tutoring
3. Continued student-teacher conferences
4. Continued teacher support
5. Continued provisions for Jane's success

Summary

Chapters 3 and 4 discuss the tests and measures available to help teachers in the decision-making process involved in the analysis of reading problems. A wide array of formal tests, informal tests, and other forms of informal assessment are presented, and an attempt is made to help you relate these to the important correlative diagnostic questions proposed for the various analytical levels. In addition, an example of how a classroom teacher might implement the analytic process is provided. You should now be more comfortable with the analytic process, the instruments available to aid you in the process, and the way to translate the teaching hypotheses into objectives for lesson plans. Together, these first five chapters provide a broad perspective of the basics of corrective reading.

The remainder of this text will elaborate on the more specific aspects of the reading curriculum: word recognition; reading comprehension; study skills and strategic reading; linguistically variant children; reading-related factors; and implementation of a reading program to meet the needs of all students.

Reference

Bond, G., Balow, B., & Hoyt, C. (1972). *Silent reading diagnostic tests.* Chicago: Rand McNally.

PART II

The Major Domains

CHAPTER 6

Word Recognition

Objectives

After you have read this chapter, you should be able to

1. explain the difference between products of word analysis instruction and the process of word analysis;
2. list the major areas of skill development for word recognition;
3. develop a sequence for instruction of an unknown word;
4. choose and develop materials and exercises appropriate for instruction in the process of word analysis skills;
5. devise an instructional program in word recognition for a corrective student.

Study Outline

I. Introduction

II. Inadequate listening vocabulary
   A. Informal assessment
   B. Instructional strategies

III. Inadequate sight vocabulary
   A. Informal assessment
   B. Instructional strategies

IV. The basic skill strands

V. Inadequate use of context clues
   A. Expectancy and picture clues
      1. Informal assessment
      2. Instructional strategies
   B. Meaning clues
      1. Informal assessment
      2. Formal assessment
      3. Instructional strategies

VI. Inadequate visual analysis

   A. Monosyllabic words
   B. Polysyllabic words
      1. Informal assessment
      2. Instructional strategies

VII. Inadequate knowledge of word parts
   A. Informal assessment
   B. Formal assessment
   C. Instructional strategies

VIII. Ineffective blending and synthesizing
   A. Informal assessment
   B. Formal assessment
   C. Instructional strategies

IX. Summary

X. References

Important Vocabulary and Concepts

analytical vocabulary

auditory blending

automaticity

context

expectancy clues

listening vocabulary

meaning clues

meaning vocabulary

perceptual unit

phonics

picture clues

productive language

psychological set

reading vocabulary

recoding

scriptal information

sight vocabulary

sight words

structural analysis

syndrome

visual synthesizing

Overview

The heart of the reading process is comprehension, or understanding what is read. Children with word recognition problems do not process print effectively enough to allow them to interact with the text and construct meaning. As a result, reading is not an interesting or pleasant experience but a frustrating, laborious task.

Instruction in word recognition is important to comprehension. However, the major goal of understanding what is read can sometimes get lost in word recognition programs. When this happens, the teacher is responsible for putting the word recognition program in proper perspective, for the students must never lose sight of the major purpose of their efforts—comprehension. Reading is a meaning-getting process.

The causes of word recognition problems are myriad, but three common types related to reading instruction are: (1) too little instruction in word recognition; (2) too much instruction in word recognition; and (3) instruction that is *imbalanced*, for example, too much phonics and no contextual analysis, in terms of the major areas or skill strands of this important domain.

The importance of developing listening vocabulary as a foundation for subsequent sight vocabulary development is discussed. The concept of **automaticity** is emphasized at both the word and word element level, because the efficient reader must learn these units to the point where little effort is needed to figure out a new word or word part.

Skill strands in word recognition programs are presented in terms of scope and sequence. Context clues, including expectancy, picture, and meaning clues, are strongly oriented to meaning and thinking. Visual analysis itself is less of a thinking skill, yet a child uses considerable thought for this skill. Segmenting unknown words visually, or in any other fashion, is not an easy task for the naive or corrective reader.

The section entitled "Inadequate Knowledge of Word Parts" centers around (1) structural analysis, which involves meaning-bearing units, and (2) phonics, which is less meaningful in orientation. Correction of blending and synthesizing deficiencies is also stressed and related to the word recognition process.

Each section begins with a general discussion followed by an explanation of informal analysis, indicating symptoms to look for and informal assessment techniques to use. Formal assessment procedures are also included, when appropriate.

Each section ends with detailed suggestions for instructional strategies. These are only samples of the many types of activities and exercises possible.

Introduction

The reading process begins by using nonvisual information (e.g., expectations about the text) to perceive such visual stimuli as letters, words, and sentences; it is completed when the message of the author is understood. Between these two points, beginning readers encounter words they do not recognize. When this happens, children must learn to analyze these words. No one knows precisely how word analysis works, but reading experts generally agree that, among other things, children need to identify the word parts, say the parts, and then reassemble them so that they cue a meaningful response.

Figuring out words unknown in print is only one of many processes used in constructing meaning from print. These processes are dynamic and interactive, changing as a child's knowledge and skills increase. For example, word analysis and word identification influence a child's ability to understand what is read. What a child understands in a passage or sentence influences the ability to decode other unknown words. These processes are symbiotic, reciprocal, and interactive. Thus, in this chapter, word recognition is conceptualized as an interaction among the skills learned (the *product* of word analysis instruction) with the way the child analyzes the unknown words (the *process* of word analysis). The more knowledge and skills children have, the easier and more efficient word recognition will be. Further, the more background and understanding children bring to the reading passage, the better will be their use of contextual analysis to decode unknown words.

The size of visual stimuli is often referred to as the **perceptual unit** or unit of analysis. Reading instruction has a long methodological history, with method being closely related to the unit of analysis. Different methods have emphasized teaching symbol-sound correspondence, using letters of the alphabet, syllables, words, sentences, and even stories. Historically, children have learned to read successfully with each method. Likewise, some children have trouble learning to read with each method, and different methods tend to yield different reading problems. You will find exercise examples in this chapter that focus on small units of analysis, such as word parts, but you will also find suggestions for teaching that use larger analytical units typically associated with a holistic or psycholinguistic approach to teaching reading. Invariably, the goal of all decoding instruction is to develop independent readers who not only comprehend what they read but who choose to read. We do not want to make decoding instruction so boring or laborious as to "turn kids off" to reading.

I believe that children with reading problems profit from learning a variety of analytic units, depending largely on the individual's specific problems. I also believe that many, if not all, beginning readers must learn to analyze words, but that this analysis is only effective when children already know the words' meanings. If the word meaning does not exist in the child's *listening* (or understanding) *vocabulary*, all the effort to analyze the word is wasted because it does not trigger a meaningful response. Unfortunately, beginning readers and many corrective readers do not know if the word exists in their understanding vocabularies until *after* they have worked to analyze the word. Only when they are sure their efforts have identified the correct word can they be sure of success.

Sadly, children have no sure way of determining whether they have misanalyzed a word or whether the word is new to them in terms of meaning. This dilemma facing the young or corrective reader disappears or lessens only with maturity in reading. The best defense against this problem is to *develop in the child, from the very beginning, the need to demand meaning from what is read.* If meaning does not result from analytic effort, the child must seek help. Further, children should have a balanced set of word analysis skills and varied techniques to allow them to approach problem-solving of unknown words with flexibility.

Teachers of corrective readers need to focus instruction on three long-term goals involving word study: (1) building a listening vocabulary, (2) building a sight vocabulary, and (3) building a balanced set of word recognition skills. A child with a deficiency in any of these three areas will have reading problems.

Inadequate Listening Vocabulary

All teachers wish to impart knowledge to students. Frequently this means teaching new concepts and elaborating on more basic ones. Words reflect these concepts. When children have opportunities to experience new areas of knowledge, they learn new words and their meanings, thereby expanding their **meaning vocabulary.** This is referred to as **listening vocabulary** when the graphic form of the word is not involved and as **reading vocabulary** when the word is in print.

Many children come to school with good listening vocabularies; they continue to add to their store of concepts and word meanings as they proceed through the curriculum. Some children, however, are deficient in their knowledge of the world and fail or falter in their attempts to analyze words unknown in print. No matter how hard children try to analyze a word, and no matter how skilled or accurate their analytical skills may be, they cannot trigger a meaningful response if the word is not in their listening vocabulary. Goodman (1968) refers to this incomplete process as **recoding.** To illustrate the point, try to pronounce the following words: miscreant, putative, egregious. If you have previously heard these words, chances are good that you will feel secure with their pronunciation. If not, chances are equally good that your pronunciation will be incorrect. Make several guesses (hypotheses) about the pronunciation of the words. For fun, try to guess the meanings from the words provided.

miscreant	*putative*	*egregious*
mistake	reputed	helpful
hero	punishable	dreadful
degenerate	ugly	powerful
relapse	childlike	tolerable

If you still feel a bit insecure with their meanings, read the following sentences, which may help clarify them.

The *miscreant* defaced Michelangelo's *Pieta.*
Charles's terrier is the *putative* sire of the litter of pups.
Crashing into the train was an *egregious* mistake.

You might have noticed that if you knew all the other words in the sentences, you may have used the context to identify the *meaning* of each word and thus you were able to understand the sentence. In all cases, however, the context may not be sufficient. Regardless, you *still* do not know how the word "sounds," it is not yet in your listening vocabulary, therefore it is not in your meaning vocabulary—you would not be able to associate a meaning with the word until you heard it used in a context from which you could derive its meaning. In reality, while reading and upon encountering such words, mature readers will attempt to use context and apply their graphophonic knowledge and do whatever they have to in order to maintain the meaning of the passage. Sometimes the word is not important enough to the overall understanding of the passage and so mature readers skip it. If it turns out the word *is* important then mature readers consult a dictionary, or ask someone. This kind of planning behavior, a strategy, is something we need to teach children.

Informal Assessment

Problems with listening vocabulary are often detectable during oral reading and present a typical **syndrome**, or set of symptoms. The children seem quite successful in analyzing words except for an occasional notable exception. When asked to figure out the word, they demonstrate knowledge of word analysis, blending skills, and use of context clues, coming close to an acceptable pronunciation, but still cannot come up with the word. This suggests that they do not know the meaning of the word being analyzed. Frequent occurrence of this behavior suggests that the children are meeting too many words with meanings they should, but do not, know.

Another good strategy is to ask the students directly if they know what a word means. A more formal assessment can be made by comparing vocabulary test scores to various subtest scores that assess word recognition skills. When vocabulary knowledge is considerably weaker than other word analysis skills, the inconsistency has been identified. The *Stanford Diagnostic Reading Test* is one of the few available group standardized tests (formal assessment) that can be used for this purpose.

Instructional Strategies

The following examples of activities are recommended to expand listening vocabularies. These activities encompass many areas of the curriculum, so they are appropriate for any age/grade level.

1. Provide many and varied first-hand experiences.
   a. Arrange field trips, preceded and followed by discussions that are deliberately planned to use and review relevant vocabulary. As Durkin (1978) states, "Experience and vocabulary do not grow together *automatically. . . .* teachers should have made some decisions beforehand about the concepts and words that ought to come alive as a result of the experience" (p. 380).
   b. Develop interest centers in the classroom, arranged and maintained by both teacher and children and utilizing appropriate charts and labels. Such interest centers also provide discussion topics.
2. Provide vicarious experiences.

a. Invite speakers to talk about relevant areas of study. Before the speaker comes and after the presentation, the teacher should initiate discussion and elaborate on important concepts and vocabulary.

b. Make full use of carefully selected, appropriate media, for example, films, filmstrips, transparencies, tapes, models, and computer simulations.

3. Provide extended opportunities for silent reading of relatively easy materials and for reading aloud to students. Explanations and elaborations by authors frequently add dimensions of meaning. This activity is particularly important for more mature readers who lack experience in a particular area; such an activity could be conceptualized as learning about the world through books. Authors often help by giving context clues that define words or terms and elaborate meanings.

4. Guide the development and use of dictionaries that relate either to a topic of special interest to the child or to a group project.

a. Have young children construct personal picture dictionaries.

b. Have students construct personal spelling dictionaries.

c. Have students construct personal vocabulary notebooks.

5. Guide the direct study of words through such activities as listing synonyms, antonyms, or affixes and searching for word derivations.

6. Use exercises such as the following with follow-up directions to use these words in written stories:

a. Exercises emphasizing sensory impressions

1) Put an X by the words that describe something you hear:

_____ sour   _____ swish   _____ clap

_____ sunny   _____ bang   _____ cold

2) Underline the words that tell how an animal moves:

slither   bright   paddle

gallop   hair   waddle

b. Exercises to develop differentiated meanings

1) Circle the words that mean almost the same as *fat:*

pudgy   chubby   overweight

skinny   clean   rotund

2) Draw a line connecting a word from list A to a word in list B that is *opposite:*

A	B
cheerful	rested
anxious	glum
tired	interested
bored	calm

Johnson and Pearson's *Teaching Reading Vocabulary* (1984) contains a wealth of suggestions for vocabulary instruction.

Inadequate Sight Vocabulary

Sight vocabulary refers to words in print that are recognized instantly and effortlessly. Mature readers perceive most words they encounter in this fashion. Most children entering school, on the other hand, begin with few or no words that they can read quickly with ease.

Children seem to learn words in three phases. At first encounter they do not recognize the word in print, although it may exist in their listening vocabularies. Then, with repeated exposure, they recognize it partially, but need to analyze its representation in graphic form to figure it out. (This is called the *analytical vocabulary* because the child says the word correctly, but *not* quickly.) Finally, after several encounters, the word is recognized instantly. Every word that children read should be considered a candidate for their sight vocabularies, with the possible exception of rare, unusual, or foreign words. As time passes, words accumulate in the child's sight vocabulary and need no further study because they are recognized automatically (LaBerge and Samuels, 1976).

The concept of sight vocabulary should not be confused with that of **sight words.** The latter term refers to a relatively small set of words in our language that do not conform to the rules or analytical techniques children beginning to read have learned. Examples are *to, of, are, come,* and *you.* Also included are words that appear so frequently that they must be thoroughly learned as soon as possible. The Dolch (1953) list of 220 words and the Moe (1972a, 1972b) lists of 210 high-frequency words account for over 50 percent of the words found in reading materials for children (and adults). Other lists of high frequency words include the *Harris-Jacobson Core Words* (1972), the *ESA (Educational Service Associates) Word List* (1977), the *Great Atlantic and Pacific Word List* (1972), Kucera and Francis's *80 Most Frequently Occurring Words* (1967), and the Fry list of *Instant Words* (1980). Johnson's (1976) *Basic Vocabulary for Beginning Readers* is provided in Appendix E. This list was chosen for reproduction because the words selected came from the speaking vocabularies of kindergarten and first grade children and a list of 500 high frequency English words. Words that were both used by children and were on the high frequency list make up Johnson's list—a total of 306 words.

Sight words should be given high priority for every child's sight vocabulary, but they should *not* be considered the only words to be learned to the point of instant recognition.

Informal Assessment

Children who have not committed words to their sight vocabularies are relatively easy to spot. They do not recognize many words on a page. They frequently are word-by-word readers. When reading orally, they analyze nearly every word, sounding out words or word parts with painful slowness. By the time they reach the end of the sentence they often have forgotten much, if not all, of what they read.

A sight vocabulary word can be recognized in about a half a second or less. The classroom teacher can assess this speed in several ways, using words that have been taught and practiced. A good source is the list of words taught in the child's present texts, one of the high-frequency word lists, or words the child has been working on recently, such as words used in a language experience story.

The following is a good group procedure for screening children. Construct a test using words from the basal series available, or use a graded word list such as the *ESA Word List* (1977) or the *Basic Elementary Reading Vocabularies* (Harris and Jacobson, 1972). On each line type three or four (depending on the maturity level of the group) words of approximately the same difficulty level. Test item difficulty is increased by using words that are similar visually (e.g., *though, through, thought*) or decreased by using visually dissimilar words (e.g., *though, paper, statue*). Duplicate copies for each member of the group and one for yourself to use as a key. A practice test is always a good idea, especially with young children, to help them know what to do when the test is given.

To prepare children for a speed test, the teacher should tell them the following:

1. This is a speed test, and not like "real reading" where you get a chance to look back and forth as much as you want.
2. You will have to hurry your "looks" (fixations). You may only get to glance once at each word, then mark the one I say.
3. Some of you may have trouble with this test, but don't worry. If you do, we'll make a time to practice these and other words. It's okay if you don't do too well.
4. If you miss a word, be ready to go on to the next line.

While administering the test, the teacher says the stimulus word twice, then allows about five seconds for pupils to respond before proceeding to the next item.

Scoring procedures are straightforward, with the number of items correct indicating the performance level. More important for corrective purposes, however, is locating the stragglers in the group. Those who have done poorly on the group test should be investigated further, using an individual procedure.

To assess individual students, make two typewritten copies of the words in list format and give one copy to the child. Ask the child to read the words to you as quickly as possible, while you check accuracy and rapidity from your copy. Remember, accurate but slow is *wrong* for sight vocabulary. Words must be read accurately and quickly. For differentiation, words read correctly but slowly are referred to as being in a child's **analytical vocabulary**.

A second procedure is to make small typewritten, or neatly printed, flash cards from the word list and flash them for about one-half second, allowing the child a moment to respond. If necessary, record the response on your copy of the word list from which the flash cards were made. These words can be used in sentences on the back of each card to test for recognition in context. Additionally, this procedure can be structured a bit differently by using a commercial or teacher-made tachistoscope or a microcomputer. DLM's *Word Radar* (1983) is a software program that presents words from basic sight word lists in a motivating arcade fashion.

Formal assessment is possible by using timed flash words from the *Gates-McKillop-Horowitz Diagnostic Reading Tests* (1982) or the flash words of the *Durrell Analysis of Reading Difficulty* (1980).

Instructional Strategies

Repetition and practice are key concepts for the improvement of sight vocabulary. Many children attain speed and accuracy simply by doing their lessons and by meeting the words in their books. Others, however, may need more practice, particularly if they are using today's readers, in which repetition of words is no longer emphasized as it was in the past, or if they are in a literature-based reading program.

Probably the most natural way of meeting common words repeatedly is through extensive recreational reading of relatively easy materials. This type of reading exposes the child to easy words, few of which are unknown. Predictable books (such as Eric Carle's *The Very Hungry Caterpillar* or Bill Martin's *Brown Bear, Brown Bear*) contain a lot of repetition and provide an excellent source for easy reading as do language experience stories.

A more direct approach may be needed for children with more serious sight vocabulary deficiencies. These children often have had an unfortunate experience with a program or teacher that has overemphasized analytical techniques or synthetic phonics. The child acquires the bad habit of looking for parts in all words rather than just unknown words. They try to "sound out" everything. Exercises that ask them to analyze words into smaller units *should be avoided.* Techniques that promote fluent reading, such as neurological impress, echo reading, and repeated readings (discussed in detail in chapter 7) are recommended.

Direct teaching of sight vocabulary words might proceed as follows (McNinch, 1981). The teacher recites a sentence containing the word to be learned and then writes the word followed by several more sentences using the word on the chalkboard, overhead, or on sentence strips.

Teacher: "I *heard* you were sick."

(writes)

heard

Mary *heard* a new joke.
Have you *heard* anything else?
John said he *heard* what you said.

Next, the teacher draws attention to the word in isolation by asking questions about it and providing practice writing it such as:

What letter does the word begin with?
What's the last letter in the word?
How many letters are in this word?
Spell the word.
Trace the word in the air.
Spell, say, spell, write the word.

Following this focus on the word in isolation, students must read the word in a phrase or sentence. The phrase, or sentence, can be created by the student. Students should also practice reading the word in whole text. The text might be one developed by the teacher or a book or language experience story.

Finally, independent practice must be provided. The word might become part of a game or the student could be asked to find the word used in other printed material such as books, magazines, or newspapers.

Three effective programs for increasing sight vocabulary are the language experience approach (LEA), Fernald's (1943) VAKT (visual, auditory, kinesthetic, tactile) approach, and intensive word practice (Moe & Manning, 1984). While the LEA can also be used to teach other word recognition skills, the VAKT approach and intensive word practice are used more specifically to help students learn *troublesome* sight words.

Many disabled readers are motivated to improve their reading skills when material that they have dictated is written down or typed for them. With the LEA, the teacher is also assured that the words used in follow-up activities are part of the child's listening vocabulary.

Any language experience story should be the result of a direct experience of the learner, or learners in the case of a group story. In addition to developing stories about field trips, an unusual classroom event, or the actions of a classroom pet, teachers plan many interesting "experiences" for students to write about. Some examples might include reading an exciting book to the students, working with clay or play-dough, making no-bake cookies, painting pumpkins for Halloween, performing a science experiment, or sharing family pictures. In the example that follows, the teacher gave each child a marshmallow and directed them to think about how it looks, feels, smells and lastly, tastes. Then a group account was dictated.

The Marshmallow

A marshmallow is soft, white and fluffy. It is shaped like a drum. It looks like a pillow. It's too small for a pillow. It can roll. The marshmallow smells sweet, airy, and delicious. It's squeezable. It's sticky. There is powder on the outside of it. It tastes like a sponge. It makes you want another one.

Following dictation, the teacher reads the entire account back to the students as they follow along. Any changes students wish to make to the account should be made at this time. (Note that this step also provides the teacher with many teaching opportunities. For example, students may notice many uses of *it* and *it's*. If not, the teacher should point them out. The teacher can then ask about the referent for *it* and discuss the nature of pronouns in a very real and meaningful context since the students themselves created the account. In this particular account, a discussion of adjectives would also be apparent. Additionally, features of words might also be important to point out. In this example, features such as compound words, syllabication between two consonants, vowel-consonant-silent e pattern, as well as the vowel-consonant pattern are among the possibilities.)

Once some material has been dictated and read by the teacher, students read it. Even if the material is just a caption for a picture drawn by the student, the words from the material are used in many ways to ensure repeated exposures. First, the student should write each word in a personal dictionary with a self-generated sentence, or picture, or both. In this way, if the child comes across one of the words again and cannot remember it, the teacher directs the child to his/her personal dictionary to find the word. The sentence and/or picture will provide the needed help. Not only does the child learn new words, but begins to develop alphabet and dictionary skills and a strategy for becoming an independent reader. Additional activities such as matching words from their stories put on cards to words found in other printed material (i.e., basal readers, story books), and playing sight vocabulary games such as BINGO, are appropriate. The teacher should insist that the word be pronounced each time it is matched or encountered in the game. Arranging word cards to form sentences also reinforces recognition of the words in other contexts. Any teacher concerned that the words children use in their language experience stories will not help them in other reading tasks need only compare those words to a word list such as Johnson's (Appendix E).

As soon as possible, students should do their own writing of stories. Their efforts at writing will help them learn the nature of written language. (For an excellent article on how to use LEA to encourage process writing see Karnowski, 1989.) "Writing also focuses children's attention on the visual features of print, aiding letter and word recognition" (Noyce & Christie, 1989). You might be thinking that students do not want to write. Disabled readers are not generally very confident of their writing abilities. However, this is all the more reason that they be given opportunities to write in a safe, pressure-free environment. Dialogue journals provide an excellent vehicle for risk-free writing. These journals are *never* graded and since the teacher responds to the child, a model for spelling and handwriting, as well as grammar and sentence structure, is always available. The function is clear—to communicate with another person. Students write in a bound notebook to their teacher about anything they want (early "writers" may even draw pictures to get across a message). The teacher writes back, in the same notebook, by responding naturally, as in conversation. The following exchanges provide an idea of what dialogue journal writing is like:

Mark	Teacher
it wa relley hot today. I got to go see a moove on Saterday.	I know what you mean about being hot! It really did feel hot in our classroom. Is it hard for you to concentrate when you feel uncomfortable? It's hard for me. What movie did you see? Did you like it? Tell me more about it.
I see the movee big it wuz funne My dad tak me we lafd hard.	I'm glad you enjoyed the movie, *Big*. I like funny movies the best. Maybe I can get my husband to take me. Do you think I would like the movie?

Children with very limited sight vocabularies can be provided with sentence starters to get them going. Initially, high frequency words can be used to create "pattern books." These are merely loose sheets of paper stapled together with each sheet being a page in the pattern book. For instance, the teacher might provide several sheets of paper each saying "I like to eat _____." The child then draws a picture of the food and the teacher writes the word for the food item on the blank line. This is done for each page. When completed, a cover with a title such as "Things I Like to Eat" by Joey can be created and attached to the stapled sheets. Of course, Joey then reads the book. Many words can be taught this way. Other examples of sentence starters are:

"I like to play _____."
"I like to go _____."
"_____ are big."
"_____ are little."
"My favorite _____ is _____."

FIGURE 6.1 Example of an intensive word practice sheet for the new sight words: *this, was, in.*

1			2		
	boy	was		this	on
	on	in		was	the
	the	this		in	boy
3			**4**		
	on	in		boy	on
	the	was		in	was
	this	boy		the	this

1. My milk is in this cup.
2. Mother was in the house.
3. This is the dog I like.

The VAKT approach begins by eliciting a word from the student that the student wants to learn. This word is written or printed on a strip of paper in crayon and is large enough for the child to trace by direct finger contact. The child is then shown how to trace the word and pronounce it at the same time. Following the teacher's example, the child traces and pronounces the word. This continues until the child feels ready to write the word from memory. If the child is successful, the session is terminated. If not, tracing continues. Words successfully written from memory should be checked for recognition later in the day or the next day.

After a period of time, which varies from child to child, the student reaches a point where tracing can be eliminated. Instead, someone pronounces the word, and the student looks at it and repeats it as often as necessary, until he or she can write it from memory. Again, if the written word is incorrect, the student looks at the word more carefully while pronouncing it, and tries once more to write it from memory. Strict use of the VAKT approach, which includes charting of the number of times a word needs to be traced before it is learned, is probably not necessary for most students. Usually the tracing technique itself is sufficient.

Intensive word practice (Moe & Manning, 1984) also uses a multisensory approach. Usually, three to six words are randomly placed among other words in each of four sections on a word practice sheet (fig. 6. 1). Sentences containing the new words show each word in a meaningful context and are placed beneath the four sections. The procedure emphasizes listening skills and following directions as well as practicing troublesome words, and can be used with a group.

First, the students are directed to fold the paper on the bottom line to separate the sentences from the word boxes. They should see only the numbered boxes. Next, the students are instructed to fold the paper again on the line that separates boxes 1 and 2 from boxes 3 and 4. Finally, the students are directed to fold the paper on the vertical line so they can only see box 1.

The teacher has previously prepared large word cards, each with one of the new words to be taught; for this example, cards are needed for *this, was,* and *in.* The directions for box 1 instruct the students to mark in some way each of the new words while the teacher pronounces the word and shows the word card. Two repetitions of the word should be sufficient. While showing the word card for *this,* the teacher may say, "I want you to draw a circle around *this.* Draw a circle around *this.*" While showing the word card for *was,* the teacher may say, "Put a line under *was.* Put a line under *was.*" Likewise, for the word card *in,* the teacher may say, "Draw a box around *in.* Draw a box around *in.* Now turn your paper over so you just see box 2."

The directions for box 2 instruct the students to mark the new words. This time, however, the teacher shows but does not pronounce the word. It is hoped that the students are mentally pronouncing the words as they look back and forth from word card to paper. The directions proceed as follows: "Put a line under _____" (while showing *was*). "Draw a box around _____" (while showing *this*). "Draw two lines under _____" (while showing *in*). At this point students are directed to refold their papers so only boxes 3 and 4 can be seen.

For box 3 the teacher pronounces the word but does not show it. All directions are oral. "Put a line under *this.*" "Draw a circle around *in.*" "Draw a box around *was.*"

For box 4 the students are simply told to circle the three words taught in the lesson. Success with box 4 indicates that the student has at least visual memory for the words taught. Not until the sentences are read at the bottom of the page can the teacher judge whether the students have learned to pronounce the words as well. Students are asked to underline the new words in the sentences, and to read the sentences.

The following exercises, and many like them that are found in developmental texts, activity books, and microcomputer software, are used to develop the habit of looking at words rapidly.

1. Exercises with flash cards. This activity can be done alone, with a partner, or with the teacher. Flash cards should be used in conjunction with sentences or other meaningful contexts. Examples can be seen in 2a and 2b below.

2. Exercises emphasizing expectancy or context clues.
   a. A snowman melts in the _____.
      sun   cold   man
   b. The bird is in the _____.
      boy   tree   table
   c. Random House's *Word Blaster* (available for TRS-80). Sentences are displayed on the screen with one word missing, and the student chooses the appropriate word from a line of five to complete each sentence. Letter-sound, sentence-structure, and contextual vocabulary clues must be used to select the correct word. The student first reads the sentence and then "blasts" a word to fit the blank from a line traveling across the screen above the sentence. When hit, the correct word falls into the blank. After two incorrect tries, the correct word automatically drops into the sentence.

3. Exercises requiring quick scanning of a group of words.
   a. See how fast you can find the word that does not belong in each list. Put a line through it.

1	2	3
boy	dog	pie
girl	look	cake
pipe	bird	much

   b. Put an X by the things you can find in the food store.

meat	soup	dogs
house	candy	cans
eggs	truck	milk

4. Activities and games using individual words.
   a. *Fish pond.* Make word cards with new (or review) vocabulary words on one side and an easy sentence on the other side with the word underlined. Affix a paper clip to each. Put in fish pond. Attach a small magnet to the end of a fishing pole. If the child fishes out a word and reads it correctly and quickly, two points are scored, if the sentence helps the child say the word, 1 point is scored.
   b. *Rocket ship.* Children take turns drawing from a stack of cards—each having a sentence containing the word being practiced. (The word should be underlined and in isolation above the sentence.) If they read the word correctly, they put the card in the slot representing the route of the trip to the moon (or wherever).
   c. *Bang.* Make a "bang" card for every five word cards. The word cards have the word of interest on one side and a sentence using the word on the other. (This 5 to 1 ratio can be changed depending on how long you want the game to last—the more "bang" cards, the longer the game will last.) Cards are placed in a bag or box and drawn out one at a time. If a word card is drawn and the word pronounced correctly, the card is kept. If the sentence needs to be read to pronounce the word, that one card is returned to the bag. If a "bang" card is drawn, *all* words collected up to that point are placed back in the bag. This element of chance allows for children of different abilities to play together and also provides the necessary repetition of new words. The first player to collect five (or three or ten) words is the winner.
   d. *DLM's Word Radar* (available for Apple II series). Presented in an arcade game format, *Word Radar* provides practice in matching *isolated* words that appear frequently on sight word lists. Words are practiced at eight levels (twenty-four words in each of eight lists increasing in word length), at nine different speeds (1 is slowest, 9 is fastest), and at three difficulty levels (level 1 has four words on the screen at a time; level 2 has eight words; and level 3 has twelve words). Student progress sheets and worksheets are included with a manual that explains a variety of uses. This software provides a motivating way to practice basic sight words.

The Basic Skill Strands

Knowledge of and ability to use five important categories of skills give students the needed flexibility to identify and analyze unknown words. Sometimes children need to use only one of the skills. At other times, two or more are needed and are used either separately or together as parallel processes. The five skill strands are listed below.

1. Context clues
   a. expectancy clues
   b. picture clues
   c. meaning clues
2. Visual analysis
3. Knowledge of word parts
   a. structural analysis
   b. phonic analysis
4. Blending and synthesizing
5. Dictionary skills

These skill strands are recognized by many reading instructional systems, although the skills themselves may be labeled somewhat differently. These strands are usually organized so that a skill is introduced in a series of lessons, then reviewed from time to time. In a basal series, the early lessons often review skills before introducing new skills. This gives teachers an opportunity to assess whether students have retained the skills. Some series also provide end-of-reader tests for assessing skill development.

The skills are usually sequenced from easy to difficult, being arranged according to logic and author experience. Thus, the skill sequences vary from one reading series to another, differences ranging from slight to considerable. When a child changes from one reading program to another that is quite different, teachers must monitor progress carefully to see that the child does not falter or fail during the transition.

Each reading series has its own scope and sequence (fig. 6.2). Teachers must know the scope and sequence of the skills program used in their school and also the skills taught in preceding materials as well as those that will follow. Teachers aware of the skills sequence can facilitate transition from level to level by using appropriate assessment and instructional strategies. If a school system is not using a skills system, teachers must do their own analyses with the knowledge that the children, in general, have received skills instruction randomly or on a basis other than that represented here. In whole language classrooms, these skills are generally learned when opportunities present themselves, and always in the context of whole text.

As can be seen, teachable units are much smaller than the major strand labels identified in the scope and sequence chart. The concept of major skill strands is roughly equated to that of level 3 analysis, that is, areas within the domain of word recognition. The skills listed in the scope and sequence chart are more specific than the strands, representing elements at level 4 analysis. Precise analytical units associated with a specific reading system must be determined from the materials of that system. For example, in the Rand Reading System (Fay, 1978), children learn their letters in the readiness book.

FIGURE 6.2 Example scope and sequence chart: word recognition.

Emerging Abilities
1. Learning letter names
2. Developing awareness of letter-sound relationships
3. Hearing likenesses and differences in beginning and ending phonemes
4. Recognizing rhyming sounds
5. Demonstrating left-to-right orientation
6. Tracing, matching, and copying letters and words
7. Demonstrating awareness of word boundaries in writing
8. Pointing to known words while being read to

First Grade
1. Picture dictionary (begin alphabetizing skill)
2. Begin using initial consonants in a modified cloze (use of context)
3. Begin consonant digraphs with context
4. Begin consonant blends with context
5. Begin short vowels with context
6. Begin spelling patterns
7. Begin final consonants with context
8. Begin initial and final consonant substitution with context
9. Begin common inflectional endings with context
10. Begin long vowels with context
11. Begin common suffixes with context
12. Begin compound words with context

Second Grade
1. Review previous letter-sound correspondences
2. Begin unusual consonants and consonant digraphs (c, g, silent t) with context
3. Begin unusual vowels (y) with context
4. Begin vowel digraphs and diphthongs with context
5. Introduce schwa with context
6. Begin r-controlled and l-controlled vowels with context
7. Introduce concept of syllabication (# of vowel sounds = # of syllables)
8. Continue compound words
9. Continue suffixes
10. Begin prefixes with context
11. Begin spelling changes involved in suffixes and inflected endings

Third Grade
1. Review previous letter-sound correspondences
2. Begin difficult consonant blends (triple letters)
3. Begin unusual and difficult vowels and vowel clusters
4. Introduce structural analysis (concept of roots and affixes, compounds)
5. Introduce more complex spelling patterns
6. Introduce two and three-syllable words (syllable patterns)
7. Inductive teaching of consistent phonics rules and their application
8. Begin dictionary skills of using diacritical markings and pronunciation spellings

Focus will now be given to problems corrective readers have that are typically associated with the major skill strands.

Inadequate Use of Context Clues

Expectancy and Picture Clues

Two important context clues, **expectancy clues** and **picture clues**, relate directly to understanding what is about to be read. Expectancy clues are related to **psychological set**, that is, when people are introduced to a topic, certain related concepts rise to the thresholds of their minds. These ideas, especially the words associated with them, become more readily available from memory storage, if present. In essence, the nonvisual information, or schemata, that the reader has for a topic is activated. When teachers introduce a new story to develop background and experiences, they promote the use of expectancy clues. For example, when children know they will be reading a story about how birds build their nests, the words they expect to meet are quite different from those expected in a story about a fire in the basement. Teachers might begin by asking students what they already know about birds building nests and then writing these ideas down so the students can see the words they have used.

Pictures also function as clues to readers, suggesting certain sets of words that may occur in a story. A picture of two youngsters playing on a raft in a pond elicits many words in the mind that are different from a picture of the same children working to build a raft for the pond. Thus, both expectancy and picture clues help the reader anticipate words that may occur in a selection or segment of a story. These concepts are closely related to ideas regarding a reader's ability to organize mentally the material about to be read (this topic will be discussed in a later chapter.) Obviously, this ability is also related to background and experience, or **scriptal information** (Pearson and Johnson, 1978), as will be discussed in chapter 7. Some children who have problems with context clues do not have the conceptual development to deal with the ideas found in many classroom reading materials. Understanding is thus unlikely, and decoding such content has little value. More familiar material must be used with these children. Their own language experience stories would be an appropriate beginning.

Informal Assessment

Children will have problems with expectancy and picture clues if they cannot anticipate what may happen (what words may be present) in a story about a given topic, a given set of illustrations, or both. A good way to informally assess a child's ability to use these clues is to ask questions before reading.

> "The selection we are going to read today is about Neil Armstrong, the first man on the moon. What special words do you think we will meet in this selection?"
> "This paragraph will tell us how the pioneers kept warm in the winter. Before we read, let's guess how they might have done it."
> "You're right, Shayne. This is a picture of the wolf in bed waiting for Little Red Riding Hood. What words do you think we will need to read in this part of the story?"

Notice that these activities are done orally; the teachers have no objective measures of expectancy, but still they can identify those who are having considerable trouble anticipating forthcoming events and the words possibly associated with them. Children with problems may not be able to use expectancy clues adequately, but the same problems may also reflect inadequate experiential, conceptual, or language background. The best way to differentiate among these is to sample behavior across a wide variety of content.

Instructional Strategies

Strategies to improve the development of expectancy clues generally give the stimulus (the subject or topic of concern or a picture portraying it) and ask the child to respond by generating or identifying possible words that may appear. This process calls for **productive language** and differs from reading in that reading is a receptive language process. The following activities are suggested.

1. Activities to develop use of expectancy clues.
   a. Have small groups or individuals prepare to write a story about a given topic of interest. Before writing, teachers should promote the discussion of words to be used in the story, writing some on the chalkboard as the discussion proceeds.
      1) For beginning readers, use techniques involved in the LEA, in which the teacher does the writing.
      2) As soon as possible, use of the Fernald (1943) technique or modifications thereof are recommended.
   b. Use exercises requiring knowledge of a particular topic.
      1) These words are about cars, airplanes, or both. Mark the words about cars with a *C*; mark the ones about airplanes with an *A*; and mark those about both with a *B*.

____ hood	____ landing	____ engine
____ wings	____ wheels	____ garage
____ body	____ bumper	____ tail

2. Activities to develop use of expectancy through picture clues.
   a. Display a picture with several different items on it, such as the produce in a market, candies in a store window, or a barnyard scene. Ask the children to name the items; write them down for further reference.
   b. Show a set of two to four pictures (comic strips are a good source). Tell the children the pictures can be arranged to tell a story. Ask them to arrange the pictures. They may then choose partners and tell each other (or the teacher) their stories.
   c. Call attention to a picture and talk about what may be expected to come next in the story. Verify predictions after the story is read.

Meaning Clues

Meaning clues are more specific to the content being read than expectancy and picture clues. **Context**, as related to meaning clues, is defined as the words surrounding a target word. The target word represents the unknown word to be decoded. Meaning clues often exist within the sentence being read, but they can also exist within phrases or between sentences. Context usually restricts alternative words that fit meaningfully into the slot represented by the target word. Consider the following examples:

As he began to rise into the air, the vaulter's pole _____.
She put the cake mix in the bowl then _____ one-half cup water.

Meaning clues can be used effectively for analyzing words unknown in print only if the surrounding words are easily read. When the reading matter is too difficult, the reader becomes discouraged and may guess more and demand less meaning from the passage.

Informal Assessment

Children who do not use meaning clues probably lack scriptal data, have poorly developed language, or have not been taught how to use such clues. These children can be identified by comparing their analysis of unknown words in isolation to their analysis of unknown words in context. Analysis of a word in context should be easier than analysis of the same word in isolation because language and context limit the word choices that fit meaningfully. If children have learned to *demand meaning* from every sentence they read, they will be aware of their problem and the problem word. If not, a major weakness and teaching task have been identified.

Teachers should suspect inadequate use of context when a child makes wild attempts at an unknown word. Wild guessing indicates misuse of context and lack of word analysis skills. Also, many substitutions that graphically resemble the actual word but are semantically incorrect (e.g., horse and house), and substitutions that are not self-corrected indicate inadequate use of meaning clues.

Teachers can structure a set of tasks to evaluate the child's ability. Select a few words the child does not know, using one of the methods discussed earlier in this chapter. Present the words first in isolation, then in context. If trouble occurs consistently with the words *in both* settings, the child is probably not using context as an aid to word recognition. The following illustrates the two settings, words in isolation and words in context.

Word in Isolation	Words in Context
train	We heard the whistle as we walked along the _____ tracks.
night	It was very dark that _____.
stone	Tim felt a sharp _____ under his foot.
wrong	The car was going the _____ way down the one-way street.

Formal Assessment

The use of meaning clues may be assessed with standardized instruments that contain subtests on words in isolation and words in context. A few are available, such as the group-administered *Silent Reading Diagnostic Test* (1972) and the individually administered *Gates-McKillop-Horowitz Reading Diagnostic Tests* (1982).

Instructional Strategies

Strategies for developing the use of meaning clues should be presented in larger discourse units in order to take advantage of all available language clues. Prerequisite to these strategies is the use of easy materials. If the child has to guess too many words, language clues will be obscured. I recommend beginning with a ratio of about one target word for every twenty words. Once children understand how the process works and what they are supposed to do, the ratio can be decreased.

The standard deletion ratio of one deletion every fifth word suggested for *assessing* comprehension (Bormuth, 1967, 1968; Rankin & Culhane, 1969) is *inappropriate* for *teaching* the use of context clues as an aid for analyzing unknown words because it distracts from the analytical task at hand and asks the child to guess too frequently. The task can be discouraging for corrective readers who are already frustrated with the reading task. Alternatives to reduce this frustration include using a sentence or two with one word deleted, using a multiple choice format (maze), and adding letters or other word parts to the slot. The following are representative activities.

1. Exercises utilizing thought units of a paragraph.

    One day when the lion was looking for food, he walked into a trap. The trap was made of strong _____, and the lion couldn't get out. The lion jumped this way and that way. He tried and tried. All day _____, the lion worked to get out of the trap. But he couldn't get ____.

2. Riddles with meaning clues that give the answer.

    It has four legs.
    It has a back.
    You sit on it.
    It is a ____.
    dog   cat   chair

3. Exercises using the meaning of a sentence.

    a. He climbed it to paint the ceiling.
        lake   looking   ladder
    b. The car is in the ____.
        house   church   garage

4. Exercises using context and word parts in different locations.

    a. The car is in the g____.
    b. He is cl____ing the ladder.

With all of these exercises, the most important aspect is incorporation of a teacher-led discussion (Valmont, 1983). This discussion points out the clues that lead to a certain word being suggested. For example, in the riddle exercise, the first two clues (four legs, a back) also describe a dog and a cat. You must have the third clue (something to sit on) before dog and cat are eliminated and chair becomes the answer. Any unknown word can be approached the same way. The context provides certain clues, and several words are suggested. The teacher is responsible for leading a discussion of what the clues are, why some words fit better than others, and which words are equally acceptable.

In summary, meaning clues are important aids in analyzing unknown words. These clues help the reader anticipate words that may occur in the selection. In addition to the anticipation factor, context serves as a language clue to the unknown word and is a means to verify the accuracy of the thought unit containing the unknown word. Probably the single most important word recognition skill is using context clues effectively (Heilman, 1976).

Using context and other meaning clues alone is not enough for effective, efficient word recognition, however. Both younger and poorer readers may rely too heavily on context (Gough, 1984; Stanovich, 1980). Overemphasizing these and neglecting other decoding skills can lead to unfortunate learning outcomes (Chall, 1967). When this happens, children guess too often when they encounter new, unknown words, resulting in a distorted or misunderstood message. This outcome must be corrected immediately; if it is allowed to continue, the child may develop the bad habit of *not* expecting meaning from the passage.

Inadequate Visual Analysis

During the course of reading, children may become aware that they do not know a word after they have *looked* at it. The symbol (word) has not cued a meaningful response, and the context has not been a sufficient aid; therefore, they must figure out the word some other way. First, they must visually inspect the word and try to break it into smaller parts, which then will be "sounded out." Thus, visual analysis *precedes* phonic or structural analysis. Phonic exercises that emphasize "sound it out" fail to communicate to some children that they have to segment visually *before* they sound.

Visual segmentation of an unknown word embedded in a sentence where context clues are not helpful presents especially difficult analytic problems. Durkin (1978) claims that decoding in such circumstances occurs at the syllable level, where only visual clues can be used. She gives eight syllabication generalizations to help decode syllables. A problem with this procedure is that the children must memorize and be able to apply all of the rules before precision can be attained. The following might be a simpler, but less precise, set of *content rules* to help younger students begin visual segmentation of words into syllables.

1. Every syllable has one vowel sound.
2. Syllables contain *about* 3 letters (plus or minus 2 letters).
3. Syllables are often divided between two consonants (plan-ter, pic-ture).
4. In a syllable with more than one vowel letter, the final *e* or the second vowel is often silent.

These four content rules, plus basic knowledge of letter-sound rules, are needed before children can begin to analyze unknown words independently. (For a listing of the more consistent phonic and syllabication content rules, see Appendix F.)

Monosyllabic Words

Children must also be able to apply at least three basic phonic process rules. The following process rules are modified from Durkin's (1978) presentation on blending syllables. They are presented under visual analysis because once children have unsuccessfully tried to use the initial consonant plus context clues strategy, they are frequently unaware of how to continue. The analytical process must begin with visual

FIGURE 6.3 Examples of applying the process rules for analyzing unknown words.

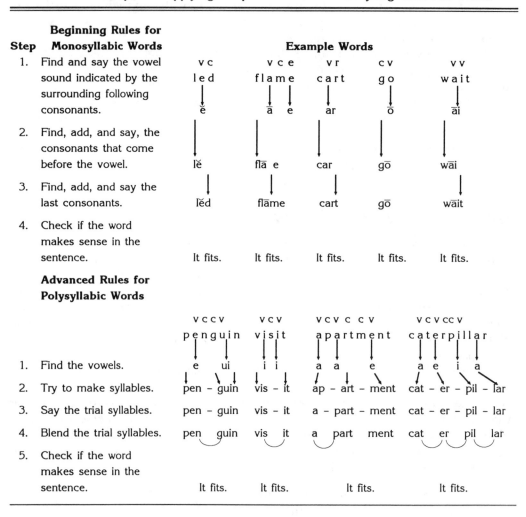

Step	Beginning Rules for Monosyllabic Words			Example Words			

Step	Beginning Rules for Monosyllabic Words
1.	Find and say the vowel sound indicated by the surrounding following consonants.
2.	Find, add, and say, the consonants that come before the vowel.
3.	Find, add, and say the last consonants.
4.	Check if the word makes sense in the sentence.

Advanced Rules for Polysyllabic Words

1.	Find the vowels.
2.	Try to make syllables.
3.	Say the trial syllables.
4.	Blend the trial syllables.
5.	Check if the word makes sense in the sentence.

segmentation of unknown words, then proceed to sounding and blending. The three basic phonic process rules are as follows:

1. Find and say the sound for the vowel or vowel cluster as determined by the surrounding *following* consonants.
2. Find, add, and say the sound for the consonant(s) that come(s) *before* the vowel(s).
3. Find, add, and say the sound for the consonant(s) that come(s) *after* the vowel(s).

The process is first illustrated in figure 6.3 using monosyllabic words, which are recommended to begin teaching the analytical process. The first syllabication content rule is all that is needed for beginners to decode "little" words. The words are ordered from easy to hard, suggesting a developmental sequence implied in content rules going from simple consonants and short vowels to the more complex letter rules. Thus, for children beginning to learn, the three-step process remains constant, but the difficulty level is increased when specific words involve more complex phonic rules.

Polysyllabic Words

Once children become facile at analyzing unknown monosyllabic words, the focus of the process changes to polysyllabic words. The remaining three syllabication rules must then be learned. This process is quite difficult for some children, and they simply give up when asked to analyze "big" words. They must be encouraged to use the following rules:

1. Find the vowels.
2. Try to make syllables using the consonants before and after the vowels.
3. Say the "trial" syllables.
4. Blend the trial syllables.
5. Verify with the meaning of the sentence.

This process, while helpful, is not precise, and children must be cautioned that if the word they come up with does not fit, they must try to resegment the syllables or try different possible vowel sounds. In the advanced syllabication process in figure 6.3, notice that no effort has been made to ask children to figure out syllables as they are technically defined in the dictionary (Arnold & Miller, 1980).

Once a child begins this process, another word or word part may be recognized, and the steps may be short-circuited somewhat. The identification of vowels and adding consonants frequently triggers this guessing. For example, a child may easily recognize "ment" in "apartment" after analysis begins. Such short circuiting should be encouraged. Notice, also, that the division of apartment in step 2 is incorrect, but the child comes up with the word anyway.

As children develop word recognition skills, they are constantly adding to their skills repertoire. Consider the following possible solutions for figuring out a new word as a child adds analytical units (the products of instruction) to the memory store. In the example, replacing an X with letters implies that the child can visually identify and say the word part.

Target sentence:
I want something to eat.

When a child can read a few words but does not yet have any word analysis skills:
I want xxxxxxxxx to eat. (Child fails.)

Add visual segmentation and ability to sound beginning consonants:
I want sxxxxxxxx to eat. "I want spaghetti to eat."
(Child fails, but the guess is sensible.)

Add knowledge of common word endings:
I want sxxxxxxing to eat. "I want s-s-s-ing to eat."
(Child fails.)

Add knowledge of one common word:
I want somexxing to eat. "I want some-ing—something-to eat."
(Child may succeed by approximation.)

Add knowledge of two common words:
I want something to eat. "I want some-thing to eat."
(Child succeeds.)

Two other important abilities develop when visual analysis skills are taught: discrimination and memory. Visual discrimination training helps a child see differences among letters, word parts, and words, while memory helps a child recall these differences quickly without having to resort to a slower, more analytical approach. (For more information on these, see chapter 12.)

Informal Assessment

Children having problems with visual analysis often have learned their symbol-sound correspondences but cannot visually identify them when they are embedded in new words or in other materials. Sometimes this is inappropriately considered a lack of ability to apply phonics skills, when, in fact, it reflects inability to visually segment word parts. For example, Larry has learned several of his consonant sounds as well as some words. He has just successfully completed an exercise in consonant substitution with the following phonograms: *an, et,* and *ill.* His efforts to read orally proceed as follows:

Sentence:	Will you let Dan go with me?
Larry:	No response. Then, "I don't know the first word."
Teacher:	"Think about our workbook lesson this morning."
Larry:	No response.
Teacher:	"What is the first letter?"
Larry:	"W."
Teacher:	"What sound does it make?"
Larry:	"Wah, as in want."
Teacher:	"Good! Now what does the rest of the word say?"
Larry:	"Ill."
Teacher:	"Now sound them together."
Larry:	"Wah-ill—will. Will you . . ." Child does not continue.

Teacher returns to original strategy, making note that Larry did his lesson satisfactorily, but cannot segment the initial consonant and phonogram from the whole word. Training in this skill is considered advisable.

Another symptom of poor visual analysis is continued use of inappropriate word parts even when they do not work. Trying a word element is acceptable, but if it does not work, it should be rejected and another tried. Inflexibility suggests a problem. The following is an example of flexibility in efforts to analyze a word, trying different word parts.

Target sentence:	Yes, you may go with father.
Child's first trial:	"Yes, you may go with fat-her." (Child rejects this trial because sentence does not make sense.)
Child's second trial:	"Yes, you may go with fa-ther, no, father." (Child accepts this trial because the sentence makes sense.)

Few standardized tests assess visual analysis skills. One that does is the "Word Synthesis" subtest and the "Phonics" subtest of the *Silent Reading Diagnostic Test* (Bond et al., 1972). The *Gates-McKillop-Horowitz Diagnostic Reading Tests* (1982) also has one subtest that requires the student to segment visually and then pronounce "nonsense" words.

Instructional Strategies

Instruction in visual analysis focuses on encouraging children to look for known parts embedded in unknown words and then try to segment other "reasonable" word parts, that is, elements that may represent a word part. You should recall the content and process rules described earlier and begin instruction with these rules if needed. The following activities aid this instruction.

1. Give the children sets of unknown words that contain word parts they already know.

    a. After a lesson on variants (discussed later), provide exercises such as the following:

        Draw a circle around the word endings you see. Then use each word to complete the sentences.

        > look   looks   looking

        Johnny _____ very tired today.
        "_____ out!" shouted Susan, as the car came speeding toward them.
        "What are you _____ for?" asked Mother.

    b. After lessons on initial consonant blends provide exercises such as this. Here are some words. If they start with a consonant, mark a C and circle the consonant. If they begin with a consonant blend, mark a B and circle the blend.

_____	cat	_____	slip
_____	bring	_____	sing
_____	try	_____	wall

    c. After lessons in various structural analysis (also called morphemic analysis) skills, ask the children to look for the relevant unit in the unknown words.

        1) Put a line between the compound words.

            sweetheart   playground   nighttime

            Use each of these compound words in a sentence.

        2) Draw a circle around each affix. Then complete each sentence using the base (or root) word.

            rewrite   careful   happiness

            The little boy touched his new baby sister with _____.
            I will _____ a letter to grandmother.
            Dad told me I did a good job and that made me _____.

Children soon learn that if they segment the word in the wrong place, they may not be able to sound the "odd" word parts. They should be encouraged to try again and break the word apart in a different place.

"Here are some words that have been divided for you. Which one helps you most to sound it out? Put an X on that word."

t/hi/nk   th/in/k   th/ink   Be sure you *think* before you speak.
spr/ing   s/pri/ng   sp/ri/ng   Today is sunny and warm and feels like *spring*.

This exercise has no right or wrong answer, especially if the child arrives at the correct pronunciation. This type of skill is probably best done in an individual setting where the teacher can encourage the child to resegment the word if it was inappropriate on the first trial.

Inadequate Knowledge of Word Parts

When children cannot figure out an unknown word from meaning clues alone, they must resort to analysis. Essentially, this means they must break the word down into smaller elements, as just discussed. Then they must look for a part that they already know. Common word parts typically taught are presented in figure 6.4. Two major skill categories concerned with this knowledge are phonics and structural analysis. **Structural analysis** deals with such meaningful word parts as derivatives (affixes), variants (word endings), and compounds. **Phonics**, on the other hand, deals with letter-sound relationships or word parts that do not necessarily have meaning. Examples would include consonants, vowels, digraphs, and many syllables. With phonics, students focus on learning what various word parts say, whereas with structural analysis the focus can be twofold: what the word part says and what it means.

Before children can use structural analysis and phonics skills effectively and efficiently, every letter and common word part should be so well known that children can recognize them instantly and automatically (LaBerge & Samuels, 1976). When this level is attained, children do not have to spend an unusually long time analyzing unknown words. With practice, students in primary grades continually add word parts to their "instant recognition" repertoire. Notice the similarity of the concept to that of sight vocabulary, when words become so familiar they can be recognized instantly and automatically.

Practice is the key to automaticity. Some children quickly attain the level of instant recognition, but others need practice before they thoroughly learn the word parts. Teachers must monitor students to determine who needs a little or a lot of practice. They also must be creative in providing ample practice that does not become deadly dull drill. The best solution may be providing many opportunities to read easy and interesting material.

Informal Assessment

Teachers must answer three questions about students learning word parts:

1. Does the child know the word part?
2. Can the child recognize the word part quickly?
3. Can the child identify the element embedded in an unknown word?

Knowledge of word parts (fig. 6.4) is assessed informally through observation of appropriate workbook activities and through oral reading during conferences.

Automaticity requires accuracy as well as alacrity. To assess this skill with a group of children, an exercise similar to the one below, which provides three or four word elements per line, is recommended. The teacher gives the stimulus, silently counts

FIGURE 6.4 Common word elements.

1. Consonants

a. *one sound (usually)*

b, d, f, h, j, k, l, m,
n, p, q, r, t, v, y, z

b. *more than one sound*

c: cat, city
g: get, gem
s: sit, his, sure
x: box, exam, xylophone

2. Consonant blends

bl, br
cl, cr
dr, dw
fl, fr
gl, gr
pl, pr

sc, sch, scr, shr, sk,
sm, sn, sp, spl, spr,
st, str, sw
thr, tr, tw

3. Consonant Digraphs

a. *one sound (usually)*

ck, gh, ng, nk, sh

b. *more than one sound*

th: thing, they
wh: when, who
ch: chair, chorus, choir

4. Vowels (long, short, or controlled)

a, e, i, o, u, (y)

5. Vowel clusters

ai: mail, said
ay: say
ea: heat, head
ee: sheep
ei: receive, weigh
ie: believe, tie
ew: few
ey: key, they
oa: road, broad
oe: hoe
oi: boil
ou: though, bough, bought
ow: mow, now
oy: toy
ue: blue

6. Prefixes

ab, ad, ante, anti, auto,
be, bi, com, con, co,
de, dis, en, ex,
in, im, inter, ir,
mis, non, op, out,
per, post, pre, pro,
re, sub, super,
trans, un

7. Suffixes

able, age, al, ate, ble,
er, est, ful, ise, ize, ish,
ist, ite, ity, ly, less,
ment, ness, ship, some,
tion, ure, ward

8. Phonograms

a	e	i	o	u
ab	ear	ib	ob	ub
ack	eat	ic	ock	uck
		ice		
		icle		
ad	ed	id	od	ud
		ide	od	
		if		
ag	eg	ig	og	ug
ake		ight		
		ike		
al	ell	il		
am	em	im	om	um
ame			ome	ump
an	en	in		un
		ine		ung
		ing		
ank		ink		unk
ap		ip	op	up
are			ore	
ash		is		us
				ush
at	et	it		ut
ate		iz		
awe	ez		ow	
aw				
ay				

9. Variants

ed, es, ing, s, 's

one-two-three, and goes on to the next element without giving children time to be analytical.

Teacher says	*Child marks element*		
1. mm—man—mm	h	b	m
2. ing—laughing—ing	ed	s	ing
3. tion—motion—tion	tion	ilk	ton

With practice the children soon learn to work as quickly as they can with this type of exercise. Children who have difficulty with this activity should be assessed individually. The stimulus in this exercise is the sound and not the symbol, and it is not exactly like real reading. Measurement specialists are critical of assessment techniques of this nature, citing lack of construct validity, however, if the child can match the written version to the oral version the teacher can be more certain that the child can also produce the oral equivalent for the written word.

The easiest and most accurate way to determine speed is to give a child a list of words containing the elements recently taught and ask for the list to be read as quickly as possible. If the elements on the list can be pronounced quickly, one after another (about one-half second per unit), the child has attained the desired level of instant recognition. Flash cards may also be used instead of lists of elements; they are easy to incorporate into a game.

The teacher must observe a child reading orally to answer the question regarding the use or application of knowledge of word parts embedded in unknown words. This is best done when the teacher can note when a child comes to a word that should be easy to analyze but is not. This may occur during a reading lesson or any other time when oral reading is done. This behavior may also be observed when the child comes to the teacher to ask for a word that is not known but should be. Care needs to be taken, however, for two reasons. First, a child must exhibit this behavior rather frequently before it can be considered a problem. Second, this behavior suggests other problems, such as ineffective knowledge of word parts, inability to use meaning clues, or both.

Formal Assessment

Many tests or subtests assessing knowledge of word parts are available, such as the *Silent Reading Diagnostic Test* (1970), the *Stanford Diagnostic Reading Test* (1974), and the text-related tests discussed in chapter 3. These tests assess accuracy but not speed. Teachers use their own judgment regarding this ability, or they can informally assess this skill as mentioned above.

Instructional Strategies

Once the teacher determines that a child has a specific weakness, corrective instruction begins. The examples that follow are organized around the scope and sequence chart in figure 6.2. Teachers designing corrective lessons for word parts should present them within the context of familiar, meaningful language.

1. Exercises to teach initial consonants
   a. *Personal dictionaries.* As children use words in their language experience stories or come across them in reading their storybooks, place them on

alphabetically-organized pages to create a dictionary. A sentence and a picture should accompany each word.

b. *Choosing the beginning letter.* Instruct the children to read the sentence in order to write in the missing letter. The material has been read to the students and they are familiar with it.

1. The cow jumped over the __oon.

    r   n   m

2. Humpty Dumpty sat on a __all.

    w   t   c

c. *Choosing the correct word.* Instruct children to read the sentence in order to write in the missing word. Again, the material is familiar.

1. Sam ate the _____.

    ram   ham   slam

2. Jack and Jill went up the _____.

    bill   will   hill

2. Exercises to teach initial blends and digraphs

a. Make a word by using these letters.

    <u>br   sl   cl</u>   <u>ch   wh   sh</u>

    The __ock struck one.   __icken Little said, "The sky is falling!"
    He __oke his crown.   Mary's lamb was __ite as snow.
    Don't __am the door.   Cinderella lost her __oe.

b. Make a word that starts like the one that has a line under it.

    1) We have a good <u>place</u> to _____.
    2) Let's <u>try</u> to _____ the squirrel.
    3) I <u>think</u> he is in _____ grade.
    4) <u>When</u> did the bicycle _____ break?

3. Exercises to teach vowel sounds

a. Instruction: Choose the right word. It must have a long vowel sound.

    1) She ate the candy _____.

        can   cane   mane

    2) Grass is _____.

        seen   mean   green

b. Instruction: Choose the right word. It must have a short vowel sound.

1) Joey saw the big _____ run.

hat   rat   cape

2) Playing games is _____.

fun   cute   sun

4. Exercises to teach phonograms or spelling patterns
   Instruction: Put in the right word.
   a. Jack climbed the _____.

   wild   hall   hill

   b. Mark the words that end like <u>night</u>.

   ___fight   ___bright   ___light
   ___bite   ___fright   ___recite

   c. Instruction: Should the vowel sound be long or short? Write L for long and S for short.

   had ___   up ___   meat ___   stay ___
   goat ___   pig ___   nose ___   side ___

5. Exercises to teach variant endings
   Instruction: Write on the line the word that makes sense.
   a. Three _____ are on the desk.

   book   books   booked

   b. The baby is _____.

   cry   cries   crying

6. Exercises to teach derivatives or affixes
   a. Make a word that means the same as the key word.

   sad   =   _____ + happy
   come back   =   _____ + turn
   trouble   =   _____ + fortune

   b. Draw a circle around the root word. Pick 3 of the words and use each in a sentence.

   timeless   recharge   unbreakable
   disagree   kindness   enjoyment

7. Exercises to teach compounds
   a. Combine these words to make compound words. In the sentences that follow, fill in the missing words by writing one of the compound words on each line.

   note   ball
   foot   book
   card   board

    1. I left my science _____ at home.

    2. The _____ box was too big to carry.

    3. I watched the _____ game Sunday.

  b. Make a new word by drawing a line from the word on the left to the right word on the right. Then write a sentence using the word.

    every   some
                  thing
                  can

Ineffective Blending and Synthesizing

After children successfully segment a word visually and say the word parts, they must then reassemble the parts to form a recognizable word. This reassembly process is referred to as blending and synthesizing. **Auditory blending** refers to a sounding process; the child says the word parts and blends them together to cue a meaningful response. This process is generally used by immature readers when they are learning to read, and it is a very important skill at that level of learning. **Visual synthesizing** is a more mature process and is used by readers who can analyze words mentally, without having to resort to overt sounding and blending of word parts. For typical learners, a gradual shift from auditory blending to visual synthesizing occurs as the analytical techniques and word parts become learned. Visual synthesizing is probably a faster process than auditory blending and should be the ultimate goal.

Some children have trouble with blending and synthesizing because the reading program has overemphasized learning word parts in isolation; a few children may not be able to blend sounds orally and must learn to compensate through visual synthesizing.

Informal Assessment

A child must know the word parts before assessment of blending and synthesizing can be meaningful. A child who cannot yet say the various word parts obviously cannot put them back together. Assuming that the word parts are known, children who are having auditory blending problems can be identified relatively easily. The teacher says the word parts slowly, with a one-second interval between parts, and asks the child to respond by saying the whole word. This is an example of auditory blending:

Objective	*Teacher*	*Child*
letters	s – a – m	sam
letters and phonogram	s – am	sam
syllables	sam – ple	sample
combination	s – am – pling	sampling

Both the stimulus and response are at the oral level; a child who does this task successfully still may not be able to deal with the task in a more reading-like setting. Instead, the stimulus must be provided in printed form, separating the letters or word parts with dashes and spaces. This is an example of auditory blending when the stimulus is in print.

Child reads and says:	Child says
b – a – by	baby
d – an – cing	dancing

When the child says the parts out loud and blends them together, the process is auditory blending. When the child simply looks at the word parts and rather quickly says the whole word aloud without sounding out the parts, the process is visual synthesizing.

Formal Assessment

Several tests and subtests are available for the assessment of blending and synthesizing, including the *Roswell-Chall Auditory Blending Tests* (1963) and the blending subtest of the *Sipay Word Analysis Tests* (1974). Teachers must choose subtests carefully, as titles are sometimes misleading.

Instructional Strategies

With early instructional strategies, separated word parts are presented to the student to reassemble. Corrective work begins with known word parts in known words so that the learner understands the task.

in – to	into
a – way	away

If the word parts are pronounced by the teacher and the child responds by saying the whole word, this is auditory blending, with the stimulus and the response both at the oral level.

Perceptual unit	Teacher says	Child says
syllables	chil – dren	children
structural elements	some – thing	something
phonic elements	p – ain – ter	painter

It is wise to begin with more natural word divisions represented by syllabic utterances and then proceed to more artificial phonic elements. Children need practice with these elements, because they are likely to segment words into elements other than syllables; therefore they must be able to blend them to cue an appropriate response.

When the stimulus is changed from word parts said by the teacher to written word parts read by the children, the task is considered either auditory blending or visual synthesizing, depending on whether the response is primarily auditory or visual. The following exercises develop both skills.

1. When the words are in isolation:

Print	Child reads
gra vel	gravel
gr avel	gravel
gr av el	gravel

2. When the words are in context:
   a. The men walked toward the <u>gra</u> <u>vel</u> pit.
   b. Add the right word part. The men walk___ toward the gravel pit.

    c. End of line segmentation
       The men walked to-
       ward the gravel pit.

Summary

Word recognition is presented as an interaction between the *process* of figuring out unknown words and the *products* of instruction, or knowledge of word parts. Several factors influence this interaction. One of the most important is that the word exist in the reader's listening vocabulary. The text also must not be so difficult that the reader is unable to use context clues. Readers are not able to use their understanding of language when material is too difficult, and they are forced to resort to more artificial analytical techniques.

Another factor influencing this interaction is the size of the child's sight vocabulary. As sight vocabulary increases, the number of unrecognized words decreases. Eventually, the student encounters few unknown words; when they are encountered, they are probably not in the meaning vocabulary. Analytical techniques seldom help mature readers who encounter unknown words because the problem is lack of meaning rather than lack of appropriate word recognition facility.

Context clues such as expectancy, or anticipation of words likely to occur in the selection, play an indirect but vital part in the word analysis process. Meaning clues, or knowledge of the language surrounding an unknown word, also contribute immeasurably to the analytical process.

For the beginning reader, however, knowledge of word parts is an important way of relating visual symbols to words that are already in the meaning vocabulary. Disregarding context clues for the moment, the process of word recognition probably includes the following steps or stages:

1. The reader knows by looking that the word is not recognized.
2. The word is segmented visually into parts.
3. Some of the parts may be recognized.
4. The reader attempts to analyze the remaining unknown parts. The more techniques the reader has for doing this, the more successful is the outcome.
5. The word is reconstructed by auditory or visual means, or both, to approximate the word and cue a meaningful response.
6. The word is confirmed or rejected based on the meaning of the sentence when the word choice is made.

Children without reading problems probably use bits and pieces of this process intuitively. However, children with problems probably need direct instruction to clarify the process at points where the problems exist. The teacher must use an analytic process to help identify areas of strength and weakness. Ultimately, children assume responsibility for analyzing words independently, always checking for sentence sense and understanding of the passage being read.

References

Arnold, R. D., & Miller, J. (1980). Word recognition skills. In P. Lamb & R. D. Arnold (Eds.), *Teaching reading: Foundations and strategies* (2nd ed.). Belmont, CA: Wadsworth.

Bond, G. L., Balow, B., & Hoyt, C. (1972). *Silent reading diagnostic test.* Chicago: Rand McNally.

Bormuth, J. R. (1968). Cloze test readability: Criterion reference scores. *Journal of Educational Measurement, 5,* 189–196.

Bormuth, J. R. (1967). Comparable cloze and multiple-choice comprehension test score. *Journal of Reading, 10,* 291–299.

Carle, E. (1987). *The very hungry caterpillar.* New York: Scholastic.

Chaffin, J., Maxwell, B., & Thompson, B. (1983). *Word Radar.* Allen, TX: Developmental Learning Materials.

Chall, J. S., (1967). *Learning to read: The great debate.* New York: McGraw-Hill.

Dolch, E. (1953). *Dolch basic sight vocabulary.* Champaign, IL: Garrard.

Durkin, D. (1978). *Teaching them to read* (3rd ed.). Boston: Allyn and Bacon.

Durrell, D. D. (1980). *Durrell analysis of reading difficulty.* New York: Psychological Corporation.

ESA Word List. (1977). In E. C. Kennedy, *Classroom approaches to remedial reading.* Itasca, IL: F. E. Peacock.

Fay, L. (1978). *Young America basic reading program.* Chicago: Rand McNally.

Fernald, G. M. (1943). *Remedial techniques in basic school subjects.* New York: McGraw-Hill.

Fry, E. B. (1980). The new instant word list. *The Reading Teacher, 34,* 284–290.

Gates, A. I., McKillop, A., & Horowitz, E. C. (1982). *Gates-McKillop-Horowitz reading diagnostic tests.* New York: Teachers College Press.

Goodman, K. S. (1968). The psycholinguistic nature of the reading process. In K. S. Goodman (Ed.), *The psycholinguistic nature of the reading process.* Detroit: Wayne State Press.

Gough, P. B. (1984) Word recognition. In P. D. Pearson (Ed.), *Handbook of reading research.* New York: Longman.

Great Atlantic and Pacific Word List. (1972). From Otto, W., & Chester, R. Sight words for beginning readers. *Journal of Educational Research, 65,* 436–443.

Harris, A. J., & Jacobson, M. D. (1972). *Basic elementary reading vocabularies.* New York: Macmillan.

Heilman, A. W. (1976). *Principles and practices of teaching reading* (4th ed.). Columbus, OH: Merrill.

Johnson, D. D. (1971). A basic vocabulary for beginning reading. *Elementary School Journal, 72,* 29–34.

Johnson, D. D., & Pearson, P. D. (1984). *Teaching reading vocabulary.* New York: Holt, Rinehart and Winston.

Karnowski, L. (1989). Using LEA with process writing. *The Reading Teacher, 42,* 462–465.

Kucera, H., & Francis, W. (1967). *Computational analysis of present-day American English.* Providence, RI: Brown University Press.

LaBerge, D., & Samuels, S. J. (1976). Toward a theory of automatic information processing in reading. In H. Singer & R. B. Ruddell (Eds.), *Theoretical models and processes of reading* (2nd ed.). Newark, DE: International Reading Association.

Martin, B. (1982). *Brown bear, brown bear, what do you see?* Toronto: Holt, Rinehart and Winston.

McNinch, G. H. (1981). A method for teaching sight words to disabled readers. *The Reading Teacher, 35,* 269–272.

Moe, A. J. (1972a). *High frequency words.* St. Paul, MN: Ambassador.

Moe, A. J. (1972b). *High frequency nouns.* St. Paul, MN: Ambassador.

Moe, A. J., & Manning, J. C. (1984). Developing intensive word practice exercises. In J. F. Baumann & D. D. Johnson (Eds.), *Reading instruction for the beginning teacher: A practical guide.* Minneapolis, MN: Burgess.

Noyce, R. M., & Christie, J. F. (1989). *Integrating reading and writing instruction in grades K–8.* Boston: Allyn and Bacon.

Pearson, P. D., & Johnson, D. D. (1978). *Teaching reading comprehension.* New York: Holt, Rinehart and Winston.

Rankin, E. F., & Culhane, J. W. (1969). Comparable cloze and multiple-choice comprehension scores. *Journal of Reading, 13,* 193–198.

Roswell, F., & Chall, J. (1963). *Roswell-Chall auditory blending test.* LaJolla, CA: Essay Press.

Sipay, E. R. (1974). *Sipay word analysis tests.* Cambridge, MA: Educators Publishing Service.

Stanovich, K. E. (1980). Toward an interactive-compensatory model of individual differences in the development of reading fluency. *Reading Research Quarterly, 16,* 32–71.

Valmont, W. J. (1983). Cloze and maze instructional techniques: Differences and definitions. *Reading Psychology, 4,* 163–167.

Word Blaster. (1981). New York: Random House.

CHAPTER 7

Reading Comprehension: Part 1

Objectives

After you have studied this chapter, you should be able to

1. list and describe the major factors affecting the comprehension process;
2. tell what behaviors a less skilled comprehender is likely to exhibit;
3. explain the various theories of the comprehension process;
4. develop informal assessment activities for word meanings;
5. devise an instructional program in vocabulary development for a corrective student.

Study Outline

I. Background

II. Factors affecting the comprehension process
  A. Factors within the reader
    1. Linguistic competence
    2. Decoding ability
    3. Prior knowledge or experience
    4. Interests and attitudes
  B. Factors within the written message
    1. Words
    2. Sentences, paragraphs, and longer units of discourse
  C. Environmental factors

III. Theories of the comprehension process
  A. Schema theory

  B. Reading comprehension as concept-driven
  C. Reading comprehension as data-driven
  D. Reading comprehension as interactive
  E. Reading comprehension as transactive

IV. Skilled versus less skilled comprehenders

V. Assessment and instructional strategies for comprehension
  A. Assessing decoding skills
  B. Instructional strategies for increased reading fluency
  C. Assessing knowledge of word meanings
    1. Informal measures
    2. Formal measures

Important Vocabulary and Concepts

abstract referent
associative words
comprehension processes
comprehension products
concrete referent
homophones
integrative processing
linguistic competence
macroprocessing

microprocessing
phonological system
schema
semantic system
specialized vocabulary
structured overview
syntactic system
transactive

Overview

Even with all the emphasis that has been placed on reading achievement in recent years, something still seems to be wrong. While many programs teach decoding skills successfully, the lament continues to be heard that "Johnny still doesn't understand what he reads!"

In dealing with the products of comprehension, such as finding the main idea, drawing conclusions, and predicting outcomes, the processes involved in achieving those products are frequently ignored. In other words, if Johnny has trouble predicting outcomes, he usually is confronted with several skill sheets on predicting outcomes without being taught *how* to predict an outcome, or the process of predicting outcomes. The difference between the two is considerable.

In this and the following chapter, you will be introduced to thinking about comprehension as a process. More specifically, you will learn what to look for in the less skilled comprehender to determine at what level comprehension is breaking down. This will enable you to do a better job of assessing comprehension. Once you have determined where the comprehension process is not working, you will be shown, by example, how to teach that aspect of the process that has not been internalized by the student.

Word meanings and the ability to interact with and organize text will be discussed at length. For study purposes, the discussion is divided into two chapters. The first deals with recent theory about the comprehension process and the crucial element of word meanings, while the second examines comprehension of whole text.

These two chapters will help you think of comprehension as a process and not simply as a list of products or skills. A basic understanding of comprehension terminology and a working knowledge of questioning skills are assumed. Any terms considered new are defined or explained.

Introduction

Many attempts have been made to define reading comprehension. Nearly every text concerned with teaching reading includes a unique definition or set of definitions. It is my conviction that comprehension is central to reading. Therefore, in this chapter, I will not define reading comprehension per se, but instead will analyze the process of comprehension by examining some of the factors that influence it. Such analysis should be helpful in the application of the analytic process discussed earlier.

Concern for understanding comprehension is not new. Early authors, such as Edmund Burke Huey (1908), wrote that to understand reading would be to understand the most intricate workings of the mind; Thorndike (1917) defined reading as thinking. Russell (1961) and Anderson (1977) view reading as an application of basic cognitive processes subject to the same constraints as memory and problem-solving. More recently, the contributions of linguists and psycholinguists have also focused on comprehension processes (Adams & Collins, 1979; Carroll & Freedle, 1972; Goodman, 1967, 1968, 1973; Kavanagh & Mattingly, 1972; Smith, 1988; Spiro, Bruce, & Brewer, 1980).

Historically, reading experts have tried to explain reading comprehension by describing what successful comprehenders do. A frequently cited study by Davis (1944) lists nine skills considered basic to successful comprehension:[1]

1. Knowledge of word meanings
2. Ability to select appropriate meaning for a word or phrase in the light of its particular contextual setting
3. Ability to follow the organization of a passage and to identify antecedents and references in it
4. Ability to identify the main thought of a passage
5. Ability to answer questions that are specifically answered in a passage
6. Ability to answer questions that are answered in a passage, but not in the words in which the question is asked
7. Ability to draw inferences from a passage about its contents
8. Ability to recognize the literary devices used in a passage and to determine its tone and mood
9. Ability to determine a writer's purpose, intent, and point of view, i.e., to draw inferences about a writer. (p. 186)

Since Davis' study, others (Schreiner, Hieronymous, & Forsythe, 1969; Spearritt, 1972) have supported some of the same nine abilities listed but not all, and not always in the same order. The single exception is knowledge of word meanings; nearly everyone considers this one skill important to comprehension (Johnson, 1986; Tierney & Cunningham, 1984). The other skill areas have been combined into a category labeled "reasoning ability" and are commonly referred to in developmental texts as literal, inferential, and evaluative or critical-creative thinking skills.

---

[1] From F. B. Davis, "Fundamental Factors of Comprehension in Reading." *Psychometrika* 9 (1944): 186. Used with permission.

The widely used skills-centered approach to reading comprehension (Simons, 1971) deals predominantly with the **products of comprehension.** Representative skills (Rosenshine, 1980, p. 537) taught in these approaches include:

1. Literal:
   Locating details
2. Simple inferential:
   Understanding words in context
   Recognizing the sequence of events
   Recognizing cause and effect
   Comparison and contrasting
3. Complex inferential:
   Recognizing the main idea, title, topic
   Drawing conclusions
   Predicting outcomes

Consider the following example: Through an assessment technique Terry is found to have difficulty drawing conclusions from a passage, a *product* of comprehension. The usual procedure is to give Terry additional practice in drawing conclusions. Unfortunately, whether such practice affects the *process* of drawing conclusions is not certain. On the other hand, if the underlying tasks involved in drawing conclusions were known, the procedure would be to determine the stage at which the process broke down and proceed with appropriate instruction from that point. What is really needed, then, is a better understanding of comprehension processes.

Factors Affecting the Comprehension Process

Before discussing specific characteristics of the less skilled comprehender, the **process of comprehension** must be examined to learn what strategies are used by the skilled comprehender. With this in mind, areas of difference between skilled and less skilled comprehenders will be easier to recognize. The ultimate goal is to design appropriate reading comprehension instruction for the less-skilled comprehender.

Key factors of the comprehension process are best grouped into three categories: factors within the reader, factors within the written message, and factors within the reading environment (Pearson & Johnson, 1978).

Factors within the Reader

Some factors within the reader that affect reading comprehension are linguistic competence, decoding ability, prior knowledge or background experience, and interests and attitudes.

Linguistic Competence

Linguistic competence refers to what the reader knows about language. According to Pearson and Johnson (1978), three systems are involved in learning language: phonological, syntactic, and semantic. The **phonological system** refers to knowledge of individual sounds in the language, knowledge of how these sounds are blended together to make words, and knowledge of stress, pitch, and juncture. Briefly, stress refers to such differences as:

The DOG broke the cup (not the cat).
The dog BROKE the cup (as opposed to knocking it over).

Pitch refers to intonation differences as in:

We'll leave in an hour.
We'll leave in an hour!
We'll leave in an hour?

Juncture refers to the differences between NITRATE and NIGHT RATE or between ICING and I SING.

Goodman (1985) terms this first important system the **graphophonic system** which includes the orthographic and phonic systems, as well as the phonological. Because the particular cues in reading are also visual, the reader must have knowledge of the particular orthography used by the language being read. In our case this is an alphabetic system, whereas Japan uses a combination of Chinese characters and syllabic orthography. The reader must have knowledge of the relationships between the oral and written language using an alphabetic system, better known as phonics.

The **syntactic system** refers to word order in sentences, punctuation, and the use of capital letters. Syntactic knowledge helps the reader determine whether a string of words makes a grammatically acceptable English sentence. For example:

The dog chased the cat.
            vs.
Chased dog the cat the.

Syntactic knowledge, sometimes called "sentence sense," also helps the reader to know that two different word orders have the same meaning:

The dog chased the cat.
            or
The cat was chased by the dog.

Or again:

His friend said, "The doctor is ill."
            or
"The doctor," said his friend, "is ill."

Knowledge of syntax even enables the reader to utilize context clues to read and answer questions on material that has no real meaning:

The illzoo was a bab. That forn, the sossy illzoo larped and was mitry. What was the illzoo? When did the sossy illzoo larp? Who was sossy?

In short, syntax is the primary means by which the reader determines the relation-ships among words.

Simply being able to pronounce words and answer certain questions correctly does not ensure that understanding has taken place. Because the sentences about the illzoo had no real meaning (the reader was not able to relate the nonsense words to anything already available in his or her head), the importance of the semantic system becomes obvious. The **semantic system** refers to knowledge of word meanings, the underlying concepts of words, and the interrelationships among concepts. Semantic knowledge enables the reader to organize the text into a coherent structure and recognize the relative importance of the various concepts found in text (i.e., main ideas versus supporting details). Pragmatic knowledge can also be considered a part of this system. Pragmatic meaning is always partly found in the text and partly found in the context of the literacy event. The reader's schemata must be called upon to achieve pragmatic comprehension (e.g., understanding the humor in a comic strip) (Goodman, 1985, p. 832).

In summary, if the phonological, syntactic, and semantic information provided for the reader on a page of print closely matches the phonological, syntactic, and semantic abilities available in the reader's head, understanding is likely to occur.

Decoding Ability

When a reader approaches text in order to construct meaning, decoding will occur more naturally. However, the construction of meaning will be difficult if the reader cannot readily pronounce many of the words in the passage, or is overly concerned with accurate word pronunciation. The reader who has to devote too much attention to decoding, or to correct pronunciation as in the case of oral, round robin reading, cannot also attend to processing the meaning of the material (LaBerge & Samuels, 1974; Stanovich, 1980). Readers who identify words quickly and automatically, on the other hand, do not have to focus on decoding and can give their full attention to comprehension, especially when reading silently.

A weakness in decoding ability does *not* imply, however, that comprehension cannot occur. In fact, comprehension must be the goal for decoding to occur more readily. Consider the following argument presented by Pearson and Johnson (1978).

> Comprehension helps word identification as much as word identification helps comprehension. That is, having understood part of the message helps you to decode another part. In short, context can help to short circuit the amount of attention you have to pay to print. (p. 15)

Decoding ability has been discussed in more detail in chapter 6, but you may conclude from this brief discussion that decoding is made easier if the reader is reading for meaning. Concern with comprehension instruction is important at every stage of reading development. The reader must *expect* and *demand* that material read *makes sense.*

Prior Knowledge or Experience

What readers bring to the reading task is critical to their understanding of what is read. A reader's background brings personal meaning to the printed page; thus not all readers comprehend material in exactly the same way. For example, if a young reader who has never been out of the city tries to read a book about life on the farm, so many words and events will be unfamiliar that the "reading" will probably become more of a word-calling situation. Even if the reader uses all of his or her linguistic competence to make predictions about what will occur in print, words such as silo, harvester, and trough and events such as birthing a calf or hauling hay have little or no meaning. Adult readers experience the same frustrations if they try to understand material in an area they consider difficult, such as a physics text, a medical journal, or legal documents. This does not imply that the reader cannot understand material concerning something not experienced, but rather that a reader must have a repertoire of relevant concepts to interpret the printed page. Consider another young reader who has always lived in the Deep South and has never experienced heavy snows. This reader is asked to read a story about a blizzard. Even though the reader has never experienced a blizzard, some relevant concepts available to the reader might be ice, the wind of a hurricane, and the possible tragedy of its aftermath.

In summary, for maximum comprehension to occur, the reader must be able to relate the printed material to personal experiences. Direct, firsthand experiences are best. At the very least, vicarious or secondhand experiences, such as listening to stories on a variety of concepts, seeing relevant pictures, and watching films and filmstrips, must be provided.

Interests and Attitudes

Closely related to prior knowledge and experience are interests and attitudes. Shnayer (1969) reports that interest in a topic enables readers with reading ability from two years below grade level to one year above grade level to read beyond their measured ability. Thus, a reader will better understand a book about explorers if he or she has an interest in history and the concept of exploration. Readers' attitudes are closely related to their interests. Attitudes are learned and probably reflect previous experiences. A reader with a poor attitude toward reading has little motivation to pick up a book and read, much less comprehend. Because attitude is influenced as much by factors within the reading environment as by factors within the reader, attitude and motivation will be discussed further in chapter 12.

Factors within the Written Message

As Smith and Johnson (1980, p. 133) state, "Reading comprehension is not entirely dependent on the reader." Elements in the written message must be considered, including the words themselves, sentences, paragraphs, and longer units of discourse, such as stories.

Words

What makes some words easier to learn than others? The most often researched characteristics of words are frequency and imagery (Gorman, 1961; Hargis & Gickling, 1978; Jackson, 1977; Ollila & Chamberlain, 1979; Paivio, 1967, 1970; van der Veur, 1975; Winnick and Kressel, 1965; Wolpert, 1972). Frequency refers to how often a word occurs in the language. Several studies (Ekwall & Shanker, 1983; Jorm, 1977) have demonstrated that passages containing words that occur frequently are more easily comprehended than passages containing words that do not occur frequently.

Imagery refers to how easily a word is visualized. A word with a **concrete referent**, such as *dog,* is probably easier to learn than a word with an **abstract referent**, such as *love.* Passages with heavy concentration of words with low imagery (abstract words) will probably be more difficult to understand than passages containing a large number of words with high imagery (Thorndyke, 1977).

Results of a study by Jorm (1977) are of interest. Jorm analyzed the effects of word imagery, length, and frequency on the reading ability of good and poor readers aged eight to eleven years. While word length had little effect on either type of reader, Jorm found that high frequency words were easier to read for both good and poor readers. He also found that imagery was a facilitating factor in word recognition only for poor readers. Jorm explains that since disabled readers are more likely than good readers to use a whole word method for word recognition, visual imagery was an aid for this type of learning. On the basis of this information, teachers are advised to carefully examine materials to be used with poor readers for the occurrence of high imagery words.

Teachers working with corrective readers must be concerned with the level of material. The ratio of known words to unknown words is of greatest importance. In fact, the ratio of difficult words in a text is the most powerful predictor of text difficulty (Anderson & Freebody, 1981), and a reader's knowledge of key vocabulary predicts comprehension of text better than reading ability or achievement (Johnston, 1984). If students are provided with material at their instructional reading level, the number of known words approximates 95 out of 100. Children are often taught the "five-finger method" to determine if a library book is easy enough for them to read. The idea is analogous to the instructional reading level criterion; if the child can count more than five words on the page that are unknown, the book is probably too difficult. (See appendix A for help in determining readability of text material.)

Sentences, Paragraphs, and Longer Units of Written Discourse

Comprehension of written material demands much more than understanding each word in the selection. Words must be understood in relation to other words. For example, the action of a sentence (verb) works together with the actor or agent (who or what is doing the action) and with the object (who or what received the action) (Fillmore, 1968). In the sentence, "Charles is reading a magazine," the action is reading, the agent is Charles, and the object is the magazine. In the sentence, "The water is boiling," the action is boiling, the agent is not stated, and the object is the water. In the sentence, "Sue ran," the agent is Sue, the action is ran, and there is no object. The types of relationships that might exist among actors, agents, actions, and objects include those of cause, purpose, condition, and time (Pearson & Johnson, 1978, p. 40). For example, who or what caused the event and what was the outcome of the event represent causal relations. The descriptions and identifications given about the event may represent relationships of time or condition.

Readers seldom read isolated sentences, but they must comprehend relationships within sentences if they are to comprehend a paragraph (called **microprocessing**, see Irwin, 1986, p. 3). Just as sentence comprehension is more than understanding each word, paragraph comprehension is more than understanding individual sentences (called **integrative processing**, Irwin, 1986, p. 5). Paragraphs are structured to function in longer units of written discourse. To understand paragraphs, the reader must recognize the actor or agent of the paragraph, that is, who or what the paragraph is about. The reader must also recognize the relations existing within and between paragraphs, such as cause and effect, question and answer, sequence, enumeration, generalization, or comparison and contrast (Hittleman, 1983).

As with sentences, a reader does not often read isolated paragraphs. Paragraphs exist in the context of longer selections. According to Robinson (1983, p. 92), paragraphs serve specific functions: introductory, expository, narrative, descriptive, definitional, persuasive, transitional, or summary and concluding. The skilled reader recognizes a paragraph's function within the total context of the selection.

Specific relationships also exist within stories. Stemming from the work of Bartlett (1932), several studies have attempted to specify the logical relations existing within stories (Mandler & Johnson, 1977; Rumelhart, 1975; Stein & Glenn, 1979; and Thorndyke, 1977). Stories are usually organized in consistent, predictable patterns. The reader expects relations that specify themes, setting, characters, goals, and resolutions. Thorndyke (1977) states that some story structures (e.g., fairy tales and fables) become more familiar with experience and that stories with several cause-effect relations are easier to comprehend than those without causal relations.

In summary, recognizing organization is apparently a key to understanding written material. The reader must identify who or what the material is about, discover the relationship between actors or agents and actions, and determine the function or purpose of the material. This "process of synthesizing and organizing individual idea units into a summary or organized series of related general ideas is called **macroprocessing**" (Irwin, 1986, p. 5).

Environmental Factors

Essentially two environments affect reading comprehension—the home and the school. The preceding emphasis on prior knowledge and experience should explain the important role of the home environment in providing the language base necessary for reading comprehension. The child with an extensive language base comes to school better equipped for the comprehension process than a child who has not been spoken to frequently, read to, taken on trips, or participated in other concept-developing activities.

The school environment refers, for the most part, to the child's classroom, teacher, and peers. The atmosphere of the entire school and the attitude of administrators and other teachers also affect reading comprehension, even if only in a more general, indirect sense.

While the classroom teacher most directly influences reading comprehension, classmates provide a source of competition or approval or a standard for comparison. Unfortunately, classmates may also have an emotionally negative influence as sources of ridicule or harassment.

In short, teachers can do much to affect comprehension both instructionally and emotionally. Teachers influence comprehension by the following:

1. Establishing a comfortable, risk-free atmosphere where students do not fear ridicule or penalty for failure. Provide the kind of teacher feedback that encourages curiosity, risk-taking, and creativity.

2. Providing a model for their students. Reading will be seen as a valuable, enjoyable, and relevant activity if students see their teachers reading and are read to by their teachers.

3. Providing direct instruction. This includes preparing students for reading by discussing backgrounds of stories and essential vocabulary, and by helping students establish purposes for reading with appropriate follow-up activities.

4. Choosing appropriate materials for instruction. Teachers must know their students' strengths, weaknesses, and reading levels. Frustrating material does nothing to help comprehension.

5. Planning the type of questions they will ask. Teachers' questions are often poorly planned with respect to the objectives of the lesson (Bartolome, 1969) and do not demand much thinking beyond a literal level (Bartolome, 1969; Durkin, 1981; Guszak, 1967). Instructional strategies in this chapter and the next will emphasize this most important aspect of comprehension instruction.

Theories of the Comprehension Process

Schema Theory

Recently, linguists, cognitive psychologists, and psycholinguists have used the concept of schema (plural, schemata) to understand how key factors affecting the comprehension process interact. The term itself is not new (Kant, 1787, 1963; Bartlett, 1932), but the concept has only recently become the focus of research related to reading comprehension (Adams & Collins, 1979; Anderson, 1977; Bobrow & Norman, 1975; Clark, 1973; Nelson, 1974, 1977; Rumelhart, 1975, 1980; Rumelhart, Lindsay, & Norman, 1972; Rumelhart & Ortony, 1977; Schank & Abelson, 1977; Smith, Shoben, & Rips, 1974; van Dijk, 1972).

Simply put, schema theory states that all knowledge is organized into units. Within these units of knowledge, the schemata, is stored information. A **schema**, then, is a generalized description or a conceptual system for understanding knowledge—how knowledge is represented and how it is used.

According to this theory, schemata represent knowledge about concepts: objects and the relationships they have with other objects, situations, events, sequences of events, actions, and sequences of actions. A simple example would be to think of your schema for *dog*. Within that schema you would most likely have knowledge about dogs in general (bark, four legs, teeth, hair, tails) and probably information about specific dogs, such as collies (long hair, large, Lassie) or springer spaniels (English, docked tails, liver and white). You may also think of dogs within the greater context of animals and other living things, that is, dogs breathe, need food, and reproduce. Your knowledge of dogs might also include the fact that they are mammals and thus warm-blooded and bear their young as opposed to laying eggs. Depending upon your personal experience, the knowledge of a dog as a pet (domesticated and loyal) or as an animal to fear (likely to bite or attack) may be a part of your schema. And so it goes with the development of a schema. Each new experience incorporates more information into one's schema.

What does all this have to do with reading comprehension? Individuals have schemata for everything. Long before children come to school, they develop schemata (units of knowledge) about everything they experience. Schemata become theories about reality. These theories not only affect the way information is interpreted, thus affecting comprehension, but also continue to change as new information is received. As stated by Rumelhart (1980):

> schemata can represent knowledge at all levels—from ideologies and cultural truths to knowledge about the meaning of a particular word, to knowledge about what patterns of excitations are associated with what letters of the alphabet. We have schemata to represent all levels of our experience, at all levels of abstraction. Finally, our schemata *are* our knowledge. All of our generic knowledge is embedded in schemata. (p. 41)

The importance of schema to reading comprehension lies in how the reader uses schema. This issue has not yet been resolved by research, although investigators agree that some mechanism activates just those schemata most relevant to the reader's task. At this time, three basic models have been offered to explain how schemata are activated. These have been termed concept-driven, data-driven[2] (Bobrow & Norman, 1975), and interactive (Ruddell & Speaker, 1985; Rumelhart, 1985). A fourth model has also emerged called the transactional psycholinguistic model (Goodman, 1985), which attempts to integrate and unify knowledge gained about reading from fields other than reading, "such as cognitive psychology, ethnography, linguistics, child language development, artificial intelligence, semiotics, rhetoric, literature, philosophy, and brain study" (Goodman, 1985, p. 813). This model takes a **transactive** view; that is, "both the knower and the known are changed in the course of knowing" (Goodman, 1985, p. 814). More specifically, readers' and writers' schemata are changed through transactions with the text as meaning is constructed. Readers' schemata are changed as new knowledge is assimilated and accommodated (Piaget, 1971). Writers' schemata are changed as new ways of organizing text to express meaning are developed. A complete explanation of these models is beyond the scope of this book; the interested reader is referred to the sources cited. A brief description of each model follows to help you understand how key factors interact in the process of comprehension.

Reading Comprehension as Concept-Driven

Concept-driven models (Goodman, 1967; Hochberg, 1970; Kolers, 1972; Levin & Kaplan, 1970; Neisser, 1967; Smith, 1973, 1988) view readers as actively engaging in hypothesis testing while reading. In other words, a reader has certain expectations about the text that activate schemata relevant to those expectations. For example, if the reader reads the title, "Betsy and the Red Balloon," schemata about previous experiences with balloons will be activated. Certain expectations then exist before the story is even read. The Directed Reading–Thinking Activity (Stauffer, 1969, 1975) specifically encourages activation of relevant schemata by asking the reader to speculate on the story content from the title. Reading the story then becomes an effort to verify hypotheses.

Reading Comprehension as Data-Driven

Data-driven models (Geyer, 1970; Gough, 1972; LaBerge & Samuels, 1974; Smith & Spoehr, 1974) view the reader as beginning with printed stimuli (the words) and processing the letters and sounds into words and eventually into meaning—a part-to-whole process. The kinds of schemata activated initially involve letter-sound relationships, syntactic knowledge, and word meanings. Reading instruction that stresses phonics at beginning stages with little regard for interpretation of material encourages this kind of processing.

---

[2] In the literature, concept-driven models are also termed top-down, inside-out, reader-based, prediction-based, schema-driven, and hypothesis-testing. Data-driven models may be called bottom-up, outside-in, text-based, text-driven, and decoding.

Reading Comprehension as Interactive

A third class of models views reading as a combination of concept-driven and data-driven processing (Ruddell & Speaker, 1985; Rumelhart, 1985). Information from several knowledge sources (schemata about letter-sound relationships, word meanings, syntactic relationships, event sequences, and so forth) are considered *simultaneously*. The implication is that when information from one source, such as word recognition, is deficient, the reader will rely on information from another source, for example, contextual clues or previous experience. Stanovich (1980) terms the latter kind of processing interactive-compensatory because the reader (*any* reader) compensates for deficiencies in one or more of the knowledge sources by using information from remaining knowledge sources. Those sources that are more concerned with concepts and semantic relationships are termed higher-level stimuli; sources dealing with the print itself, that is phonics, sight words, and other word attack skills, are termed lower-level stimuli. The interactive-compensatory model implies that the reader will rely on higher-level processes when lower-level processes are deficient, and vice versa. Stanovich (1980) extensively reviews research demonstrating such compensation in both good and poor readers.

Reading Comprehension as Transactive

This most recent fourth model of the reading process views reading as integrated with other language processes, and with its functional use. Reading is seen as a "literacy event, an event in which writer and/or reader transact with and through a text in a specific context with specific intentions" (Goodman, 1985, p. 814). This transactional view is in keeping with a holistic philosophy about learning which attempts to integrate all areas of the curriculum and place learning within the context of students' own experiences (a meaningful environment). In a transactional view, the reader has a highly active role. It is the individual transactions between a reader and the text characteristics (i.e., physical characteristics such as orthography—the alphabetic system, spelling, punctuation; format characteristics such as paragraphing, lists, schedules, bibliographies; intrinsic purposes [macrostructure or text grammar], such as that found in telephone books, recipe books, newspapers, letters; and wording of texts, such as the differences found in narrative and expository text) that result in meaning. "It makes what the reader brings to the text as important as the text itself in text comprehension" (Goodman, 1985, p. 827).

According to Goodman (1985):

> How well the writer knows the audience and has built the text to suit the audience will make a major difference in text predictability and comprehension. However, since comprehension results from reader-text transactions, what the reader knows, who the reader is, what values guide the reader, what purposes or interests the reader has will play vital roles in the reading process. It follows then that what any reader comprehends from a given text will vary from what other readers comprehend. Meaning is ultimately created by the reader. (p. 838)

Skilled Versus Less Skilled Comprehenders

This is an appropriate time to consider the reader having difficulty with comprehension. The characteristics of less skilled comprehenders must be known in order to help them become skilled.

A thorough review of the literature on good and poor comprehenders by Golinkoff (1975–1976) reveals that good comprehenders are adaptable and flexible. They seem to be aware that reading is a process for gaining information or expanding one's knowledge about the world. More specifically, in terms of three comprehension subskills that Golinkoff uses to compare good and poor comprehenders, the skilled comprehender is a master at decoding, accessing single word meanings, and extracting relations between words in sentences and larger units of text.

Poor comprehenders, on the other hand, are less adaptive and flexible in their reading style. They make more decoding errors and take more time to decode. They tend to read word-by-word, which implies one of three things: they are unfamiliar with the printed words (decoding), they are unaware of the clues to proper phrasing (syntactic aspects), or they are unaware that reading involves using what they already know about the concepts and contextual constraints found in the text to construct meaning. This last characteristic is also supported by McKeown's (1985) research on the acquisition of word meanings from context (semantic aspects).

Such characterizations have led to the conclusion that poor comprehenders are more concerned with pronouncing words correctly than with getting meaning from the printed page. This is not necessarily the case, however. Stanovich (1980) gives evidence that in some situations poor readers rely *more* on contextual information than good readers. To cope with a large number of visually unfamiliar words, some poor readers depend too much on the syntactic and semantic clues available.

Kolers (1975) presents evidence that such dependence on syntactic and semantic clues to avoid decoding may be a common source of reading difficulty. Kolers' subjects, good and poor readers between ten and fourteen years of age, read sentences in normal and reversed type. The poor readers made ten times as many substitution errors as the good readers. Also, the reading speed of the poor readers was less affected by the reversed type than that of the good readers. The poor readers guessed frequently and paid relatively little attention to the typographical (graphemic) aspects of the print. These results were interpreted to indicate an overreliance on syntactic and semantic clues.

Stanovich (1980) distinguishes between two types of contextual processing when discussing differences between good and poor comprehenders. The first type involves relating new information to known information and imposing structure on the text (text organization). The second type is the contextual hypothesis-testing strategy that allows previously understood material to help with ongoing word recognition. Good readers use both types of contextual processing whereas poor readers are more adept at the second type. In itself this is not a problem; however, if processing is being used to aid word recognition, the reader is depleting valuable cognitive-resources— resources that could otherwise be employed for making inferences or relating new information to old. Stanovich views the comprehension problem as a direct result of slow and nonautomatic word recognition skills that require the poor reader to draw on the wrong kinds of knowledge sources. As stated by Stanovich (1980):

> Given that the ability to use prior context to facilitate word recognition is not a skill that differentiates good from poor readers, there appear to be two general types of processes that good readers perform more efficiently than poor readers. Good readers appear to have superior strategies for comprehending and remembering large units of text. In addition, good readers are superior at context-free word recognition. There is some evidence indicating that good readers have automatized the recognition of word and subword units

to a greater extent than poor readers. However, good readers recognize even fully auto-mated words faster than poor readers. . . . In short, the good reader identifies words automatically and rapidly. . . . The existence of this rapid context-free recognition ability means that the word recognition of good readers is less reliant on conscious expectancies generated from the prior sentence context. The result is that more attentional capacity is left over for integrative comprehension processes. (p. 64)

Thus poor comprehenders apparently do not use the strategies that good com-prehenders do. Research by Olshavsky (1976–1977) reveals that poor readers are not proficient in using context to aid reading fluency, or in using their knowledge of the language to add information that is not in the text but would help in under-standing of the material (making inferences). Olshavsky concluded that, in general, poor readers use fewer strategies than good readers.

Good comprehenders also utilize nonverbal strategies to aid comprehension. Levin (1971) states that good comprehenders usually produce mental images while reading text. He points out that poor comprehenders understand stories as well as good comprehenders if illustrations of the story are provided. He concludes that poor comprehension may be due partly to failure to produce mental images auto-matically while reading.

Rumelhart (1980, p. 48) offers additional explanations of failure to comprehend a selection, assuming that the words are automatically recognized.

1. The reader does not have the appropriate schemata necessary (lack of con-ceptual background).
2. The reader has the appropriate schemata, but clues provided by the author are insufficient to suggest them.
3. The reader interprets the text but not in the way intended by the author.

These breakdowns are likely when reading something in a new field of study, some-thing abstract, vague, technical, or too difficult.

In conclusion, comprehension demands that the reader be active, attentive, and selective while reading. Poor reading comprehension seems related to either too much dependence on the printed word or too much dependence on contextual information (pictures included). Poor reading comprehension also implies a failure to impose structure and organization on the text as evidenced by word-by-word reading.

Assessment and Instructional Strategies for Comprehension

The remainder of this chapter examines assessment of comprehension difficulties at the word level and suggests instructional strategies. Assessment and instructional strategies are related to the subskills of decoding or recognition of individual words and the access of the meaning of these words.

Assessing Decoding Skills

The importance of quick and automatic word recognition to comprehension is made clear in the numerous studies reviewed by Stanovich (1980). For assessment strategies related to decoding refer to chapter 6.

Instructional Strategies for Increased Reading Fluency

The instructional strategies provided here are intended to increase reading fluency which in turn should enable the weak decoder to focus more on meaning than on individual words (Samuels, 1988). The increased amount of practice reading whole text should also increase the automatic recognition of words.

Predictable Language

This strategy (Walker, 1988) takes advantage of the rhythmic, repetitive, and redundant language structures in children's storybooks and nursery rhymes. The assumption is that word identification is facilitated by the predictive nature of the material. Choose a book that contains a predictable pattern such as Bill Martin's *Brown bear, Brown bear* ("Brown bear, brown bear, what do you see? I see a pink elephant looking at me. Brown bear, brown bear, what do you see? I see a yellow bird looking at me . . ."). The material should be read for the children aloud completely through first so they can hear the whole story. During this reading, emphasize the predictable parts using an enthusiastic voice. Now the children are ready for a second reading. During the second reading, ask the students to join in whenever they feel they know what to say. During subsequent readings, an oral cloze procedure can be used so students get practice predicting upcoming words in text. Finally, students are ready to read the book on their own using the predictable language pattern and picture clues to aid them. Students can also be asked to write their own story, using the same predictable pattern found in the book, only changing the characters and/or setting. For example, brown bear might become Furry Fox with a whole new list of animals that he sees.

Neurological Impress Method (NIM)

In this method (Heckelman, 1969) the student and teacher read orally in unison. Sitting side by side, with the teacher slightly behind on the right side so that he or she can read into the child's right ear, the student reads out loud with the teacher. Actually the teacher's voice will be a bit ahead of the student's, especially if the student has a limited sight vocabulary. The teacher thus models fluent and expressive reading and allows the student to experience the way that feels. The teacher does not stop when the child falters. The child is directed to continue to read with the teacher the best he or she can. The teacher should move a finger along the line of print being read so the student can follow more easily. This method does take some getting used to; initially using short, rhythmic, and repetitive materials, such as poems or nursery rhymes might prove helpful.

Repeated Readings

This procedure is exactly as it sounds, a self-selected passage is reread orally until it is read accurately and fluently (Samuels, 1979). Repeated readings encourage the use of contextual meaning and sentence structure to predict upcoming words and to correct miscues. The student chooses the material to be read. The teacher should make a copy of the passages that will be used for repeated reading so that notations can be made as the student reads. The student reads and the teacher records errors and speed. These numbers are charted on a graph. The student then practices re-reading the material silently. (During this time the teacher can work with another student.) The student then rereads the passage aloud for the second time while the teacher records errors and speed using a different color pen. Again these numbers are charted and any progress noted. This procedure is followed until a speed of 85 words per minute is achieved. There has been a substantial amount of research showing that repeated readings "helps students remember and understand more, increases their oral reading speed and accuracy, and seems to improve students' oral reading expression (Dowhower, 1989). Additionally, a modification that supports a cooperative learning approach through the use of partners, called Paired Repeated Reading (Koskinen & Blum, 1986), also seems to be effective and easy to manage in regular classrooms.

Echo Reading

Echo reading is similar to both the Neurological Impress Method and Repeated Readings in that the student is following a teacher's model and may need to repeat the reading that is being imitated. In echo reading (Walker, 1988), the teacher reads one sentence of text aloud with appropriate intonation and phrasing. The student then tries to imitate this oral reading model. The text reading continues in this fashion until the teacher feels the student can imitate more than one sentence at a time. This technique allows for the student to read text fluently that otherwise, he or she may not have been able to do. This technique can also be used in conjunction with repeated readings or neurological impress to model particularly troublesome sentences. Echo reading is quite helpful for the student who needs a model of fluent reading, for instance, students who focus too much on the words in a passage rather than the meaning, or those who show no concern for whether their oral reading sounds like fluent language.

Readers Theater

This technique provides a realistic opportunity for students to read orally and practice their use of intonation, inflection, and fluency. In Readers Theater (Sloyer, 1982), students provide a dramatic interpretation of a narrative passage through an oral interpretive reading. Character parts are assigned or selected by participating students, and appropriate parts for oral reading are identified, and then practiced silently. Following practice, the students then read their scripts orally for an audience. (Props and costumes are not necessary.) The mood of the story is conveyed through proper intonation and phrasing. This technique is especially helpful not only for fluency, but also for comprehension. When deciding what should be included in the script, the students must decide what is important in terms of dialogue and narration to the understanding of the story. Once again, the opportunity for repeated readings is present.

Assessing Knowledge of Word Meanings

Informal Measures

When assessing knowledge of word meanings, the degree of word knowledge should be considered. According to Dale, O'Rourke, and Bamman (1971), levels of familiarity with a word proceed from total ignorance ("I never saw it before"), to an awareness ("I've heard of it, but I don't know what it means"), to a general knowledge ("I recognize it in context—it has something to do with . . ."), and finally to accurate knowledge ("I know it"). Dale et al. state that in a vocabulary program concentration on levels 2 and 3 is probably best to move these *almost known* words into the category of *known* words. Therefore, in testing students' vocabulary knowledge for the purpose of discovering what students' vocabulary needs are, determining words that are at least at an awareness level is recommended.

Dale et al. (1971, p. 20) suggest four methods of testing awareness vocabulary that are easily adaptable by classroom teachers for informal assessment.

1. Identification. In this simple, most direct method, the student is asked to reply orally or in writing whether the meaning of a word is known as it is used in some material. The meaning is identified according to its definition, use, or an associated word.
2. Multiple choice. The student selects the correct meaning of the tested word from three or four definitions or examples.
3. Matching. The tested words are presented in one column and the matching definitions are presented, out of order, in another column.
4. Checking. The student checks the words he does or does not know.

Within these four groups are a variety of techniques a teacher can use to test vocabulary. Some examples follow.

Identification.   A list of words, preferably related to material the student will be asked to read, is constructed in an easy-to-read sequence. The students are asked to define (orally or in written form) checked words later. In preparation for a story on skydiving, the following list may be used:

____ sport   ____ hover
____ speed   ____ harness
____ target   ____ daredevil
____ parachute   ____ coordination
____ ripcord   ____ plummet

Multiple choice.   Words are presented in context, and several answers are provided. The student selects the best response. For example:

A. Mary was <u>hungry</u>. She wanted her _____.
                            (flower, coat, snack)

B. He bought an <u>expensive</u> gift.
   1. very beautiful
   2. did not cost too much
   3. cost a lot

Matching.   Several types of matching exercises evaluate vocabulary development. Three useful types with examples follow.

A. Matching words with definitions
   1. ____ census   a. A town near a large city
   2. ____ suburb   b. Areas where people live close
   3. ____ urban   together in towns and cities
                           c. Where people live on the surface of the earth
                           d. A count of people
                           e. The study of where people live and carry on their activities

B. Matching affixes with definitions
1. ____ pre   a. three
2. ____ es   b. someone who
3. ____ er   c. not
4. ____ bi   d. against
5. ____ un   e. two
                                         f. more than one
                                         g. before

C. Matching words with related words or phrases. These are matches of associations and not definitions. Lines are drawn to the matches. (The first match is done for you.)
1. owl   flies high
    eagle   called wise
2. canine   puppy
    feline   kitten
3. lions   pride
    geese   gaggle
4. carat   diamond
    caret   editing

Checking. The fourth method involves checking by the student. This alerts both the student and the teacher to vocabulary strengths and weaknesses. Two types of self-checking tests follow.

A. If the underlined word in the sentence is used correctly, the student puts a check beside it. If both sentences in the unit are incorrect, the student checks "neither" (Gipe, 1977).
1. ____ a. The gooey bramble stuck to the roof of his mouth.
    ____ b. The bramble caught on Mary's coat.
    ____ c. Neither
2. ____ a. Graphite will erase the mark Jim made with his pencil.
    ____ b. Graphite will leave a mark on the paper.
    ____ c. Neither
3. ____ a. The cat's cries were luminous in the night.
    ____ b. The cat's eyes were luminous in the night.
    ____ c. Neither.
4. ____ a. Our friend brought good tidings.
    ____ b. We bought some tidings from our friend.
    ____ c. Neither.

B. The student indicates on a chosen list of words how well he knows the word. The code to use might be:
+ means "I know it well."
✓ means "I know it somewhat."
O means "I've seen it or heard of it."
– means "I don't know it at all."

The following type of list, drawn from a science book, is best used analytically before a new story or unit of study.

_____ hypothesis
_____ experiment
_____ interact
_____ substance
_____ element

These testing methods are first of all intended to help the teacher determine strengths and weaknesses in students' vocabularies. They should also serve as a source of motivation for students. Once students are sensitized to words and recognize that they can expand their vocabularies, they develop a sense of excitement about words. A teacher who is enthusiastic about developing vocabulary will, in turn, enhance the child's enthusiasm. Many exercises on word meanings are found in workbooks and teacher's manuals accompanying basal readers. These exercises also serve as informal tests for vocabulary at an awareness level.

For assessment of full conceptual knowledge of vocabulary, the tasks required must be more sensitive to the specific dimensions of the vocabulary items than those used for assessing an awareness level. Simpson (1987) suggests a hierarchy of four processes that in turn suggest formats for assessing full conceptual knowledge. The four processes are:

(1) Students should be able to recognize and generate the critical attributes, examples, and nonexamples of a concept. . . .
(2) Students should be able to sense and infer relationships between concepts and their own background information. . . .
(3) Students should be able to recognize and apply the concept to a variety of contexts. . . .
(4) Students should be able to generate novel contexts for the targeted concept. (p. 22)

Simpson also provides examples of alternative formats for these four processes.

Formal Measures

The vocabulary subtests in most standardized reading achievement tests probably are not valid measures of knowledge of word meanings for disabled readers (Bond & Tinker, 1967, p. 281). Many disabled readers are not able to identify or pronounce the words in the test. This does not necessarily mean that they do not know the meanings. Oral administration of the test, as is possible with informal measures, would invalidate the norms for the test, however.

Examples of standardized tests that contain vocabulary subtests more appropriate for use with disabled readers are the *Gates-McKillop-Horowitz Reading Diagnostic Tests* and the *Stanford Diagnostic Reading Test*.

Instructional Strategies for Word Meanings

The usual types of corrective instruction for vocabulary often are not successful with the corrective student. As noted earlier in this chapter, teachers usually provide additional practice when children demonstrate a weakness in a specific area. This instructional strategy is frequently disappointing.

General Instructional Strategies

While meaning vocabulary is certainly learned incidentally through experience and reading (Nagy, Anderson, & Herman, 1987), this way of learning vocabulary is slow and not at all predictable (Dale & O'Rourke, 1986). Readers with limited meaning vocabularies must receive direct and intense instruction in vocabulary (Gipe, 1977; Hare, 1975; Jackson & Dizney, 1963; Nagy, 1988; Pany & Jenkins, 1978; Petty, Herold, & Stoll, 1968; Wixson, 1984). Planned lessons for vocabulary development may include firsthand experience, such as field trips, in-class demonstrations, or laboratory experiences in math or science. Related discussions before, during, and after the experience use the key vocabulary words.

Vocabulary is usually taught by other than firsthand experiences, however. Words should be taught that help corrective readers comprehend material on their instructional reading levels and understand content area class discussions. These words are found in the readers and content area materials being used in the classroom.

Most methods of teaching new vocabulary involve the use of context. Typically, teachers present new vocabulary words by writing sentences on the board. Meanings are discussed, and the material is then read. For corrective readers this kind of vocabulary instruction may not be enough, however. According to Goodman (1985), "it is a mistake to think that vocabulary-building exercises [alone] can produce improved comprehension. Language is learned in the context of its use. Word meanings are built in relationship to concepts; language facilitates learning, but it is the conceptual development that creates the need for the language. Without that, words are empty forms. So vocabulary is built in the course of language use including reading. It is probably more accurate to say that people have big vocabularies because they read a lot than that they read well because they have big vocabularies" (p. 838).

As noted earlier in the discussion of schema theory and comprehension, schemata relevant to the reader's task (in this case, learning the meaning of a new word) must be activated. Vocabulary instruction that provides this activation is most effective. Research by Wittrock, Marks, and Doctorow (1975) indicate that students learn and retain many new vocabulary words when the words are introduced in familiar, meaningful sentences and stories. Therefore, vocabulary instruction that helps students to (1) relate new vocabulary to what they already know, (2) develop broader understanding of word knowledge in a variety of contexts, (3) become actively involved in learning new words, and (4) develop strategies for independent vocabulary acquisition is desirable (Carr & Wixson, 1986). Marzano and Marzano (1988) provide four clear principles for vocabulary instruction:

1. Wide reading and language rich activities should be the primary vehicles for vocabulary learning. Given the large number of words students encounter in written and oral language, general language development must be encouraged as one of the most important vocabulary development strategies.

2. Direct vocabulary instruction should focus on words considered important to a given content area or to general background knowledge. Since effective direct vocabulary instruction requires a fair amount of time and complexity, teachers should select words for instruction that promise a high yield in student learning of general knowledge or of knowledge of a particular topic of instructional importance.

3. Direct vocabulary instruction should include many ways of knowing a word and provide for the development of a complex level of word knowledge. Since word knowledge is

stored in many forms (mental pictures, kinesthetic associations, smells, tastes, semantic distinctions, linguistic references), direct vocabulary instruction should take advantage of many of these forms and not emphasize one to the exclusion of others.

4. Direct vocabulary instruction should include a structure by which new words not taught directly can be learned readily. Again, given the large number of words students encounter and the limited utility of direct instruction, some structure must be developed to allow the benefits of direct vocabulary instruction to go beyond the words actually taught. (pp. 11–12)

Research by Gipe (1978–1979, 1980) indicates that new word meanings are effectively taught by providing appropriate and familiar context. A four-step procedure is recommended. Students are given a passage in which the first sentence uses the new word appropriately, thereby providing valuable syntactic and semantic information. The context is composed of familiar words and situations. The second sentence of the passage describes some of the attributes of the new word. As with the first sentence, terms are already familiar to the students. The third sentence defines the new word, with care being taken to use familiar concepts. The last sentence gives the students an opportunity to relate the new word to their own lives by asking them to write an answer to a question about the word's meaning or to complete an open-ended statement that requires application of the word's meaning. An example of a complete passage follows:

The boys who wanted to sing together formed a *quintet*. There were five boys singing in the *quintet*. *Quintet* means a group of five, and this group usually sings or plays music. If you were in a *quintet*, what instrument would you want to play?

Talk Through (Piercey, 1982) is another technique that recognizes the importance of helping students relate what they already know to a word that is unfamiliar or has multiple meanings. In *Talk Through*, the teacher identifies key concept words, perhaps prior to a content area reading selection, that students are likely to find difficult. These words may be totally new, introduced previously, or possessing a different meaning from the common meaning.

The teacher begins by using the word in a sentence on the chalkboard.

The frog has gone through a complete *metamorphosis* from its days as a tadpole.[3]

At this point the teacher helps relate the meaning of the new word to students' own lives and personal experiences. The teacher *asks* students for input, as opposed to telling them what the word means. For example,

"Jerry, remember when you brought in a tree branch that had a cocoon attached to it? What made that cocoon?"

Jerry answers, "The caterpillars in the trees in my backyard made that cocoon."

"Class, does anyone remember what happened to the cocoon?—Lisa?"

Lisa responds, "One day a butterfly came out of it."

"Yes, and right after that happened remember I read you the story of *The Very Hungry Caterpillar* by Eric Carle. What happened to *that* caterpillar?—Tony?"

---

[3] The author wishes to thank Mr. Herbert Ellis, Jr., a former student, for the ideas behind this example.

Tony relates, "The caterpillar ate one bite out of lots of different things, leaves, apples, tomatoes, and then it went to sleep inside a cocoon. Then one day it became a butterfly."

The next step the teacher takes is to write the word of interest in isolation,

metamorphosis

then writes

meta   +   morphe
(over)   (shape or form)

and says, "metamorphosis comes from two Greek words—over and shape or form— combined to mean the shape or form of something changes over to a different shape or form. Our experience with the cocoon and the story of *The Very Hungry Caterpillar* showed us that the *shape* or *form* of a caterpillar changed *over* to the shape or form of a butterfly. That is what metamorphosis means."

At this point the teacher seeks to relate the new word further to students' lives.

"What else goes through a metamorphosis that you are familiar with?"

Responses: "We had some mealworms once to feed out pet chameleon. They changed into beetles."

"I think some caterpillars change into moths."

"My mom told me that flies lay eggs that hatch out little white worms. And then later on those worms turn back into flies."

"I saw a movie once where a man turned into a wolf."

"Frogs must change—it's in the sentence on the board."

And so it goes! The concept of metamorphosis is more meaningful now than if the students were simply told what it meant and then told to read the text containing the subject matter.

Corrective readers also must be taught how to use context clues and structural analysis clues to help them determine the meanings of unknown words (chapter 6). The easiest vocabulary exercises employ simple associations. Students use knowledge already in their schemata to work with synonyms, antonyms, homophones, **associative words** that often occur together (e.g., green-grass, bacon-eggs), and classifying (e.g., animal: dog, cat, horse).

The following activities can be used as the core of lessons designed to promote vocabulary development. For these activities to be considered instructional, student and teacher must interact. If they are done independently, they become practice activities.

Synonyms

Children are often taught that synonyms are words that have the same meaning. This is not exactly true, however. Synonyms have *similar* meaning, which allows us to express the same idea in a variety of ways.

The study of synonyms is probably the easiest and most efficient place to start expanding students' vocabularies because it starts with a familiar word. The child already has a schema for the known word; by comparing synonyms the child sees the relationships between words and is able to further generalize and classify words, thus enhancing the schema. Some characteristic synonym activities follow.[4]

1. Underline the word that means about the same as the word underlined in the sentence. (Note that this activity encourages the use of context clues.) We almost missed Sue's name because she wrote so <u>tiny</u>.

    large   small   big   hot

2. Match the words with about the same meaning.

    1. ____ large   a. unhappy[5]
    2. ____ tiny   b. big
    3. ____ hen   c. chicken
    4. ____ sad   d. small

3. Circle the two words that could complete each sentence.
    a. The clown did a _____ right in front of us.
        treat   stunt   trick
    b. The neighborhood kids play baseball in the _____ lot.
        empty   vacant   full
    c. A large tree _____ blew down in the storm.
        branch   leaf   limb

4. Use the words in the box to complete the paragraph. Each word will be used twice, and it will have a different meaning each time. A synonym has been provided in parentheses for each space.

keen   slim   serious

    The hikers were (eager) _____ to reach the cabin. The approaching storm could be (dangerous) _____. Already, a (sharp) _____ wind was blowing, and the possibility of finding a cave to shelter in was (unlikely) _____. "Come on," said the guide, a tall, (thin) _____ woman. Her expression was (solemn) _____.

This format is easily adapted to language experience stories with the use of a thesaurus.

Comparing synonyms helps students see the relationships between words of similar meaning and also recognize that fine distinctions often should be made. Before these fine discriminations are possible, however, gross discriminations, as in the first three exercises, must be mastered. For example, the word *tiny* from the first set of exercises has many "synonyms" (little, small, minute, diminutive, miniature, microscopic, and so on). However, all of these terms are not interchangeable. The use of contextual clues and a dictionary will help the student determine the most appropriate shade of meaning for the following sentences.

---

[4] From Dale, O'Rourke, & Barbe, *Vocabulary building: A process approach.* Columbus, OH: Zaner–Bloser, 1986, p. 85

[5] Note how the structural clue, the prefix *un,* can help with this task.

1. We all agreed that Mary's feet were _____ but smaller yet were Sue's
   small   tiny

   _____ feet.
   small   tiny

2. The doll was an exact _____ of a real British soldier.
   miniature   diminutive

The meanings of synonyms, while similar, are not exactly the same. Choosing a synonym depends on how the word is used. Dale, O'Rourke, and Barbe (1986) provide an excellent example for synonyms of the word *get*. The student is directed to write the best word to use in place of *get. Buy, catch,* and *win* are the synonyms.

1. I will <u>get</u> the ball you throw.
2. The fastest runner will <u>get</u> a prize.
3. Will you <u>get</u> a new sweater at the store? (p. 85)

This type of activity is especially valuable during editing of students' written stories.

Antonyms

Just as no two synonyms are exactly alike in meaning, no two antonyms are exact opposites. To develop the concept of opposites, however, antonyms can be grouped according to their general meaning. Most activities suggested for synonyms can be modified for antonyms:

1. The student is instructed to change the underlined word so the sentence will have almost the opposite meaning.

   Jack <u>hates</u> to read.
   Spot is a <u>fat</u> dog.
   It is a <u>hot</u> morning.

   The study of antonyms is readily adapted to the use of structural analysis clues. The teacher can purposely present pairs of words to illustrate how opposites result from the addition of certain prefixes and suffixes (e.g., happy-unhappy; fear-fearless)

2. Antonym trees are useful to help study the formation of antonyms (fig. 7.1). Given a root word at the base of the tree, students prepare "leaves" for the tree by writing words that mean the opposite of the root word. Students soon discover the use of prefixes and suffixes in forming antonyms. Some antonyms formed from prefixes and suffixes are listed below (Dale et. al., 1971, p. 57).

   Prefixes Forming Antonyms

<u>in</u>doors	vs.	<u>out</u>doors	<u>pre</u>paid	vs.	<u>post</u>paid
<u>in</u>flate	vs.	<u>de</u>flate	<u>post</u>test	vs.	<u>pre</u>test
<u>in</u>hale	vs.	<u>ex</u>hale	<u>sub</u>ordinate	vs.	<u>super</u>ordinate
<u>under</u>fed	vs.	<u>over</u>fed	<u>pro</u>gress	vs.	<u>re</u>gress

   Suffixes Forming Antonyms

worth<u>y</u>	vs.	worth<u>less</u>	lion	vs.	lion<u>ess</u>

beardless	vs.	bearded	widow	vs.	widower
useless	vs.	useful	hero	vs.	heroine

3. The student is told to read the sentence and choose the word that best completes the sentence.

<u>Cowardly</u> means the opposite of a person who is ____.
timid   courageous   fearful

Was the bread <u>fresh</u>, or had it become _____?
burned   stale   delicious

Homophones

Words that sound alike but are different in spelling and meaning are called **homophones.** Homophones may confuse encoding and decoding tasks (e.g., distinguishing between *reed* and *read*) but may help the comprehension task (e.g., the reader knows *reed* refers to a tall grass).

As with synonyms and antonyms, the student needs much practice discriminating between one homophone and another. In the activities that follow, several approaches are presented.

1. Students practice exercises in which they are given a word and asked to supply its homophone. This task begins simply by giving letter-space clues.

   bear, <u>b</u> <u>a</u> r e   stare, <u>s</u> <u>t</u> <u>a</u> i <u>r</u>
   cite, <u>s</u> <u>i</u> g <u>h</u> <u>t</u>   hour, <u>o</u> <u>u</u> r

FIGURE 7.1 Antonym tree. Students make leaves with words opposite in meaning to the "root" word at the base of the tree.

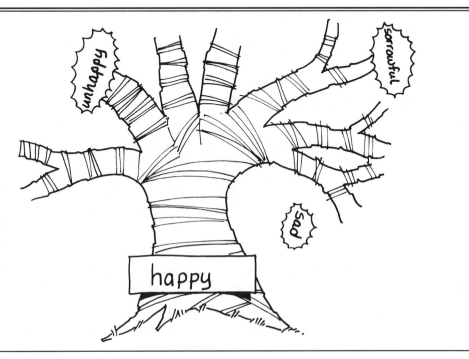

2. The student is directed to choose the correct homophone using context clues.
   a. They met on the (stairs, stares).
   b. They spent a (weak, week) at the beach.
   c. We stayed for the (hole, whole) game.
   d. (Meet, Meat) me at six o'clock.
3. The student is directed to supply the correct homophone utilizing definition clues.
   a. It stops a bike. It sounds like break. _____
   b. It's an animal skin. It sounds like fir. _____
   c. Boats stop here. It sounds like peer. _____
   d. It's taking what doesn't belong to you. It sounds like steel. _____

Associative Words

Unexpected responses for associative activities are not uncommon. The teacher must be flexible regarding acceptable responses for association activities.

- The student is directed to underline the word that best fits the sentence. Responses should be discussed as to why one choice is better than another.

   The sky is so _____ it looks like the ocean.
      blue   orange   red

- The student matches the word in the first column with one from the second column that is usually associated with it.

   1. ___ tall   a. tiger
   2. ___ electric   b. buildings
   3. ___ green   c. energy
   4. ___ ferocious   d. sky
   5. ___ blue   e. fields

Classifying or Categorizing Activities

Instruction in classifying and categorizing develops an understanding of word relationships. Once a new word is identified as belonging to an already familiar category, all attributes of the known category can be assigned to the new word, and the new word becomes known. This is also an example of how schemata are expanded. Consider the familiar category, colors, and *azure* as the unfamiliar word. Once azure is identified as a color, it receives all the attributes that may be associated with color (e.g., hue, shade, brilliance). Even further, once azure is identified as the color of the blue sky, it will take on the additional attributes of the already familiar word *blue*.

A teacher can present classification or categorization activities in many ways. The following general formats can be modified to accommodate many categorizing needs. The same formats provide the basis for classification games.

1. Direct categorization. The student is given a worksheet with category titles and a set of words to be categorized. The student lists the words under the appropriate category title.

Word sorting (Gillet & Temple, 1990, pp. 255–260) is also used to involve students in categorizing. For example, a group (or individual) may be given a set of words that represent several different common elements:

blue   pencil   desk
paper   book   apple
green   red   peach

The group sorts the words (e.g., blue, green, red; paper, pencil, desk; apple, peach) and reads out the words in one group to the rest of the class. Those listening must determine the category title (e.g., colors; things used to write or things found in school; fruits).

2. Categorizing by omission. The student is given a set of words (e.g., four, too, six, eight) and asked to indicate the word that does *not* fit the category represented by the majority of the words. Subsequent discussion reveals the category title.

3. Structured vocabulary overview. In preparation for, or in review of, a unit of study it is helpful to fit words into categories. For example, a unit on algae might call for the categories of "Microscopic" and "Nonmicroscopic." The specialized vocabulary items to be classified might be desmids, Irish moss, brown kelp, and diatoms. "Fresh Water" and "Sea Water" are two additional titles for classifying these same words.

4. Looking for common elements. The student is given a group of words that all have something in common. The student decides what the words have in common. For example, given the words buffalo, prairie dog, and eagle, the student may conclude that all these make their habitat in the Great Plains.

5. Word maps. The Frayer model of concept attainment (Frayer, Frederick, & Klausmeier, 1969) provides a basis for word map activities. This model offers a structure that encourages the independent learning of new word meanings. Briefly, concepts are presented in relation to relevant and irrelevant attributes, examples and nonexamples, and supraordinate, coordinate, and subordinate aspects of the concept. Using the Frayer model leads readily to thinking about new words in relation to known, related words. A new concept can be "mapped" using the following structures:

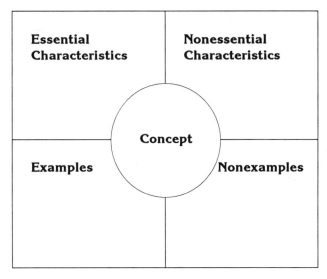

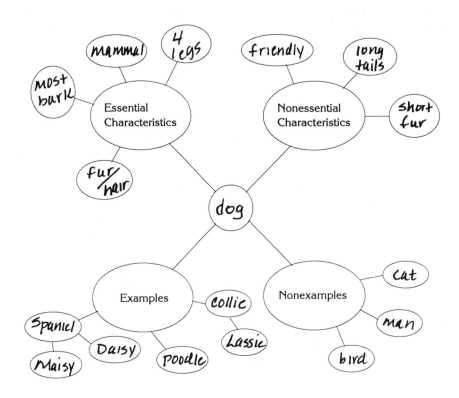

Similarly, Schwartz and Raphael (1985) present a word map that describes three types of relationships: "(1) the general class to which the concept belongs, (2) the primary properties of the concept and those that distinguish it from other members of the class, and (3) examples of the concept" (p. 200). An example of a word map is graphically displayed here.

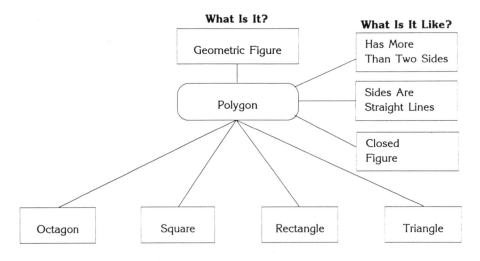

Specialized Vocabulary

The **specialized vocabulary** of content areas must also be taught directly. Content area materials may introduce ten or more technical (a meaning of a common word form specific to a content field, Harris & Hodges, 1981) or unfamiliar words on a page. These words are not usually repeated often, nor are they unimportant words to the understanding of the material. They are usually labels for important concepts being discussed. For example, in the area of social studies, abstract words such as *culture, technology,* and *adaptation* may be unfamiliar but extremely important to understanding the material. Not all words in content area materials are new in terms of pronunciation, however. Common words such as *mouth, matter, suit,* or *recess,* may be confusing if a specialized meaning is attached to them. While most students associate the word *recess* with time out to play, a different meaning is presented in the following sentence: "When it was time to do his homework, Bob hid in the *recess* hoping that his mother would not find him." *Mouth* may refer to the facial cavity, to a part of a musical instrument, or to the place where a stream enters a larger body of water. Content area materials abound with words that have multiple meanings.

Instructional Strategies for Specialized Vocabulary. Under most circumstances assessment of specialized vocabulary for a content area is not necessary. Instead the teacher may safely assume that the specialized words are unknown and proceed with teaching strategies.

Most teachers at all levels agree that specialized vocabulary representing a crucial concept is best introduced before the lesson. For example, the teacher may (1) give the students a sentence using the new word and assume that the context will teach the meaning or (2) give the students a list of words (perhaps as part of a study guide or simply to copy from the board) and direct them to look up each word's meaning in the book's glossary and copy it down. This second technique assumes that the definition per se will be clearly understood by the students.

These techniques are essentially useless without discussion. New words can be discussed in many ways that greatly enhance understanding of their meaning and, in turn, understanding of the material read. The new concept should be related to something already familiar to the students (Gipe, 1980). For example, the students may be studying history and are about to confront the word *tariff,* which is unfamiliar. While *tariff* is new, the word *tax* is probably not. Thus, any discussion about the new word should include mention of taxes and experiences students have had with them, such as not being able to buy a 29¢ item unless they have more money for the tax.

New terms are probably best taught as new concepts. In addition to relating the new word to familiar concepts, the specific characteristics of the new concept must become part of the students' understanding as well. Eventually the students must be able to distinguish examples and nonexamples of the particular concept. For instance, if the concept of *symmetry* is new, the teacher may first provide the students with pictures or three-dimensional models of objects that demonstrate symmetry (fig. 7.2). A discussion of what the objects have in common should follow.

One specific technique developed not only for introducing new vocabulary but also for introducing overall organization of a selection to include important concepts is the **structured overview.** This particular technique, developed by Richard Barron (1969), uses a graphic representation of terms that are indispensable to the essence

FIGURE **7.2** Pictures used to teach the concept of symmetry.

of the selection to be read. The graphic representation makes this technique doubly attractive for the corrective reader. The steps for developing and using a structured overview are as follows:

1. List the vocabulary words that are important to understanding the selection. (This analysis could include both familiar and new words.)
2. Arrange these words so they show the interrelationships among the concepts represented.
3. Add to the diagram vocabulary that the students understand and that further helps to show relationships.
4. Evaluate the diagram. Does it clearly depict the major relationships? Can it be simplified, but still communicate the important ideas?
5. Introduce the lesson by displaying the diagram (perhaps as a transparency using an overhead projector). Explain why you arranged the terms the way you did. Encourage the students to contribute any information they have. Give each student familiar vocabulary terms on slips of paper. As you discuss the overview, the students then help construct it by placing their vocabulary terms in logical positions.
6. As the selection is read, continue to relate the new information to the structured overview.

An example of a structured overview was developed for a section of a social studies text dealing with explorers coming to the New World (fig. 7.3). Students had previously studied the Incan, Aztec, and Mayan cultures.

Other examples of content area structured overviews can be found in Richard A. Earle's *Teaching Reading and Mathematics* (1976) and Judith Thelan's *Improving Reading in Science* (1976).

Burmeister (1978) presents teaching strategies for words that have both common and specialized meanings. She suggests a two-part activity: part 1 demonstrates the common meanings, and part 2 uses sentences with blanks for the unique meanings. The students fill in the blanks in part 2. Burmeister provides examples for several content areas; a few items follow for clarification.

FIGURE 7.3 Example of a structured overview for social studies.

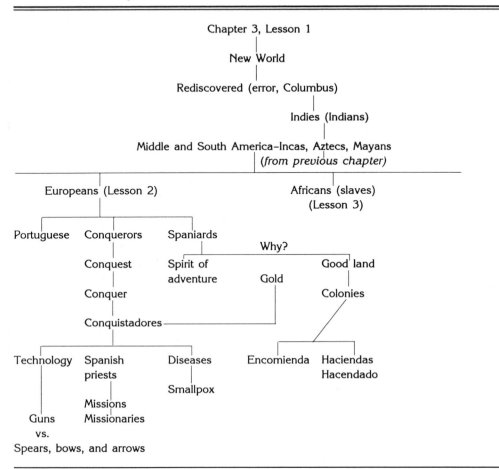

Mathematics

Part 1

Term	Common Use
1. difference	You know the *difference* between right and wrong.
2. root	The tree *root* was growing through the sidewalk.
3. base	Jim made it to first *base*.

Part 2
1. The subtraction operation finds the (difference) between two numbers.
2. Find the square (root) of 9.
3. The (base) of the triangle is 10 cm. long.

Activities that reinforce the idea that words may have several meanings are worthwhile. Such activities are commonly found in reading workbooks (fig. 7.4). Similar activities can easily be developed by the teacher for any lesson; simply use the dictionary and put together a list of sentences directly from the material of interest.

FIGURE 7.4 Examples of workbook activites for words with more than one meaning. (From Skills Handbook for *All Sorts of Things* of the READING 360 series by Theodore Clymer and others. © Copyright 1973, 1969 by Ginn and Company [Xerox Corporation]. Used with permission.)

Words with More Than One Meaning

You know that a word can have more than one meaning. Read each sentence below and think of one word that will fit in both blanks. The word you need rhymes with the word after each sentence.

1. I walked back to the camp with a pack on my back . (**sack**)

2. The bus went past an old house built in the past . (**fast**)

3. We will rest the rest of the time to keep from getting tired. (**best**)

4. A bump on the head caused him to head for the doctor. (**bread**)

5. Watch me wind my new watch . (**splotch**)

6. A light tap caused the electric light to go on. (**bright**)

7. He struck the palm tree with the palm of his hand. (**calm**)

8. Before he had walked 200 feet , his feet hurt. (**meet**)

9. We lit a fire just before they were ready to fire the rocket. (**tire**)

Which Meaning Is the Right One?

The glossary meanings are given for each word below. In the blank before each sentence, write the number of the meaning which fits the word as it is used in the sentence.

ferry　1. a boat that carries people and goods back and forth across a body of water, such as a river or bay. **2.** to carry people and goods across a stretch of water in a boat. **3.** to cross a stretch of water on a ferry.

observation　1. the act or power of seeing and noting something. **2.** something seen and noted. **3.** the fact of being seen: to try to avoid observation. **4.** a remark: to make an observation. **5.** for use in viewing or looking closely at something: an observation tower.

pedestal　1. the support or base on which a column or statue stands. **2.** the base of a tall lamp, vase, or the like.

spiral　1. a winding coil that gradually widens. **2.** to wind around a central point in circles that gradually grow larger. **3.** shaped like a spiral.

tablet　1. a flat sheet of some material, such as bronze, bearing an inscription. **2.** sheets of paper fastened together, used for writing letters, notes, or the like.

　2　　1. The boat will ferry them across.

　1　　2. We rode a ferry to the island.

　2　　3. The pedestal of the lamp was broken.

　1　　4. The statue stood on a pedestal.

　5　　5. They stood on the observation platform.

　1 or 4　　6. He made an observation about the weather.

　1　　7. There were words carved on the tablet.

　2　　8. Did you write on the tablet?

　2　　9. The road spirals around the mountain.

　1　　10. The spiral wound around the tower.

Once new words and concepts are introduced, they can be practiced in many ways. Probably the most effective activities are those that require students to relate the new words to their own experiences and to use or apply the concept involved. *Word Theater* (Barnell Loft) is an example of published material that attempts to involve students actively with the use and application of new words (fig. 7.5).

Published materials are not required. The new word probably will not be learned unless students see its relevance or use in their own lives and have opportunities for appropriate application.

Some excellent general formats for specialized vocabulary instruction and practice follow. Each activity is easily modified to fit the needs of the teacher in any content area.

Word Pairs (Stevenson & Baumann, 1979)
Use a table that allows students to show the relationship of various word pairs. Students may add word pairs to the list. The word relationships should be discussed.

Example:

Word Pair	Almost the Same	Opposite	Go Together	Not Related
land-sea		X		
ship-galleon	X			
merchant-commerce			X	
pirate-bread				X

Semantic Mapping (Johnson & Pearson, 1984; Stevenson & Baumann, 1979)

1. Select a word central to the material to be read (e.g., transportation), or from any other source of classroom interest. Write it on the chalkboard.
2. Ask the class to think of as many words as they can that are related in some way to the word you have written. Jot them on paper.
3. Have individuals share the words they have written. As they do, write the words on the board and attempt to put them into categories.
4. Number the categories and have the students name them:
   a. Kinds of transportation
   b. Places we can travel to
   c. Reasons for transportation
5. Discuss the words. This is crucial to the success of semantic mapping. Students then learn meanings of new words, new meanings for known words, and see relationships between words.
6. If time permits, select one word from the existing semantic map and begin to develop a new one (e.g., start a new map with the word *exploration*).

Constrained Categorization (Stevenson & Baumann, 1979)
Give students a chart with relevant category titles listed across the top and various letters listed along the side. Have students fill in the chart using a word that fits the category and also begins with a certain letter. Some of the words should be available in the material read. Others can be researched by groups or individuals.

FIGURE 7.5 Example skit card from *Word Theater* by Richard A. Boning. Copyright 1978, Barnell Loft, Ltd., Baldwin, NY. Reprinted with permission.

WORD THEATER

(2)   SKIT C 178

Write _____ **trade** _____ on the chalkboard.

You and your friend are talking about your parents' jobs. You say that your parents work for a company that trades all over North America. Your friend asks if it *does business* in Canada and Mexico. You say it *buys and sells* in all North American countries.

ANSWER

to do business/to buy and sell

1. Do you know the names of any companies that trade all over the country?

2. Has any person or company ever not traded fairly with you or with anyone you know?

© 1978 Barnett Loft, Ltd., Baldwin, NY   AW

Steps

1. The cast reads and translates the skit into their own words.

2. The cast writes the word on the chalkboard.

3. The audience pronounces the word and thinks about its meanings.

4. The vocabulary concept is *dramatized* by the cast.

5. The audience attempts to tell the precise meaning as evidenced by the skit.

6. The cast gives the definition.

7. The audience answers the two questions.

8. The audience writes the word and the meaning in their notebooks.

9. The pupils utilize one or more of the reinforcers mentioned in the **Instructions to the Teacher**.

10. After each session the pupils review all the words introduced in that session.

11. The cast creates very short sentences featuring the key word, and inserts them in their SPREAD THE WORD BUTTONS.

Example:

	Solids	Liquids	Gases
S	salt		
C		coffee	carbon dioxide
I	ice		
E		ether	ethylene
N			neon
C		cleaning fluid	
E	earth		

Semantic Feature Analysis

1. Select a category *(shelters)*
2. List, in a column, some words within the category *(tent, hut)*.
3. List, in a row, some features shared by some of the words *(small, exquisite)*.
4. Put pluses or minuses beside each word beneath each feature.
5. Add additional words.
6. Add additional features.
7. Complete the expanded matrix with pluses and minuses.
8. Discover and discuss the uniqueness of each word.
9. Repeat the process with another category.

	large	small	exquisite	lovely	rustic
villa	+	–	+	+	–
cabin	–	+	–	–	+
shed	–	+	–	–	+
barn	+	–	–	–	+
tent	–	+	–	–	–

From *Teaching Reading Vocabulary*, 2d ed., by Dale D. Johnson and P. David Pearson. Copyright © 1984 by Holt, Rinehart and Winston. Reprinted by permission of CBS College Publishing, New York.

Other beginning categories:

games	vegetables	pets
occupations	food	clothing
tools	buildings	animals
plants	transportation	

Later categories:

moods	sizes	entertainment
feelings	shapes	modes of
commands	musical instruments	communication

Do You Know Your Sports? (Chant & Pelow, 1979)

Note to the teacher: Many words may be categorized under two headings. For instance, *center* refers to a position played in football or basketball. *Yards* relates to the

FIGURE 7.6 Sport terms include compound words and can be used to study the latter.

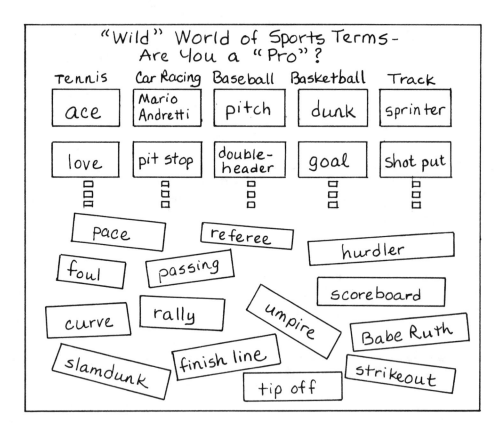

number of yards on a golf drive or the number gained or lost on a particular play in football. Simply color code the answer key to include more than one answer. In addition, many compound words may be found among sports terms (fig. 7.6). Why not use these terms to study compound words?

Summary

A student who is successful with these basic vocabulary activities will be ready for instruction in some of the more difficult aspects of vocabulary development (e.g., analogies, connotative and denotative meanings, figures of speech, and word origins). Because these aspects of vocabulary are not easily learned, a firm vocabulary base is essential. For examples of strategies and other suggestions related to these aspects, Dale, O'Rourke, and Bamman's *Techniques of Teaching Vocabulary* (1971), chapter 4 in Pearson and Johnson's *Teaching Reading Comprehension* (1978), and more recent texts on developmental reading are suggested.

References

Adams, M. J., & Collins, A. M. (1979). A schema-theoretic view of reading. In R. O. Freedle (Ed.), *Discourse processing: Multidisciplinary perspectives*. Norwood, NJ: Ablex.

Anderson, R. C. (1977). The notion of schemata and the educational enterprise. In R. C. Anderson, R. J. Spiro, and W. E. Montague (Eds.), *Schooling and the acquisition of knowledge*. Hillsdale, NJ: Erlbaum.

Anderson, R. C., & Freebody, P. (1981). Vocabulary knowledge. In J. Guthrie (Ed.), *Comprehension and teaching: Research reviews* (pp. 77–117). Newark, DE: International Reading Association.

Barron, R. F. (1969). The use of vocabulary as an advance organizer. In H. Herber and P. Sanders (Eds.), *Research in reading in the content areas: First year report*. Syracuse, NY: Syracuse University Press.

Bartlett, F. C. (1932). *Remembering: A study in experimental and social psychology*. New York: Cambridge University Press.

Bartolome, P. I. (1969). Teachers' objectives and questions in primary reading. *The Reading Teacher, 23*, 27–33.

Bobrow, D. G., & Norman, P. A. (1975). Some principles of memory schemata. In D. G. Bobrow and A. M. Collins (Eds.), *Representation and understanding: Studies in cognitive science*. New York: Academic Press.

Bond, G. L., & Tinker, M. A. (1967). *Reading difficulties: Their diagnosis and correction*. New York: Appleton-Century-Crofts.

Burmeister, L. E. (1978). *Reading strategies for middle and secondary school teachers*. Reading, MA: Addison-Wesley.

Carr, E., & Wixson, K. K. (1986). Guidelines for evaluating vocabulary instruction. *Journal of Reading, 29*, 588–595.

Carroll, J. B., & Freedle, R. O. (Eds.). (1972). *Language comprehension and the acquisition of knowledge*. Washington, DC: V. H. Winston.

Chant, S. A., & Pelow, R. A. (1979). *Activities for functional reading and language: Preschool through middle school*. Paper presented at the annual meeting of the International Reading Association, Atlanta.

Clark, E. V. (1973). What's in a word? On the child's acquisition of semantics in his first language. In T. E. Moore (Ed.), *Cognitive development and the acquisition of language*. New York: Academic Press.

Dale, E., O'Rourke, J., & Bamman, H. A. (1971). *Techniques of teaching vocabulary*. Palo Alto, CA: Field Educational Publications.

Dale, E., O'Rourke, J., & Barbe, W. (1986). *Vocabulary building: A process approach*. Columbus, OH: Zaner-Bloser.

Davis, F. B. (1944). Fundamental factors of comprehension in reading. *Psychometrika, 9*, 185–197.

Dowhower, S. L. (1989). Repeated reading: Research into practice. *The Reading Teacher, 42*, 502–507.

Durkin, D. (1981). Reading comprehension instruction in five basal reading series. *Reading Research Quarterly, 14*, 515–544.

Earle, R. A. (1976). *Teaching reading and mathematics.* Newark, DE: International Reading Association.

Ekwall, E. E., & Shanker, J. L. (1983). *Diagnosis and remediation of the disabled reader.* Boston: Allyn and Bacon.

Fillmore, C. J. (1968). The case for case. In E. Bach and R. T. Harms (Eds.), *Universals in linguistic theory.* New York: Holt, Rinehart and Winston.

Frayer, D. A., Frederick, W. C., & Klausmeier, H. J. (1969). A schema for testing the level of concept mastery. (Tech. Rep. No. 16). Madison, WI: University of Wisconsin R & D Center for Cognitive Learning.

Geyer, J. J. (1970). Models of perceptual processes in reading. In H. Singer and R. B. Ruddell (Eds.), *Theoretical models and processes of reading.* Newark, DE: International Reading Association.

Gillet, J. W., & Temple, C. (1990). *Understanding reading problems: Assessment and instruction* (3rd ed). Glenview, IL: Scott, Foresman/Little, Brown.

Gipe, J. P. (1977). *An investigation of the effectiveness of four techniques for teaching word meanings with third and fifth grade students.* Unpublished doctoral dissertation, Purdue University, West Lafayette, IN.

Gipe, J. P. (1978–1979). Investigating techniques for teaching word meanings. *Reading Research Quarterly, 14,* 624–644.

Gipe, J. P. (1980). Use of a relevant context helps kids learn new word meanings. *The Reading Teacher, 33,* 398–402.

Golinkoff, R. M. (1975–1976). A comparison of reading comprehension processes in good and poor comprehenders. *Reading Research Quarterly, 11,* 623–659.

Goodman, K. S. (1973). Psycholinguistic universals in the reading process. In F. Smith (Ed.), *Psycholinguistics and reading.* New York: Holt, Rinehart and Winston.

Goodman, K. S. (1967). Reading: A psycholinguistic guessing game. *Journal of the Reading Specialist, 6,* 126–135.

Goodman, K. S. (Ed.). (1968). *The psycholinguistic nature of the reading process.* Detroit: Wayne State University.

Goodman, K. S. (1985). Transactional psycholinguistic model. In H. Singer and R. B. Ruddell (Eds.), *Theoretical models and processes of reading* (pp. 813–840). Newark, DE: International Reading Association.

Gorman, A. (1961). Recognition memory for nouns as a function of abstractness and frequency. *Journal of Experimental Psychology, 61,* 23–29.

Gough, P. B. (1972). One second of reading. In J. F. Kavanagh and I. G. Mattingly (Eds.), *Language by ear and eye.* Cambridge, MA: MIT Press.

Guszak, F. J. (1967). Teachers' questions and levels of reading comprehension. In T. C. Barrett (Ed.), *The evaluation of children's reading achievement.* Newark, DE: International Reading Association.

Hare, S. Z. (1975). *An investigation of the effectiveness of three methods of teaching reading vocabulary.* Unpublished doctoral dissertation, University of South Carolina, Columbia.

Hargis, C., & Gickling, E. (1978). The function of imagery in word recognition development. *The Reading Teacher, 31,* 870–874.

Heckelman, R. G. (1969). A neurological-impress method of remedial reading instruction. *Academic Therapy, 4,* 277–282.

Hittleman, D. R. (1983). *Developmental reading, K–8: Teaching from a psycholinguistic perspective.* Boston: Houghton Mifflin.

Hochberg, J. (1970). Components of literacy: Speculation and exploratory research. In H. Levin and J. Williams (Eds.), *Basic studies in reading.* New York: Basic Books.

Huey, E. B. (1977). *The psychology and pedagogy of reading.* Cambridge, Mass.: MIT Press. (First published in 1908 by Macmillan.)

Irwin, J. W. (1986). *Teaching reading comprehension processes.* Englewood Cliffs, NJ: Prentice-Hall.

Jackson, J. (1977). *The effect of method of presentation and degree of imagery on learning responses to printed words.* Unpublished doctoral dissertation, University of New Orleans.

Jackson, J. R., & Dizney, H. (1963). Intensive vocabulary training. *Journal of Developmental Reading, 6,* 221–229.

Johnson, D. D. (1986). Journal of Reading: A themed issue on vocabulary instruction. *Journal of Reading, 29,* 580.

Johnson, D. D., & Pearson, P. D. (1984). *Teaching reading vocabulary.* New York: Holt, Rinehart and Winston.

Johnston, P. H. (1984). Prior knowledge and reading comprehension test bias. *Reading Research Quarterly, 19,* 219–239.

Jorm, A. (1977). Effect of word imagery on reading performance as a function of reader ability. *Journal of Educational Psychology, 69,* 46–54.

Kant, E. (1963). *Critique of pure reason* (2nd ed.). (N. Kemp Smith, Trans.). London: Macmillan. (Originally published 1787.)

Kavanagh, J. F., & Mattingly, I. G. (Eds.). (1972). *Language by ear and eye.* Cambridge, MA: MIT Press.

Kolers, P. A. (1972). Experiments in reading. *Scientific American, 227,* 84–91.

Kolers, P. A. (1975). Pattern-analyzing disability in poor readers. *Developmental Psychology, 11,* 282–290.

Koskinen, P. A., & Blum, I. H. (1986). Paired repeated reading: A classroom strategy for developing fluent reading. *The Reading Teacher, 40,* 70–75.

LaBerge, D., & Samuels, S. J. (1974). Toward a theory of automatic information processing in reading. *Cognitive Psychology, 6,* 293–323.

Levin, H., & Kaplan, E. L. (1970). Grammatical structure and reading. In H. Levin and J. Williams (Eds.), *Basic studies in reading.* New York: Basic Books.

Mandler, J. M., & Johnson, N. S. (1977). Remembrance of things parsed: Story structure and recall. *Cognitive Psychology, 9,* 111–151.

Marzano, R. J., & Marzano, J. S. (1988). *A cluster approach to elementary vocabulary instruction.* Newark, DE: International Reading Association.

McKeown, M. (1985). The acquisition of word meaning from context by children of high and low ability. *Reading Research Quarterly, 20,* 482–496.

Nagy, W. E. (1988). *Teaching vocabulary to improve reading comprehension.* Newark, DE: International Reading Association.

Nagy, W. E., Anderson, R. C., & Herman, P. (1987). Learning word meanings from context during normal reading. *American Educational Research Journal, 24,* 237–270.

Neisser, U. (1967). *Cognitive psychology.* New York: Appleton-Century-Crofts.

Nelson, K. (1977). Cognitive development and the acquisition of concepts. In R. C. Anderson, R. J. Spiro, and W E. Montague (Eds.), *Schooling and the acquisition of knowledge.* Hillsdale, NJ: Erlbaum.

Nelson, K. (1974). Concept, word and sentence: Interrelations in acquisition and development. *Psychological Review, 31,* 267–285.

Ollila, L. O., & Chamberlain, L. (1979, May–June). The learning and retention of two classes of graphic words: High-frequency nouns and non-noun words among kindergarten children. *The Journal of Educational Research,* pp. 288–293.

Olshavsky, J. E. (1976–1977). Reading as problem solving: An investigation of strategies. *Reading Research Quarterly, 12,* 654–674.

Paivio, A. (1970). On the functional significance of imagery. *Psychological Bulletin, 73,* 385–392.

Paivio, A. (1967). Paired associate learning and free recall of nouns as a function of concreteness, specificity, imagery, and meaningfulness. *Psychological Reports, 20,* 239–245.

Pany, D., & Jenkins, J. R. (1978). Learning word meanings: A comparison of instructional procedures and effects on measures of reading comprehension with learning disabled students. *Learning Disabled Quarterly, 9,* 21–32.

Pearson, P. D., & Johnson, D. D. (1978). *Teaching reading comprehension.* New York: Holt, Rinehart and Winston.

Petty, W T., Herold, C. P., & Stoll, E. (1968). *The state of knowledge about the teaching of vocabulary.* Cooperative Research Project No. 3128. Champaign, IL: National Council of Teachers of English.

Piaget, J. (1971). *Psychology and epistemology.* New York: Grossman.

Piercey, D. (1982). *Reading activities in content areas.* Boston: Allyn and Bacon.

Robinson, H. A. (1983). *Teaching reading, writing and study strategies: The content areas.* Boston: Allyn and Bacon.

Rosenshine, B. V. (1980). Skill hierarchies in reading comprehension. In R. J. Spiro, B. C. Bruce, and W F. Brewer (Eds.), *Theoretical issues in reading comprehension.* Hillsdale, NJ: Erlbaum.

Ruddell, R. B., & Speaker, R. (1985). The interactive reading process. In H. Singer & R. B. Ruddell (Eds.), *Theoretical models and processes of reading* (pp. 751–793). Newark DE: International Reading Association.

Rumelhart, D. E. (1975). Notes on a schema for stories. In D. G. Bobrow, and A. M. Collins (Eds.), *Representation and understanding: Studies in cognitive science.* New York: Academic Press.

Rumelhart, D. E. (1980). Schemata: The building blocks of cognition. In R. J. Spiro, B. C. Bruce, and W. F. Brewer (Eds.), *Theoretical issues in reading comprehension.* Hillsdale, NJ: Erlbaum.

Rumelhart, D. E. (1985). Toward an interactive model of reading. In H. Singer & R. B. Ruddell (Eds.), *Theoretical models and processes of reading* (pp. 722–750). Newark, DE: International Reading Association.

Rumelhart, D. E., Lindsay, P. H., & Norman, D. A. (1972). A process model for long-term memory. In E. Tulving and W. Donaldson (Eds.), *Organization and memory*. New York: Academic Press.

Rumelhart, D. E., & Ortony, A. (1977). The representation of knowledge in memory. In R. C. Anderson, R. J. Spiro, & W. E. Montague (Eds.), *Schooling and the acquisition of knowledge*. Hillsdale, NJ: Erlbaum.

Russell, D. H. (1961). *Children learn to read*. Boston: Ginn.

Samuels, S. J. (1988). Decoding and automaticity: Helping poor readers become automatic at word recognition. *The Reading Teacher, 41,* 756–761.

Samuels, S. J. (1979). The method of repeated readings. *The Reading Teacher, 32,* 403–408.

Schank, R. C., & Abelson, R. P. (1977). *Plans, scripts, goals and understanding*. Hillsdale, NJ: Erlbaum.

Schreiner, R. L., Hieronymous, A. N., & Forsyth, R. (1969). Differential measurement of reading abilities at the elementary school level. *Reading Research Quarterly, 5,* 84–99.

Schwartz, R. M., & Raphael, T. E. (1985). Concept of definition: A key to improving students' vocabulary. *The Reading Teacher, 39,* 198–205.

Shnayer, S. W. (1969). Relationships between reading interest and comprehension. In J. A. Figurel (Ed.), *Reading and realism*. Newark, DE: International Reading Association.

Simons, H. D. (1971). Reading comprehension: The need for a new perspective. *Reading Research Quarterly, 6,* 338–363.

Simpson, M. L. (1987). Alternative formats for evaluating content area vocabulary understanding. *Journal of Reading, 31,* 20–27.

Sloyer, S. (1982). *Readers theatre: Story dramatization in the classroom*. Urbana, IL: National Council of Teachers of English.

Smith, F. (1973). *Psycholinguistics and reading*. New York: Holt, Rinehart and Winston.

Smith, F. (1988). *Understanding reading* (4th ed.). Hillsdale, NJ: Erlbaum.

Smith, R. J., & Johnson, D. D. (1980). *Teaching children to read*. Reading, MA: Addison-Wesley.

Smith, E. E., Shoben, E. J., & Rips, L. J. (1974). Structure and process in semantic memory: A featural model for semantic decisions. *Psychological Review, 81,* 214–241.

Smith, E. E., & Spoehr, K. T. (1974). The perception of printed English: A theoretical perspective. In B. H. Kantowitz (Ed.), *Human information processing: Tutorials in performance and cognition*. Hillsdale, NJ: Erlbaum.

Spearritt, W. (1972). Identification of subskills of reading comprehension by maximum likelihood factor analysis. *Reading Research Quarterly, 8,* 92–111.

Spiro, R. J., Bruce, B. C., & Brewer, W. F. (Eds.). (1980). *Theoretical issues in reading comprehension*. Hillsdale, NJ: Erlbaum.

Stanovich, K. E. (1980). Toward an interactive-compensatory model of individual differences in the development of reading fluency. *Reading Research Quarterly, 16,* 32–71.

Stauffer, R. G. (1975). *Directing the reading-thinking process*. New York: Harper & Row.

Stauffer, R. G. (1969). *Teaching reading as a thinking process.* New York: Harper & Row.

Stein, N., & Glenn, C. (1979). An analysis of story comprehension in elementary school children. In R. Freedle (Ed.), *New directions in discourse processing.* Norwood, NJ: Ablex.

Stevenson, J., & Baumann, J. (1979). *Vocabulary development: Semantic feature analysis and semantic mapping.* Microworkshop presented at the Twenty-fourth Annual Convention of the International Reading Association, Atlanta.

Thelan, J. (1976). *Improving reading in science.* Newark, DE: International Reading Association.

Thorndike, E. L. (1917). Reading as reasoning: A study of mistakes in paragraph meaning. *Journal of Educational Psychology, 8,* 323–332. Reprinted in *Reading Research Quarterly* (1971), 6, 425–434.

Thorndyke, P. (1977). Cognitive structures in comprehension and memory of narrative discourse. *Cognitive Psychology, 9,* 77–110.

Tierney, R. J., & Cunningham, J. W. (1984). Research on teaching reading comprehension. In P. D. Pearson (Ed.), *Handbook on reading research.* New York: Longman.

Van der Veur, B. (1975). Imagery rating of 1000 frequently used words. *Journal of Educational Psychology, 67,* 44–56.

van Dijk, T. (1972). *Some aspects of text grammars.* The Hague: Mouton.

Walker, B. J. (1988). *Diagnostic teaching of reading: Techniques for instruction and assessment.* Columbus OH: Merrill.

Winnick, W., & Kressel, K. (1965). Tachistoscopic recognition thresholds: P-A learning and immediate recall as a function of abstractness-concreteness and word frequency. *Journal of Experimental Psychology, 70,* 163–168.

Wittrock, M. C., Marks, C., & Doctorow, M. (1975). Reading as a generative process. *Journal of Educational Psychology, 67,* 484–489.

Wixson, K. K. (1984). *Vocabulary instruction and children's comprehension of basal stories.* Paper presented at the National Reading Conference, St. Petersburg, FLA.

Wolpert, E. (1972). Length, imagery values and word recognition. *The Reading Teacher, 26,* 180–186.

CHAPTER 8

Reading Comprehension: Part 2

Objectives

After you have studied this chapter, you should be able to

1. develop informal assessment activities for understanding sentences, paragraphs, and longer units of discourse;
2. devise an instructional program for a student having difficulty at any of the above levels;
3. think about reading comprehension as a process rather than a set of skill products.

Study Outline

Important Vocabulary and Concepts

causal patterns
deficit type reader
difference type reader
integrative processing

replaced words
ReQuest Procedure
scriptally implicit
semantic webbing

macroprocessing	story frames
mapping	story grammar
microprocessing	structured comprehension
paraphrasing	text organization
phase-out/phase-in strategy	textually explicit
QARs	textually implicit
repeated words	

Overview

This chapter continues the discussion of reading comprehension begun in chapter 7 and views reading comprehension as a task of making connections between the text organization and one's prior knowledge. Three levels of text organization are considered: the sentence, the paragraph, and longer units of written discourse. Assessment and instructional strategies are related to each of these levels.

Introduction

As noted at the beginning of chapter 7, reading comprehension is a complex skill affected by many factors. It was also pointed out that knowledge of word meanings is a critical subskill of reading comprehension. In addition to vocabulary knowledge, reading comprehension requires a number of thinking and reasoning skills. Gaining insights into relevant "subprocesses like attention, perception, encoding, comprehension, memory, information storage, and retrieval" (Pearson, 1985, p. 725) is a task that researchers, especially cognitive psychologists, have begun to pursue furiously.

No longer is it acceptable to consider material "comprehended" if the reader can recall elements of the text. As Pearson (1985) has stated "no longer do we regard text as a fixed object that the reader is supposed to 'approximate' as closely as possible as s/he reads. Instead we now view text as a sort of blueprint for meaning, a set of tracks or clues that the reader uses as s/he builds a model of what the text means" (p. 726). It is only when readers actively construct logical connections among their own prior knowledge, ideas in the text, the specific task at hand, and the situation they are in, and can express these ideas in their own words that the text is considered comprehended. **Text organization** refers to establishing the relationships among words, sentences, paragraphs, and longer units. As such, it is a key to reading comprehension. Teachers also need to recognize the importance of prior knowledge to reading comprehension (Irwin, 1986; Pearson, 1985).

Assessment and Instructional Strategies

Assessing the Ability to Organize Text: Informal Measures

In constructing relations between words, the reader must be able to operate at (1) a sentence level, (2) a paragraph level, and (3) a level involving longer passages or series of paragraphs (Irwin, 1986; Pennock, 1979). Language provides signals, some of which were discussed early in chapter 7, that cue the reader to the relationship at hand (Bormuth, 1969). To measure a reader's ability to understand at each of the levels, the teacher can use, with some modifications, the same types of activities employed to teach sentence reading strategies, paragraph reading strategies, and longer selection reading strategies.[1]

Assessing Sentence Level Strategies

According to Irwin (1986), in the comprehension process the reader must first construct meaning "from the individual idea units in each sentence" and "decide which of these ideas to remember" (p. 3). This initial task of chunking and selective recall of individual idea units is termed **microprocessing**. The following assessment strategies can be used to find out if the reader is able to operate at this microprocessing level.

1. Can the student recognize *who* or *what* a sentence is about? In other words, can the student identify the subject of the sentence? Give the student sentences that state the subject directly. These sentences, and any of the suggested types of sentences and paragraphs in the following sections, may be taken directly from the material being used in the classroom. For example:

Joe went into the house.
The books on the table are Bob's.

2. Can the student recognize the predicate, or *what is being done,* in the sentence? Provide the student with sentences. For example:

Sue *kissed her mom and dad goodnight.*
They *became interested in the story right away.*

3. Can the student recognize *where* someone is or something is done? Some key signal words are: *under, over, in, at, to, between, among, behind, in front of,* and *through.* Give the student sentences containing these words. For example:

Our class saw a film *in the gym.*
There was one girl *among the group of boys.*

4. Can the student recognize *when* something happens? Some key signal words are: *before, after, while, later, as, now,* and *then.* Provide the student with sentences containing these words. For example:

We can watch TV *after we do our homework.*
While it was raining, I read a good book.

5. Can the student understand and use language signals that indicate information has been replaced? Some key signal words are: *I, you, he, she, it, they, we, us, them, their, his, her, your, our, him, this,* and *these.* Give the student sentences that contain these key signal words and their referents. For example:

After *Mary* finished dinner, *she* started to read.
Bill wrote a story about *his* vacation.

---

[1] Discussion of the three assessment categories is based on Daniel R. Hittleman, *Developmental Reading, K–8,* 2d ed., pp. 208–216. Copyright © 1983 Houghton Mifflin Company. Used with permission.

6. Can the student recognize that words or information are sometimes left out of sentences, but the author wants the reader to mentally put the words in? The key signal is if the reader can ask *what* or *did what* where the words seem to be omitted. Provide the student with sentences that make sense but seem incomplete. For example:

The rest of the family ate popcorn while Mary made more. *(More what?)*
The teacher told the class to start writing so they began.
(Began doing what?)

7. Can the student understand how some information in a sentence can be moved without changing the meaning of the sentence, or how punctuation can affect meaning? Give the student pairs of sentences that do and do not mean the same. The student should be able to recognize the sentence pairs that mean the same. For example:

The airplane picked up speed as it came down the runway.
As it came down the runway, the airplane picked up speed.

Before John worked on his car model, he ate lunch.
Before he ate lunch, John worked on his car model.

Or, given three sentences, can the student indicate which one does not mean the same? For example:

Father said, "Carol, come and play."
"Father," said Carol, "come and play."
"Carol, come and play," said Father.

8. Can the student understand that different sentences can have the same meaning? Provide the student with pairs of sentences that do and do not mean the same. The student should be able to recognize the sentence pairs that mean the same. For example:

In the fall of the year the trees are painted with many colors.
Leaves on the trees have many colors in the fall.

The old horse nibbled at the grass.
The old horse was thin and feeble.

In addition to items 7 and 8, the student should be given one sentence and then asked to give another sentence that means the same, or says the same thing in another way.

Assessing Paragraph Level Strategies

Individual idea units must also be connected into a coherent whole. Making these connections requires recognizing pronoun referents, inferring causes, and identifying main ideas. "The process of understanding and inferring the relationships between individual clauses and/or sentences can be called **integrative processing**" (Irwin, 1986, p. 5). The following strategies can be used to assess integrative processing.

1. Can the student recognize *who* or *what* a paragraph is about? Key signals for determining the subject of a paragraph are repeated and replaced words. **Repeated words** are those found in almost every sentence of the paragraph. Given the following paragraph, the student should be able to recognize the repeated word and tell what (or who) the paragraph is about.

The city of Bern, Switzerland, starts its holiday season each year with *onions*. The fourth Monday in November is "*Onion* Market Day." On this day farmers display *onions* in the public square. Red, yellow, and white *onions* are piled in colorful mounds. Wreaths and garlands of *onions* are on view. Visitors can sample free *onion* cake and hot *onion* soup.

Replaced words are substitutes for words that would normally be repeated. The pronoun is the most common substitute. Given the following paragraph, the student should be able to mentally substitute each replaced word with its referent and thus recognize who (or what) the paragraph is about.

Two *scientists* "camped" for a week on the bottom of the sea. *Their* underwater home was a cabin shaped like a barrel. *The men* did not spend all *their* time in *their* underwater bubble. *They* went out to explore the sea bottom.

2. Can the student determine the *main idea* of the paragraph? This task is very much analogous to determining a category title for a set of words. Pearson and Johnson (1978) discuss several types of main idea organizations that are useful for both testing and teaching. Each of these organizations could be tested by asking the student to locate the sentence that best expresses the main idea of the paragraph. The material should correspond to the student's instructional level.

a. Explicit main idea is stated at the beginning of a paragraph.

Polar bears are well adapted to life in the Arctic. Their color makes them hard to see against a snowy background. A jacket of fat keeps them warm and helps them float in the water. Hair on the soles of their paws gives them good footing on ice.

b. Explicit main idea is stated at the end of the paragraph.

The color of polar bears makes them hard to see against a snowy background. A jacket of fat keeps them warm and helps them float in the water. Hair on the soles of their paws gives them good footing on ice. Polar bears are well adapted to life in the Arctic.

c. Main idea is implicit, that is, not stated.

The color of polar bears makes them hard to see against a snowy background. A jacket of fat keeps them warm and helps them float in the water. Hair on the soles of their paws gives them good footing on ice.

Recognizing explicit main ideas is easier than determining implicit main ideas. Both tasks are simplified by providing multiple choice responses. Example choices should include the four types of distractors shown in the following example:

1. Polar bears are fat, hairy, and white. *(too specific)*
2. Polar bears are good swimmers. *(not mentioned)*
3. Life in the Arctic. *(too general)*
4. Polar bears are well adapted to life in the Arctic. *(right level of generality)*

Assessing Strategies for Longer Units of Written Discourse

Authors organize their ideas in such a way that an isolated paragraph may not have a main idea and can only be understood in relation to other paragraphs. Karlin

(1975) emphasizes that comprehension is aided when the reader sees the relationships among ideas in a passage or story and recognizes the structure, overall function, or purpose of the material.

According to Irwin (1986), "ideas are connected and retained in memory more effectively if they are organized around an overall organizational pattern. The main topics in an organized text make up a kind of summary. The process of synthesizing and organizing individual idea units into a summary or organized series of related general ideas can be called **macroprocessing**" (p. 5). Obviously, these relationships are more realistically studied in the context of several paragraphs. Assessment of macroprocessing abilities may proceed as follows.

Does the student recognize **causal patterns** within a paragraph or paragraphs? Sometimes causality is cued by key words such as *because, since, for, hence, so, therefore,* and *as a result.* Many times, however, causal relations are not signaled at all, forcing the reader to provide the signal mentally. With corrective readers, both assessment and instruction should begin with the use of key words. Initially, the teacher must find out if the student recognizes cause-and-effect relationships. This is most appropriately done through questioning. Some examples follow. These paragraphs are read silently or orally, and students may look back at the passage after the key question is asked.

Single paragraph

The boy was being very selfish. He did not want to share his toys. *Because* of this, he played alone.

Ask: Why did the boy play alone? (Key word is in italics.)

Series of paragraphs

In the early years of our country the Mississippi River was important for both trading and travel. First it was used by the Indians, then by the Spanish explorers. Finally French fur traders used the river.

Later, the river helped many settlements get started. But *as* the railroads came, river traffic almost disappeared. Then came World War I.

As a result the United States was shipping so many goods to help with winning the war, river traffic once again became important. The railroads could not carry all the goods. Today the river remains busy.

Ask: What caused Mississippi River traffic to almost disappear? Why did river traffic once again become important? (Important key words are in italics.)

Other paragraph relationships are assessed in similar fashion. Common key words (Hittleman, 1983) for the major relationships found in passages are:

- Enumeration: one, two, three, another, more, also
- Generalization: for example
- Comparison or contrast: but, however, although, yet, even though
- Sequence: first, second, third, last, before, after, while, then, later, finally
- Question and answer: why, how, when, where, what

The reader is *not* required to label the function or purpose of a paragraph or a series of paragraphs, but should be able to recognize the characteristics, or key words, for each type.

Paragraph frames (Cudd & Roberts, 1989) can also be used to assess awareness of text organizational patterns. Similar to story frames (Cudd & Roberts, 1987;

Fowler, 1982), paragraph frames use a cloze format and provide the key words representing the organizational pattern of the text. If the material were sequentially organized, the paragraph frame would provide key words such as first, next, then, later, and last or finally. For example, after reading about the life cycle of a butterfly, the student would be asked to complete the following paragraph frame.

The beautiful butterfly we see in the garden has gone through four stages. First, an adult butterfly _____

_____.

Then, _____.

Next, _____.

Finally, _____.

Paragraph and story frames are not only useful for assessing awareness of text organization, but also provide a useful instructional tool for focusing on the structure of text material whether it be narrative or expository. Using story and paragraph frames for instruction is suggested later in this chapter and also in chapter 10.

Assessing the Ability to Organize Text: Formal Measures

Most standardized reading tests, both survey and diagnostic, include items that measure sentence or paragraph meaning or both. However, standardized test scores only indicate the existence of a problem understanding sentences or paragraphs in general. The teacher still must examine individual items to determine the specific difficulty the child has in comprehending sentences or paragraphs. Once a standardized test determines that the student does not understand sentences and paragraphs, further diagnosis by informal procedures, such as a story retelling, or completion of a story map or story frame, are generally useful.

Instructional Strategies for Text Organization

No easy way has been found to improve comprehension skills. Because of the complex interrelationship of the many factors operating during comprehension, better understanding cannot be assured by having a student experience a certain activity. However, if the teacher is aware of the factors within the reader, the text, and the environment and tries to account for these factors in instruction, the chances for improvement seem greater.

Strategies especially relevant for the poor comprehender follow and are organized according to the three major assessment categories: sentence level, paragraph level, and longer units. Underlying all comprehension strategies is the assumption that the teacher is aware of and utilizes good questioning techniques. The right questions must be asked at the right times to help both the teacher and the student further understand the comprehension process. Appropriate questioning techniques are exemplified whenever they are especially important. A good questioning technique models appropriate strategies and teaches children to ask themselves questions while reading; this ensures active participation and helps the children realize that the material being read should and must make sense.

In summary, corrective reading students are most likely to improve in comprehension if their special needs are considered. The results of a study by Taylor (1979), especially relevant here, suggest that poor readers' comprehension, more so than good readers, suffers when their use of prior knowledge is restricted. Also, when provided with easy, familiar material, poor readers comprehend adequately. Thus the best way to begin instruction in comprehension for the corrective student is to use short, easy, familiar (in terms of background) material.

Instructional Strategies for Sentences

The main purpose of instruction at the sentence level is to teach children how to note the important details of a sentence, how to use word order and punctuation to indicate the meaning of the sentence, and to realize that the same thing can be said more than one way. According to Kamm (1979), focusing on the details of a sentence is an analysis task that should begin with simple sentences such as: "The dog ran." (Language experience stories provide an excellent source for such sentences.) This sentence is read aloud, and the child is asked to identify the action. If the response is "running" or "ran," the sentence is shown to the child and the specific word representing the action underlined. The next question asks who or what is running, and if the child responds "the dog," the word is underlined twice. The child then sees "The dog ran."

Through sentence expansion, the child is shown that the action and agent do not change even if words are added. For example, the sentence may be expanded to "The brown dog ran down the street." The following sequence would then apply:

- What is the action? *(ran)* Underline once.
- Who or what ran? *(dog)* Underline twice.
- What color is the dog? *(brown)*
- Where did the dog run? *(down the street)*
- How else could you describe the dog? *(black, spotted, lost, frightened)*
- Where else could the dog have run? *(away, in the house, across the street)*

A follow-up activity for this type of instruction would be to transform sentences into telegrams, teaching the reader that recognition of just the important words still gives the meaning of the sentence.

Sentence expansion also allows instruction in word order. Using just the form, "The brown dog ran down the street," the child is asked: "Why might the dog run down the street?" In most responses a prepositional phrase will be added. All forms of open-ended sentences or sentence fragments aid teaching word order. For example:

The brown dog _____ .
The brown dog ran _____ .
Down the street _____ .

Weaver (1979) developed a procedure for training students in sentence organization skills that was shown to transfer to reading comprehension performance. The major purpose of the strategy is to teach children how to group words into organizational units. Briefly, the first step is to form word groups by identifying the action word, or verb. Then a series of questions are asked to help students group the remaining words and determine how these groups are related to the verb. Application of this strategy proceeds as follows.

At first, sentences containing the words to be grouped are developed. The sentences should be short (five to fifteen words), easy for the student (i.e., containing familiar words), declarative, and in the active voice. As the student progresses, sentences increase in difficulty. Each word of the sentence is written on a separate card. No word is capitalized (except proper names and I), and no punctuation cards are included. The words are then presented to the student in scrambled order. A list of the steps of the strategy in the order to be followed is also given to the student. The teacher then demonstrates and explains how to follow the steps to unscramble the sentence. For example:

car   to   ran   the   the   boy

WH questions
1. WHo
2. WHat
3. WHere
4. WHen
5. WHy
6. HoW

Steps
1. Find the action word. (Expected response: *ran*)
2. Ask WH question, for example, "Who did this action?" (Expected response: boy)
3. Put the words together. (Expected response: *boy ran*)
4. Does the order make sense? *(boy ran versus ran boy)*
   If no, have all orders been tried?
5. Is the thought complete? If yes, go to step 7.
   If no, find helping words (auxiliary verbs, function words).
6. Go back to step 3.
7. Can the sentence be completed by adding the remaining words?
   If yes, go to step 2. If no, have all the WH questions been asked?
8. Have all the words been used? If yes, STOP. If no, go to step 2.

In this example it was possible for the child to respond that "the car ran," and this combination of words alone does make sense. However, after adding the rest of the words, "the car ran to the boy," the order is no longer sensible, and the words would be reordered as directed in step 4.

This technique assumes that the student understands the concepts of verb and action word, WH questions, sensibility, and complete sentences. Eventually, a time element is introduced, and students are encouraged to keep track of their progress by trying to decrease the time required to solve the sentence anagram (i.e., as soon as the student can solve a six-word sentence within a set time limit 80% of the time, seven-word sentences are given). Weaver points out, however, that accuracy will probably precede speed. A student may need many opportunities for practicing and refining sentence organizational skills before becoming concerned with time.

Another useful strategy to help students group units of sentences is practice in sentence combining (Jenkins & Pany, 1981). For example, the sentences "The dog ran down the street" and "The dog is brown" can be combined as "The brown dog ran down the street." Hughes (1975) observed that training in sentence combining was most effective for lower and middle ability students.

Another aspect of sentence comprehension is synthesis (Kamm, 1979). At this stage the learner is involved in paraphrasing sentences. This **paraphrasing** takes two forms: rearrangement of the words in the sentence or substitution of words with appropriate synonyms.

One way to begin teaching paraphrasing is to provide the students with a set of four to seven sight words. These words are taken from the student's personal word bank. The student is then shown how to form as many different sentences as possible. Each word is used only once. For example, *Bob-what-Mary-does-says* can become:

1. Bob does what Mary says.
2. Mary does what Bob says.
3. What Mary says Bob does.
4. Mary says what Bob does.
5. Bob says what Mary does.
6. What Bob says Mary does.

Once the sentences are developed, the teacher instructs the student to find those that mean the same thing and asks questions as follows. "What action goes with Bob in sentence 1?" Response: *does.* "What action goes with Mary in sentence 1?" Response: *says.* "Find any other sentences where 'Bob does' and 'Mary says' are together." Response: *sentences 3 and 4.* The conclusion to be drawn is that sentences 1, 3, and 4 mean the same thing even though the word order is different. "What about sentences 2, 5, and 6?" Response: *They have the same meaning because in all three Mary does and Bob says.*

After this kind of direct instruction, the student is allowed to practice with a new set of sentences or sentence pairs. Sentences similar to those used for assessing sentence level strategies are appropriate. Instruction in comprehension should provide the student with a strategy for unlocking meaning. Therefore, the teacher must ask questions that the children should ask of themselves when the time comes to work independently. Incorrect responses must be discussed as well as correct responses so that the children understand which features are important.

Comprehension instruction that focuses on deriving meaning from single sentences or pairs of sentences is also discussed by Durkin (1978–1979). She suggests providing a sentence and asking the children to name everything it tells. Her example, "The little kindergarten boy was crying," elicits the responses that tell about the boy. All the facts of the sentence are written on the board. If a child speculates on why the boy was crying, this response leads into a list of what the sentence does *not* tell. This latter particular approach is an application of "negative type questions" (Willford, 1968). Such questions represent an attempt to move away from the "right answer syndrome" (Caskey, 1970) to more speculation and predicting. As an example, Willford (1968) relates:

Watch a five- or six-year-old. You put a picture up and say, "Okay, what can you do with a horse?" Out of a group of 10, five of them have had an experience. The others don't know what you can do with a horse. We turn it completely around and say, "What can't you do with a horse?" You ought to see the different responses we get. Every child can tell you what you can't do with a horse. "What can't you do?" "Well you can't take a horse to bed with you." Someone else might say, "You can too if you live in a barn." This kid never thought about this. So now we find, what can you do with a horse? You can take a horse to bed with you if you live in a barn. You can flip the thing over by using a negative question as a stimulus to get a variety of answers. Kids love to do this. You may get more conversation from a single picture than any single thing you can do. (p. 103)

Sentence level instruction should move from a literal level of understanding to an implied or inferred level. Heilman and Holmes (1978), in *Smuggling Language into the Teaching of Reading,* give two excellent activities for this level of instruction. To help students understand the strategy involved, the directions and questions here have been modified.

1. Choose the best meaning for the following sentence:
   The moving van stopped in front of the empty house.
   a. The truck was probably empty.
   b. The truck was there to pick up furniture.
   c. The truck contained furniture for the people moving into the house. (p. 68)
      Questions: Why did you make the choice you made?
      What clues were in the sentence?
2. Fill in the blank. Only one word makes sense. Put two lines under any words that helped you decide what the *one* word had to be.
   a. The score was <u>tied</u> <u>seven</u> to <u>(seven)</u> .
   b. The <u>right</u> hand <u>glove</u> will <u>not</u> <u>fit</u> on your <u>(left)</u> hand.
   c. The <u>umpire</u> said, " <u>(Strike)</u> three, you're <u>out</u>!"

(Note how important background knowledge is at the implied or inferred level.)

At all levels of meaning instruction, children should be directed to form mental pictures of what they are reading. While an imagery strategy may not benefit all poor readers (Levin, 1973), imagery instructions may facilitate the reading comprehension of "difference" type poor readers (Gambrell, 1982). Cromer (1970) distinguishes between a **deficit type** reader—one whose reading vocabulary and comprehension are poor—and a **difference type** reader—one whose reading vocabulary is adequate but whose comprehension is poor.

Imagery instruction begins by having children "make a picture in their heads" for specific things, such as a favorite animal or a place they have visited. These pictures are then shared so that each child can respond and listen to others' descriptions. The students are now ready to form mental pictures about the reading material. For example, if the reading contained the phrase, "As I was walking alone on that cold winter afternoon," appropriate questions would be: "Where are you walking?" "What does the sky look like?" "How do you feel?" "How are you dressed?" Materials for imagery instruction should not have overly elaborate descriptions. Material already rich in imagery leaves nothing for the student to visualize.

Instructional Strategies for Paragraphs

Instruction in comprehension must include teaching the reader to see the relationship among ideas in a paragraph. As with sentences, however, the corrective student must be taught literal meanings of paragraphs before implicit meanings. A technique that moves quite well from the sentence level to the paragraph level, **structured comprehension**, was developed by Marvin Cohn (1969). Cohn suggests that material selected for this technique be somewhat difficult for the students to read in their usual fashion. Passages from content area materials are recommended. Only a selection of two or three sentences is needed for this technique, as instruction proceeds sentence by sentence and can become tedious if the selection is overly long. Once the sentences are selected, the background is given to the students to put the sentences into their appropriate context. The next step is for the students (or the teacher) to read just the first sentence aloud. Any decoding errors are simply corrected. The students are then directed to ask themselves, "Do I know what this sentence means?" They may ask the teacher as many questions as necessary to understand the sentence. Once the students' questions have been answered, the teacher asks several questions about each sentence. These questions must be prepared in advance, because Cohn recommends that certain questions always be asked if the opportunity presents itself (see below). The students may look back to the text for answers, but the answers must be written. The questions asked should require only two or three words to answer; questions requiring longer answers are put in a multiple choice format.

Questions always to be asked seek the following information:

1. Clarification of the referent for a pronoun
2. Clarification of meaning when a word has multiple or unusual meanings
3. The meaning of figurative expressions
4. Definition of causal or other relationships left implicit

Answers for each question are discussed. For incorrect answers, the teacher demonstrates why and explains the reasoning behind the correct answer. Correct answers, when put back into the text, make sense; incorrect answers do not. This procedure also helps students *demand* that material read be meaningful.

Initially Cohn recommends that literal meanings be stressed more than relationships or implied information. Beginning with emphasis on the literal meaning provides more success for students and also allows them the opportunity to develop appropriate questioning techniques. The passive reader may become more actively involved through this process. An example showing possible teacher's questions for a structured comprehension lesson can be examined in figure 8.1.

Another technique, similar to structured comprehension, is called the **ReQuest Procedure** (*Re*ciprocal *Quest*ioning Procedure) developed by Anthony Manzo (1969, 1985). This procedure, which is used with individuals or small groups, aids students in setting their own purposes for reading. The teacher guides the students through the silent reading of as many sentences of a selection as are necessary to enable them to complete the passage independently. Once again, as in structured comprehension, questions are exchanged by student and teacher, sentence by sentence. Every question asked by a student or teacher must be answered from recall, or an explanation must be given for why it cannot be answered. Teachers' questions serve as models for the kinds of questions students should ask of themselves while reading. Also, when responding to students' questions, the teacher gives reinforcement such as, "That was an excellent question," or "You might want to reword the question in this way . . . ," or "I think your questions are really improving." When the teacher thinks students are ready to proceed independently (no more than three paragraphs should be handled reciprocally), a general purpose-setting question is asked: "Did we raise the best question or purpose for which to read this selection?" (Manzo, 1985). At this point, the rest of the selection is read silently.

FIGURE 8.1 Structured comprehension lesson.

Background: The student is told that the Constitution is a list of the rights that the American people have. Soon after the Constitution was written, the people wanted to add more rights. These additional rights are called the Bill of Rights.

Passage: "The Bill of Rights says that every person can speak freely. A person can criticize the government or its officials if he believes that they are not doing a good job. We call this freedom of speech."

—Herbert H. Gross, et al., *Exploring Regions of the Western Hemisphere*

Questions

Sentence 1

1. Does "speak freely" mean you won't have to pay before speaking?
2. Is the Bill of Rights a person?
3. How can the Bill of Rights "say" anything?
4. This sentence means:
    a. that the Bill of Rights thinks no one should have to pay to speak;
    b. an important right of all people is to be able to say whatever they think is important to say;
    c. a new law was passed that has cured people who couldn't speak, so that now they can speak.

Sentence 2

1. What does "criticize" mean?
2. What does "its" refer to?
3. Who does "he" refer to?
4. Who does "they" refer to?
5. This sentence means:
    a. if the government or the people who are leaders in the government are not doing a good job, anybody can say that they aren't;
    b. when the government does not do a good job, the people must believe that they are doing a good job anyway;
    c. it is impossible for the government to do a bad job.

Sentence 3

1 . Who does "we" refer to?
2. What does "this" refer to?
3. "Freedom of speech" means no one can charge to hear a speech. True or false?
4. This sentence means:
    a. all people have the right to speak out if the government does not do what it's supposed to do;
    b. the Bill of Rights is also called freedom of speech;
    c. the government can say anything it wants to for free.

Both of these techniques help move the student from literal understanding of sentences to understanding the relationship between sentences, and eventually entire selections. The techniques also actively involve the students in the comprehension process by having them ask questions about meaning and by emphasizing the importance of expecting material to make sense.

A recent technique born from Manzo's ReQuest Procedure which proceeds in a paragraph-by-paragraph manner is called reciprocal teaching (Brown & Palincsar,

1982; Palincsar & Brown, 1984, 1986). Its major purpose, training in comprehension monitoring skill, will be discussed in detail in chapter 10, "Strategic Reading." Briefly, four strategies are modeled by the teacher. The teacher gradually encourages the students to take on the "teacher" role. The four strategies are:

1. summarize the paragraph.
2. ask a main idea, or high level, question.
3. clarify difficult parts.
4. predict what the next paragraph will present.

(For best results with poor comprehenders use small groups of 2–3 students.)

Sometimes the problem of not understanding material can be attributed to inappropriate phrasing. Even material used in a structured comprehension lesson can be rewritten into phrase units to aid the reader (Cromer, 1970). This technique, referred to as "chunking" (Walker, 1988), "facilitates comprehension and fluency by using thought units rather than word-by-word reading" (p. 101). An example from Heilman and Holmes (1978, p. 127) follows.

> This material
> is written
> in short phrases
> so that you
> can practice
> seeing words
> in thought units.
> This helps you
> read faster.
> However,
> remember also
> that reading
> in phrases
> or thought units
> helps the reader
> get the meaning.

Echo reading (see earlier discussion in chapter 7) could also be used to model appropriate phrasing.

Before readers can determine the main idea of a paragraph or see relationships between ideas, they must be able to recognize significant details. Newspaper articles are a ready source of materials that lend themselves to the kind of questioning involved in teaching children to look for details (fig. 8.2). The following questions may be asked regarding this particular article:

1. Who was involved in this event? *(residents of the nursing home, policemen, firemen)*
2. What took place? *(a fire)*
3. Where did it take place? *(Bryn Mawr Nursing Home in Minneapolis, Minnesota)*
4. When did it take place? *(Saturday, September 22, 1979)*
5. How or why did it take place? *(Police believe the fire was caused by arson.)*

FIGURE 8.2 Type of newspaper article that helps children look for details. (From *New Orleans Times-Picayune,* September 23, 1979. Used with permission of the Associated Press, New York.)

The Times-Picayune   **Sunday, September 23, 1979**

Nursing Home Hit in Arson?

By JOHN LUNDQUIST

MINNEAPOLIS (AP) - Police said they believe the nursing home fire which claimed the life of one elderly resident and injured three others Saturday was the work of an arsonist.

A 38-year-old female resident of the Bryn Mawr Nursing Home, who was not identified, was taken into custody about 3 1/2 hours after the blaze broke out, police said.

Charges were not filed immediately, police said.

Teams of firemen who responded to the three-alarm blaze helped many of the elderly at the home to safety from second floor windows. The residents were carried down ladders in rescue baskets or down stairways in their wheelchairs.

One fireman, Jeff Bartholomew, about 30, suffered smoke inhalation when he took off his mask and put it over the face of a woman he helped out of the two-story building, said Capt. Cecil Klingbile, one of the station fire chiefs on the scene.

"He took a lot of smoke when he did that," said Klingbile, who aided in the rescue.

Bartholomew was treated and released.

The Hennepin County medical examiner identified the dead woman as Fanny Anttila, 85.

Two elderly women in serious condition suffering from smoke inhalation were identified as Rose Seiger, 80, and Esther Cotter, 79.

A 75-year-old man, whose identification was being withheld until relatives had been notified, was in critical condition with second-degree burns.

Twenty-five other people were taken to hospitals but they were not admitted. David Lesperance, associate administrator, said they were "disposition cases," meaning the hospital was arranging accommodations for them.

One of the displaced residents was Richard Fobes, 71, who sat in a waiting room with his two sons.

"I was sitting in the recreation room on the first floor when the fire broke out," he said. "They (nursing home workers) told us to get in our rooms, and pretty soon they came and got us outside."

Fire Capt. Ronald Knoke said 44 firefighters from nine engine and four hook-and-ladder companies answered the alarm.

He said the fire was discovered at 9:54 a.m. (CDT) in the closet of a resident room, then spread down the hall to other parts of the second floor. Firefighters had the blaze under control at 10:28 a.m.

Knoke said most of the danger was from smoke, because of the age of the residents.

Menus, recipes, and directions also teach recognition of details in written materials.

Activities similar to locating key words in sentences also may be expanded to paragraphs. The key words become the significant details and are either underlined or listed. Telegrams may be written using just key words to see if the reader gets the correct message.

Once a student learns how to find significant details, the next natural step is main idea instruction. Significant details are listed on the board and examined for similarities. As previously stated, this task is similar to providing a category title. To further aid the corrective reader, the relationship between the main idea and supporting details can be represented in several pictorial ways (fig. 8.3).

FIGURE 8.3 The main idea and supporting ideas can be pictorially represented to aid the corrective reader.

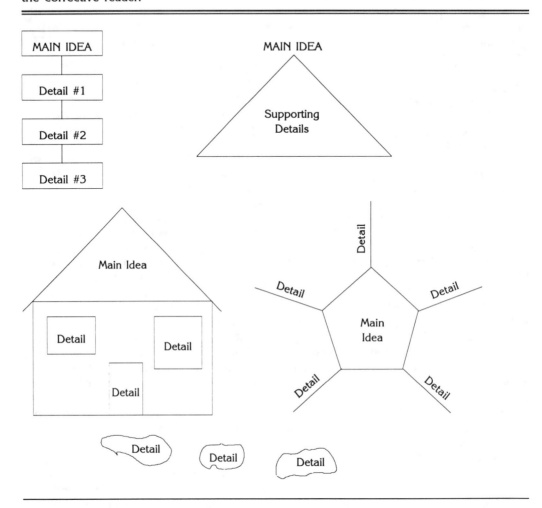

Instruction in main ideas begins by using a topic sentence with the main idea explicitly stated. The following questions may be asked:

What do most of the key words seem to point out?
What key words occur more than once?
What do these words relate to?
Is there a sentence that would summarize these ideas?

Using the paragraph about polar bears, the student is first directed to find the key words or significant details, words that occur more than once, and a sentence that summarizes these details.

Polar bears are well adapted to life in the Arctic. Their color makes them hard to see against a snowy background. A jacket of fat keeps them warm and helps them float in the water. Hair on the soles of their paws gives them good footing on ice.

The first step is to underline key words, as shown in the paragraph. These key words aid in determining the significant details. In searching for recurring words, students are first led to discover the pronoun referents. Ask: "Who or what is the first sentence about?" Response: *polar bears.* Ask: "Who or what does the word *their* refer to in the second sentence?" Response: *polar bears.* "In the same sentence you see the word *them.* What does *them* refer to?" Response: *polar bears.* In actuality then, the term *polar bears* occurs quite frequently in this paragraph, which is a clue to the main topic of the paragraph. Significant details about polar bears should then be discussed by asking, "What does this paragraph tell us about polar bears?" A diagram may be used, such as those shown in figure 8.3.

Going back to the paragraph, ask, "Can you choose one sentence that includes all of the supporting details or summarizes those details?" Elicit the response that the first sentence does this. The teacher explains why this sentence summarizes the others if students have difficulty (1) recognizing that the first sentence describes the main idea of the paragraph or (2) determining why polar bears are well adapted to life in the Arctic. (Chapter 9 presents additional instructional strategies for main ideas.)

The usefulness of activities such as the structured comprehension lesson for teaching paragraph understanding should now be apparent. Instruction in this area helps the student know what to look for in a paragraph to determine its meaning. After instruction, the following activities should be easier for students:

1. Find the sentence that does not belong in this paragraph.

   Tommy was baking a cake for Mother's birthday. He sifted flour, added two eggs, and put it in the oven to bake. It seemed to take forever to be done. At last the potatoes were ready. The frosting was chocolate with marshmallows. (Heilman & Holmes, 1978, p. 65)
   Possible questions to ask regarding this paragraph are:

   • What is this paragraph about?
   • Which sentence doesn't seem to belong? Why?

2. In this activity, the student attempts to determine implied information.

   Tomorrow is the big day. John has been practicing ever since school started. Now is his chance to show all his friends his special tricks. This is the time of year when spooky things are really popular. He doesn't even need to wear a costume to scare people. After the parade the older kids get to put on a show for the little ones. Gee! It will be great fun to see their faces turn white. It's a good thing it will be on the last day of the school week. They will have the weekend to recover from their fright. (Heilman & Holmes, 1978, p. 70)

   • What day of the week will something important take place?
     a. Saturday   b. Sunday   c. Friday

To help students answer this question, the teacher directs their attention to the appropriate sentences. "What sentences in the paragraph mention the word *day?*" Response: *first and eighth sentences.* "Does the first sentence help us to know what day it is?" Response: *no, only tomorrow.* "What about the eighth sentence?" Response: *yes, the last day of the school week is Friday.*

- What holiday do you think it is?
  a. Halloween   b. Christmas   c. Easter

Once again the relevant sentences are discussed. First, the teacher elicits key words associated with Halloween, Christmas, and Easter. Next, the students look for key words in the paragraph. Once the words *spooky, costumes, trick or treat, scary,* and *frighten,* elicited for Halloween, are also found in the paragraph, the holiday becomes apparent.

- How long has John been practicing?
  a. about two weeks   b. about two months   c. about two hours

"What sentence mentions practicing?" Response: *the second sentence.* "When does school start?" Response: *late August or early September.* "When is Halloween?" Response: *late October.* "How much time is between late August or early September and late October?" Response: *about two months.*

As noted before, prior knowledge and experience are important for success in implied information activities. Most of the guiding questions require the readers to think about something they already know or have experienced. Additional activities and discussion of implicit main ideas can be found in Pearson and Johnson's (1978) *Teaching Reading Comprehension* (chapter 5).

The questions in the foregoing examples represent the direction that instruction in paragraph comprehension should take. Children must be shown how to deal with paragraph information. Teachers instruct best by modeling or thinking out loud with their students to reveal the strategies they themselves use. Once shown the strategy, children can practice and apply this type of thinking to material read independently. Students can write their own paragraphs and plan a lesson for transmitting the main idea to other students. This gives students the opportunity to practice the question-asking strategies involved.

Instructional Strategies for Longer Units

Recall that one major difference between good and poor comprehenders is that good comprehenders apparently organize the material as they read, but poor comprehenders do not. While the poor comprehender must learn organizational techniques, in the interim the reader should receive as much help as possible in organizing the material. Most of this instruction will guide students in asking the right questions about the textual material they read. Instruction is geared toward helping children think about what they already know in relation to what they are reading, and organize what is being read while reading.

Standard instructional techniques, such as Stauffer's (1981) Directed Reading-Thinking Activity (DRTA) (see figure 8.4), can be modified to suit the particular needs of the corrective student. Modifications found in the literature are Hittleman's idea map (1983, pp. 224–229); Schwartz and Sheff's (1975) and Singer's (1978) emphasis on student involvement in questioning for comprehension; and Manzo's (1975, 1985) guided reading procedure (GRP). Semantic webbing (or mapping), a visual technique that specifically aids readers in organizing what they read, can be used to improve comprehension (Freedman & Reynolds, 1980; Reutzel, 1985; Sinatra, Stahl-Gemake, & Berg, 1984). Some types of cloze training (Aulls, 1978; Carr, Dewitz, & Patberg, 1989) also aid comprehension of longer selections.

FIGURE 8.4 Example directed reading-thinking activity.

A DRTA lesson usually contains the following components which will be highlighted in the example presented.

I. Building Background for the Reading Selection
II. The DRTA Cycle
    a. Students set purposes, make predictions
    b. Silent reading
    c. Students verify predictions, satisfy purposes
III. Comprehension Check
IV. Rereading Parts of the Selection for Specific Purposes
 V. Enrichment, or Follow-up, Activities

DRTA Lesson

Teacher Goals:

1. To help students discover how to use the clues in text to anticipate upcoming text using both prior knowledge and context clues.
2. To expose students to a more expository (informational) writing style.

Student Objectives:

1. Each student will participate in the lesson by:
    a. offering answers to the opening riddle.
    b. making predictions about what (who) the text will be about.
    c. verifying their predictions by citing evidence in the text.
    d. answering comprehension questions following the silent reading and verification of predictions.
    e. writing their own "first person" riddle.

Materials:

Text: *A Not So Ugly Friend* by Stan Applebaum and Victoria Cox. This text is from The Satellite Books published by Holt, Rinehart and Winston and is a Level 10 book, meaning it is intended for use with second-semester second grade readers. The text begins by using a riddle format, each page providing clues for the reader about what is being described; in other words, who is the "not so ugly friend." For example, from the first page "I can't see you. I have no eyes, but I can feel you walking. I have no nose, but I have a mouth and I can taste. Do you know what I am?" Midway through the book the answer to the riddle is revealed, and then the book becomes informational about the earthworm and how valuable earthworms are to us—why we should consider them friends.

Procedures:

    To develop *background* for this lesson, introduce the idea of "first person" riddles, as the text is written in this format. It may be an unusual format for the students. These "practice" riddles will relate to people and things very familiar in the students' lives. In teaching new concepts it is much better to relate the unfamiliar to the familiar. For example, one practice riddle is: "I am something you drink. I come from a cow, and I'm white. Babies really like me a lot. Do you know what I am?" The riddles will be on individual index cards so that students can take turns reading them. After each riddle is solved, students must tell what the important clues were in the riddle that helped them solve it. At this point, students should be anxious to solve yet one more riddle, the one in the text.

    The *DRTA Cycle* will begin by introducing the title of the selection. Students will be told that this text is written like the riddles they just solved. The cover of the text may also be used if desired. Predictions will be made based on the key question "What or who do you think is the not so ugly friend?" Students' predictions will be written on the chalkboard. Once all predictions are made, each student is asked to choose one they think is correct. Their purpose for reading then is to verify

(continued)

FIGURE 8.4 Example directed reading-thinking activity (*continued*).

whether or not their prediction is accurate. With this text, proceed one page at a time, reading silently. After each page, students will reevaluate their predictions, and make changes, although they must be able to use the clues to justify their changes or new predictions. Once the answer is revealed in the text, discuss the clues as a group. At this point a new key question is introduced, "What does the earthworm do for us?" Again, write their ideas on the board. Students again read the rest of the selection silently to verify their predictions. Discuss their predictions and which ones were supported and what new information they discovered.

The questions for the *comprehension check* include vocabulary items that may be new, or are important to the understanding of the text. Sample questions are:

1. Who is this book about? (earthworm) textually explicit
2. Who is telling the story? (earthworm) textually implicit
3. Can earthworms *really* talk? (no) scriptally implicit
4. What is soil? (dirt, earth) scriptally implicit; possibly textually implicit
5. What does it mean to make the soil richer? (better for plants, helps plants grow better, provides nutrients) scriptally implicit
6. Why does the earthworm come out of the ground when it rains? (because the water fills the earthworm's underground hole) textually implicit
7. Why doesn't the earthworm like to be out in the sun? (because the sun dries out its skin) textually implicit
8. Where do earthworms come from (or how are they born)? (eggs) textually explicit
9. What did you learn about earthworms that you did not know before? (answers will vary) textually explicit, textually implicit
10. Can we think of earthworms as our friends? (yes, no, give reasons) scriptally implicit, textually implicit, textually explicit

Following the questions, students will be asked to *reread for the specific purpose* of completing a semantic map of the selection to help them organize what they have read. The core question of the map is "What does an earthworm do?" The students are allowed to look back to the text since this is a rereading activity. Each idea can then be read aloud if desired.

The *enrichment* activity for this lesson should be done individually. The students are to write three "first person" riddles that ask "Who Am I?" or "What Am I?" as their last line. These can then be posted later for other students to solve.

The goal of all of these comprehension strategies is to help students become more actively involved with text. Instruction focuses on encouraging flexibility, risk-taking, and depth of thinking. Questions mold the student's thinking—not to test for right and wrong answers. As Schwartz and Sheff (1975) state, "Instruction should provide a type of questioning that consciously directs the reader to become involved in understanding what he reads."

Examples cannot be given for all of the techniques mentioned, so you are strongly encouraged to consult the original sources. McNeil's (1987) *Reading Comprehension,* Flood's (1984) *Promoting Reading Comprehension,* and Cooper's (1986) *Improving Reading Comprehension* provide examples for some of these techniques and others as well.

Detailed examples for several comprehension instructional techniques will be provided here. Some aid students in organizing the material they read, others encourage self-questioning while reading. All initially require direct instruction by the teacher.

Semantic webbing, also called mapping, constructs a visual display representing relationships in the content of a story or expository selection (Freedman & Reynolds,

1980; Davidson, 1982). The technique is especially helpful for disabled readers, because it visually demonstrates how main ideas are logically related to subordinate ideas (Sinatra, Stahl-Gemake, & Berg, 1984). This is consistent with findings by Pirozzolo and Rayner (1979) that indicate that reading and learning disabled students are strong in the spatial mode of conceptualization. Cleland (1981) taught the process of semantic webbing to remedial second graders and found the technique helped them "to perceive relationships and organize their thoughts. Rereading is made more purposeful and retelling of stories is enhanced" (p. 645).

Four steps are basic in constructing a web, or map.

1. Answer the *core question.*
2. Use the answers to the core question as *web strands.*
3. Provide *strand supports,* facts, events, inferences, and generalizations taken from the story that distinguish one web strand from another.
4. Decide what *strand ties* exist, that is, how strands are related to each other. (Dotted lines may be used to indicate strand ties or location on the map itself, such as grouping.)

Before using a semantic web with students, the teacher must organize the content of the selection conceptually. For instance, in step 1, the core question, the focus of the web for *The Three Little Pigs* is chosen by the teacher (fig. 8.5) and placed in a central position. Answers to the core question elicited through discussion (i.e., the eight characters) become the web strands. The strand supports are facts, events, inferences, and generalizations that distinguish the characters from one another. Strand ties in this example are represented by placing the man with straw beside Pig #1, the man with twigs beside Pig #2, and so forth. Placement in sequential order also indicates the repetitive pattern in this story. The relationship between Pig #3 and the wolf is actually more complex than the strand supports in the figure indicate, however. The story contains a series of episodes in which the wolf tries to trick the pig and the pig outsmarts the wolf. If the teacher thinks further exploration of a part of the web would be beneficial, a section, such as the wolf and Pig #3, may be "blown up" to examine the more complex relationships.

Questions based on **story grammar** (a structure that describes the elements essential to a well-formed story) may improve children's comprehension by enhancing their schemata (Fitzgerald & Spiegel, 1983). In Mandler and Johnson's (1977) story grammar, the story elements are described as: a setting (who, where, and when); a beginning or initiating event (the problem for the hero); a reaction (what the hero says or does in response to the problem); a goal (what the hero decides to do about the problem); an attempt (the effort or efforts to solve the problem); an outcome (the consequence or result of what the hero does); and an ending (a brief wrap-up of the whole story).

Sadow (1982, p. 520) suggests five generic questions to be asked about a story:

1. Where and when did the events in the story take place and who was involved in them? *(setting)*
2. What started the chain of events in the story? *(initiating event)*
3. What was the main character's reaction to this event? *(reaction)*
4. What did the main character do about it? *(action: goals and attempts)*

FIGURE 8.5 Semantic web for *The Three Little Pigs.*

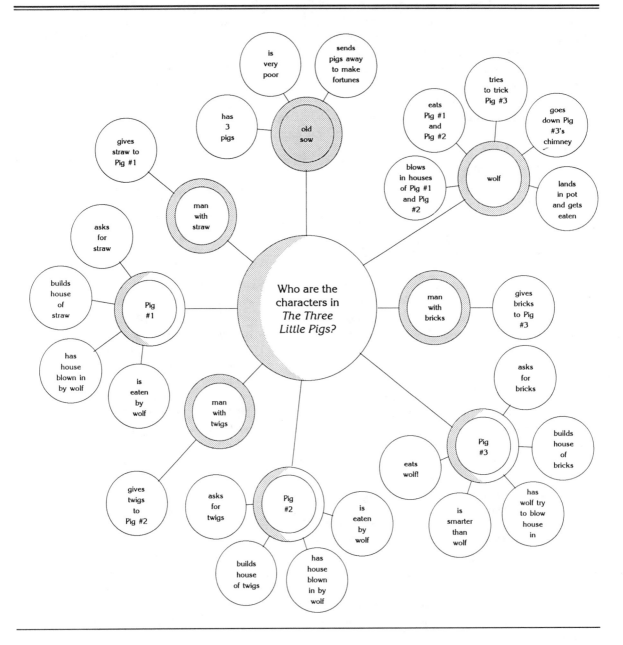

5. What happened as a result of what the main character did? *(consequence, outcome)*

A format such as that in figure 8.6 can help students see the structure of stories. Or, a story frame (Cudd & Roberts, 1987; Fowler, 1982) could be provided as follows.

FIGURE 8.6 Story map for *Goldilocks and the Three Bears.*

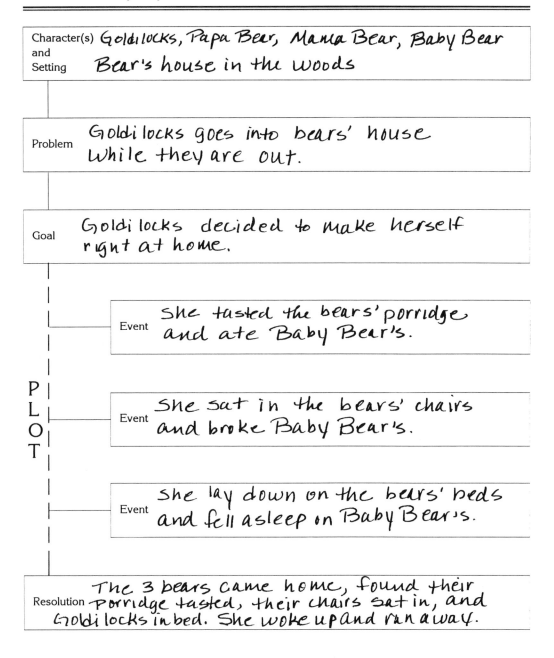

Character(s) and Setting: Goldilocks, Papa Bear, Mama Bear, Baby Bear
Bear's house in the woods

Problem: Goldilocks goes into bears' house while they are out.

Goal: Goldilocks decided to make herself right at home.

PLOT

Event: She tasted the bears' porridge and ate Baby Bear's.

Event: She sat in the bears' chairs and broke Baby Bear's.

Event: She lay down on the bears' beds and fell asleep on Baby Bear's.

Resolution: The 3 bears came home, found their porridge tasted, their chairs sat in, and Goldilocks in bed. She woke up and ran away.

Title: *Goldilocks and the Three Bears*

In this story, the problems start when _____

_____

After that, _____

_____

Next, _____

_____

Then, _____

_____

This was a problem because _____

_____

After that, _____

_____

Next, _____

_____

Then, _____

_____

The problem was solved when _____

_____

In the end, _____

_____

Questions based on story grammar and asked in conjunction with developing story maps help students see the underlying organization of ideas and relationships in a story (Beck & McKeown, 1981). For instance, in *The Three Little Pigs,* once the web strands (characters) are identified, the initiating event is asked about in order to begin eliciting information about each strand: "What caused the three pigs to go out on their own?" The responses provide strand supports for the old sow. Likewise, the reaction (in this example, three separate reactions for each pig) is elicited by asking: "What does each pig decide to do?" The goals, attempts, and outcomes follow by asking: "What does Pig #1 (Pig #2, Pig #3) decide to build?" "What is the first problem for the pigs?" "What happens to Pig #1?" "What is the next problem for the pigs?" "What happens to Pig #2?" "What is the problem for Pig #3?" "What happens to Pig #3?" "How is Pig #3 different from Pig #1 and Pig #2?" The ending is addressed by a question regarding a theme or a moral, such as, "Which pig is the hero, and why?" These questions develop the story map; however, questioning in the form of extension or enrichment can continue once the map (web) is completed.

Semantic webs may also be introduced in incomplete form as organizers in advance of reading. In an example suggested by Cleland (1981) and seen in figure 8.7, three distinct responses are indicated; students reading the selection will know to look for three major reasons for Joel's decision. A similar approach but one that provides more detail from the story is the cloze story map (Reutzel, 1986).

The real benefit from using semantic webbing lies in its teacher-directedness. The teacher guides the children in constructing the web by pointing out relationships between ideas and characters and events in the material read. The technique is *not* reserved for stories, but like DRTAs, works as well with expository material. In using content area material, Davidson (1982) observed that "as students interact with one another by sharing maps and asking questions about various elements in each others' maps, they gain insights about the various reasoning processes used by others." (p. 56).

FIGURE 8.7 Using semantic webs as advance organizers.

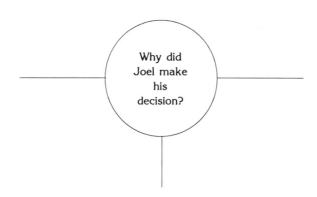

For detailed examples of a wide variety of mapping ideas you should refer to Heimlich and Pittelman's (1986) *Semantic Mapping: Classroom Applications.*

Reutzel[2] summarizes the ways story maps or webs help teachers and students to

- plan and execute more purposeful, focused reading lessons;
- organize readers' efforts toward specific comprehension objectives;
- focus questions and discussion on the important aspects of the text;
- create a workable structure for storage and retrieval of important information learned from the text;
- provide a visually coherent summary of the text;
- furnish a structure for guiding prereading experiences;
- supply students with a model for organizing and integrating text information in the content areas;
- present events and concepts in divergent visual patterns designed to emphasize specific types of relationships;
- experience a visual representation of text arrangements to encourage sensitivity to varying text patterns;
- summon the correct collection of background experiences and knowledge to facilitate comprehension of the text;
- encourage students to think about and monitor their reading.

Because of this last aspect, monitoring, the technique of mapping will be discussed as an instructional strategy in chapter 10 as well as additional comprehension monitoring training techniques.

Another type of comprehension instruction that the corrective reader needs when dealing with longer selections can be demonstrated using the selection in figure 8.8. The steps incorporate bits and pieces from techniques such as DRTA, but probably reflect the Shwartz and Sheff (1975) and Singer (1978) viewpoints more specifically. Remember that the corrective reader must be taught a highly structured step-by-step

[2] From "Story Maps Improve Comprehension," by D. Ray Reutzel, *Reading Teacher,* January 1985, page 403. Reprinted with permission of the author and the International Reading Association, Newark, Delaware.

FIGURE 8.8 Teaching active comprehension. ("The Hare and the Fox." From *Basic Reading*, Book C. © J. B. Lippincott Company, 1975, p. 37. Used by permission.)

The Hare and the Fox

A small, brown hare was sitting near a creek sunning himself, when he saw a fox. The fox was getting a drink in the small stream.

The hare ran from his nest, but the fox saw him hopping in the grass. Quick as a wink, the fox was running to catch the hare.

The brown hare ran into a hole in an old log. The hole was too small for a fox.

As the hare ran from the hole, he saw the fox digging to get into it.

When the fox got inside the old log, he did not find a hare. All he saw was a hole as long as the log.

procedure for approaching text, and such instruction should begin with small amounts of material.

The ultimate goal of all reading instruction is to develop independent readers. Comprehension instruction must bring the corrective reader to the point of active communication with the text. While this kind of involvement is being encouraged with the student-teacher interaction found in the structured comprehension lesson, for example, the teacher must also teach students to ask *themselves* questions of what they are reading. The teacher-posed questions of a structured comprehension lesson or a DRTA provide models for students. However, a gradual transfer from teacher-posed to student-posed questions is desirable in developing independent readers. This transfer, referred to by Singer (1978) as the **phase-out/phase-in strategy**, promotes active comprehension.

A most important procedure for teaching active comprehension is to ask a question that requires another question as the response. Using "The Hare and the Fox," a lesson may proceed as follows with the teacher asking questions to elicit initial student questions.

Teacher: "Look at the title. What questions could you ask about this story after reading just the title?"
Possible student questions:
"What will the hare and the fox be doing?"

"What is a hare?"
"What will happen to the hare?"
"What will happen to the fox?"
"Will the fox chase the hare?"
"Will the fox catch and eat the hare?"
"Will the hare get away?"

The teacher then asks questions paragraph by paragraph.

Teacher, paragraph 1: "What else would you like to know about the hare? What else about the fox?"
Possible student questions:
"Is it a baby hare?"
"Is the hare a fast runner?"
"Is the fox a fast runner?"
"Is the fox hungry?"

Teacher, paragraph 2: "What would you like to know more about when the fox starts running to catch the hare?"
Possible student questions:
"Will the fox catch the hare?"
"Will the hare get away?"

Teacher, paragraph 3: "Is there anything you'd like to know when the hare runs into the log?"
Possible student questions:
"Will the hare be safe?"
"Will the fox get in the log?"
"Will the fox wait for the hare to come out of the log?"

Teacher, paragraph 4: "What would you like to ask when the hare runs from the log?"
Possible student questions:
"Why did the hare run from the log?"
"Is the fox waiting outside to catch the hare?"
"Where will the hare run to next?"
"Will the fox be able to catch the hare?"

Teacher, paragraph 5: "After you read the last paragraph, what questions about the hare and the fox do you still have?"
Possible student questions:
"Did the fox run out of the log to chase the hare some more?"
"Where did the hare go?"
"Did the hare get away from the fox?"
"What happened to the fox and the hare next?"

This lesson sequence supplies example questions for each paragraph in order to provide more structure for the corrective reader. This procedure is not necessary for every lesson, however. The teacher may receive such a variety of questions at the initial stage that the students will be motivated enough to read the rest of the story. When students are able to find answers to their own questions, they become active comprehenders. With this particular example, the reader is not told in the text what happens to the hare and the fox. Answers to the last set of questions could be used as the basis for creative writing or a language experience story. In any case, the students become involved in reading; situations or problems are identified, and further understandings are sought while reading. Comprehension is the result.

Corrective readers also benefit from direct instruction in how to answer questions. They need to know about the different sources of information available for answering questions (Raphael & Pearson, 1985). As Raphael (1982) has pointed out, many poor comprehenders do not realize that it is both acceptable and necessary to use one's prior knowledge about the world to answer some types of comprehension questions. Thus, instruction in **question-answer relationships (QARs)**, is especially helpful to the corrective reader.

Raphael's classification scheme for QARs is based on Pearson and Johnson's (1978) question taxonomy of **textually explicit** (the answer to the question is directly stated in one sentence in the text), **textually implicit** (the answer to the question is in the text but requires some integration of text material as the answer might span several sentences or paragraphs), and **scriptally implicit** (the answer must come from the reader's prior knowledge).

An introductory lesson in QARs must first define all the question types. The first question-answer relationship (QAR) is termed "Right There" since the answer is directly stated in a single sentence. The second QAR is termed "Think and Search" because the answer requires information that spans several sentences or paragraphs. The third QAR is termed "On My Own" because readers must rely totally on their own background knowledge for the answer.

After several research studies, Raphael (1986) has added a fourth QAR, "Author and You," which recognizes that for some questions the answer comes from the reader's background knowledge but only in connection with information provided by the author. Consider the nursery rhyme, *Little Miss Muffet*, and the following questions as examples of each type.

> Little Miss Muffet sat on a tuffet,
> Eating her curds and whey.
> Along came a spider that sat down beside her,
> And frightened Miss Muffet away.

1. What did Miss Muffet sit on?

   Response: a tuffet
   QAR: Right There

2. Why did Miss Muffet get up from the tuffet?

   Response: a spider sat beside her and scared her away
   QAR: Think and Search

3. What are curds and whey?

   Response 1: something to eat
   QAR: Right There
   Response 2: In making cheese, the milk is allowed to sour. The curds are the thicker part which separates from the watery part, the whey. (Probably something like cottage cheese.)
   QAR: On My Own

4. What do you think Miss Muffet did when she first saw the spider?

>   Response: She probably threw her curds and whey up in the air, screamed, and jumped up as fast as she could to get away.
>   QAR: Author and You

Depending on the age and ability of the students, follow-up lessons will be needed for practice in recognizing the category types and using this knowledge in answering comprehension questions. Raphael (1986) suggests beginning QAR instruction with first- and second-grade students by introducing only a two-category distinction: "In The Book" and "In My Head." Middle grade students can learn the three (or four) categories in one lesson although the types can still be distinguished by the two headings "In The Book" ("Right There" and "Think and Search"), and "In My Head" ("Author and You" and "On My Own"). Sample text is presented with the questions, responses, and QAR provided, and the *reasons for each classification are discussed*. Once students understand category differences, then other samples of text, questions, and responses can be provided so they can identify the QAR. Finally, students, when provided text and questions only, will have learned to recognize the key words in questions that cue them as to whether the answer lies in the text or in their heads. At this point, students are well on their way in using text organization as an aid to comprehension.

Summary

Poor comprehenders generally do not view reading as a meaning-getting task; therefore, comprehension instruction for the corrective reader must emphasize understanding as the paramount purpose of reading. Instruction includes use of short selections, concrete words and examples, and appropriate questions. It must be direct, that is, involve teacher-student interaction. Teachers should verbalize for their students the strategies they themselves use while trying to comprehend text. These strategies might include finding the main idea or predicting an outcome. Comprehension instruction is not limited to intermediate grades and beyond; it *must* be taught from the first grade. Many techniques presented in this chapter can be adapted as listening activities. To be good comprehenders, students must first realize that written materials should make sense. Until this realization has been internalized by the student, no instruction in comprehension is likely to help.

References

Aulls, M. W. (1978). *Developmental and remedial reading in the middle grades,* Abridged edition. Boston: Allyn and Bacon.

Beck, I. L., & McKeown, M. B. (1981). Developing questions that promote comprehension of the story map. *Language Arts, 58,* 913–917.

Bormuth, J. R. (1969). An operational definition of comprehension instruction. In K. S. Goodman and J. T. Fleming (Eds.), *Psycholinguistics and the teaching of reading.* Newark, DE: International Reading Association.

Brown, A. L., & Palincsar, A. S. (1982). Inducing strategic learning from texts by means of informed, self-control training. *Topics in Learning and Learning Disabilities, 2,* 1–17.

Carr, E., Dewitz, P., & Patberg, J. (1989). Using cloze for inference training with expository text. *The Reading Teacher, 42,* 380–385.

Caskey, H. J. (1970). Guidelines for teaching comprehension. *The Reading Teacher, 23,* 649–654, 669.

Cleland, C. J. (1981). Highlighting issues in children's literature through semantic webbing. *The Reading Teacher, 34,* 642–646.

Cohn, M. L. (1969). Structured comprehension. *The Reading Teacher, 22,* 440–444, 489.

Cooper, J. D. (1986). *Improving reading comprehension.* Boston: Houghton Mifflin.

Cromer, W. (1970). The difference model: A new explanation for some reading difficulties. *Journal of Educational Psychology, 61,* 471–483.

Cudd, E. T., & Roberts, L. L. (1987). Using story frames to develop reading comprehension in a first grade classroom. *The Reading Teacher, 41,* 74–79.

Cudd, E. T., & Roberts, L. L. (1989). Using writing to enhance content area learning in the primary grades. *The Reading Teacher, 42,* 392–404.

Davidson, J. L. (1982). The group mapping activity for instruction in reading and thinking. *Journal of Reading, 26,* 52–56.

Durkin, D. (1978–1979). What classroom observations reveal about reading comprehension instruction. *Reading Research Quarterly, 14,* 481–533.

Fitzgerald, J., & Spiegel, D. L. (1983). Enhancing children's reading comprehension through instruction in narrative structure. *Journal of Reading Behavior, 15,* 1–17.

Flood, J. (Ed.). (1984). *Promoting reading comprehension.* Newark, DE: International Reading Association.

Fowler, G. L. (1982). Developing comprehension skills in primary students through the use of story frames. *The Reading Teacher, 37,* 176–179.

Freedman, G., & Reynolds, E. G. (1980). Enriching basal reader lessons with semantic webbing. *The Reading Teacher, 33,* 677–684.

Gambrell, L. B. (1982). Induced mental imagery and the text prediction performance of first and third graders. In J. A. Niles and L. A. Harris (Eds.), *New inquiries in reading research and instruction.* Thirty-first Yearbook of the National Reading Conference, Rochester, NY.

Heilman, A. W., & Holmes, E. A. (1978). *Smuggling language into the teaching of reading.* Columbus, OH: Merrill.

Heimlich, J. E., & Pittelman, S. D. (1986). *Semantic mapping: Classroom applications.* Newark, DE: International Reading Association.

Hittleman, D. R. (1983). *Developmental reading, K–8: Teaching from a psycholinguistic perspective.* Boston: Houghton Mifflin.

Hughes, T. O. (1975). *Sentence combining: A means of increasing reading comprehension.* Bloomington, IN: ERIC Clearinghouse on Reading, ED 112 421.

Irwin, J. W. (1986). *Teaching reading comprehension processes.* Englewood Cliffs, NJ: Prentice-Hall.

Jenkins, J. R., & Pany, D. (1981). Instructional variables in reading comprehension. In J. T. Guthrie (Ed.), *Comprehension and teaching: Research reviews.* Newark, DE: International Reading Association.

Kamm, K. (1979). Focusing reading comprehension instruction: Sentence meaning skills. In C. Pennock (Ed.), *Reading comprehension at four linguistic levels.* Newark, DE: International Reading Association.

Karlin, R. (1975). *Teaching elementary reading: Principles and strategies* (2nd ed.). New York: Harcourt Brace Jovanovich.

Levin, J. R. (1973). Inducing comprehension in poor readers: A test of a recent model. *Journal of Educational Psychology, 65,* 19–24.

Mandler, J. M., & Johnson, N. S. (1977). Remembrance of things parsed: Story structure and recall. *Cognitive Psychology, 9,* 111–151.

Manzo, A. V. (1985). Expansion modules for the ReQuest, CAT, GRP, and REAP reading/study procedures. *Journal of Reading, 28,* 498–502.

Manzo, A. V. (1975). Guided reading procedure. *Journal of Reading, 18,* 287–291.

Manzo, A. V. (1969). The ReQuest procedure. *Journal of Reading, 13,* 123–126.

McNeil, J. D. (1987). *Reading comprehension: New directions for classroom practice.* Glenview, IL: Scott, Foresman.

Palincsar, A. S., & Brown, A. L. (1986). Interactive teaching to promote independent learning from text. *The Reading Teacher, 39,* 771–777.

Palincsar, A. S., & Brown, A. L. (1984). Reciprocal teaching of comprehension-fostering and comprehension-monitoring activities. *Cognition and Instruction, 1,* 117–175.

Pearson, P. D., & Johnson, D. D. (1978). *Teaching reading comprehension.* New York: Holt, Rinehart and Winston.

Pennock, C. (Ed.). (1979). *Reading comprehension at four linguistic levels.* Newark, DE: International Reading Association.

Pirozzolo, F. J., & Rayner, K. (1979). Cerebral organization and reading disability. *Neuropsychologia, 17,* 485–492.

Raphael, T. E. (1982). Question-answering strategies for children. *The Reading Teacher, 36,* 186–190.

Raphael, T. E. (1986). Teaching question answer relationships, revisited. *The Reading Teacher, 39,* 516–522.

Raphael, T. E., & Pearson, P. D. (1985). Increasing students' awareness of sources of information for answering questions. *American Educational Research Journal, 22,* 217–235.

Reutzel, D. R. (1986). Clozing in on comprehension: The cloze story map. *The Reading Teacher, 39,* 524–528.

Reutzel, D. R. (1985). Story maps improve comprehension. *The Reading Teacher, 38,* 400–404.

Sadow, M. W. (1982). The use of story grammar in the design of questions. *The Reading Teacher, 35,* 518–522.

Schwartz, E., & Sheff, A. (1975). Student involvement in questioning for comprehension. *The Reading Teacher, 29,* 150–154.

Sinatra, R. C., Stahl-Gemake, J., & Berg, D. N. (1984). Improving reading comprehension of disabled readers through semantic mapping. *The Reading Teacher, 38,* 22–29.

Singer, H. (1978). Active comprehension: From answering to asking questions. *The Reading Teacher, 31,* 901–908.

Stauffer, R. G. (1981). Strategies for reading instruction. In M. Douglas (Ed.), Forty-fifth Yearbook of the Claremont Reading Conference, Claremont, CA.

Taylor, B. H. (1979). *Good and poor readers, recall of familiar and unfamiliar text.* Paper presented at the 24th Annual Meeting of the International Reading Association, Atlanta.

Weaver, P. A. (1979). Improving reading comprehension: Effects of sentence organization instruction. *Reading Research Quarterly, 15,* 129–146.

Willford, R. (1968). Comprehension: What reading's all about. *Grade Teacher, 85,* 99–103.

CHAPTER 9
Study Skills

Objectives

After you have studied this chapter, you should be able to

1. list and describe the major study skills;
2. identify prerequisite skills for a given study skill;
3. recognize sources of material other than stories for teaching study skills;
4. develop informal assessment activities for any study skill;
5. develop instructional activities for any study skill.

Study Outline

I. Background

II. Study skills and the corrective reader

III. Assessment strategies for locational skills
  A. Formal measures
  B. Informal measures
    1. Alphabetizing
    2. Book parts
    3. Reference materials
    4. Library skills

IV. Instructional strategies for developing locational skills
  A. General teaching strategy
  B. Specific activities
    1. Alphabetical order
    2. Parts of books
    3. Using an index

V. Assessment strategies for organizing information
  A. Assessing ability
  B. Informal measures

  1. Classifying words, phrases, and sentences
  2. Main ideas and supporting details
  3. Sequencing
  4. Summarizing and synthesizing

VI. Instructional strategies for organizing information
  A. Classifying
  B. Main ideas and supporting details
  C. Sequencing
  D. Summarizing and synthesizing
  E. Note-taking
  F. Outlining

VII. Assessment strategies for interpreting graphic and pictorial materials
  A. Formal measures
  B. Informal measures

Important Vocabulary and Concepts

arrays
content words
equal status relationships
expository material
Herringbone technique
locational skills
main ideas
mapping
paraphrase

semantic webbing
study skills
subordinate relationships
summarizing
superordinate relationships
synthesizing
thought units
topic

Overview

It is not enough to teach students how to recognize new words and how to improve their understanding of what they read. If a major goal of reading instruction is to develop truly independent readers, closer attention must be paid to the area of study skills and strategic reading. When a student has no difficulty in reading class but cannot transfer knowledge of reading skills to materials other than basal readers or stories, the weakness may be in the area of study skills or strategic reading.

Study skills will be introduced in this chapter in a kind of hierarchy, that is, skills seen as prerequisites for other study skills will be discussed before more complex skills. This presentation will help you do a better job of assessing and teaching study skills.

More specifically, the study skills of (1) locating and organizing information and (2) interpreting graphic and pictorial material will be discussed at length. You will soon see that the techniques used to aid reading comprehension are also used to develop the study skill of organizing information. One major difference in teaching the study skills discussed here is the type of material used. The instructional examples given throughout this chapter deal with nonstory, or content area, material. Many examples of specific instructional techniques are provided; although teachers know that study skills should be taught, they are often at a loss regarding how to proceed. As a result, many developmental readers are corrective readers in the area of study skills.

This chapter will help you to become familiar with what study skills are, to recognize the importance of teaching them, and to teach them effectively. New terms will be defined or explained.

Introduction

According to Cooper, Warncke, Ramstad, and Shipman (1979, p. 137) **"Study skills are the tool aspects of reading which allow the reader to extend and expand his basic reading skill." Any discussion of study skills assumes that the reader has some basic knowledge of word recognition and comprehension skills—one cannot "extend and expand" something that is not present. Only minimum reading skill is necessary, however, as word recognition, comprehension, and study skills are all interrelated. Growth in one area aids growth in another. Instruction in study skills and strategic reading therefore should not be delayed until a reader has well-developed word recognition and comprehension skills.

The material used to teach study skills differs from that used to teach basic word recognition and comprehension skills. The narrative material of the basal reader or language experience story does not provide an opportunity to learn and apply study skills. For example, the various uses of book parts to locate information cannot be taught when a book's table of contents lists only titles of stories. Being able to use a table of contents is an important study skill, although other book parts typically found in content area textbooks (e.g., title page, index, copyright) more readily help children realize that specific parts of books can help them locate specific kinds of information. Other study skills, such as using the card catalog or interpreting a bar graph, simply cannot be taught most effectively with narrative material.

An increasing number of secondary teachers complain that "Johnny can't read the textbook" or that "Johnny doesn't know how to find information for his term project." A student who may otherwise be a good reader, or one who was thought *not* to have a reading problem in elementary school, often cannot deal independently with secondary level textbooks. At present, direct teaching of study skills seems to be overlooked or ignored during the elementary school years. Part of the problem may be that the elementary level teacher judges a reader's progress only in the areas of comprehension and word recognition skills and by using narrative material in the basal reader. The teacher then assumes that the reader can apply this reading skill to the more factual material in content area textbooks. Thus, an otherwise good reader suddenly has a problem upon entering the intermediate grades where content area reading increases.

This sequence of events is not excusable, however; school system curriculum guides suggest teaching some study skills as early as first grade (fig. 9.1). The teacher must also provide ample opportunity to apply the skills in material other than the basal reader. The use of study skills is *not* central to reading a story but *is* central to reading a content area textbook and other materials such as newspapers, encyclopedias, and magazines. Study skills should be taught in the context in which they will be used.

Another unfortunate part of the problem may be that teachers themselves are not knowledgeable regarding the study skills intended for use by children (Askov, Kamm, & Klumb, 1977). As Cooper et al. (1979, p. 138) point out, reading experts do not agree as to what specific skills should be taught, although most suggested skills fall into one of four categories: locating information, organizing information, interpreting graphic and pictorial materials, and adjustment of reading rate.

Cooper et al. (pp. 138–145) provide an extensive taxonomy of study skills for the interested reader. However, a corrective reading text more appropriately emphasizes study skills considered basic or prerequisite to the others. During discussion of these skills, the interrelation of word recognition and especially comprehension skills will become apparent. It should be recalled that the corrective reader is probably not having difficulty with all aspects of reading. Thus, a student who is having trouble with content area material may not have a reading problem in general, only difficulty with specific study skills or with strategic reading.

FIGURE 9.1 Example of the kinds of study skills suggested for introduction in first grade. (From *Minimum Standards/Maximum Goals for Reading in Louisiana, Grades 1–12*, Louisiana State Department of Education, 1977, p. 35.)

*	A. Alphabetizes with first letter
	B. Follows directions
***	1. Two-step oral directions
*	2. Simple written directions
	C. Locates information
	1. Parts of a book
*	a. Title page
*	b. Table of contents
*	c. Page numbers
	2. Dictionary
*	a. Picture dictionary
*	b. Word meaning
*	c. Word spelling
	3. Graphic materials
*	a. Calendar
*	b. Picture maps
*	c. Simple charts
	4. Library
*	a. Selects a book
***	b. Signs for a book

Key:
* skill introduced
** skill ongoing
*** skill mastered

In summary, study skills are tools that enhance the reader's understanding of content area textbooks and other informative materials. The basic or prerequisite skills are found in figure 9.2. The rest of this chapter presents specific assessment and instructional strategies for the first three of the four major categories listed previously. Strategies for study appropriate for corrective readers and adjustment of reading rate will be discussed in chapter 10.

Study Skills and the Corrective Reader

Once again, to meet the needs of the corrective reader, the teacher first determines the reader's deficiencies in a particular area. Remember that the corrective reader has moderate reading problems or learning gaps. The teacher should be able to provide appropriate instruction for these students within the classroom in a relatively short time.

Particularly the underlying tasks necessary for success for study skills must be determined. For example, Jerry must have certain prerequisite skills to use an index. The study skills checklist in figure 9.2 arranges the subskills within each category according to an underlying hierarchy so that prerequisite skills can be easily identified. Thus, for Jerry to use an index, he must be able to alphabetize by first, second, and third letters.

FIGURE 9.2 Study skills checklist.

Study Skill	Knows	In Progress	Does Not Know	Not Assessed
I. Locating information				
A. Alphabetizes by first letter				
B. Alphabetizes by second letter				
C. Alphabetizes by third letter				
D. Knows and uses book parts (table of contents, index, glossary)				
E. Knows and uses reference materials (e.g., dictionary, thesaurus, encyclopedia, directories)				
F. Uses the library (card catalog, Dewey Decimal System)				
II. Organization information				
A. Knows and uses specialized vocabulary				
B. Categorizes information				
C. Recognizes main ideas/supporting details				
D. Sequences events				
E. Summarizes/synthesizes information				
F. Takes effective notes				
G. Outlines effectively				
III. Interpreting graphic and pictorial materials				
A. Uses pictures				
B. Uses graphs				
C. Uses tables				
D. Uses maps				
IV. Has and uses a study strategy (chapter 10)				

To help corrective readers, the weak skill and, equally important, deficient prerequisite skills must be identified. If Jackie cannot use the encyclopedia and other reference materials, she may not be able to alphabetize properly or know how to use the various book parts. Exercises on using reference materials without first learning these prerequisite skills will probably be unsuccessful.

In summary, this chapter stresses the need to consider underlying tasks. This emphasis is especially relevant for the corrective reader who characteristically has learning gaps.

Assessment Strategies for Locational Skills

Formal Measures

Most standardized achievement tests include subtests on a limited range of **locational skills**, usually titled "work-study" skills. The most common skills tested are interpretation of tables and graphs and use of reference materials (e.g., *Iowa Test of Basic Skills; Comprehensive Test of Basic Skills*). Because the range of skills tested is small and the yield is simply a grade equivalent, stanine, or other standard score reflecting a general level of achievement only, the information obtained by the teacher for instructional purposes is minimal. The standardized test may indicate a weakness, but informal assessment will be needed to pinpoint the specific teachable units.

Informal Measures

Teacher-made tests, if constructed with some thought, are a valuable source of information for instructional decision making (Kennedy, 1977). In the checklist (fig. 9.2), the skill of actually locating information has the prerequisite skills of being able to alphabetize by first, second, third, and beyond letters. Most teachers will have no difficulty devising an instrument to determine whether students have these prerequisite skills.

Alphabetizing

Some sample exercises for assessing the ability to alphabetize follow. They are presented in an order of increasing difficulty.

1. Present letters and have students provide the letter that comes immediately before and after.

(q)	r	(s)		f	
	c			v	

2. Present a random listing of letters to students and have them arrange the list in alphabetical order.

   x, c, r, j, d, s, u, t, a, m.

3. Provide students with a random listing of familiar words that begin with different letters. Ask the students to arrange the list alphabetically, or place words alphabetically in their word banks or personal dictionaries.

   the, dog, cat, me, house, baby.

4. Provide students with a random listing of words that begin with the same letter but have different second letters. Ask the students to arrange the list alphabetically.

   cat, come, cup, city, cent.

5. Provide students with a random listing of words that are sometimes different in the first or second letter. Ask the students to arrange the list alphabetically.

   give, bed, foot, jump, gave, bad.

6. Provide students with a random listing of words that are all alike in the first and second letters but differ in the third. Ask them to arrange the list alphabetically.

   bowl, boat, boy, bottle.

7. Provide the students with a list of words that vary to any extent. Ask the students to arrange the list alphabetically.

   such, as, to, try, come, camp, look, like, boy, road, read.

Book Parts

Knowledge of book parts can be checked simply by asking the student to locate a particular part and then describe its purpose or how it might be used. Figure 9.3 shows an example of a skills test for assessing knowledge of book parts in a written format. Book parts that should be tested are the title page; date of publication page; table of contents; lists of tables, graphs, maps, illustrations, and so on; preface or forward; glossary; index; appendix; and bibliography or references.

Reference Materials

The ability to recognize and use a variety of reference materials needs to be assessed. Activities for assessing the more common information sources should come first. For example, use of the dictionary and encyclopedia can be assessed by the following activities.

Dictionary

1. Students must be able to alphabetize and interpret diacritical marks to use a dictionary or glossary. An exercise similar to the following, containing words that the students already know how to pronounce, is recommended.

   Directions to students: Use the pronunciation key at the top of the page and circle the correct dictionary respelling of the numbered words. The first one has been done for you.

Pronunciation key				
fat	āpe	cär	ten	ēven
hit	bīte	gō	yü-few	tool
book	up	für	ə = a in ago	

1. dad

   dād   (dad)   däd   dəd

2. look

   look   look   lōk   lŏk

FIGURE 9.3 Skill test for parts of a book. (From *The Reading Corner*, by Harry W. Forgan, Jr. Reproduced by permission of Scott, Foresman and Company. © 1977.)

Name _____

KNOW YOUR BOOK

Directions:

Use your _____ book to answer these questions.

1. What is the title of this book?

2. Who are the authors?

3. When was the book copyrighted?

4. What is a copyright?

5. What company published the book?

6. What edition is this book?

7. What kind of information is in the preface?

8. Why do some books have more than one edition?

9. Give an example of how the table of contents can help you.

10. Is there a list of tables, maps, or diagrams?

11. How can this help you?

12. How are new words shown?

13. Is there a glossary?

14. How can the glossary help you?

15. Where is the index located?

16. When will you use the index?

17. Is there an appendix?

18. What information is presented in the appendix?

3. main

　　man　　män　　mān　　mãĭn

4. cute

　　cute　　kute　　kut　　kyüt

About ten items should be given.

2. Provide students with sets of guide words from the dictionary (e.g., *mill/mind*). Ask questions about the sets: Which word will be found at the bottom of the page? Why is *mill* written before *mind*? Where will you find *mill* on this page?

3. Provide students with guide words from two pages of the dictionary. Then give them other words and ask them to choose the page where the word will be found, or whether it can be found on either page. For example:

domain/door　　　　　　　　　　　*downcast/drain*

dragon	double
doze	doorway
donkey	downstairs
dog	dome

4. Have students write in the guide words for the pages in their personal dictionaries.

5. Provide students with a list of words and have them write the guide words of the page where they found each word.

6. Provide the students with several dictionary entries. The students should study each entry and be able to answer the questions that follow. Try to include a variety of parts of speech, accents, syllables, and diacritical marks. The reader should note that dictionary activities assume knowledge that is typically taught as a decoding skill. For example, students must be able to recognize syllables, accents, and diacritical markings before a task like the following can be used.

Example:

freight (frāt), *n.* 1. a load of goods shipped by train, ship, truck, airplane, etc. 2. the cost of shipping such goods. *v.* 1. to load with freight. 2. to send by freight.

A. What is the vowel sound heard in this word? __(long a)__

B. How many syllables does this word have? __(one)__ If more than one, on what syllable is the accent? _____

C. The letter *n* means __(noun)__.

D. The letter *v* means __(verb)__.

E. If the guide words on a page of the dictionary were *framework* and *free*, would *freight* be on that page, on the page before, or on the page after? _(after)_

F. Which definition and part of speech for *freight* is being used in the following sentence? (second; noun) The *freight* for the package was $2.75.

Encyclopedia. According to Hittleman (1983, p. 297), in order to use information from an encyclopedia effectively, a reader must be able to use the encyclopedia index, information on the spine of each volume, guide words, cross references, and bibliographies at the end of articles. Each of these items needs assessing. An example skill test for assessing encyclopedia knowledge may proceed as follows:

Students are provided with a picture of a set of encyclopedias (fig. 9.4), or the actual set can be displayed in the classroom. Questions are then asked about the set.

1. How many volumes are in this set of encyclopedias?   (14)
2. To find out more about the climate in Alaska, which volume would you use?   (1)
3. What number and letters are on the volume you would use to find information about each topic in the following list:

Topic	Number	Letter(s)
climate	(2)	(B–C)
polar	(9)	(O–P)
bees	(2)	(B–C)
eskimos	(3)	(D–E)
whales	(13)	(W–X)
zebras	(14)	(Y–Z)

Exercises in workbooks accompanying basal series often can be used as skills tests. Figure 9.5 represents such an exercise.

In addition to the dictionary and encyclopedia, students should be able to use the thesaurus, directories (e.g., *The Yellow Pages*), almanacs, and periodicals. Assessment tasks are just as easily constructed for these materials as for the dictionary and encyclopedia. An example skill test on when to use each type of reference material is seen in figure 9.6.

Library Skills

The last major area dealing with locational skills is the use of the library. To use the library effectively the reader must be able to use the card catalog, the particular classification scheme of the library (most likely the Dewey or Library of Congress classification), and special collections (e.g., periodicals, records, filmstrips, and vertical files). Some sample skill tests follow.

1. Provide students with a sample set of cards found in the card catalog and questions about the cards.

FIGURE 9.4 Students can be taught to use encyclopedias by giving them a picture of a set and asking relevant questions.

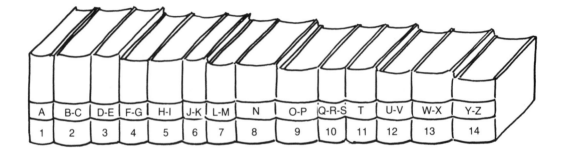

FIGURE 9.5 Skill test for using an index. (From Skills Handbook for *All Sorts of Things* of the READING 360 series by Theodore Clymer and others. © Copyright 1973, 1969 by Ginn and Company [Xerox Corporation]. Used with permission.)

Read the Index

An index is an alphabetical list which tells where items can be found in a book.

Part of an index is given below. Read the index, then use the index to answer the questions below.

Plays
"Bake a Cake," 10
"Long, Long Ago," 51
"Tick-Tock," 25

Poems
"A Busy Day," 26
"Dogs Can Play," 16
"Music For You," 3

Songs
"Happy Time," 30
"It Rained All Day Long," 32

Stories
Animal, 17
Folk Tales, 52
Humorous, 34

1. On what page can a poem about dogs be found? __*16*__
2. On what page can you read about long ago? __*51*__
3. What is "It Rained All Day Long"? __*Song*__
4. Which page has a poem about music? __*3*__
5. What kinds of stories are listed in the index? __*Animal*__, __*Folk Tales*__, __*Humorous*__
6. What is the name of the play that could be about a clock? __*Tick-Tock*__
7. Look under **Plays** in the index. What are the titles of the plays? __*Bake a Cake*__, __*Long, Long Ago*__, __*Tick-Tock*__
8. "It Rained All Day Long" is the name of one song listed in the index. What is the name and page number of the other song listed in the index? __*Happy Time*__, __*30*__
9. In what kind of book would you find an index like the one above? _____
_____

Directions: Study the three types of cards found in the card catalog and then answer the questions.

	F	Dahl, Roald
A	Dah	James and the giant peach, a children's story.
		Illustrated by Nancy Ekholm Burket. Knopf 1961 118p illus

FIGURE 9.6 Skill test for reference materials. (From *The Reading Corner* by Harry W. Forgan. Reproduced by permission of Scott, Foresman and Company. © 1977.)

Name _____

Appendix Item **64**
Skill Test for Reference Materials

Directions:
Listed below are some kinds of information you may need to obtain. There is also a list of reference materials that contain information. Match reference books with the information by placing the letter of the reference material in front of the information. You can use the letters more than once. Remember, sometimes the information might be found in two or three different types of material, but one would be the best source.

A. Encyclopedia
B. Atlas
C. Thesaurus
D. Dictionary
E. Telephone Book
F. Almanac

_____ 1. . Pictures of the human body

_____ 2. Address of a friend

_____ 3. Maps

_____ 4. How televisions work

_____ 5. Pronunciation of a new word

_____ 6. Words that mean the same

_____ 7. Where to buy flowers in your community

_____ 8. Information about animals

_____ 9. Information about the number of telephones in the United States

_____ 10. Words that mean the opposite

_____ 11 . The population of the United States

_____ 12. Who won the World Series last year

_____ 13. The telephone number of a store

_____ 14. A map that shows where corn is grown

_____ 15. To find out what causes bumps when you hit your head

_____ 16. To find out what stores sell sports equipment

_____ 17. To find the correct spelling of a word

_____ 18. To find out what parts of United States get the most rainfall

_____ 19. To find the high and low temperatures of different states in United States

_____ 20. To find pictures of poisonous snakes

B	F Dah	James and the giant peach, a children's story. Roald Dahl Illustrated by Nancy Ekholm Burket Knopf 1961 118p illus

C	F Dah	Children's Story Roald Dahl James and the giant peach, a children's story. Illustrated by Nancy Ekholm Burket. Knopf 1961 118p illus

Questions:
1. Which card (A, B, or C) is the title card? __(B)__
2. Which card (A, B, or C) is the subject card? __(C)__
3. Which card (A, B, or C) is the author card? __(A)__
4. How many pages does this book have? __(118)__
5. What does *illus* mean? __(illustrated; the book has pictures)__
6. Who is the publisher of the book? __(Knopf)__
7. When was this book published? __(1961)__
8. Why are there three cards for one book? __(if you know just the title or author or subject, you will still be able to find the book)__
9. What do the numbers or letters in the upper left corner of the card tell you? __(how to locate the book on the shelf)__
10. The author's name begins with __(D)__
11. If the author's name begins with Mc, it is filed as if it began with __(M)__
12. Why do we have a card catalog? __(to help us locate books in the library)__

Another set of cards follows for which the same questions could be asked.

	910	McFall, Christie
	McF	Underwater continent: the continental shelves.
A		With illus. by the author.
		Introduction by Jaap W. Boosman.
		Dodd 1975 120p illus bibl

	910	Underwater continent: the continental shelves.
	McF	Christie McFall
B		With illus. by the author.
		Introduction by Jaap W. Boosman.
		Dodd 1975 120p illus bibl

	910	Continental shelf
	McF	Christie McFall
C		Underwater continent: the continental shelves.
		With illus. by the author.
		Introduction by Jaap W. Boosman. Dodd 1975 120p illus bibl

2. Have the students use the card catalog to locate books. Begin by locating the correct drawer for suggested book titles (fig. 9.7).

Directions: On the blank in front of each one of the book titles, write the number of the drawer in the card catalog where you would find the book listed.

___ 1. *The Phantom Tollbooth*   ___ 4. The Sign of the Beaver
___ 2. *Charlotte's Web*   ___ 5. *Football: You Are the Coach*
___ 3. *A Kitten Is Born*   ___ 6. *101 Ways to Fix Hamburger*

Once all assessments have been made, the teacher interprets and summarizes total results. Once again figure 9.2 is referred to. If a copy of the checklist for each student is available while scoring skills tests, areas of strengths and weaknesses for

FIGURE 9.7 Learning to use the library card catalog starts by locating the correct drawer for book titles.

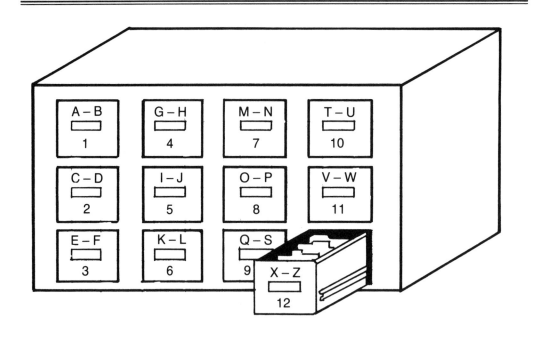

these and other study skills are easily marked. When all checklists are marked, the teacher can group the students for instruction in skill areas.

Instructional Strategies for Developing Locational Skills

Instructional strategies for the corrective reader do not differ essentially from those used to teach developmental reading. The major difference is that analysis has identified a specific need. An attempt should be made with corrective readers to provide lessons that are motivating and relevant to their experiences. Rather than using the students' textbooks and workbooks, more unusual materials are employed. Some items that are atypical, yet provide good sources for work in the entire area of study skills, follow.

catalogs	newspapers
TV program guides	globes
diaries	*Guinness Book of World Records*
job applications	How-to-make-it books
maps	ingredient labels
menus	advertisements
travel brochures	driver's manual
thesauruses	insurance forms

encyclopedias   weather maps and reports
magazines   police reports

General Teaching Strategy

With some modifications, the exercises used for assessment can also serve as the basis for a lesson. The student is first made aware of the purpose for learning the skills. For alphabetizing, students are shown that being able to alphabetize allows them to use such valuable resources as the dictionary, telephone directory, and encyclopedia. Once the purpose of the lesson is established, some motivation for pursuing the lesson may be necessary. For example, in order to play a new game, such as an alphabetizing relay, participants must know how to alphabetize.

The teacher is now ready to teach the skill to the students directly. Usually this means demonstrating how a random list of words can be arranged alphabetically. The teacher should explain the actual process used to alphabetize, showing how words are compared by first letters (or by second or third letters, depending on the specific purpose of the lesson). After the explanation, the teacher invites student feedback to see if the explanation was clear. This may mean simply asking a student to reexplain the procedure just described.

Once the students demonstrate that they understand the explanation, the teacher gives them a chance to practice the new skill with no penalties for errors. This practice stage also allows the teacher to clarify any misunderstandings. When the teacher is satisfied that the students understand the process, they are redirected to the immediate purpose, in this case the alphabetizing relay. After the relay, the teacher may evaluate each student with a worksheet exercise on the same material.

An important part of the strategy is to give the students many opportunities to apply the newly learned skill in appropriate situations. For example, soon after the actual alphabetizing lesson, perhaps later in the day or week, a new science term may be introduced. The teacher asks the students how they can find out what the word means and also check on its pronunciation. If no one says the dictionary, the teacher simply suggests using the dictionary and reemphasizes the skill taught in the alphabetizing lesson (in this case, where the word would be found in the dictionary using the first letter as a guide).

Another planned application is development of a classroom directory. The students first list their names, last names first, on the chalkboard one at a time. Then, using the skills taught in the initial alphabetizing lesson, they alphabetize the list. The directory is completed by looking up the names in the telephone directory and copying the address and telephone information. A periodic check with similar activities should be planned to ensure that the skill is being maintained.

Thus, the steps of the lesson are as follows:

1. Establish the purpose of the lesson.
2. Provide motivation for the lesson.
3. Teach the skill directly.
   a. Demonstrate and explain process.
   b. Check students' understanding of explanation.
   c. Allow for students to practice new skill.
   d. Review purpose and complete the original task (motivation).

4. Allow independent practice (e.g., a follow-up worksheet).
5. Provide application opportunities.
6. Plan for distributed practice (periodic checks).

Specific Activities

This general format can be used in planning lessons to develop the locational skills and many other reading skills. Some especially worthwhile activities for corrective readers having difficulty with locational skills follow.

Alphabetical Order

Directions: Look at each row of words. For each row, circle the word that would come first in the dictionary. Underline the word that comes last in the dictionary.

Example:	grew	grade	go	(gasp)
1. boy	down	city	over	
2. little	lot	lake	letter	
3. dance	date	days	dark	

Activities are often found in reading workbooks. Figures 9.8 through 11 demonstrate alphabetizing activities. Figure 9.9, which illustrates reasons for knowing how to alphabetize, is particularly valuable.

Parts of Books

Have the students locate the table of contents in any content area textbook.[1] Ask questions such as the following:

1. On what pages do you find the chapter called "The Founding of our Nation?" (173–202)
2. On what page does the chapter called "The Civil War Divides the Nation" begin? (263)
3. Does this book include a chapter on what the United States is like today? (yes, chapter 13)
4. If you wanted to read about the settlers moving westward across the Appalachian Mountains, which chapter would you go to? (chapter 8, "Exploring the North Central States")
5. How many pages are in the chapter called "Exploring the New World?" (24)
6. Does this book have an index? (yes, begins on page 463)

Using an Index

Have the students locate the index in any content area textbook. Use the index to find answers to questions. Students write the answer, the page on which they found it, and any heading from the index that helped them (fig. 9.5).

---

[1] Used for this example was the Table of Contents from H. H. Gross et al., *Exploring Regions of the Western Hemisphere.* Chicago: Follett, 1966.

FIGURE 9.8 Alphabetizing activity for the relative position of letters in the alphabet. (From Skills Handbook for *All Sorts of Things* of the READING 360 series by Theodore Clymer and others. © Copyright 1973, 1969 by Gin and Company [Xerox Corporation]. Used with permission.)

Directions: To find words in the dictionary you need to know the position of the letters in the alphabet very well. Fill in the blanks using the words *before* or *after*. The first one has been done for you.

1. **f** is (after) **e** and (before) **g**
2. **v** is _____ **s** and _____ **w**
3. **q** is _____ **r** and _____ **n**
4. **l** is _____ **m** and _____ **o**
5. **k** is _____ **p** and _____ **g**
6. **n** is _____ **p** and _____ **m**
7. **s** is _____ **t** and _____ **u**
8. **sa** is _____ **sc** and _____ **se**
9. **cr** is _____ **ch** and _____ **cw**
10. **tr** is _____ **ti** and _____ **tw**
11. **re** is _____ **ra** and _____ **ro**
12. **br** is _____ **bu** and _____ **bi**

FIGURE 9.9 The value of alphabetizing. (From *Mysterious Wisteria* Activity Book. Copyright 1972 by The Economy Company, Oklahoma City. Reprinted with permission.)

Using the ABC's

Jan had missed the school bus, and her mother and father had already left for work. So Jan decided she would take a taxi to school. She looked in the yellow pages to find the taxi listings. Just as she found the number, she remembered that she didn't have enough money. It would still be too early to reach Mom or Dad. She looked up Aunt May's number in the white pages and called her. In ten minutes Aunt May was there to pick her up for school.

At school Jan, Lisa, and Matt worked on a special report about reptiles. Jan went to a set of science books and took the one marked *R*. She turned to the part about reptiles and looked in a list at the end for articles about lizards. Lisa and Matt kept that book, and Jan went back to the shelf to get the book marked *L*. She quickly found the article about lizards and read it. Then she was ready to write her part of the special report.

Would **marmot** come before **market**? Yes (No)
Would **scare** come before **scatter**? (Yes) No
Would **alligator** come before **allow**? (Yes) No
Would **blue** come after **blunt**? Yes (No)
Would **manner** come after **manager**? (Yes) No
Would **queer** come before **question**? (Yes) No
Would **trace** come after **trash**? Yes (No)
Would **pickles** come before **picnic**? (Yes) No
Would **disappear** come after **distance**? Yes (No)

Plan 11, Pages 79-88

Study Skills: Locating words alphabetically

Directions: For the first part, have pupils underline the parts of the story that tell when Jan used the alphabet. For the second part, have them answer the questions by circling **yes** or **no**.

Exploration: Have pupils list and illustrate other instances in which they would use knowledge of the alphabet.

FIGURE 9.10 Alphabetizing by four letters and using guide words. (From *Mysterious Wisteria* Activity Book. Copyright 1972 by The Economy Company, Oklahoma City. Reprinted with permission.)

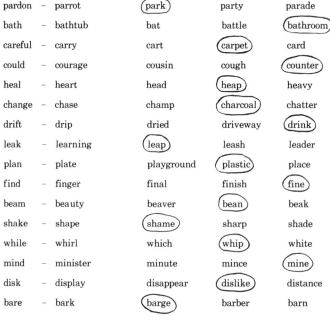

ABC Guides

Circle the word that would come between the two words on the left. The first one has been marked for you.

pardon	–	parrot	(park)	party	parade
bath	–	bathtub	bat	battle	(bathroom)
careful	–	carry	cart	(carpet)	card
could	–	courage	cousin	cough	(counter)
heal	–	heart	head	(heap)	heavy
change	–	chase	champ	(charcoal)	chatter
drift	–	drip	dried	driveway	(drink)
leak	–	learning	(leap)	leash	leader
plan	–	plate	playground	(plastic)	place
find	–	finger	final	finish	(fine)
beam	–	beauty	beaver	(bean)	beak
shake	–	shape	(shame)	sharp	shade
while	–	whirl	which	(whip)	white
mind	–	minister	minute	mince	(mine)
disk	–	display	disappear	(dislike)	distance
bare	–	bark	(barge)	barber	barn

Plan 18, Pages 131-136

Study Skills: Locating words alphabetically by the first four letters

Directions: Have pupils read the instructions on the page. Discuss with them why **park** is circled. Have pupils complete the page independently.

Exploration: Give pupils the words **care - cart.** Have them list words they think of that would come after **care** and before **cart.**

Give the students a variety of resource books. Ask them to decide which resource would be most appropriate for locating information to answer questions the teacher either asks or has written for them to answer independently. For example, ask whether a dictionary, telephone book, thesaurus, almanac, atlas, or encyclopedia would be used to find the following:

1. Address of a friend
2. Words that mean the same
3. Information about a certain animal
4. Population of the United States
5. Winner of the World Series in 1980

FIGURE 9.11 Alphabetizing to the second letter. (From Skills Handbook for *All Sorts of Things* of the READING 360 series by Theodore Clymer and others. Copyright 1973, 1969 by Gain and Company [Xerox Corporation]. Used with permission.)

The Alphabet Is Important

Number the following groups of words according to their alphabetical order. The first one has been done for you.

_2_	proud	_3_	branches	_1_	happiness
_1_	peace	_2_	boy	_3_	house
_3_	purple	_1_	because	_2_	hear
_3_	country	_3_	women	_3_	drink
_2_	change	_2_	white	_2_	doing
_1_	call	_1_	waters	_1_	desert
_3_	follow	_1_	things	_3_	swift
_1_	father	_2_	together	_1_	sometimes
_2_	fields	_3_	turquoise	_2_	stand

Assessment Strategies for Organizing Information

The study skill area of organizing information is most related to comprehension skills as discussed in chapter 8. However, instead of such skills as finding main ideas, sequencing, summarizing, and synthesizing being end products to reading story material, they are prerequisite to the more commonly recognized study skills of note-taking and outlining. Thus, to be able to take effective notes and develop good outlines, the student must be able to apply the notions of main ideas, sequence, and supporting details to content-related material.

Assessing Ability

The best and most direct way to assess the ability to organize information is simply to ask students to make an outline (or map) or to take notes from a short selection. The selection should be easy for the students in regard to word identification and comprehension skills to ensure that the study skill itself is actually being assessed.

If a student has difficulty in outlining or note-taking, additional practice may not necessarily be the solution. The student may be having difficulty with one of the prerequisite skills: classifying words, phrases, or sentences; main ideas; sequencing; summarizing or synthesizing; or knowledge of specialized vocabulary. These prerequisite skills should therefore be assessed before providing instruction that the student may not be ready for.

Informal Measures

Classifying Words, Phrases, and Sentences

Being able to distinguish main ideas from supporting details is a prerequisite to summarizing, outlining, or drawing inferences from **expository** (explanatory, content area type) **material.** However, before a student can identify main ideas in paragraphs, he or she must be able to distinguish **superordinate** (general or main idea), **subordinate** (specific or supporting details), and **equal status** (equally general or equally specific) **relationships** among words, phrases, and sentences. For instance, if Othell has trouble categorizing *hammer, axe,* and *lathe* as specific examples of tools, he will have difficulty identifying the main idea and supporting details in paragraphs discussing the role of tools within a social studies technology unit.

Some assessment strategies for classifying words, phrases, and sentences follow.

Categorizing.   Give students a list of category titles, such as *birds, mammals, planets,* and *reptiles.* Test items group the members (specific or subordinate relationships) of each category title (general, superordinate relationships). The student must identify the correct category for the series of items. For example:

1. deer, whale, dog (mammals)
2. Mars, Saturn, Venus _____
3. robin, oriole, bluejay _____
4. alligator, chameleon, salamander _____

Another format combines the specific examples with the general topic. Students are directed to circle the word that represents the general topic. For example:

1. deer (mammal) whale dog
2. Mars Saturn planets Venus
3. birds robin oriole bluejay
4. alligator chameleon salamander reptiles

A third format provides the specific items at the top of the page with the skeleton of an outline format to be completed by placing the specific items under appropriate general headings. For example:

butterfly	dog	beetle
Mrs. Jones	firefly	iguana
trout	frog	terrapin
sandpiper	mouse	swallow
sparrow	haddock	herring

I. Insects   II. Reptiles
  A.   A.
  B.   B.
  C.   C.

III. Mammals   IV. Fish   V. Birds
  A.   A.   A.
  B.   B.   B.
  C.   C.   C.

Phrases and sentences are assessed in much the same way. Some examples follow.

Directions: Circle the phrase or sentence that describes all the other items in the list.

1. cows and pigs   farm animals
   ducks and chickens   sheep and goats
2. Streets fell apart.   Cars were lost.
   Windows rattled.   An earthquake occurred.
3. Scientists dig up fossils.
   Scientists learn about dinosaurs.
   Scientists look at the size and shape of bones.
   Scientists study where the bones were found.
4. They wanted to have their own church.
   They were separatists.
   They were Englishmen.
   They had secret church meetings.

Main Ideas and Supporting Details

When the student is able to classify words, phrases, and sentences, the next skill to be assessed is that of locating the main idea (superordinate topic) and supporting details (subordinate topics) in a single expository paragraph (Aulls, 1978). As discussed in chapter 8, main ideas may be explicit or implicit, and some paragraphs have no main idea at all. For assessment, paragraphs with stated main ideas should be used, as students must be able to recognize stated main ideas before being asked to determine an implicit main idea. Recall from chapter 8 that main ideas may be stated in the first or last sentences of a paragraph or somewhere in between. Students should be given paragraphs with the main idea stated in each of the three positions and asked to underline the appropriate sentence. The *Barnell Loft Specific Skill Series* (Boning, 1985) provides placement tests, as do their booklets, "Getting the Main Idea," at levels 1 through 12, which are a ready source for assessment paragraphs.

Teachers may also employ the content area materials being used in their schools; however, the students should be assessed with material at their instructional or independent reading level.

Sequencing

Sequencing is an important prerequisite skill to outlining because outlines reflect a chronological, forward-moving summary of material read. Sequencing is an especially important skill for studying history and conducting science experiments in which time order (first, second, third, and so on) may be critical to understanding the material. The easiest way to assess this ability is to give the student pictures, phrases, or sentences that relate a sequence of events. The items are out of order, and the student must sequence the items. For example:

> *Directions:* Put a "1" in front of the event that would come first; a "2" for second; a "3" for third.
> __ The air becomes warm.
> __ Ice and snow cover the ground.
> __ Green leaves appear on the plants.
>
> __ Put the pan on the burner.
> __ The water boils.
> __ Pour the water in the pan.

Paragraph frames can be readily adapted for use in sequencing (see earlier discussion in chapter 8 for an example).

Summarizing and Synthesizing

The essential difference between **summarizing** and **synthesizing** is that a summary usually contains the essential ideas of *one* selection, while synthesizing summarizes information from *several* sources. Thus, a student must be able to summarize before he or she can synthesize. The most obvious application of these skills is in writing a report or term paper. Summarizing and synthesizing skills relate to the ability to paraphrase material read. Specifically, readers must be able to locate the main idea and supporting details, apply literal and inferential thinking skills, and interpret the information in their own words. These skills are the essence of comprehension in general.

Methods that involve "retelling" of material read (not to be confused with recall) are appropriate for assessment. In a retelling, the reader's ability to interact with, interpret, and draw conclusions from the text are assessed. Other assessment procedures are likely to include questions that ask about main ideas and inferred information. These questions may take the following general form.

> What is this section about?
> What was learned from this experiment?
> What was the purpose of the article?
> How would you describe this period of history?
> Could this poem mean something else?
> Explain that in your own words.

Most teacher's manuals have questions that ask students to summarize or synthesize information at the end of chapters or units. When some students consistently have difficulty with these questions, an analysis should be made in the areas of main ideas, supporting details, and paraphrasing (chapter 8).

Instructional Strategies for Organizing Information

The strategies suggested here demonstrate how teachers can provide both instruction and practice in using materials that require students to apply these study skills independently. Many of the instructional strategies presented in chapter 8 can be adapted for use in content areas. I attempt to suggest strategies in the most commonly taught content areas, where reading problems may be the prime cause of difficulty. The most valuable instructional strategies employ the concepts and specialized vocabulary found in the content area material the students will be using.

Classifying

Aulls (1978) suggests that teaching the classification skills of superordinate, subordinate, and equality relationships, which are so important to main ideas and supporting details, involves:

> (1) an introductory teacher directed lesson; (2) a teacher directed reinforcement lesson which reviews the introductory lesson but uses different examples; (3) a pupil directed review activity where pupils work individually, in pairs or in small groups using worksheets, games or learning centers; (4) an application to one of the weekly content area reading assignments; and, (5) a posttest of ten to twenty test items. . . . Approximately 80 percent accuracy is suggested as a criterion. (p. 95).

The introductory lesson concentrates on the meaning of general (superordinate), specific (subordinate), or equal word, phrase, or sentence relationships. The discussion involves the students in making decisions first about pairs of items. For example, the teacher may ask:

"Is *beetle* the general or specific word in the pair 'beetle–insect'?" *(response)*
"How can you tell? Use the rule: Is the *(specific)* a type of *(general)*? If beetle fits the first blank it is the specific word. The word that fits the second blank is the general word."
Responses should compare "beetle, a type of insect" and "insect, a type of beetle" to conclude that beetle is the specific word.

Many examples should follow. For phrases or sentences the rule may vary:

"Does (specific) describe (general)?"

An example would be:

"Does *Englishmen* describe *Separatists* or does *Separatists* describe *Englishmen?*"

Gradually introduce the equal relationship concept by comparing three items instead of pairs. For example:

"Wanted to have their own church" *(specific)* describes "Separatists" *(general)*.
"Secret church meetings" *(specific)* describes "Separatists" *(general)*.

These two sentences demonstrate that "wanted to have their own church" and "secret church meetings" both describe "Separatists," so they are *equally specific.* Continue these lessons until students achieve 80 percent accuracy with four items.

Categorization activities similar to those found in chapter 8 and the activities found under the assessment section in this chapter for classifying words, phrases, and sentences can also be used as bases for lessons. In addition, with disabled readers especially, some "real life" application is needed to show these students how skills that help them read better can also help them *outside* the classroom in their daily lives. An example of one such activity follows.

The Yellow Pages lists, alphabetically, categories of services available in the area. The companies providing those services are in turn listed alphabetically under their particular heading; for example, Ed's Moving Company would be found under "Movers," along with a telephone number and sometimes additional information. As in a dictionary, guide words give the first and last service listed on a page. Students are given hypothetical situations and asked to determine what service is needed; this is a classification task.

Similar activities can be devised using mail order catalogs, tables of contents, indexes, the library card catalog (subject cards), almanacs, and newspapers.

Main Ideas and Supporting Details

Students who can distinguish general, specific, and equal word, phrase, and sentence relationships are ready to be taught how to identify main ideas and supporting details. Aulls (1978) suggests moving from classifying lessons to identifying the general topic of a picture. A **topic** differs from a main idea in that it is usually a word or phrase that represents the major subject of a picture, paragraph, or article. **Main ideas** are statements in paragraphs that give the most important ideas regarding the topic. Thus, the topic must be identified before an important idea about it can be identified.

Direct teaching is essential before students are asked to practice a new skill. The teaching sequence suggested for classifying skills also applies here. Initial lessons involve pictures and paragraphs with one topic and several details supporting that topic. For example:

> There are many kinds of seeds. There are small seeds and large seeds. There are seeds with wings that can fly through the air. There are seeds with stickers that catch on your clothes. There are seeds that can float on the water.

After reading the paragraph, students are asked to identify the topic of the paragraph from some listed words.

___ wind   ___ wings
___ seeds   ___ stickers

Based on the previous discussion about classifying words, phrases, and sentences as general, specific, and equal, the students are often helped with the rule, "Does ____ describe _____?" More specific to the example is the question: "Are (small seeds) specific kinds of seeds?" "Are (seeds with wings) specific kinds of seeds?" Practice should follow with more paragraphs of the same simple structure.

Finally, students who can identify the topic of a paragraph are ready for instruction in main ideas. Students learn that the main idea is the most important thing that the author wants the reader to understand about the topic (Aulls, 1978).

Instruction proceeds from the writer's point of view. The teacher may suggest a topic and one important piece of information about it. For example, the teacher writes "Water is moving all the time" on the board and points out that this statement is the main idea the writer wishes to make in the paragraph. Students are then invited to supply some specific statements that describe the main idea. Some possible responses may include:

Water moves in the ocean.
It runs over rocks in streams.
It falls over waterfalls.
It ripples on the lake.

If students can understand main ideas from the writer's point of view, they may better understand main ideas from the reader's point of view.

Instruction proceeds to paragraphs with the main idea stated in the first sentence, followed by paragraphs with the main idea stated last, and finally to paragraphs with the main idea stated somewhere in between.

Content area textbooks can be used to help students apply what they have learned. The teacher may use an illustration that summarizes one of the written sections well. Science and social studies textbooks often lend themselves best to this type of activity. For example, a section may discuss the concept of the water cycle, while an accompanying illustration clearly shows the whole process. Students are asked to think of a sentence that explains the main idea of the picture and thus the concept of the water cycle. Supporting, or specific, details are then found in the text and listed as brief items below the sentence (fig. 9.12).

Sequencing

Many activities are suitable as bases for sequencing lessons other than the more common exercises that ask the student to put comic strip frames in the proper sequence. The teacher wants to encourage students to think logically. By first relating sequencing to events common in their daily lives, the teacher helps students realize that events usually occur in a sensible step-by-step fashion. Initially, activities take a very simple form.

Example: What would you do first?

1. Put the cake in the oven to bake, or combine eggs and water with the mix?
2. Put on your shoes or put on your socks?
3. Get dressed or get out of bed?

Having students follow simple written directions to make or cook something also reinforces the idea that certain steps precede others. Remind students to look for key words (e.g., *first, second, third, next, then, finally, last*) and other hints of sequence (refer to chapter 8). For example, if a science selection deals with the growth stages of insects, the word *stages* is a hint that a sequence of events is going to be related. Students must be made aware of these hints. Many times the stages are listed, giving a numerical hint of what comes first, second, and so forth. (Be careful though; all listings are not sequential.) Having students write directions for making something so that other students can follow them also reinforces the importance of proper sequencing.

Figure 9.12 Example of illustration that helps student identify main idea and supporting details. (From Joseph Abruscato et al. *Holt Elementary Science,* p. 126. Copyright © 1980 by Holt, Rinehart and Winston, Publishers. Used with permission.)

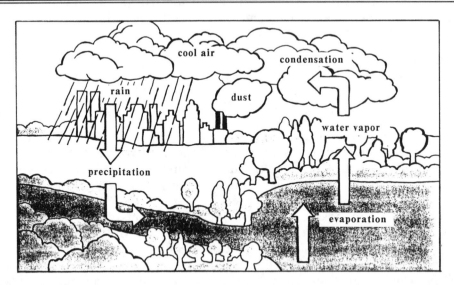

Main Idea: The evaporation and condensation of water over and over again is called the water cycle.
Supporting Details: When water evaporates, it changes into a gas called water vapor. Water vapor is cooled as it is carried up by warm, rising air. The cooling changes it back into a liquid. The vapor condenses into a cloud. Clouds bring precipitation.

Summarizing and Synthesizing

Often techniques used to teach summarizing skills do not differ very much on the surface from activities requesting identification of main ideas. However, in summarizing, instead of the main ideas being explicitly stated, the reader is asked to infer a main idea or draw a conclusion about what has been read.

One method to help students learn to summarize is teaching them to **paraphrase**, or restate text in their own words. Instruction in paraphrasing begins at a sentence level. Initially, two sentences are compared for meaning. For example:

Do the following sentence pairs have the same meaning?

The harbor was safe for small boats.
Small boats were protected in the harbor.

In order to get to the New World, the Pilgrims needed a ship.
The Pilgrims needed a ship to take them to the New World.

Most of the Pilgrims were farmers, weavers, or shopkeepers.
The Pilgrims were farmers.

At this initial level of instruction, the student must simply recognize one sentence as a paraphrase of another sentence.

The next stage in the instructional sequence moves from recognition of paraphrased sentences to production of paraphrased sentences. One method is to have students give synonyms for the **content words** (nouns, verbs, adjectives, adverbs) in a sentence, as in the following examples.

Automobiles, airplanes, and dirigibles are operated by gasoline engines.
Cars, planes, and blimps are run by gasoline engines.

When students can paraphrase sentences with ease, instruction proceeds to short paragraphs. Synonyms again are used. However, instead of trying to substitute one word for another, with paragraphs one thought unit is substituted for another. The following word problem demonstrates this procedure.

Oranges are priced at 3 for 90¢. How much would you pay for 4 oranges?

The first step is to divide the paragraph into **thought units**, or short phrases that contain only one idea. The thought units for this example might be listed as:

oranges are priced
3 for 90¢
how much (would you pay)
for 4 oranges

The next step is to paraphrase each thought unit. One student may suggest:

oranges cost
30¢ each
How much will 4 oranges cost?

The paraphrases may vary; the concern is that all the thought units are represented in the paraphrase.

The last step is to compare various paraphrases for meaning changes. If the meaning is the same, the paraphrase is acceptable. No personal translation is incorrect as long as the meaning is the same. For example:

Oranges cost 90¢ for 3. How much will I have to pay for 4?
3 oranges cost 90¢. 4 oranges will cost how much?

In paraphrasing, other skills, such as sentence combining (chapter 8), can be applied. In fact, many comprehension skills are involved in paraphrasing: vocabulary knowledge (synonyms), literal understanding of words and sentences, sentence combining and sentence expansion. The following example demonstrates the use of sentence combining to paraphrase.

Original: There is a plant that helps people tell the time. The plant has flowers that may be white, red, yellow, or pink. These flowers open in the late afternoon. The flowers close in the morning. The plant is named the "four-o'clock." [From *Specific Skill Series, Primary Overview, Drawing Conclusions–Booklet C* (level 3), by Richard Boning, 1985, Baldwin, NY: Barnell Loft.]

Paraphrase: There is a plant, called the "four-o'clock," which helps people tell time. Its flowers, which can be white, yellow, red, or pink, open at about four o'clock in the afternoon, and close in the morning.

As noted previously, synthesizing paraphrases and combines information from more than one source. To teach this skill, at least two different sources must be used. The easiest way to introduce the concept of synthesizing is to give the students two different versions of the same story and have them look for similarities and differences. Children's stories, such as *The Three Bears, Jack and the Beanstalk,* and *Cinderella,* are usually available in different versions. Summaries that make use of topics and specific details for each version can be listed on the board and then compared.

The next step is to apply this idea to content area material. Choose a topic that is presented in different ways (usually different texts or different levels of the same textbook series). As an example, two versions of difficulties the Pilgrims faced follow.

Version 1

Sickness. There was terrible sickness in Plymouth that first winter. There were some days in February when only six or seven people were well enough to take care of the ones who were sick.

By spring, about half of the Pilgrims and sailors were dead. Three whole families died during this terrible time. [From . . . *if you sailed on the Mayflower* (p. 48) by Ann McGovern, 1969, New York: Scholastic Book Services.]

Version 2

Hard times. New England winters are long and cold. Icy winds blow across the land. The Pilgrims were not used to such cold weather, nor did they have proper clothing. They got wet going to and from the *Mayflower.* So many became sick that at one time only six or seven settlers were well enough to look after the others. They moved the sick to the Common House and used it as a hospital. By the end of the winter, half the Pilgrims had died. [From *Exploring Regions of the Western Hemisphere* (pp. 120–121) by H. H. Gross, et al., 1966, Chicago: Follett.]

Next, guide the students to summarize each version, using topics and specific details. Paraphrasing should be encouraged. Example summaries follow for each version.

Version 1

Sickness in Plymouth *(topic)*
  terrible sickness *(detail)*
  first winter *(detail)*
  February—only six or seven people well enough to care for others *(detail)*
  by end of winter, half the Pilgrims and sailors died *(detail)*
  3 whole families died *(detail)*

Version 2

Hard times for Pilgrims *(topic)*
  long, cold New England winters *(detail)*
  icy winds *(detail)*
  Pilgrims not used to such winters *(detail)*
  Pilgrims didn't have the right clothes *(detail)* they got wet *(detail)*
  so many became sick *(detail)*
  at one time only 6 or 7 settlers well enough to care for others *(detail)*
  moved sick to Common House *(detail)*
  Common House used as hospital *(detail)*
  by end of winter, half the Pilgrims died *(detail)*

Students then compare the summaries and put a check mark by the details that occur in both versions. The teacher may wish to point out that details found in both versions are probably important and should be included in any written synthesis of the information.

Depending on the teacher's purpose and the needs of the students, the teaching sequence may proceed to a written synthesis of the two versions. Sentence-combining strategies (chapter 8) are useful at this stage. For example, the Pilgrim's "first winter" from version 1 can be described with details from version 2 such as "long, cold, New England, icy winds" and result in the following sentence:

The Pilgrim's first New England winter was long and cold with icy winds.

This kind of instruction also helps prepare students for writing reports that reflect a little more understanding than copying information from an encyclopedia.

Jeanne Day (1980) has developed a strategy for applying basic rules of summarizing. Teachers developing lessons for teaching summarization will find these rules useful.

1. Delete trivial or unnecessary details. (For instance, a detail found in only one version in the previous example, that is, the Pilgrims got wet, could be omitted.)
2. Delete redundant material.
3. Use a category heading for items mentioned within a single category. (For example, if the text mentions *roses, lilies,* and *petunias,* substitute the word *flowers.*)
4. Combine component actions into one encompassing action. (For example, instead of noting that James ate five doughnuts on Monday, ten doughnuts on Tuesday, ten more doughnuts on Wednesday, and so on, say James ate fifty doughnuts in one week.)
5. Identify a topic sentence, or what seems to be the author's summary.
6. If a topic sentence is not apparent, make up your own.

Any summarization strategy involves teacher modeling and discussion of students' ideas and responses. In teaching the strategy, material that students find easy (independent level) should be used initially. (The teaching strategy presented later in the strategic reading chapter, called reciprocal teaching, will serve as a model for teaching summarization skills.)

Note-Taking

Instruction in the previous skills of summarizing and synthesizing leads directly to instruction in note-taking. In essence, when taking notes on printed material, the student is summarizing the material. If notes are being taken on material presented orally, the process assumes the additional skill of auditory comprehension (chapter 12). In either case, the ability to summarize and translate information into one's own language is imperative.

Note-taking is a most complex skill, as evidenced by the prerequisite skills already discussed. While direct instruction is necessary, the procedure for improving note-taking is not clearly defined. Research by Dunkeld (1978) on taking notes while reading does offer some helpful suggestions. First, students are introduced to note-taking while reading or listening to a familiar story (e.g., *The Three Bears*). Second, in the early stages of note-taking, a textbook with subheadings is used. Third, the teacher demonstrates the format of good notes on the chalkboard or overhead using students' own examples. Fourth, students are encouraged to use their notes during class discussions.

Thus, to teach note-taking, teachers provide students with many short practice sessions with the clear purpose of improving their skills. At the end of each session, students share their notes, so that the variety of note-taking styles (use of key words, phrases, full sentences) can be discussed.

Outlining

The underlying skills needed for note-taking and outlining are similar. As with note-taking, outlining involves identification of main ideas and specific details. With outlining, however, these elements must be properly related. Outlines utilize any of the following formats: phrases or topics; sentences; paragraphs; or graphic representations. Instruction in outlining skills begins with easy material and much teacher guidance, discussion, and practice.

The first sessions in outlining should provide a completed outline of the material for the students on a worksheet, chalkboard, or overhead transparency. The assumption here is that the students will better understand the function of outlining if they can see how the writer organized the selection. After students have read the material, the reasons for selecting certain topics as main ideas and others as supporting details for the outline are discussed. For example, if the selection being read is about bees and how they communicate, the outline may appear as follows:

I. Bees communicate with each other.
    A. One bee discovers honey.
    B. Other bees soon appear.
II. Bee gives message.
    A. Scout bee returns to hive.
    B. Scout bee begins to dance.
    C. Dance tells story.

The discussion emphasizes that the major headings represent the main ideas in the selection. The subheadings provide more specific details that explain the major headings. The outline could be used before the actual reading to help students anticipate the selection's content. Through these activities, students eventually recognize the ways in which written material follows an outline. The teacher is responsible for choosing material that is simple and well-organized.

A later stage may provide students with the supporting details and instruction for filling in the main headings. Then a complete skeleton outline can be provided with a few random topics filled in and instruction for completing the outline. Eventually only the structure of the outline is given. Finally, after much practice at each stage, students will be able to formulate outlines without assistance. Examples of outlines for early instruction can be found in figures 9.13 and 9.14.

In addition to the above techniques, the strategies of mapping (Hanf, 1971), semantic webbing (Freedman & Reynolds, 1980) and the Herringbone technique (Tierney, Readence, & Dishner, 1985) are useful for developing outlining skill. **Mapping, semantic webbing,** and **Herringbone** are graphic representations of the relationships of ideas in a selection. The visual result clearly reveals the major topic, main idea, and supporting details. Such graphic representations have also been called **arrays** (Hansell, 1978). Hansell provides a definition: "An array is essentially a free form outline which requires that students decide how to arrange key words and

FIGURE 9.13 Selecting main headings for an outline. (From *Mysterious Wisteria Activity Book*, p. 56. Copyright 1972 by The Economy Company, Oklahoma City. Reprinted with permission.)

Paris

Many people think of Paris as one of the most beautiful cities in the world. It has been called the City of Light because of the beauty of its lights at night. Colorful flower beds and famous statues line paths through lovely public gardens throughout the city. Children in Paris go to the parks to enjoy puppet shows and to sail their toy boats in the ponds.

Over the years Paris fashions have been famous throughout the world. When women want to know the latest in fashion, they look to the fashion shows in Paris. Many well-known designers of women's clothes live and work in Paris.

The city of Paris is also famous for its art. Priceless art treasures are on display in several museums. Paintings and statues are among the most popular kinds of art seen in Paris. Many people from all over the world come to Paris each year to study in the outstanding schools of art.

Put the main headings where they belong.

City of fashion
City of art
City of beauty

I. <u>City of beauty</u>
   A. Lights
   B. Gardens
   C. Parks

II. <u>City of fashion</u>
   A. Worldwide fame
   B. Fashion shows
   C. Fashion designers

III. <u>City of art</u>
   A. Museums of art
   B. Kinds of art
   C. Schools of art

Plan 17, Pages 127-130

Comprehension: Selecting main headings for an outline

Directions: Have pupils read the selection and complete the outline.

Exploration: On the board write **cleaning a cut, treating with medicine,** and **bandaging.** Have pupils list the materials needed under each heading.

phrases to show how the author fit them together" (p. 248). Therefore, in maps, webs, and arrays the student constructs an organizational design of ideas by selecting relevant information, sorting this into its proper place, and relating all facts to the whole and to the other facts. Figure 9.15 shows an example of an array for the African folktale, *Anansi the Spider*. In this folktale, Anansi buys all the stories in the world from the Sky God. To pay for the stories, Anansi captures and gives to the Sky God a hive of hornets, a jaguar, and a great python. The diagram shows how these events fit together by the arrangement of key words and arrows designating direct relationships.

FIGURE 9.14 Outlining by relating subheading to main heading. (From *Mysterious Wisteria* Activity Book, p. 100. Copyright 1972 by The Economy Company, Oklahoma City. Reprinted with permission.)

Make an Outline

If you wanted to use the following ideas in a report about the ocean, how would you set up an outline?

Use these words for the main headings in the outline.

Bottom of the ocean
Movement of the ocean
Life in the ocean

Put these words under the main headings in the outline.

Seaweeds
Tides
Shelves
Waves
Slopes
Fish
Floor
Shellfish
Whales
Currents

The Ocean

I. Bottom of the ocean
   A. Shelves
   B. Slopes
   C. Floor

II. Movement of the ocean
   A. Tides
   B. Waves
   C. Currents

III. Life in the ocean
   A. Seaweeds
   B. Fish
   C. Shellfish
   D. Whales

(Arrangements under each heading may vary.)

Plan 31, Pages 230-234

Study Skills: Outlining by relating subheadings to main headings

Directions: Have pupils read the instructions and complete the page independently.

Exploration: Have pupils write an article with content based on these headings and subheadings.

FIGURE 9.15 Example array. (From Hansell, T. Stevenson. 1978. Stepping up to outlining. *Journal of Reading,* 22: 248–252.)

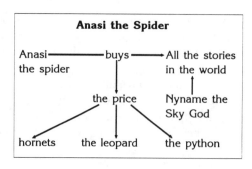

Hansell's research suggests certain steps in teaching students how to prepare arrays. First, the teacher selects ten to twenty key words or phrases (assuming passages of 400 to 800 words) from the material. Next, the teacher develops questions that require students to organize what they already know about the passage, for example, "How would you capture a jaguar?"

Once this teacher preparation has been accomplished, the students are assigned to small groups. Each group receives several strips of paper that contain the key words and phrases from the passage. This step allows the teacher to pronounce and explain any of the key words or phrases if necessary. After the paper strips have been distributed, the teacher asks the organizing questions. At this point the students actually read the passage, but they are now reading for two very definite purposes: (1) to check their answers to the organizing questions against what is stated in the passage and (2) to find out how the key words and phrases are related.

The students, still in groups, compare the strips of paper to select the most important idea. This strip is placed at the top or the center to stress its importance. The other strips are positioned around it in a way that reflects the relationships of the material. This positioning must be done with teacher guidance; the teacher asks appropriate questions, encourages, and makes suggestions while moving from group to group. When the group is satisfied with the position of all the paper strips, one member copies the array onto a piece of paper, drawing arrows to show connected ideas and the direction of relationships.

The last step is for each group to share their arrays and discuss reasons for the arrangement and placement of arrows. The teacher asks extending questions at this time.

Hansell recommends at least four teacher-guided arrays be constructed before expecting students to do an unguided array. In an unguided array, students select the key words and phrases themselves. Eventually, by moving from free-form arrays to skeletal outlines, students are ready to prepare individual outlines. The array approach is useful because it focuses on the primary reason for outlining in the first place, that is, to identify relevant ideas and fit them into a meaningful pattern. Unfortunately, the focus of most instruction in outlining is on the format, which assumes students understand the relationships presented in the material—a "cart before the horse" approach. Instruction in array formation puts the horse back in front of the cart.

The **Herringbone technique** (Tierney, Readence, & Dishner, 1985, p. 203) is a structured outlining procedure useful for helping students organize information from text. This strategy utilizes six basic comprehension questions to obtain the important information: who, what, where, when, how, and why.

As with arrays, the teacher must make some specific preparations for teaching the Herringbone technique. Important preparation questions for the teacher to ask include:

1. What are the major concepts my students should understand from this material?
2. What are the important vocabulary items?
3. How will my students learn this information?
4. Which concepts do I expect *all* my students to master and which do I expect only my better students to achieve?

The teacher introduces the lesson as usual, with concern for developing motivation and conceptual background. Then the Herringbone technique is introduced.

Figure 9.16   The herringbone form.

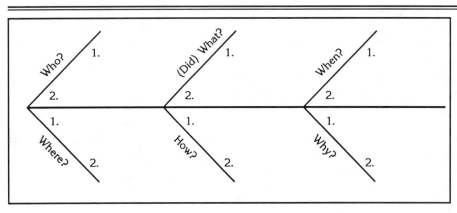

The Herringbone form (fig. 9.16) can be easily provided to students as a ditto. Students are told they will be seeking answers to the questions that appear on the form. The answers themselves can also be written right on the form. The first few lessons that involve the Herringbone technique are walked through by the use of an overhead transparency and teacher guidance.

As students read the assigned material they will be noting answers to the following questions.

1. Who (person or groups) was involved?
2. What did this person or group do?
3. When was it (the event from question 2) done?
4. Where was it done?
5. How was it done?
6. Why did it happen?

The answers to these questions help the student recognize the important relationships in the material. An example follows.

For a chapter entitled "Europeans Rediscover the Western Lands" in a social studies textbook, the students were instructed to read the topic, "Columbus Tries to Get Help from Portugal," and to answer the six key questions. The answers to be recorded on the Herringbone form were as follows:

Who?	Columbus, King of Portugal, King's experts
What?	Columbus went to the King to ask for ships and supplies to sail west to reach the Indies. King's experts thought Columbus was wrong.
When?	———
Where?	Portugal
How?	———
Why?	Columbus wanted to prove (1) that it was possible to sail straight west to reach the Indies, because the earth is round; and (2) that this route was shorter than going around Africa. King's experts knew the earth was round but thought the distance was much greater than Columbus thought.

As seen in this example, texts do not always contain all the information needed to answer the six key questions. The teacher must decide whether the missing information is important enough to look for elsewhere. The Herringbone technique readily reveals these information gaps. The teacher can also use the textual answers as springboards for further discussion and research. Figure 9.17 shows the information recorded on the Herringbone form.

It can be seen that mapping, webbing, and array tasks and the Herringbone technique use processes employed in both note-taking and outlining. More importantly, they give students a structure for observing relationships in text that further enhance comprehension and remembering of information. When these techniques are used as prewriting strategies as well, students will quickly begin to understand text organization.

Assessment Strategies for Interpreting Graphic and Pictorial Materials

The skills to be discussed in this section differ considerably from those discussed in the previous sections. While the previous skills overlapped with the comprehension skills discussed in Chapter 8, the reading of graphic and pictorial materials requires a unique set of skills.

Formal Measures

As stated early in this chapter, the interpretation of tables and graphs is a subtest commonly found on standardized achievement tests. However, if the information from such a test is not readily available to the teacher (i.e., tests are machine scored), the instructional benefits are minimal. Informal measurements developed by the teacher *will* provide a readily available source of information.

Informal Measures

Graphic and pictorial materials help readers understand text by explaining, clarifying, or providing additional information. A reader must have skill with the following materials:

1. Pictures. Students must be able to utilize pictures that present or clarify concepts, afford new experiences vicariously, or stimulate discussion. Political cartoons are included in this category.
2. Time lines. Students should be able to recognize time lines as graphic presentations of events in chronological order. Both the time and the event are presented on a time line.
3. Tables and charts. Students must be able to read the variety of facts presented in a table or chart. These may be in single column or multicolumn formats.
4. Graphs. Many types of graphs clarify and illustrate comparisons. Students should be able to read and interpret circle graphs, line graphs, bar graphs, and picture graphs.

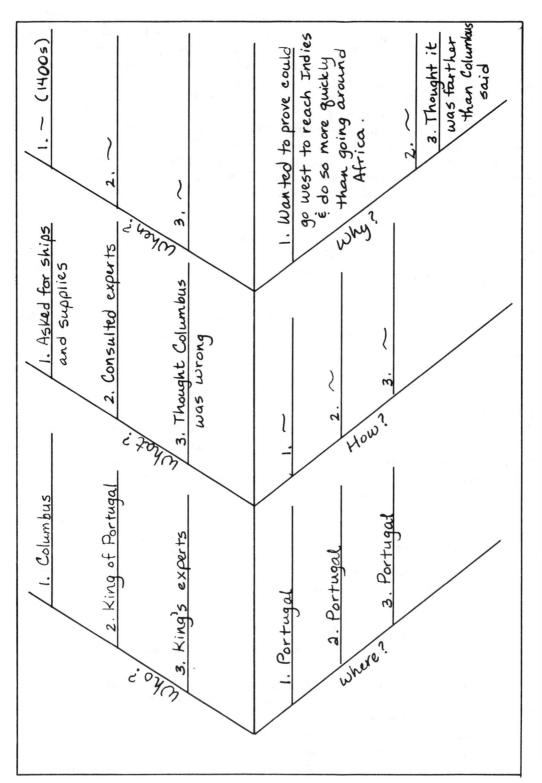

5. Map and globes. Students must be able to interpret a legend and its symbols, the scale indicated, the directions of north, south, east, and west, and the lines of latitude and longitude to read maps and globes effectively.

To assess whether students can use the five items listed above, the teacher simply has to develop a set of questions that can be answered only if the picture, time line, table, chart, graph, map, or globe has been read properly. These informal measures are quite easily constructed. The *Wisconsin Design for Reading Skill Development* has many examples in the study skills component. Scholastic Book Services' *Real Life Reading Skills* and *Map and Graph Skills* also provide teachers with such informal instruments.

Instructional Strategies for Interpreting Graphic and Pictorial Materials

General Teaching Strategy

Interpretation of pictorial and graphic material is best taught according to a five-step procedure (Cooper et al., 1979).

1. Explanation of the use or purpose of the material being taught.
2. An understanding of the meanings of the words used to describe the material being learned.
3. The teaching of the specific skills needed for use of the tool or material.
4. A demonstration of the use of the material or tool.
5. The guidance of the students through the initial usage of the material. (p. 259)

The activities described in the remainder of this section point out how the teacher can follow each of the five steps. Because a large amount of visual information is available, teachers soon discover that disabled readers who master interpretation of pictorial and graphic materials greatly enhance their understanding of content area materials.

When explaining the use and purpose of pictures, examples must be available for students to view during the lesson. The explanation may begin by giving students a sentence describing a scene that can be easily sketched. For example, the students may be asked to draw a picture to correspond to the following sentence:

The ball rolled down the street and hit a big tree.

The resulting drawings are shared, with a discussion of the techniques used to indicate "rolled" and "hit." (Refer to step 3.) Students should experience a need to indicate the passage of time in their drawings. Some may resolve this problem by showing several pictures that indicate the ball getting closer to the tree; others may use dotted lines to show the ball moving toward the tree (fig. 9.18). Both solutions are found in content area material.

At this point, an example from a textbook is appropriate. The following sentence was taken from a science text: The paramecium pinched in the middle and split in two. First, this sentence may be difficult to visualize if the important words are unfamiliar (e.g., *paramecium, pinched, split*). Therefore, step 2, understanding or at least recognition of the key words, is important. The picture itself attempts to clarify concepts in the text that would otherwise be difficult to understand, as the picture associated with the preceding sentence clearly demonstrates (fig. 9.19). In this case,

FIGURE 9.18 Pictures drawn by seven-year-old boy (*left*) and eight-year-old girl (*right*) showing rolling ball hitting a tree.

FIGURE 9.19 Illustration clarifying concept of paramecium splitting in two.

the picture provides the reader with a better understanding of the sentence than the words themselves. The whole illustration shows how a paramecium reproduces itself. This kind of concept is best illustrated by a series of pictures (recall the rolling ball sentence). Other concepts are better described using arrows, or dotted lines if direction or distance is involved (fig. 9.20).

Some illustrations have legends (a step 2 term) that the reader must use to understand the concepts involved. Students must be taught how to use these legends for pictures, maps, and titles and column headings in tables and how to relate the pictorial or graphic information back to the text. Guidance is essential initially and can be given only by direct instruction. A variety of pictorial and graphic materials with questions relevant to interpretation is the basis of such instruction. Figure 9.21 is a familiar example. The following questions would be appropriate to use with this graph.

1. What kind of graph is this? Circle one.

    bar graph   circle graph   picture graph

FIGURE 9.20 *Use of arrows (left) and legend (right) to aid reader in understanding concepts involved. (Right-hand illustration adapted from* Science for You *by Gerald S. Craig and others. © Copyright 1965 by Ginn and Company [Xerox Corporation]. Used with permission.)*

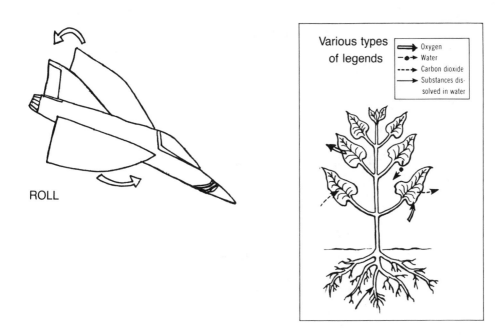

2. This graph shows that (50) children like horses best.
3. Two animals are liked the same. What are these two animals? (cats) (hamsters)
4. How many children like dogs best? (100)
5. How many children were asked what their favorite pet was? (200)

To maintain their competence in this area, students must have many opportunities to use and apply these skills.

Real World Usage

The best reinforcement activity for developing graphic and pictorial skills is real world usage. For instance, after the lesson on the bar graph, the class could collect its own data and construct its own graph. Not only will the teacher be teaching graph skills but math skills as well.

Teachers must be alert to the many opportunities in daily life that help students appreciate the need for learning graphic and pictorial skills. Bus schedules, newspaper weather maps, TV guides, and city street maps are obvious items that can be brought into the classroom. Students who have been taught to graph their own progress on spelling tests could also use this skill to graph progress in a weight loss program. Who hasn't been asked to draw a map giving directions from "my house" to "your house." Students can help make maps from "classroom to cafeteria" or "from school

FIGURE 9.21 Students can be instructed in interpreting graphic materials by asking a series of relevant questions. (From *Read Better—Learn More, Book B* of the READING 360 series by Theodore Clymer and others. © Copyright 1972 by Ginn and Company [Xerox Corporation]. Used with permission.)

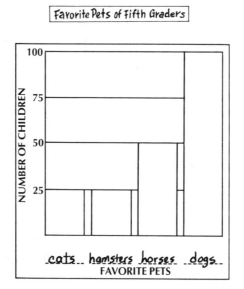

to the ice skating rink." Most large shopping malls have maps that locate the stores. In the Southeast and on the East Coast, hurricane tracking maps are free to teachers in large quantities during the hurricane season.

Knowing the students and the community in which they live broadens the opportunity to practice graphic and pictorial skills. The least that can be done for disabled readers is give them skills needed for daily life.

Summary

Students considered to be successful readers are often at a loss when given an assignment to "report on one of the following topics" or to "take notes on chapter 6 in your history book for homework." Such assignments assume the student can locate and organize information and interpret graphic or pictorial information. In short, the student must be an independent reader *and learner*—not just a reader who can recognize words in print and understand the message.

Knowing *how* to learn is what study skill instruction is all about. Study skills must be taught directly. Teachers must "extend and expand" reading to include a variety of material. Also, study skills must be taught from the beginning. If students are to be independent learners and readers they must know how to find information they need, how to organize information, and how to interpret the visual aids accompanying information ("reading to learn"). Teachers therefore must provide reading instruction within content area classes where students can see the application of the study skills.

Another vital aspect of study skill instruction is to teach students the value of strategic reading. This particular aspect of study skill instruction is the content of chapter 10.

References

Askov, E. N., Kamm, K., & Klumb, R. (1977). Study skill mastery among elementary school teachers. *The Reading Teacher, 30,* 485–488.

Aulls, M. W. (1978). *Developmental and remedial reading in the middle grades.* Boston: Allyn and Bacon.

Boning, R. (1985). Getting the main idea. *Specific skills series.* Baldwin, NY: Barnell Loft.

Cooper, J. D., Warncke, E. W., Ramstad, P., & Shipman, D. A. (1979). *The what and how of reading instruction.* Columbus, OH: Merrill.

Day, J. D. (1980). *Training summarization skills: A comparison of teaching methods.* Unpublished doctoral dissertation, University of Illinois, Urbana.

Dunkeld, C. (1978). Students' notetaking and teachers' expectations. *Journal of Reading, 21,* 542–546.

Freedman, G., & Reynolds, E. G. (1980). Enriching basal reader lessons with semantic webbing. *The Reading Teacher, 33,* 677–684.

Hanf, M. B. (1971). Mapping: A technique for translating reading into thinking. *Journal of Reading, 14,* 225–230, 270.

Hansell, T. S. (1978). Stepping up to outlining. *Journal of Reading, 22,* 248–252.

Hittleman, D. R. (1983). *Developmental reading, K–8: Teaching from a psycholinguistic perspective.* Boston: Houghton Mifflin.

Kennedy, E. C. (1977). *Classroom approaches to remedial reading.* Itasca, IL: F. E. Peacock.

Tierney, R. J., Readence, J. E., & Dishner, E. K. (1985). *Reading strategies and practices: A compendium* (2nd ed.). Boston: Allyn and Bacon.

CHAPTER 10

Strategic Reading

Objectives

After studying this chapter, you should be able to

1. identify ways to determine whether students know about and are able to use reading strategies;
2. describe the three stages of studying;
3. give examples of skimming versus scanning;
4. explain what happens in comprehension monitoring;
5. describe techniques for teaching self-questioning skills and postreading organizational skills.

Study Outline

Important Vocabulary and Concepts

arrays

Assignment Mastery

comprehension monitoring

prereading

reciprocal teaching

scanning

during reading
GRS
K-W-L
mapping
metacognition
postreading

skimming
SQ3R strategy
studying
think-links
understanding questions

Overview

How do you intend to read this chapter? The steps you follow make up your plan, or strategy. If you are a good strategic reader you might proceed in the following manner.

1. Look through the entire chapter and ask questions. How long is this chapter? How much time will I need to read it? Do the headings refer to familiar ideas, or does this material seem difficult? Do the figures (tables or graphs) appear helpful?

2. Decide upon purposes for reading. I want to know more about some of the terms used. The figures appear interesting. I want to know more about the techniques they represent.

3. Read the material. At the same time try to paraphrase sections (note-taking) and continue asking questions. Do I know what this means? Do I see how I can apply this with students? Also decide what needs further clarification from the instructor.

4. Question yourself after the material has been read. Can you go to the objectives listed at the beginning of the chapter and honestly say you have met them? Can you outline, from memory mostly, the important points? (Your outline should resemble the study outline already provided.) Can you explain the meaning of the terms listed at the beginning of the chapter?

If you have never tried to study text chapters systematically, why not try it now, using the list above if you like. See whether employing a strategy helps you remember more. If you are convinced that using some kind of strategy helps you remember more of what you read, you will be more likely to teach good reading strategies to your students.

Introduction

Strategic readers understand that for the purpose of learning or remembering specific information, a different set of strategies is needed from that which they might use when reading for enjoyment. When the purpose for reading is to study, readers process text material with the expectation of learning or remembering something specific. Good strategic readers: (1) think about what they already know about the topic; (2) clarify their purpose for reading; (3) focus their attention on the content; (4) monitor whether or not they are understanding what they read; (5) use fix-up strategies (e.g., look back, reread, read ahead, consult a dictionary) when they do not understand; (6) fit new material into what they already know; (7) take notes; (8)

think aloud to be sure of their understanding; (9) create mental images to aid understanding of difficult concepts; (10) summarize what they have read by mapping or using some other form of graphic organizer; (11) evaluate their understanding of what they read, whether or not their purpose was achieved; and, if necessary, (12) seek outside sources for additional information (Orange County Public Schools, 1985, 1986). Thus, an important characteristic of **studying**, as pointed out by Anderson (1978), is that it is student-directed instruction. In other words, a teacher is *not* available to ask guiding questions, point out or clarify important concepts, or help with decisions about what to do next when material is not understood.

Nevertheless, teachers need to demonstrate the variety of strategies available for the purpose of studying so that students can become independent learners. Garner (1987) proposes six guidelines for effective strategy instruction.

1. Teachers must care about the processes involved in reading and studying, and must be willing to devote instructional time to them.
2. Teachers must do task analyses of strategies to be taught.
3. Teachers must present strategies as applicable to texts and tasks in more than one content domain.
4. Teachers must teach strategies over an entire year, not in just a single lesson or unit.
5. Teachers must provide students with opportunities to practice strategies they have been taught.
6. Teachers must be prepared to let students teach each other about reading and studying processes. (pp. 131–138)

Assessing Awareness of Strategic Reading and Study Habits

One quick way to determine whether students are aware of and use study strategies is to administer a questionnaire similar to the one found in figure 10.1 If you worry about students answering honestly, you can give the questionnaire on an anonymous basis to the entire group. A tally of the responses to each item indicates areas where students need instruction.

Another way to assess students' strategic reading abilities is through observation. After directing a group of students to study some reading materials for a test, observe their behavior. Some type of survey of the material should be apparent, such as a quick perusal of the title and headings or looking at pictures, charts, or graphs. Often in a survey of the material, a reader quickly reads the first and last paragraph in the various sections of the material or the introductory and summary passages.

After a survey of the material, most students start reading from the beginning. Observable behaviors, such as note-taking, underlining, looking back at previously read text, or rereading, indicate that the reader is actively studying the material.

A number of behaviors are possible when readers complete their reading. Some readers go back and try to outline the material. Others choose to go back and take notes or underline certain information.

FIGURE 10.1 Questionnaire to determine study strategies and habits. (From *The Reading Corner* by Harry W. Forgan, Jr. Reproduced by permission of Scott, Foresman and Company. © 1977.)

Appendix Item 69
Skill Test for Study Skills and Habits

Name _____

Directions:
Put a check mark (✓) in the column that describes how often you do the following. Be honest. I shall help you learn to study if needed.

	Never	Sometimes	Usually
1. Do you look over what you are going to read before you read it?			
2. Do you form questions about the selection before you read it?			
3. Do you use a slower rate when you are reading your textbooks?			
4. Do you try to pronounce and define words that are in bold print or italics?			
5. Do you read the tables, graphs, and diagrams in your textbooks?			
6. Do you answer questions as you go along?			
7. Do you outline the important ideas and facts as you read?			
8. Do you reread the materials you do not understand?			
9. Do you review what you have read when you have finished?			
10. Do you set a time for study?			
11. Do you have a place to study at home or near your home? Are your supplies ready?			
12. Are you able to concentrate when studying?			
13. If you are doing math problems, do you read them carefully and then reread them to see if your answer is correct?			
14. If you must turn work in to your teacher, are you proud of it? Is it neat and well organized?			

Both the questionnaire and the observable behaviors indicate three phases in the process of studying. A student may consistently exhibit behavior for one of the phases but not for all three. These phases will be discussed in detail in the next section.

Instructional Strategies for Developing Strategic Reading Habits

Stages of Studying

Behaviors observed in skilled readers studying reveal three stages (Anderson, 1978). These stages are: prereading, during reading, and postreading.

Briefly, the **prereading** stage is characterized by attention to the overall theme of a selection. The student prepares to read the selection by considering what he or she already knows about the topic. Headings, subheadings, graphs, tables, and new vocabulary words are typical items of concern at this stage. The student also clarifies a specific purpose for reading which helps in focusing attention on the content to be read.

The **during reading** stage is more difficult to describe because of the wide variety of possible behaviors. Ideally, this stage is characterized by active involvement with the print. Recently, the term *comprehension monitoring* has been used to describe what should be happening at this stage (this will be discussed in detail in a later section). Readers who monitor their comprehension continually ask themselves, "Do I understand this material?" (Baker, 1979). If material is *not* understood, fix-up strategies must be used. The reader also tries to relate any new information to what is already known.

In the **postreading** stage, students engage in activities that help them retain information. The most commonly used activities are organizational (outlines, maps); translational (paraphrases, formulating of questions); and repetitional (recitations, rehearsals) (Anderson, 1978). Instructional strategies for each stage will now be presented.

Prereading

Throughout this text I have emphasized trying to understand the processes involved in the various reading domains. Even for the domain of strategic reading, task requirements, or underlying processes, are important considerations. When the purpose is to learn and remember information, students must look over the material: titles, headings, illustrations, tables, introductions, summaries, and topic sentences. The prereading stage thus demands that students be proficient in **skimming** and **scanning.** "*Skimming* and *scanning* both refer to rapid reading during which the reader does not direct attention to all of the information on the page. *Scanning* is fast reading to obtain answers to specific questions. . . . while *skimming* is rapid reading to find out what something is about or a general idea" (Schachter, 1978, p. 149).

Flexibility in rate of reading is a skill that can and should be taught directly to every student. Young children can be asked to skim or scan pictures for particular objects or colors. They can scan magazines for a specific letter of the alphabet, or catalogs for objects beginning with a specific sound. Just about any type of printed material can be used to teach skimming and scanning, including telephone books (both yellow and white pages); menus; catalogs; newspapers; or textbooks.

Direct instruction for skimming and scanning.   Corrective readers often demonstrate a tendency to read every word. As students progress through the grades, teaching them when and how to vary their reading rate takes on increasing importance. An introduction to skimming and scanning uses a technique that shows the student what is meant by flexible reading rate or skimming and scanning. For example, ask a student to look up a classmate's phone number in the telephone book (father's name: William Jenkins). Point out that he or she would not start at the beginning and read the whole book or even start at the beginning of the *J*s and read through all of the names beginning with *J*. Instead, using alphabetizing skills, the student finds the general location and then scans to locate Jenkins, William. If asked, students are usually able to identify other instances from real life where they skim or scan material, for example, scanning the TV schedule to decide what channel to watch or a recipe to see if the needed ingredients are available.

In direct instruction, students are taught to skim or scan for a variety of purposes. Initially, directions are simple, with activities chosen specifically to teach the concepts of skim and scan. Eventually, activities are more directly related to what students will be expected to do on their own as strategic readers. Some specific activities follow.

1. Direct the students to scan a passage that is easy to read and underline ten verbs. The teacher may set time limits on this task and gradually decrease the time allowed.

2. Direct the students to locate five items on a menu that sell for less than three dollars.

3. With the librarian's help, give students copies of brand new book arrivals. Have each student skim the book (consider a time limit) and briefly share the general idea of the book.

4. Give students a list of questions to answer from the classified ads. Examples are: How much does the 1981 Mustang cost? What breed of cat was lost? Where can you call to buy a used dishwasher? How much does a thirty-foot sailboat cost?

5. Questions similar to those in activity 4 can be used with content area material. Tables of contents and indexes are ready sources for similar questions. Question starters are: Find the place where. . . . Locate the page on which. . . . List the chapters that. . . .

6. More directly related to studying is an activity that uses a content area textbook and a question guide. Students are told to look specifically for the answers to the questions and *not* to read every word. Sample directions include the following:

- Look at the paragraph headings for pages 17 through 24. After reading *just the headings,* write a sentence or two that tells what this section is about.
- List the steps that tell how a bill is passed.
- Read the section "The President Wears Many Hats" to find out how many different jobs the President has.

Accessing prior knowledge. Poor readers often start reading without first thinking about the subject of what they are reading. They fail to realize that they may already know something about the material, and that this knowledge can help them during their reading. There are several useful strategies teachers can demonstrate that will help these readers focus on what they already know about a subject.

An uncomplicated procedure discussed by Ogle (1986) that can be used with any content or grade level, individually, or with groups, is the **K-W-L** strategy. The "K" step requires that the student identify what is already known about the subject. If a group is applying the strategy this step involves a brainstorming of all the information the group already knows about the subject. The "W" step requires that the student reflect on what is already known and determine what still needs to be learned. Thus, the "W" becomes a question, "What do I want to find out?" The "L" step actually occurs *after* the material is read. The student writes down what was learned. The student should make sure that any questions they had identified at the "W" stage were answered. A chart similar to that found in figure 10.2 could be used to provide a graphic structure for the reader.

FIGURE 10.2 Chart for the K-W-L Strategy.

K ——— What Do I **KNOW**	W ——— **WHAT** Do I Want to Learn	L ——— What Did I **LEARN**

FIGURE 10.3 What Do You. . .

Know You Know	Think You Know	Think You Will Learn	Know You Learned?

Modifications of the K-W-L strategy have also been developed. The *What Do You. . .* chart (IRA, 1988, p. 15) seen in figure 10.3 combines aspects of K-W-L and DRTA formats. Such a chart encourages the student to focus on the subject, the title, or the cover of a book, and distinguish between what is known for certain and what is predicted to be covered.

Depending on the age and ability of the students, a simplified version of such organizational charts might focus only on accessing prior knowledge and making predictions. Such a version is "What do you know/What do you think" (Richards, 1988, personal communication). Given a topic, title, or book cover, the student states what is *known* ("just the facts") before stating what is predicted. For example, given the title and cover of the story *Goldilocks and the Three Bears*, the stated facts might include:

> This is a story about a girl, Goldilocks, and three bears.
> There are three bears in this story.
> The bears have a house in the woods (based on cover illustration).
> The girl has yellow hair (based on cover illustration).
> There are two big bears and one small bear (based on cover illustration).

The predictions then, are based on the known facts, and also the reader's familiarity with other stories of a similar nature. Responses to the question "What do you think?" might include:

> I think this story will tell about what happens to Goldilocks and the bears.
> I think the bears will scare the girl.
> I think Goldilocks visits the bears in their house in the woods.
> I think that Goldilocks will make friends with the little bear.
> I think that the bears will help Goldilocks.

When a book cover or illustration is used, a three-column map can be prepared and responses written down as seen in figure 10.4. Thus, even very young students can learn to be strategic readers beginning with familiar narrative material, and moving into more difficult, expository material.

FIGURE 10.4 Three Column Map for *Goldilocks and the Three Bears*.

What Do You See?	What Do You Know?	What Do You Think?
a girl with yellow hair	Goldilocks is a girl	The bears will scare Goldilocks
two big bears, one little bear	There are three bears	Goldilocks will hide from the bears
house in the woods	This is a fairy tale	The story will begin "Once upon a time. . ."

A variation of the DRTA that focuses on accessing prior knowledge is discussed by Richek (1987). The variation DRTA SOURCE helps students recognize that readers use both the text and their prior knowledge when making DRTA predictions. In DRTA SOURCE students stop after making predictions and identify which part of the prediction was based on something in the text and which part on prior knowledge. The value of this strategy is that it helps students become aware of how important their own prior knowledge is to reading.

During Reading

A wide variety of behaviors are seen in the second stage of studying. Good strategic readers generally start at the beginning and read through the material, engaging in what is termed **comprehension monitoring.** With this process, students constantly evaluate their level of understanding of what is being read. The ability to monitor one's own comprehension is so critical to studying that this topic deserves further elaboration.

Comprehension monitoring.   Research in the area of comprehension monitoring is recent and is part of a larger area of study called **metacognition.**

> Metacognition refers to one's knowledge concerning one's own cognitive processes and products or anything related to them, e.g., the learning-relevant properties of information or data. For example, I am engaging in metacognition (metamemory, metalearning, metaattention, metalanguage, or whatever) if I notice that I am having more trouble learning A than B; if it strikes me that I should double-check C before accepting it as a fact; if it occurs to me that I had better scrutinize each and every alternative in any multiple-choice type task situation before deciding which is the best one; if I sense that I had better make a note of D because I may forget. (Flavell, 1976, p. 232)

Metacognitive activities of interest for the during reading stage of studying include keeping track of the success with which one's comprehension is proceeding and, if comprehension breaks down, taking action to remediate the failure. The actual processes involved in monitoring one's comprehension are currently being researched in an increasing number of studies (Baker, 1979; Baker & Anderson, 1981; Baker & Brown, 1984; Brown, 1975, 1980; Brown & Campione, 1978; Garner, 1987; Markman, 1977, 1979, 1981; Wagoner, 1983). The research gives ample evidence that poor comprehension monitoring ability is characteristic of poor readers. However, little specific information about the monitoring processes of successful readers is documented.

Research by Markman (1979) and Harris, Kruithof, Terwogt, and Visser (1981) indicates developmental differences in comprehension monitoring, with initial development implicated at an earlier age than previously thought (Flavell, Speer, Green, & August, 1981). However, the ability to monitor comprehension is not a unitary phenomenon, but instead varies according to the task requirements (Chi, 1978). Therefore, comprehension monitoring ability is not likely to develop simply with maturity; it depends on knowledge, experience, and instruction (Brown & DeLoache, 1978).

Beginning readers and less able readers are generally deficient at evaluating their understanding of text (Baker & Brown, 1984; DiVesta, Hayward, & Orlando, 1979; Garner, 1980; Markman, 1979; Myers & Paris, 1978; Paris & Myers, 1981; Winograd & Johnston, 1980). Poor readers have less insight into the procedures they use during reading (Smith, 1967; Strang & Rogers, 1965) and are less likely to seek clarification of poorly understood information (Strang & Rogers, 1965). Poor readers also have difficulty in relating prior knowledge to the reading material (Sullivan, 1978). If the reader does not know whether the text has been understood, the teaching of techniques for remediating comprehension failure could be premature.

Teaching strategic reading behaviors to corrective readers is especially important since it will put them "in control of their own learning activity" (Palincsar & Ransom, 1988, p. 788). Instruction in strategic reading behaviors will require that students learn and use comprehension monitoring skills. Because one of the first steps in comprehension monitoring is recognizing whether or not the text has been understood (Baker, 1979), that seems a logical place to begin instruction. Once a reader has developed this initial ability, instruction can go forward (Anderson, 1978).

Self-questioning.   Recent research in the area of self-interrogation skills reveals that this is a promising area of instruction for improving comprehension monitoring skills (Andre & Anderson, 1978–1979; Brown & Campione, 1977; Duell, 1978; Frase & Schwartz, 1975; Schmelzer, 1975). Results from this research show that students remember more when they formulate questions during studying by either writing them down or verbalizing them to a friend.

When readers do not know whether they understand the text just read, Anderson (1980) recommends the use of **understanding questions** to help pinpoint the reason for comprehension breaking down. Obstacles to comprehension may occur at a word, sentence, or paragraph level. Some examples of understanding questions are: Does this sentence have any new words? Is a word I know being used in a new way? Did this sentence make sense? Does this sentence fit with what I already know about the topic? What was this section about? Can I explain this in my own words? What were the important facts? Have I read something similar to this before?

Self-generation of questions may be an effective strategy because the student is forced to pause frequently, deal with the effort to understand, determine whether comprehension has occurred, and finally become concerned about what to do if comprehension has not occurred.

Instructional strategies for teaching students how to use understanding questions are not readily available. Nevertheless, it is clear that "helping poor readers become strategic readers demands modeling of mental processes" (Duffy, Roehler, & Herrmann, 1988, p. 766). A few promising techniques for training self-questioning skills can be found in the literature. Collins and Smith (1980) recommend a modeling technique during which the teacher demonstrates the various types of understanding questions the students could ask themselves. The teacher tries to think aloud for the students, showing them where and when they would appropriately ask questions. The actual instructional method suggested by Collins and Smith (1980) proceeds in three stages similar to Singer's (1978) active comprehension lesson discussed in chapter 8. Initially, the teacher models by reading a passage aloud, pausing and asking relevant understanding questions along the way. The second stage includes the students by asking them to pose the understanding questions, gradually lessening the teacher's involvement. The third stage is silent reading by the students with teacher input only if difficulties are encountered.

Davey (1983, p. 45) provides important guidelines for the teacher modeling stage for "think-alouds" which can be found in figure 10.5. Duffy, Roehler, and Herrmann (1988) emphasize the importance of the teacher modeling the mental processes (as opposed to procedural steps) that would otherwise be invisible to the students. In

FIGURE 10.5 Guidelines for teacher modeling of "think-alouds." (Reprinted with permission of Beth Davey and the International Reading Association.)

Think aloud

To help poor readers clarify their views of reading and their use of strategies, teachers can verbalize their own thoughts while reading orally. We call these activities "think-alouds."

First, select a passage to read aloud that contains points of difficulty, contradictions, ambiguities, or unknown words. (You may want to develop your own materials for this step—short, with obvious problems.) As you read the passage aloud, students follow along silently, listening to how you think through these trouble spots. Here are some examples of points to make during think-alouds.

1. *Make predictions.* (Show how to develop hypotheses.)

"From the title, I predict that this section will tell how fishermen used to catch whales."

"In this next part, I think we'll find out why the men flew into the hurricane."

"I think this is a description of a computer game."

2. *Describe the picture you're forming in your head from the information.* (Show how to develop images during reading.)

"I have a picture of this scene in my mind. The car is on a dark, probably narrow, road; there are no other cars around."

3. *Share an analogy.* (Show how to link prior knowledge with new information in text.) We call this the "like-a" step.

"This is like a time we drove to Boston and had a flat tire. We were worried and we had to walk three miles for help."

4. *Verbalize a confusing point.* (Show how you monitor your ongoing comprehension.)

"This just doesn't make sense."

"This is different from what I had expected."

5. *Demonstrate fix-up strategies.* (Show how you correct your lagging comprehension.)

"I'd better reread."

"Maybe I'll read ahead to see if it gets clearer."

"I'd better change my picture of the story."

"This is a new word to me—I'd better check context to figure it out."

---

this way, the students will have heard examples of appropriate reasoning they can then use to read strategically for themselves.

Paris and Lipson (1982) describe a program of instruction that relies on bulletin boards and related worksheets to teach children to use what they call "focal questions," which are similar to the understanding questions already discussed. Their research indicates that metacognitive skills can be taught.

Pitts, Thompson, and Gipe (1983) discussed a procedure employing microcomputers to train students to ask understanding questions. Such questions were flashed on the monitor for students to see; obstacles such as difficult vocabulary or an unclear pronoun referent were located ahead of time by the researchers so that the understanding questions could be programmed. This aspect would be similar to the teacher modeling stage of the Collins and Smith (1980) technique.

A recent variation of Manzo's ReQuest Procedure (discussed in chapter 8) intended to provide direct instruction in comprehension monitoring is called reciprocal teaching (Palincsar & Brown, 1984). **Reciprocal teaching** is an interactive procedure in which students are taught to summarize sections of text, anticipate questions that a teacher may ask, make predictions about upcoming text, and clarify unclear sections of text. Initially, the teacher plays a major instructional role by modeling these behaviors and helping students in a collaborative effort (unlike the stages in the Collins and Smith procedure) with the wording of summaries and questions. Working specifically with seventh graders who were described as adequate decoders but poor comprehenders,[1] Palincsar and Brown were able to train the students to use the comprehension monitoring behaviors listed above after only fifteen to twenty sessions. They also trained classroom teachers to use the technique with similar success.

Reciprocal teaching can be used for either individuals or small groups. In either case, the adult teacher takes turns role-playing "teacher" with each student participant and leads a dialogue on a section of text read, usually a paragraph. After each section, the "teacher" asks a main idea question. If this is difficult, a summary is attempted. A clarification of some aspect of the text may be asked for, or a prediction about upcoming text may be given. Feedback and praise are given by the adult teacher whenever appropriate. In group sessions feedback also comes from other students.

Early training sessions require much guidance from the teacher. As students become better able to summarize and ask main idea questions, the teacher's level of participation decreases. Sessions should last about thirty minutes. Although Palincsar and Brown worked with expository passages of about 1500 words, any type or length of reading material could be used. An example of how session dialogues can proceed over time is demonstrated in figures 10.6 and 10.7.

Once students have reached a level of awareness regarding comprehension, they can deal with the question of "what to do next" (Anderson, 1980). Anderson provides the following guidelines:

1. If a reader reads something that he or she does not understand, the reader may decide to take some strategic action immediately or may store the information in memory as a pending question.
2. If the reader stores it as a pending question, he or she may formulate a possible meaning (usually one) that is stored as a tentative hypothesis.
3. If the reader forms a pending question, he or she usually continues to read.
4. If a triggering event occurs after the reader forms the pending question (i.e., too many pending questions or repetitions of the same pending question), the reader may take some strategic action.
5. If the reader takes some strategic action, he or she may:
   a. *reread* some portion of the text in order to collect more information that will either answer a pending question or form a tentative hypothesis that is related to a pending question;
   b. *jump ahead* in the text to see if there are headings or paragraphs that refer to the pending question and that might answer the pending question;
   c. *consult* an outside source (e.g., dictionary, glossary, encyclopedia, expert) for an answer to some pending question;
   d. make a *written record* of a pending question;
   e. *think/reflect* about the pending question and related information that the reader has in memory;
   f. *quit* reading the text.
6. If the strategic action is successful, the reader usually continues to read from the point at which the comprehension failure was last encountered.
7. If the strategic action is not successful, the reader usually continues to read by taking some other strategic action. (pp. 498–499)

An instructional strategy described by Babbs (1984) is appropriate for this area. Using a reading plan sheet and comprehension monitoring cards, readers are first

---

[1] The students decoded at least eighty words per minute with a maximum of two words per minute incorrect and were two grades or more behind on a standardized reading comprehension test.

FIGURE 10.6 Reciprocal dialogue from an early session, study 2, group 3, day 3. (From "Reciprocal Teaching of Comprehension-Fostering and Comprehension–Monitoring Activities" by A. S. Palincsar and A. L. Brown, 1984, *Cognition and Instruction, 1,* 161. Copyright 1984 by Lawrence Erlbaum Associates, Inc., Hillsdale, NJ. Reprinted by permission.)

Text:		Can Snakes Sting With Their Tongues?
		No—snakes' tongues are completely harmless. They're used for feeling things and for sharpening the snakes' sense of smell. Although snakes can smell in the usual way, the tongue flickering in the air picks up tiny particles of matter. These particles are deposited in two tiny cavities at the base of the nostrils to increase the snakes' ability to smell.
1.	A:	Do snakes' tongues sting?
2.	K:	Sometimes.
3.	A:	Correct.
		This paragraph is about do snakes sting with their tongue, and different ways that the tongue is for and the senses of smell.
4.	*T:	Are there any questions?
5.	C:	Snakes' tongues don't sting.
6.	*T:	Beautiful! I thought, boy, I must have been doing some fast reading there because I missed that point. A _____, could you ask your question again?
7.	A:	Do snakes' tongues really sting?
8.	*T:	Now, A _____, since you have asked the question, can you find in that paragraph where the question is answered?
9.	A:	No, snakes' tongues are completely harmless.
10.	*T:	So we'll try it again. Can you generate another question that you think a teacher might ask?
11.	A:	What are the tongues used for?
12.	*T:	Good!
13.	L:	The sense of smell.
14.	*T:	Is that correct? A _____, do you disagree? Yes.
15.	A:	That answer was right, but there are other things that the tongue can do.
16.	L:	But she only said tell one, she didn't say tell all of them.
17.	*T:	O.K.
18.	B:	It is used to pick up tiny particles.
19.	*T:	O.K. I think that this is an important point. You have the basic concept which is correct, O.K., but what the question really is saying is, is it used for smell? O.K.?
20.	B:	They are used for feeling things for sharpening snakes' sense of smell.
21.	*T:	O.K. They are used for sharpening the snakes' sense of smell. Are they used for smelling? That's the point we aren't clear on.
22.	L:	In my answer I said it is for the sense of smell.
23.	*T:	That is fine; this is what the technique is all about. What it means is not that you are right or wrong or good or bad. What it says is that we have just read something and have had a disagreement about what it says. We need to work it out.
24.	A:	My prediction is that they will now talk about the different things about snakes. Where they live, and what they eat and stuff like that.
25.	*T:	O.K. Good. What do you think they eat?
26.	A:	Animals.
27.	A:	Deserts.
28.	C:	I challenge. Snakes, all of them, don't live in the desert. They live in the woods and in swamp areas.

Note: * indicates turns taken by adult teacher (T); A, B, C, K, and L are students.

Figure 10.7 Reciprocal dialogue from a later session, study 2, group 3, day 13. (From "Reciprocal Teaching of Comprehension-Fostering and Comprehension-Monitoring Activities" by A. S. Palincsar and A. L. Brown, 1984, *Cognition and Instruction, 1*, 162–163. Copyright 1984 by Lawrence Erlbaum Associates, Inc., Hillsdale, NJ. Reprinted by permission.)

Text:		In the United States salt is produced by three basic methods: solar (sun) evaporation, mining, and artificial heat evaporation. For salt to be extracted by solar evaporation, the weather must be hot and dry. Thus, solar salt is harvested in the tropic-like areas along our southern ocean coasts and at Great Salt Lake.
1.	C:	Name three different basic methods how salt is produced.
2.	A:	Evaporation, mining, evaporation. . . artificial heat evaporation.
3.	C:	Correct, very good. My summary on this paragraph is about ways that salt is being produced.
4.	*T:	Very good. Could you select the next teacher?
		(Student selects another student)
Text:		The second oldest form of salt production is mining. Unlike early methods that made the work extremely dangerous and difficult, today's methods use special machinery, and salt mining is easier and safer. The old expression "back to the salt mine" no longer applies.
5.	L:	Name two words that often describe mining salt in the old days.
6.	K:	Back to the salt mines?
7.	L:	No. Angela?
8.	A:	Dangerous and difficult.
9.	L:	Correct. This paragraph is all about comparing the old mining of salt and today's mining of salt.
10.	*T:	Beautiful!
11.	L:	I have a prediction to make.
12.	*T:	Good.
13.	L:	I think it might tell when salt was first discovered, well, it might tell what salt is made of and how it's made.
14.	*T:	O.K. Can we have another teacher?
Text:		Table salt is made by the third method—artificial evaporation. Pumping water into an underground salt bed dissolves the salt to make a brine that is brought to the surface. After purification at high temperatures, the salt is ready for our tables.
15.	K:	After purification at high temperatures the salt is ready for what?
16.	C:	Our tables.
17.	K:	That's correct. To summarize: After its purification, the salt is put on our tables.
18.	*T:	That was a fine job, Ken, and I appreciate all that work, but I think there might be something else to add to our summary. There is more important information that I think we need to include. This paragraph is mostly about what?
19.	A:	The third method of artificial evaporation.
20.	B:	It mainly tells about pumping water from an underground salt bed that dissolves the salt to make a brine that is brought to the surface.
21.	*T:	Angela hit it right on the money. This paragraph is mostly about the method of artificial evaporation and then everything else in the paragraph is telling us about that process. O.K. Next teacher.
Text:		For thousands of years people have known salt—tasting it, using it for their lives' needs. Sometimes it has been treasured as gold; other times it has been superstitiously tossed over the shoulder to ward off bad luck. Somehow people and salt have always been together, but never is the tie more complete than when the best people are called "the salt of the earth."

(continued)

22.	C:	My question is, what are the best people called?
23.	L:	The salt of the earth.
24.	C:	Why?
25.	L:	Because salt and the people have been together so long.
26.	*T:	Chris, do you have something to add to that? O.K. It really isn't because they have been together so long; it has to do with something else. Brian?
27.	B:	(reading) "People and salt have always been together but never has the tie been so complete."
28.	*T:	Alright, but when we use the expression, "That person is the salt of the earth," we know that means that person is a good person. How do we know that?
29.	B:	Because we treasure salt, like gold.

Note: * indicates turns taken by adult teacher (T); A, B, C, K, and L are students.

taught to be aware that they may have a comprehension problem while reading (the plan sheet) and then are taught strategies for dealing with comprehension failure (the cards).

The reading plan sheet asks five questions: "(1) What is reading? (2) What is my goal? (3) How difficult is the text? (4) How can I accomplish my goal? (5) How can I check on whether or not I accomplished my goal?" (Babbs, 1984, p. 201). The questions presented on this plan sheet represent a study strategy, and you may see similarities between these questions and the strategy presented in the overview to this chapter. Students should receive practice using the plan sheet so that these questions are automatically asked before beginning to read text material.

The comprehension monitoring cards encourage the reader, in a step-by-step fashion, to evaluate their own understanding of the text read and also aid the reader in knowing what to do when a comprehension problem occurs. The nine cards are as follows with identifying numbers indicated: "(1) Click—'I understand.' (2) Clunk—'I don't understand.' (3) Read on. (4) Reread the sentence. (5) Go back and reread the paragraph. (6) Look in the glossary. (7) Ask someone. (8) What did it say? (to check comprehension at the paragraph level). (9) What do I remember? (to check comprehension at the page level)" (pp. 201–202).

A modeling procedure is recommended to teach students to use the cards. The teacher reads a sentence of text, then asks, "Did I understand that?" If the answer is yes, the Click card is raised and the teacher goes on to the next sentence. If the answer is no, the Clunk card is raised and cards 3 through 7 are selected. If the problem is with a word, the order of the strategy cards is 4-3-6-7. If the problem is with the whole sentence or with a pronoun referent, the order of the strategy cards is 4-5-3-7. The teacher models all of these possibilities over the course of several sentences.

After a complete paragraph has been modeled, the teacher should look away from the page and hold up card 8 and answer that question. If the question cannot be answered, the paragraph is reread without further use of the strategy cards.

Likewise, after a complete page has been modeled, the teacher looks away, holds up card 9, and answers the question. If the question cannot be answered, the page is reread using card 8 after each paragraph.

Once the teacher has modeled the process, Babbs (1984) recommends that each student have a turn modeling before going on to individual practice. She also states that fifteen sessions of twenty-two minutes each were allowed for learning both the reading plan sheet questions and the use of the comprehension monitoring cards. At that point the students could describe details of both of these elements from memory.

Modifications of reciprocal teaching and "Click-Clunk," which are effective for readers who experience great difficulty catching on to monitoring their reading and who are more passive readers, include the Yes/No Strategy and the "Clunk" Strategy (Richards, 1988, personal communication). In the Yes/No Strategy, the teacher and student both read silently an agreed upon portion of the text. This might be a page or a paragraph. Following the silent reading, the teacher models a "yes" and a "no." A "yes" is something that the reader liked or understood about the passage. A "no" is something not liked or not understood about the passage. Then the student shares a "yes" and a "no." For example, after reading the nursery rhyme *Jack and Jill*, the teacher might say, "My 'yes' is that I like the way Jack and Jill were doing their chores. My 'no' is that I didn't like that they got hurt." Then the student might respond with, "My 'yes' is that I like the name Jill. My 'no' is that I don't know what Jack broke." After a period of sharing Yes/Nos, and the teacher has modeled a variety of responses to text, the student will become more involved with the material and will become better able to summarize, clarify, predict and ask main idea questions about the material.

The "Clunk" strategy focuses on those aspects of the text that cause a problem for the reader. After the student has read a passage silently, the teacher asks if there were any "clunks," meaning was there anything in the text that was not understood (in this respect similar to Babbs' clunk). Once the clunk is identified, the teacher offers suggestions for fix-up strategies, thus modeling for the student such approaches as using context to determine the meaning of an unknown word, reading beyond the point of difficulty to see if more of the passage will clarify the ideas, rereading a difficult part, perhaps aloud, or perhaps emphasizing different words to clarify meaning, or referring to a glossary or dictionary to find a word's meaning.

Postreading

In the final stage of studying, activities that help the student organize and remember important information are appropriate. Outlining, paraphrasing, and reciting or rehearsal of information are common activities for this last stage. These activities are usually difficult for students to master, however.

Mapping.   One promising technique (Anderson, 1978) may aid the learner in linking ideas together. This technique is called **mapping** (Hanf, 1971) and is a graphic representation of the nature of the relationship between ideas found in the text. (Recall semantic webbing in chapter 8 and arrays in chapter 9.) Mapping is intended here as a substitute for the organizational activity of outlining. Hanf (1971) discusses three basic steps for designing a map: (1) identify the main idea, (2) identify principal parts that support the main idea (called secondary categories), and (3) identify supporting details. The skeleton of a map may be completed during the prereading stage (i.e., the title of the selection becoming the main idea or central theme and the headings becoming secondary categories that support the main idea). However, the map itself should be completed during the postreading stage from memory. The student must add the supporting details. If the student cannot complete the map, he or she knows to go back and reread the material. Thus, there is a built-in feedback device. If the student can complete some parts of the map but not others, the map provides feedback as to which categories need further study. An example of a map for the study of a science chapter entitled "Power for Work"[2] is found in figure 10.8.

Anderson (1978) has expanded upon Hanf's idea of mapping and has included a set of symbols that are used to show how two ideas are related. In addition to the relational symbols, the shape of the map represents the organizational pattern of the ideas. An example of an Anderson (1978) map is found in figure 10.9. Anderson recommends using short maps rather than maps of entire chapters.

When the K-W-L Strategy discussed earlier is combined with mapping and summarization, the technique helps students construct meaning from the text in an independent fashion. This modification of K-W-L is called K-W-L Plus (Carr & Ogle, 1987), and has been used successfully with disabled secondary readers. Basically, students must think critically about what they have read in order to organize, restructure, and apply what they have learned to the formation of a map and a written summary. Figure 10.10 shows how one ninth grader went from the K-W-L listings to a concept map. The map can then be used as an aid for preparing a written summary and also preparing for exams.

Think-links. Wilson (1981) refers to another organizational strategy called **think-links**. Upon completion of the during reading stage of study, the teacher directs the students to think about what they have read. The following steps are then taken (fig. 10.11).

1. Write the name of the person the chapter is about (Lincoln) and some words that describe his early life.
2. Ask students for examples that show Lincoln's early life was hard and record them.
3. Step 2 is repeated using other descriptive words.

After all of the words have been used, the students have actually reconstructed, graphically, the important parts of the material read.

Once the teacher has helped students develop several think-links, they can start to develop them on their own. Think-links are used to summarize any type of reading material; during the instructional process, different types are constructed with the students so they can see a variety of types.

Paragraph frames. As discussed in chapter 8, paragraph frames provide a useful instructional tool for helping students write about what they learn in content areas (Cudd & Roberts, 1989). A cloze format is used which provides sentence starters that focus on the organizational pattern of the text. Intended for students of all grade levels, the introduction of paragraph frames is easiest with sequentially ordered material. The teacher might write a brief paragraph based on a content area topic just read, using such key words as *first, next, then, now, finally,* and *after this.* The individual sentences are put on sentence strips and as a group students are asked to first review the topic read and then to arrange the sentence strips in the logical

---

[2] From *In Your Neighborhood* (pp. 91–96) by A. O. Baker, G. C. Maddox, and H. B. Warrin, 1955, New York: Rand McNally.

FIGURE 10.8 Example of a map for a science chapter entitled, "Power for Work."

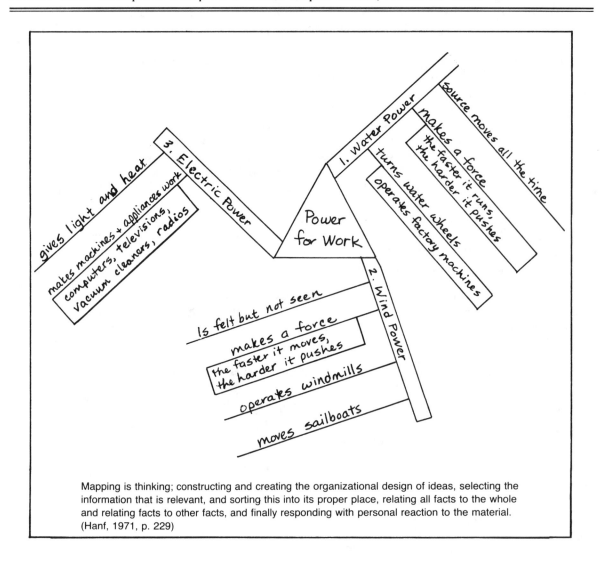

Mapping is thinking; constructing and creating the organizational design of ideas, selecting the information that is relevant, and sorting this into its proper place, relating all facts to the whole and relating facts to other facts, and finally responding with personal reaction to the material. (Hanf, 1971, p. 229)

sequence of events. The resulting paragraph is read for "correctness." Following the group work, individual students are to reorder the sentences on their own, write the paragraph, and illustrate the important parts. Figure 10.12 provides an example of a completed paragraph frame.

General Study Strategies

SQ3R

The most well-known study strategy recommended for helping students make optimum use of study time is Robinson's (1961) **SQ3R** (survey, question, read, recite,

FIGURE 10.9 Mapping procedure with relational symbols. (From "Study Skills and Learning Strategies," by Thomas Anderson. In *Cognitive and Affective Learning Strategies,* edited by H. F. O'Neil, Jr., and C. D. Spielberger. New York: Academic Press, 1979, p. 94. Used with permission. Data for map adapted from Sociology by Ian Robertson, New York: Worth Publishers, Inc., 1977, p. 83.)

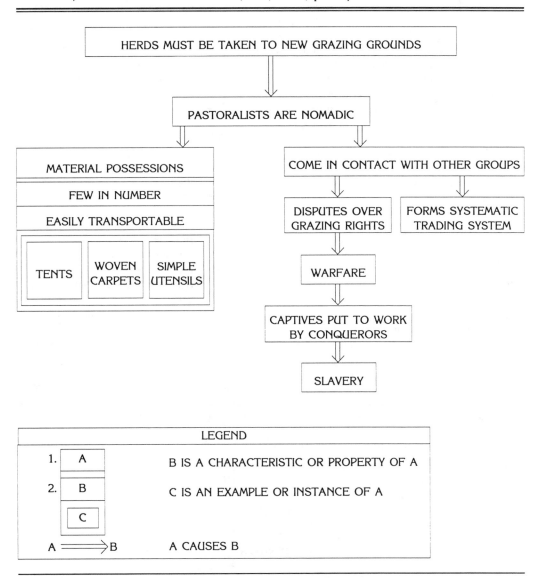

review) **Strategy.** This strategy is designed to (1) provide specific purposes for reading, (2) provide self-comprehension checks, and (3) fix information in memory (Tadlock, 1978). Briefly, in the *survey* step, the student reads the title, introductory statement, and main headings, surveys the illustrations, reads the chapter summary, and tries to construct mentally an outline of the chapter. In the *question* phase, the student again looks at the main headings. These headings are used to formulate questions to be answered in the next step. The *read* step then has the main purpose

FIGURE 10.10 Example of ninth grader's K-W-L worksheet and resulting concept map. (Reprinted with permission of Eileen Carr and the International Reading Association.)

A 9th grade disabled reader's K-W-L worksheet on killer whales

K (Know)	**W** (Want to know)	**L** (Learned)
They live in oceans.	Why do they attack people?	D — They are the biggest member of the dolphin family.
They are vicious.	How fast can they swim?	
They eat each other.	What kind of fish do they eat?	D — They weigh 10,000 pounds and get 30 feet long.
They are mammals.	What is their description?	
	How long do they live?	F — They eat squids, seals, and other dolphins.
	How do they breathe?	
		A — They have good vision underwater.
		F — They are carnivorous (meat eaters).
		A — They are the second smartest animal on earth.
		D — They breathe through blow holes.
		A — They do not attack unless they are hungry.
Description		D — Warm blooded
Food		A — They have echo-location (sonar).
Location		L — They are found in the oceans.

Final category designations developed for column L, information learned about killer whales:
  A = abilities, D = description, F = food, L = location

The 9th grader's concept map

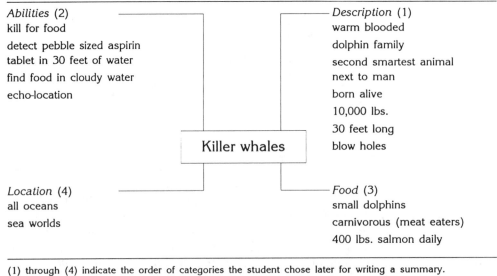

Abilities (2)		*Description* (1)
kill for food		warm blooded
detect pebble sized aspirin		dolphin family
tablet in 30 feet of water		second smartest animal
find food in cloudy water		next to man
echo-location		born alive
		10,000 lbs.
	Killer whales	30 feet long
		blow holes
Location (4)		*Food* (3)
all oceans		small dolphins
sea worlds		carnivorous (meat eaters)
		400 lbs. salmon daily

(1) through (4) indicate the order of categories the student chose later for writing a summary.

FIGURE 10.11   Think-links are used to summarize graphically the important parts of any type of reading matter.

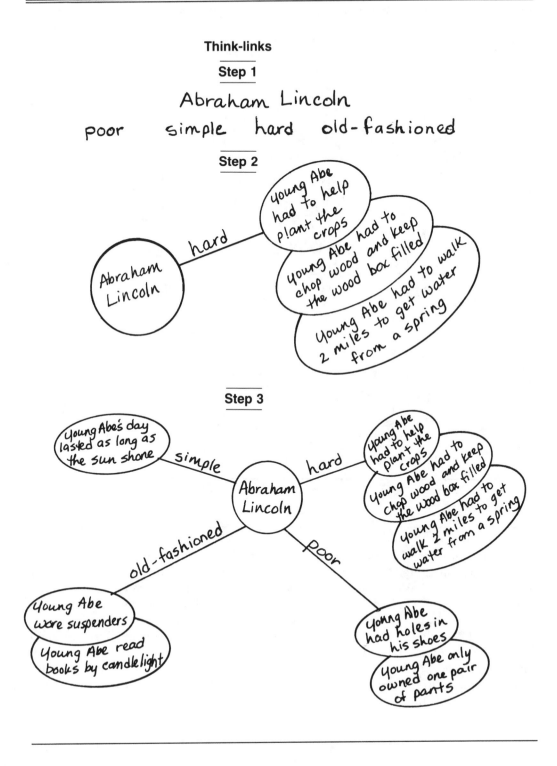

FIGURE 10.12 Example of a completed paragraph frame to include illustrations. (Reprinted with permission of Evelyn T. Cudd and the International Reading Association.)

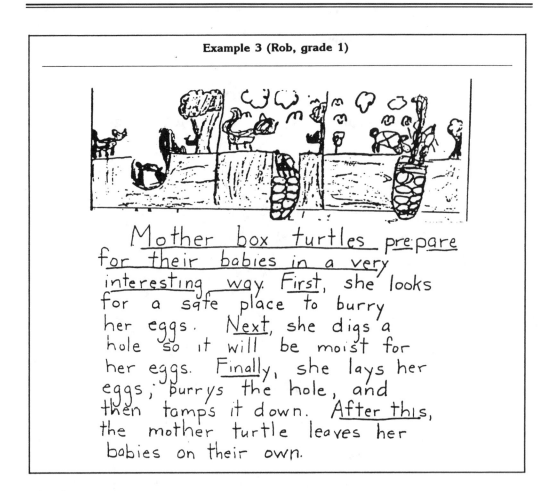

Example 3 (Rob, grade 1)

<u>Mother box turtles</u> prepare for their babies in a very interesting way. <u>First</u>, she looks for a safe place to burry her eggs. <u>Next</u>, she digs a hole so it will be moist for her eggs. <u>Finally</u>, she lays her eggs; burrys the hole, and then tamps it down. <u>After this</u>, the mother turtle leaves her babies on their own.

of finding answers to the questions formed in the question phase. The *recite* step has the student literally reciting the answers aloud to the questions. At this point the student should also be concerned about the quality of the answers; for example, does the author provide answers that satisfy the question? The last step, *review*, is done from memory, with the entire chapter or selection being reviewed in survey fashion. The mental outline is reconstructed. The author's main ideas are recalled, and new ways to use these ideas are considered. A second and even a third review should take place over as many days. For a detailed description of how to teach the SQ3R Strategy, the interested reader is referred to Forgan and Mangrum's (1985) *Teaching Content Area Reading Skills,* pages 180–182.

Assignment Mastery

A similar technique, developed by Edward Strickland (1975), is called **Assignment Mastery.** The steps themselves closely parallel those in SQ3R. They are: scanning, preparation for reading, reading, recitation and review, and reading review. The biggest difference from SQ3R is that specific questions are developed for students to ask themselves during the scanning, preparation, and reading stages. These follow:

Scanning

- How difficult does the work appear to be?
- Is it a relatively large amount of work?
- Will I have to alter my schedule to get it done?
- Are the terms generally familiar?
- What is the main theme of the assignment?
- What main headings and subheadings are there?
- What words are stressed (in italics or bold print)?

Preparation for reading (with the help of a dictionary or glossary)

- Are there related terms that I use?
- Have I learned something that changes the meaning of the term from what I thought it was?
- Does the theme of the material appear to challenge or support my ideas?

Reading

- What is the meaning of what I am reading?
- What illustrations of that meaning are given?
- Can I recall any examples from my own experience that would clarify the meaning of the material?
- What questions should I ask my instructor that will help clarify the meaning of this material?

Strickland also stresses the underlining or outlining of main themes and illustrative examples while reading.

GRS

A third technique, called the guided reading strategy (Bean & Pardi, 1979), was developed specifically for corrective readers. The **guided reading strategy (GRS)** is a modification of the guided reading procedure (Manzo, 1975) and differs from the first two techniques because it depends heavily on teacher guidance. Briefly, the steps of a GRS are as follows:

1. Survey the chapter or chapter sections, reading only the chapter title, subtitles, vocabulary lists, graphs, maps, and chapter questions.
2. Close the book and orally state everything remembered from the survey. The teacher records what is remembered on the board.
3. Students recheck the chapter for any missing information; this is added to the board.

4. A crucial step, the teacher and students discuss the results of the chapter survey and organize this information into a topical outline on the board. This organizing highlights the structure of the information and enhances the ability to remember it later.
5. Students read the chapter or selection silently.
6. Students complete a ten-item true-false quiz.
7. About a week later, students take a ten-item pop quiz.

Of these three strategies, the teacher may find that using the GRS as an introduction to the other strategies is most helpful.

PORPE

A fourth strategy, developed by Simpson (1986) for secondary and college level students as a less teacher-directed strategy, uses writing as the main learning strategy for planning, monitoring, and evaluating the reading of any content area material. PORPE (Predict, Organize, Rehearse, Practice, Evaluate) is especially useful for students preparing to take essay examinations. Once the five steps of PORPE are modeled and mastered, it becomes a learning strategy that gives the student complete independence and control. The 5 steps are briefly presented here, but interested readers are urged to refer to Simpson's (1986) detailed description of the steps, and how to teach them to students. The steps are:

1. Predict. Students are asked to generate possible essay questions on the material read.

2. Organize. Students summarize and synthesize the important ideas in the material. Charts, maps, or outlines are all possible ways for organizing the material.

3. Rehearse. Students recite the overall organizational structure of the chart, map, or outline, eventually adding important ideas and examples to this recitation. The purpose is to place these important ideas and organizational structure into longterm memory.

4. Practice. Students actually practice writing answers to the predicted essay questions from recall.

5. Evaluate. Students judge the quality of their responses from the perspective of the instructor. An evaluative checklist might be developed to aid in this process.

Summary

The techniques presented here have been chosen because they stress student involvement with text and appear in the literature as promising techniques.

Teachers must develop study strategies even for the young reader. At the early stages this may simply involve scanning printed material for a specific word or being taught to question material while reading it; that is, asking "Do I understand this?" Teacher modeling of the types of questions to ask while reading is one direct way of providing instruction in the area of self-questioning. Also, students at all levels, when given appropriate materials, can be taught to organize what they have read to aid them in remembering that material. Mapping and think-links are promising techniques because of their graphic nature.

The general study strategies discussed are most easily taught if the students have previously received instruction in the three stages of studying because these strategies include all three phases. Study strategies do not simply develop—they must be taught and practiced.

References

Anderson, T. H. (1978). *Study skills and learning strategies* (Tech. Rep. No. 104). Champaign, IL: University of Illinois, Center for the Study of Reading.

Anderson, T. H. (1980). Study strategies and adjunct aids. In R. J. Spiro, B. C. Bruce, and W. F. Brewer (Eds.), *Theoretical issues in reading comprehension.* Hillsdale, NJ: Erlbaum.

Andre, M. E. D. A., & Anderson, T. H. (1978–1979). The development and evaluation of a self-questioning study technique. *Reading Research Quarterly, 14,* 605–623.

Babbs, P. J. (1984). Monitoring cards help improve comprehension. *The Reading Teacher, 38,* 200–204.

Baker, L. (1979). *Comprehension monitoring: Identifying and coping with text confusions* (Tech. Rep. No. 145). Champaign, IL: University of Illinois, Center for the Study of Reading.

Baker, L., & Anderson, R. I. (1981). *Effects of inconsistent information on text processing: Evidence for comprehension monitoring* (Tech. Rep. No. 203). Champaign, IL: University of Illinois, Center for the Study of Reading.

Baker, L., & Brown, A. L. (1984). Metacognitive skills and reading. In P. D. Pearson (Ed.), *Handbook of reading research.* New York: Longman.

Bean, T. W., & Pardi, R. (1979). A field test of a guided reading strategy. *Journal of Reading, 23,* 144–147.

Brown, A. L. (1980). Metacognitive development and reading. In R. J. Spiro, B. C. Bruce, & W. F. Brewer (Eds.), *Theoretical issues in reading comprehension.* Hillsdale, NJ: Erlbaum.

Brown, A. L. (1975). The development of memory: Knowing, knowing about knowing, and knowing how to know. In H. W. Reese (Ed.), *Advances in child development and behavior* (Vol. 10). New York: Academic Press.

Brown, A. L., & Campione, J. C. (1978). Memory strategies in learning: Teaching children to study effectively. In H. Leibowitz, J. Singer, A. Steinschneider, H. Stevenson, & H. Pick (Eds.), *Application of basic research in psychology.* New York: Plenum Press.

Brown, A. L., & Campione, J. C. (1977). Training strategic study time apportionment in educable retarded children. *Intelligence, 1,* 94–107.

Brown, A. L., & DeLoache, J. (1978). Skills, plans, and self-regulation. In R. Siegler (Ed.), *Children's thinking: What develops?* Hillsdale, NJ: Erlbaum.

Carr, E. & Ogle, D. (1987). K–W–L plus: A strategy for comprehension and summarization. *Journal of Reading, 30,* 626–631.

Chi, M. T. H. (1978). Knowledge structures and development. In R. S. Siegler (Ed.), *Children's thinking: What develops?* Hillsdale, NJ: Erlbaum.

Collins, A., & Smith, E. E. (1980). *Teaching the process of reading comprehension* (Tech. Rep. No. 182). Champaign, IL: University of Illinois, Center for the Study of Reading.

Cudd, E. T., & Roberts, L. L. (1989). Using writing to enhance content area learning in the primary grades. *The Reading Teacher, 42,* 392–404.

Davey, B. (1983). Think aloud–Modeling the cognitive processes of reading comprehension. *The Reading Teacher, 27,* 44–47.

DiVesta, F. J., Hayward, K. G., & Orlando, V. P. (1979). Developmental trends in monitoring text for comprehension. *Child Development, 50,* 97–105.

Duell, O. K. (1978). Overt and covert use of objectives of different cognitive levels. *Contemporary Journal of Educational Psychology, 3,* 239–245.

Duffy, G. G., Roehler, L. R., & Herrmann, B. A. (1988). Modeling mental processes helps poor readers become strategic readers. *The Reading Teacher, 41,* 762–767.

Flavell, J. H. (1976). Metacognitive aspects of problem solving. In L. B. Resnick (Ed.), *The nature of intelligence.* Hillsdale, NJ: Erlbaum.

Flavell, J. H., Speer, J. R., Green, F. L., & August, D. L. (1981). The development of comprehension monitoring and knowledge about communication. *Monographs of the Society for Research in Child Development, 46* (5, Serial No. 192).

Forgan, H. W., & Mangrum, C. T. II. (1985). *Teaching content area reading skills* (3rd ed.). Columbus, OH: Merrill.

Frase, L. T., & Schwartz, B. J. (1975). Effect of question production on prose recall. *Journal of Educational Psychology, 67,* 628–635.

Garner, R. (1987). *Metacognition and reading comprehension.* Norwood, NJ: Ablex.

Garner, R. (1980). Monitoring of understanding: An investigation of good and poor readers' awareness of induced miscomprehension of text. *Journal of Reading Behavior, 12,* 55–64.

Hanf, M. B. (1971). Mapping: A technique for translating reading into thinking. *Journal of Reading, 14,* 225–230.

Harris, P. L., Kruithof, A., Terwogt, M. M., & Visser, P. (1981). Children's detection and awareness of textual anomaly. *Journal of Experimental Child Psychology, 31,* 212–230.

International Reading Association. (1988). *New directions in reading instruction.* Newark, DE: International Reading Association.

Manzo, A. V. (1975). Guided reading procedure. *Journal of Reading, 18,* 287–291.

Markman, E. M. (1981). Comprehension monitoring. In W. P. Dickson (Ed.), *Children's oral communication skills.* New York: Academic Press.

Markman, E. M. (1977). Realizing that you don't understand: A preliminary investigation. *Child Development, 48,* 986–992.

Markman, E. M. (1979). Realizing that you don't understand: Elementary school children's awareness of inconsistencies. *Child Development, 50,* 643–655.

Myers, M., & Paris, S. (1978). Children's metacognitive knowledge about reading. *Journal of Educational Psychology, 70,* 680–690.

Ogle, D. M. (1986). K-W-L: A teaching model that develops active reading of expository text. *The Reading Teacher, 39,* 564–570.

Palincsar, A. S., & Brown, A. L. (1984). Reciprocal teaching of comprehension-fostering and comprehension-monitoring activities. *Cognition and Instruction, 1,* 117–175.

Paris, S. G., & Lipson, M. Y. (1982). *Metacognition and reading comprehension.* Research colloquium presented at the annual meeting of the International Reading Association, Chicago, IL.

Paris, S., & Myers, M. (1981). Comprehension monitoring, memory, and study strategies of good and poor readers. *Journal of Reading Behavior, 13,* 7–22.

Pitts, M. M., Thompson, B., & Gipe, J. P. (1983). *Comprehension monitoring: Longitudinal unobtrusive measurements with microcomputers.* Paper presented at the annual meeting of the American Educational Research Association, Montreal.

Richards, J. C. (1988). Personal communication.

Richek, M. A. (1987). DRTA: 5 variations that facilitate independence in reading narratives. *Journal of Reading, 30,* 632–636.

Robinson, F. P. (1961). *Effective study* (rev. ed.). New York: Harper & Brothers.

Schachter, S. W (1978). Developing flexible reading habits. *Journal of Reading, 22,* 149–152.

Schmelzer, R. V. (1975). *The effect of college student constructed questions on the comprehension of a passage of expository prose.* Doctoral dissertation, University of Minnesota. *Dissertation Abstracts International, 36,* 2162A.

Simpson, M. L. (1986). PORPE: A writing strategy for studying and learning in the content areas. *Journal of Reading, 29,* 407–414.

Singer, H. (1978). Active comprehension: From answering to asking questions. *The Reading Teacher, 31,* 901–908.

Smith, H. K. (1967). The responses of good and poor readers when asked to read for different purposes. *Reading Research Quarterly, 3,* 53–84.

Strang, R., & Rogers, C. (1965). How do students read a short story? *English Journal, 54,* 819–823, 829.

Strickland, E. (Oct. 1975). Assignment mastery. *Reading World,* 25–31.

Sullivan, J. (1978). Comparing strategies of good and poor comprehenders. *Journal of Reading, 21,* 710–715.

Tadlock, D. F. (1978). SQ3R–why it works, based on an information processing theory of learning. *Journal of Reading, 22,* 110–112.

Wagoner, S. A. (1983). Comprehension monitoring: What it is and what we know about it. *Reading Research Quarterly, 17,* 328–346.

Wilson, R. M. (1981). *Diagnostic and remedial reading for classroom and clinic* (4th ed.). Columbus, OH: Merrill.

Winograd, P., & Johnston, P. (1980). *Comprehension monitoring and the error detection paradigm* (Tech. Rep. No. 153). Champaign, IL: University of Illinois, Center for the Study of Reading.

PART III

Other Considerations

CHAPTER 11

Developing Reading of Linguistically Variant Children

John G. Barnitz

Objectives

After you have studied this chapter, you should be able to

1. explain the relationship between communicative competence and reading development;
2. describe some of the basic characteristics of linguistic competence and sociolinguistic competence;
3. describe how language characteristics vary across cultural groups;
4. list some specific characteristics of Black English Vernacular and other varieties of English;
5. explain implications of language or dialect differences for assessing reading and language abilities of linguistically variant children;
6. summarize basic principles for teaching standard English;
7. describe various approaches for developing or correcting the reading of linguistically variant children;
8. appreciate and respect the language varieties of children as a first step toward developing standard English literacy.

Study Outline

I. Introduction

II. Communicative competence, language, and reading

III. Characteristics of linguistic variation
   A. Black English Vernacular
   B. Other language varieties

IV. Principles for reading and language

A. Language-reading assessment

B. Standard English language arts instruction

C. Reading instruction
   1. Language experience approach
   2. Experience-text-relationship method

Important Vocabulary and Concepts

Black English Vernacular

communicative competence

choral reading

deficit hypothesis

dialects

dialogue journals

discourse

experience-text-relationship method

language experience approach

language functions

linguistic competence

morphemes

morphology

narrative ability

nonstandard English

oral interaction

phonemes

phonology

regional dialects

social dialects

sociolinguistic competence

standard English

style shifting

syntax

Overview

Teachers frequently find that many students in a corrective reading program are children whose native tongue is either a nonstandard variety of English or another language totally. Some of these students have become poor readers because of true correlates to reading disability, while many have become poor readers as a result of teachers' unawareness of how language and dialect differences influence the reading process. Teachers' attitudes toward the speech patterns of children can either facilitate or hinder minority children's growth in literacy (Goodman & Buck, 1973). For example, as a result of the recent federal court case of *Martin Luther King Junior Elementary School Children* v. *Ann Arbor School District Board*, teachers are expected to understand and respect the language varieties minority children bring to the task of learning to read standard English (Labov, 1983; Smitherman, 1985.) A major implication of the *Ann Arbor* case is that it establishes a legal precedent for parents of children in any ethnic group to expect teachers to know linguistic facts about the language varieties children bring to school (Labov, 1983).

The primary purposes for reading this chapter, then, are threefold: (1) to understand the nature of communicative competence as it relates to reading; (2) to understand basic information about dialect and language differences; and (3) to acquire some guidelines and techniques for teaching reading of standard English to linguistically variant children in your corrective reading program.

The author wishes to thank Dr. John G. Barnitz, University of New Orleans, for contributing this chapter.

Communicative Competence, Language, and Reading

A general understanding of **communicative competence** and the relationship between language development and reading development is essential. Language competence is both a prerequisite to learning to read and an intimate part of the fluent reading process. As language is basic to reading, linguistic information is an integral part of the professional knowledge of teachers of reading. In this section, I will define some basic concepts associated with communicative competence.

Communicative competence is defined by DeStefano (1978, p. 2) as "competence in language use or as the language abilities of the speaker and listener." Hymes (1974) clearly asserts that communicative abilities not only involve the basic mastery of the language system but also the use of language in social situations. Shuy (1981) labels these two capabilities as **linguistic competence** and **sociolinguistic competence.** Linguistic competence generally refers to mastery of the formal system of language, while sociolinguistic competence is the use of language "to get things done." Sociolinguistic competence is the most important aspect of communication and of language learning. Functional use of language is basic to language production and comprehension (Halliday, 1974) and usually precedes the formal perfection of structure. Functional use of language is also crucial to school success (Shafer, Staab, & Smith, 1983), although many traditional curricula are limited only to linguistic competence.

Shuy (1981) describes **sociolinguistic competence**, which includes oral interaction, language functions, narrative abilities, and style shifting. **Oral interaction** is a basic human social skill that encompasses such abilities as beginning a conversation, switching topics, taking turns, or using tact in sharing bad news. It also includes basic pragmatic abilities, such as knowing what and what not to say, stating things directly and indirectly, being relevant, and so forth (Grice, 1975). These important social skills may transfer to reading because reading is a social activity. Such skills also help one to infer the social motives of an author and better comprehend the oral interactions of characters in a story.

Language functions, as mentioned earlier, are crucial to the social use of language. Language exists because it is useful, and children learn language when they perceive the need. For instance, sixth-grade students in their **dialogue journals** (daily journals written back and forth by the child and teacher) demonstrate a wide range of language functions: reporting opinions and personal and general facts, responding to questions, predicting future events, complaining, giving directives, apologizing, thanking, evaluating, offering, promising, and asking various types of questions (Shuy, 1988; Staton, Shuy, Peyton, & Reed, 1988). Functional language development is essential to literacy development in that the writer must use language to bring out a certain response in the reader. Conversely, an effective reader is aware of what the author is trying to *do* with language. Therefore, functional language ability is a basic reading and writing skill.

Narrative ability encompasses another set of sociolinguistic competencies, which includes not only the above two categories, but also the fluency of expression and sequencing of ideas. Many speakers are "gifted" at composing oral stories, telling lengthy jokes, and describing traffic accidents in logical and sequential manners. Future research may prove that this ability transfers to reading narratives. If children have an intuitive awareness of how narrative discourse is ordered, they can make meaningful predictions in the reading comprehension process.

Style shifting is an important language skill that refers to the ability of speakers and writers to adapt their language styles to various social contexts (i.e., different settings, participants, and topics.) Just as we vary our dress depending on the social situation (formal, semiformal, casual, "grubby"), so do we shift our language. Language *variety* is a necessary part of language competence. The more variety in our language "wardrobe," the better we can survive in diverse social contexts. I will return to this point later in this chapter.

What is crucial to remember is that sociolinguistic competence is a foundation for developing linguistic competence or the actual structures of the language: phonology, morphology, syntax, discourse structure, and vocabulary. Recall that **phonology** refers to the sounds **(phonemes)** and sound processes of a language. **Morphology** refers to the study of meaningful word structures **(morphemes). Syntax** is the system of patterns and processes in sentence formation. **Discourse** refers to a unit of communication that relates ideas to a unified theme for a particular purpose. Vocabulary, of course, is made up of the words of the language. These surface features comprise only the tip of the iceberg of language competence; sociolinguistic competence is the essence of language communication (Shuy, 1981).

Language competence is intimately related to reading development. Linguists and linguistically informed reading educators understand that children bring to school a wealth of language and cultural experiences upon which teachers can build literacy. This is even true of minority group children, who have been shown to follow stages of language acquisition similar to those of middle class children (Steffensen, 1974, 1978) and also to acquire English literacy naturally, while they were learning the language (Hudelson, 1984; Goodman & Goodman, 1978). Both first and second language English speaking children's literacy is continually emerging within natural communicative contexts (see Teale & Sulzby, 1986). Reading and writing emerge together.

Reading and language development are interdependent. Earlier studies by Strickland (1962), Ruddell (1963), and Tatham (1970) illustrate that children with more variety and complexity of sentence structures in their oral language tend to be better readers. Similarly, Chomsky (1972) found that children with more exposure to books were more advanced in oral language development. More recently, Eckhoff (1983) found that children learned sentence patterns through their reading and transferred them to their writing. Reading and writing abilities develop together (Harste, Woodward, & Burke, 1984). Teale and Sulzby (1986) illustrate conclusively that written language development is closely tied to oral language development. Reading instruction, therefore, cannot be isolated from the development of children's communicative competence, regardless of the variety of language children bring to school. In the next section, some of the characteristics of language varieties commonly found in classrooms are examined.

Characteristics of Linguistic Variation

In this section is a brief sketch of how language varies with geographical areas and social classes. Teachers must be linguistically informed of language varieties among students in their corrective reading program in order to distinguish between errors and dialect or language differences.

Most of you have enjoyed traveling to different parts of the country and meeting a wide variety of people in gas stations, restaurants, hotels, resorts, or roadside fruit stands, and you have certainly noticed how pronunciation and usage patterns differ from your own. Similarly, you will notice how children in your classroom vary in their speech performance depending on their home background or place of birth. These surface differences are part of what are called **dialects**; they are fully developed linguistic systems identifiable to particular speech communities and vary in the specific combination of pronunciation, vocabulary, and usage. Dialects identifiable to a particular geographical area are called **regional dialects.** For example, Labov (1988) studied the complexity of the regional distributions of the submarine sandwich lexicon: submarine, hoagie, po'boy, grinder, hero, wedge, torpedo and zep. Compare these and other dialect features among your classmates. How do the syntax, phonology and lexicon of different English speakers vary regionally and socially? (See Shuy, 1967, for a discussion of regional dialects.)

Dialects also vary across social classes or cultural groups. These are called **social dialects.** Compare the language of an educated businessman with that of a sanitation engineer. One's speech often reflects one's social status (Labov, 1975). The language spoken and preferred by educated members of our community for conducting important affairs is called **standard English** while the "less prestigious" varieties used in everyday communication by speakers with far less formal education and income are called **nonstandard English.** Labov (1975) explains that nonstandard English dialects, which share many common features with standard English, are fully developed, rule-governed systems. Moreover, standard English consists of a variety of features used by educated speakers and writers as they shift styles depending on the social situation (see Farr & Daniels, 1986). Teachers must respect the language and culture of children from lower social classes, while providing opportunities for them to acquire the standard variety. I will return to this point later.

Language also varies, as noted earlier, in terms of the social situation. One aspect of communicative competence is the ability to use language appropriate to the situation, whether formal or informal. These styles are additional complex aspects of language variation, common to all social classes (Labov, 1975). Thus, one's speech at a given instance is usually influenced by regional, social, and situational factors. (See Wolfram & Christian [1989] for further discussion of dialect issues in education.)

Black English Vernacular

Black English Vernacular (BEV) is a variety of English found in black communities and used in the most informal settings throughout the United States. BEV differs from the standard speech found in black and white communities (Labov, 1983). As is any ethnic variety of English, BEV is rule-governed, containing a systematic set of phonological and syntactic features, some of which are listed in Table 11.1 (adapted from Burling, 1973; Labov, 1975; and Smitherman, 1985).

Several facts should be understood about Black English Vernacular.

1. Language competence goes beyond surface characteristics, such as those listed in Table 11.1. Much communicative competence is illustrated in the different, yet rich, lexical and oral discourse features found in the black communities (Kochman, 1972).

TABLE 11.1 Some Surface Features of Black English Vernacular

Phonological Patterns and Processes	Examples	
Consonant cluster simplification	desk	des'
	past	pass
Deletion of 1 phoneme before consonants or at the end of words	tool	too
	help	he'p
Voiced *th* phoneme becomes *d* or *v*	then	den
	bathe	bave
Voiceless *th* phoneme becomes *t* or *f*	thin	tin
	bath	baf
Neutralization of short vowels before nasal consonants	ten	tin
	went	win(t)

Morphological and Syntactic Patterns	Examples
Deletion of plural morpheme	ten cent
Deletion of third person singular morpheme	The girl walk fast.
Deletion of past tense morpheme	The man walk yesterday.
Existential *it* (there)	It was three ball in the basket.
Invariant *be*	He be hollin at us.
Be deleted	My momma name Annie.

2. As Black English Vernacular is a rule-governed system, the claim that it is an illegitimate or linguistically inferior language system has been disproved in studies (Labov, 1975; Burling, 1973; Steffensen, 1978) and has been disproved in federal court (Labov, 1982; Smitherman, 1985).

3. Many surface features of Black English Vernacular are shared by white nonstandard English speakers in lower socioeconomic groups, but the distribution or frequency of specific features varies (Labov, 1975). Language varieties develop along with social, cultural, economic, or racial boundaries in a society.

4. Part of communicative competence involves knowing when to adapt language to the appropriate settings, topics, and participants in a discourse. Therefore, many black speakers shift between standard and vernacular features as appropriate to the formality of the social situation: standard English for formal situations (e.g., commerce, education, business) and nonstandard English for informal settings. Moreover, standard and nonstandard English speakers alike vary their language with the social setting.

Teachers, then, must be knowledgeable regarding the influence of language differences on learning to read standard English.

Other Language Varieties

A detailed discussion of other varieties of English found in the repertoire of culturally different children will not be undertaken here. Teachers should be aware, however, that language differences, not just dialect differences, influence children's learning to read standard English, and they should become familiar with other language varieties found in the United States.

Hispanic varieties of English are pervasive throughout the United States, and Spanish learners of English as a second language will probably need assistance in learning to read a nonnative language. The Spanish child brings to the task of reading English a certain degree of competence in the first language, but possibly a lesser degree of competence in English. Moreover, many nonnative English speakers already have some reading experience in the second language, and literacy skills may transfer to English. Nonetheless, a teacher of Hispanic children must be aware of areas where the first language, Spanish in this case, may influence the reading of English, the second language.

A few examples are in order. In the phonology of Spanish, the inventory of speech sounds varies (Troike, 1972). For example, the contrasts between *sip* and *zip, chair* and *share; bat* and *vat; den* and *then,* are easily made by native English speakers; but the Hispanic child may not readily recognize these contrasts because Spanish does not have the sounds corresponding to *z, sh,* and *v.* Similarly, vowel phonemes are fewer in Spanish than in English; thus the learning of English vowel phonemes and phoneme-grapheme correspondences become more challenging. A child benefits from auditory discrimination exercises or learning target words by sight in the context of meaningful passages. Readers often bypass phonological differences by relying on context and other clues to word identification.

Syntactic differences are also common among languages of the world. In Spanish, negative sentences are formed by placing the negative morpheme before the verb (he no go home); the placement of adjectives is different (the cap red is large); understood subject pronouns are deleted (is big); and comparatives are made differently (is more big) (Ching, 1976). Points of contrast influence the way second language readers process the sentences they read (Cowan, 1976). However, depending on the content, second language readers can compensate by using the broader context of their background knowledge (see Barnitz, 1986; Carrell, Devine, & Eskey, 1988). Through holistic sentence expansion and language experience activities, to be discussed later, a teacher can facilitate syntactic awareness of the second language learner.

Teachers should also understand lexical differences that may exist across various languages. For example, Spanish *penitencia, realizar, libreria,* and *chanza,* do not mean *penitentiary, realize, library,* and *chance,* but rather, *penance, accomplish an ambition, bookstore,* and *joke* (Thonis, 1976). Reading teachers must know that shades of meaning differ in various languages. Vocabulary instruction in context is critical to facilitating growth in reading.

Teachers are reminded, however, that other languages may have a significantly different set of contrasts with English. In Vietnamese, some of the phonemic contrasts not made are laugh/lap; pin/bin; much/mush; bad/bat. In addition, Vietnamese is a tone language, that is, the pitch of a syllable makes a difference in meaning; it also disallows consonant clusters. Vietnamese speakers learning English often either split consonant blends or simplify them, for example, stop becomes "suhtop" and cold becomes "col" (Grognet et al., 1976).

More diverse syntactic differences exist between Vietnamese and English. Possessive and past tense suffixes are deleted because separate words indicate these meanings and because, as noted, Vietnamese cannot allow consonant clusters. In addition, yes-no questions are formed by placing a question word at the end of the sentence. Grognet (1976) discusses this further.

To become more familiar with language communities in the United States, consult Conklin and Lourie (1983), Ferguson and Brice-Heath (1981), and Kachru (1982).

Principles for Reading and Language Development

Several principles may be presented to guide teachers of nonnative and nonstandard English speaking children. These and related principles are also presented in Barnitz (1980, 1982, 1988). It is most important to remember that reading is "the process of constructing meaning from written texts. It is a complex skill requiring the coordination of a number of interrelated sources of information" (Anderson et al., 1985). The language abilities children bring to school, no matter how variant, can be a rich foundation for learning and developing reading proficiency (see Goodman & Goodman, 1978). The present discussion is divided into three sections: assessing language differences in reading; developing standard English language arts as a context for reading development; and developing reading performance of linguistically variant children.

Language-Reading Assessment

Some classroom techniques for determining children's oral language performance include whole language evaluation procedures (Goodman, Goodman, & Hood, 1989), the *Oral Language Evaluation* (Silvaroli, Skinner, & Maynes, 1977), *Peabody Picture Vocabulary Test* (Dunn, 1981), *Sentence Repetition Tests* (Anastasiow & Hanes, 1974), and various informal language checksheets for assessing language functions (Shafer, Staab, & Smith, 1983), characteristics of language experience stories (Norton, 1980; Dixon, 1977), and surface dialect features (Marcus, 1977).

Language influences on reading performance also can be observed in analyzing oral reading miscues and story retellings (Goodman & Burke, 1972), analyzing results of auditory discrimination tasks and tests; and adaptations of the cloze procedure to determine how student responses differ from the expected response, according to dialect features (Casbergue, 1984).

Although assessment techniques will not be presented here, the following discussion will guide the interpretation of test results (Barnitz, 1982). These principles are important to the teacher in a corrective reading program.

- In interpreting test results, teachers must be sensitive to cultural and linguistic differences, because these differences affect test results.

Hall and Freedle (1975) cited a study by Williams and Rivers (1972) demonstrating that children's performance on tests is better if the vocabulary matches their cultural backgrounds. For example, in Louisiana the word *parish* is equivalent in meaning to *county* in other parts of the country; the words *carnival, throw,* and *krewe* have particular meanings associated with Mardi Gras; and children play *cabbage ball.* If these items appeared on an IQ test, non-Louisianans would probably be at a cultural disadvantage.

In a similar way, different cultural experiences affect the comprehension of prose. In a study by Reynolds, Taylor, Steffensen, Shirey, and Anderson (1981), urban black students comprehended a passage differently than agrarian white students. (See Andersson & Barnitz, 1984, and Barnitz, 1986 for a summary of research on cross-cultural schemata and reading comprehension instruction.)

Another example of language and cultural influences on tests can be found in auditory discrimination tests (Geissal & Knafle, 1977). Linguistically different students may not be able to hear contrasts between word pairs such as thin/tin, sherry/cherry, cot/caught, oil/erl, and Mary/merry/marry, because the linguistic rules and patterns of their dialect or native language do not permit it. Teachers must know dialect or language features in order to attribute an "error" to the appropriate cause, that is, an auditory problem versus a dialect difference. In fluent reading, these dialect homonym pairs can be interpreted by context, just like other homonym pairs, such as knight/night. Hence, caution is needed in interpreting test performance when evaluating children in corrective reading programs.

- Variations in the situation must be considered in language assessment, as situational variables affect language variation.

Straker (1980) found that bidialectal speakers were able to use their communicative competence to switch between Black English and standard English depending on the setting, topic, or audience. Hall, Cole, Reder, and Dowley (1977) also found that lower income black children produce more spontaneous language in a supermarket but are less verbal in classroom settings. If their language is evaluated in the classroom only, assessment of their total communicative competence may be incomplete and inaccurate. Similarly, Steffensen and Guthrie (1980) found that variation in the testing situation dramatically influenced the quantity and quality of language produced by black preschool children.

- Teachers must realize that performance in a nonstandard dialect does not imply a deficit in language proficiency.

Linguistic studies on language variation have disproved the **deficit hypothesis**, which states that minority children have underdeveloped, impoverished, and illogical systems of language. (See Labov, 1975, and Burling, 1973, for discussion.) Steffensen (1974, 1978) found that children who speak Black English follow the same natural stages of language development as white middle class children. Moreover, the *Ann Arbor* case marked a legal end to any claimed validity of the deficit hypothesis (Labov, 1983). This means that teachers must respect the language of minority children as different, not deficient. Children should be provided with opportunities to acquire oral and written standard English for the situational contexts in which it is expected.

Standard English Language Arts Instruction

The language arts consist of communicative competence in language, which is both oral (speaking and listening) and written (writing and reading). You will recall from your language arts methods course that these processes are interrelated in children's development of English. You must also recall from your language arts methods course the basic methods for developing each of these processes of communication. As part of the language arts curriculum, what is the role of standard English as it relates to teaching nonstandard and nonnative English speaking children?

Although linguistic research has disproved the myth that nonstandard English varieties, such as Black English Vernacular, are inferior language systems for use in one's own culture, speaking standard English has many social, political, economic, and educational advantages (e.g., professional advancement). The following guidelines are relevant (Barnitz, 1982):

1. Children should be given opportunities to learn standard English because of its social advantages. Standard English is not a prerequisite to reading (Goodman, 1972), but, because language arts are interrelated, immersion in reading standard materials facilitates the learning of standard English patterns. Moreover, as Shuy (1981) points out, children usually do not acquire features of standard English unless they are motivated and see its function in their lives.

2. To facilitate learning of standard English, three principles must become part of the philosophy of instruction (Marcus, 1977): (1) children must recognize how their home language (dialect) differs systematically with the school language; (2) they must be motivated to acquire standard English and to use language; and (3) they must practice language in real life situations. Children learn language through interaction and using language to get things done. Current research on learning standard English implies that nonstandard English speakers learn standard English features when there is substantial meaningful interaction with standard English speakers. Verbal interaction effects a gradual change in the home linguistic system of the learner (Labov & Harris, 1983; Farr & Daniels, 1986).

3. A corrective reading program based on language arts may first emphasize sociolinguistic competence, whereby children develop language to inform, entertain, persuade, inquire, narrate, encourage, and so on. Similarly, corrective instruction must be placed within a wider communicative setting of reading for information, entertainment, exposure to persuasion, and so on. Classroom strategies, such as role playing, listening to good models of children's literature, choral speaking, oral presentations, and group discussions can all be related to the passages being read.

Reading Instruction

The social use of language to "get things done" is the driving force of language. Children develop language to play, to explore, to acquire information, and so forth. Language-reading activities must be purposeful, and instruction of basic reading skills must be placed within this context. For example, children can develop their reading skills within a unit on tourism, while reading travel brochures. The reading activity may be placed within the wider social-language context of planning a trip to Disney World, including role-playing an afternoon at the travel agency. The children must interact, use language skills, and read to plan a vacation. The teacher, within this context, can embed the specific reading skills (e.g., sequencing, content vocabulary, word analysis) and language competencies (pronunciation, syntax) appropriate to the situation. Corrective reading skills instruction then, should be embedded within a functional reading activity, which in turn, is part of a wider social language arts context. Reading instruction for all children, including linguistically variant children, must be motivated by meaning. Specific methods are available for developing reading for meaning. Some of these will be described briefly.

Language Experience Approach

Inasmuch as children's language development is tied to their social, cognitive, and linguistic development, a logical strategy to use in a corrective reading program is the **language experience approach** (Allen, 1963; Hall, 1983; Stauffer, 1980). With this approach, the teacher takes advantage of children's experiences to motivate oral expression and develop reading skills. Children, either individually or in small groups, are led to dictate a story to a teacher who functions as a scribe, editor, and language expander. The teacher is free to interact with the children to elicit elaborations, when appropriate. Once the story is written down, the teacher analyzes it for specific functions and structures. The first "draft" becomes an invaluable first step in language expansion.

For example, the teacher can expand the syntax of the first draft. Fennimore (1980) suggests that a simple sentence can be expanded through systematic questioning for each potential slot in an **expanded sentence** pattern. For example, starting with a sentence such as, "The boy ran," children can be led to add words for various slots and yield a sentence such as, "The happy boy ran slowly through the yard." Children can also expand their sentences by adding other clauses. Teachers may also lead the students in sentence-combining activities to learn processes of sentence formation (O'Hare, 1973).

Wangberg (1982) suggests making pattern books with beginning readers, and this is also useful for corrective readers. Employing the language experience approach, Wangberg suggests that children make a simple book with a particular pattern, such as "This is a _____," in order to learn the syntactic pattern and the sight vocabulary for words that match pictures pasted on each page. Students thus learn language patterns along with reading skills. Syntactic awareness, the ability to predict meaning from the arrangement of meanings in a sentence, is crucial to reading and can be incorporated into reading comprehension instruction (Barnitz, 1979).

Teachers can ask questions with the language experience approach that elicit more descriptive words or phrases or alternative ways of expressing thoughts, including standard English equivalents to nonstandard dialects. Teachers can also teach vocabulary and comprehension through the use of semantic maps (Johnson & Pearson, 1984).

The language experience approach is invaluable in teaching reading to linguistically variant children. These children can dictate a story in their vernacular, which is written down in the native dialect with standard spellings. For example, notice the following hypothetical sample:

> My friend, he went to the parade. He don't like the crowd. He climb a tree and he saw the band. And he saw the float.

The teacher can rewrite the story to include standard patterns or lead the students to produce standard patterns. A second draft is thus produced by the teacher and children together to discover alternate ways of expression and the conventions of standard edited English.

> My friend went to the parade. He doesn't like crowds. So, he climbed a tree. Then, he saw the bands. He saw the floats.

The teacher and children may add connective words (e.g., so, then) and embellish the story with more description.

> My friend, Nathan, went to the Mardi Gras parade. Since he doesn't like large crowds, he climbed an oak tree on the street corner. Then he saw the marching bands and the decorated floats.

The language experience approach provides children and teachers with meaningful interaction and growth in reading.

Experience-Text-Relationship Method

Because reading integrates information in the text with the child's previous experience, teachers of minority children must expand their knowledge of the students' backgrounds, inasmuch as cultural differences affect comprehension. (See Andersson & Barnitz, 1984; Barnitz, 1985; and Carrell, Devine & Eskey, 1988 for reviews of research and interpretation for classroom practice.)

The **experience-text-relationship method** (Au, 1979) allows the teacher to motivate the children to talk about their experiences relevant to the central focus of a story or content chapter (the experience step); read natural segments of text (the text step); and relate the content of a story with the prior experiences discussed in the story (the relationship step). A sample lesson transcript from Au (1979) illustrates the teacher-student interaction in developing reading of minority children (Table 11.2). Techniques like this one allow the teacher and children to bridge the knowledge gap between the children's experiences and the text. Likewise, the experience-text-relationship method allows students to become actively involved with the text and permits culturally compatible styles of interaction between teacher and students. Au and Kawakami (1985) found that a focus on comprehension rather than on word identification, and a culturally compatible style of interaction greatly improve the quality of reading by minority children. Teachers need to recognize that students from various cultures possess culturally unique communication routines, which quite often contrast with the verbal routines of the school (Cazden, John, & Hymes, 1972; Heath, 1983). Verbal and cultural differences need not become barriers to literacy, if teachers choose materials and methods that engage the students' background experiences (see Appendix G for children's literature featuring black Americans).

Children's Literature and Choral Reading

Most of you have already acquired a knowledge of choral speaking or **choral reading** techniques from your language arts or children's literature courses. Choral reading involves the children in group recitation of a meaningful refrain or poem. Teachers select a refrain that has specific language features needed by the children. The children then recite the refrain or specific portion of the poem or story in unison. This becomes an oral language drill in disguise, but also involves the children in literature. Reading must be enjoyable. For example, in the delightful children's book, *Never Tease a Weasel,* by Jean Conder Soule (1964), the following verse occurs in various forms:

> But never tease a weasel;
> This is very good advice.
> A weasel will not like it
> and teasing isn't nice.

The language features being practiced in a frequent recitation of this verse are complete sentences, pronoun reference, standard English syntax (negative, be verb), rhyming, as well as standard English pronunciation (*This* instead of *dis, teasing* instead of *teasin,* and so forth). Tompkins and McGee (1983) suggest that children's books with standard patterns corresponding to nonstandard speech be used to help children

TABLE 11.2 Transcript of an Experience-Text-Relationship Lesson

Experience Step

Teacher: . . . Okay, let's think if we could do anything else with a frog. What would you do, Shirley?

Ann: I wouldn't touch the legs. Yuck.

Shirley: I would put it in a bucket.

Teacher: You would put it in a bucket. Okay, that's something different. What would you do with it?

Shirley: *(Inaudible)*

Ann: Yeah, you eat the legs?

Teacher: Okay, Shirley might even eat it. Good, you can eat frog, can't you?

Text Step

Teacher: . . . Shirley, why did you say Freddy laughed? Okay, read the part that you said—when Freddy laughed.

Shirley: *(Reading)* "I would take it fishing. Freddy laughed."

Teacher: Okay, who says, "I would take it fishing"?

Nathan: Mr. Mays.

Teacher: Mr. Mays. And why did Freddy laugh?

Ann: Because maybe he didn't—maybe he didn't know that he was going to use the frog.

Teacher: No, he laughed for another reason. Ellie? Who can read that?

Ellie: Because—'cause Mr. Mays didn't know what to do with the frog. That's all he could think was—he didn't know that he could use frogs was—was a bait. That's why Freddy laughed.

Teacher: Okay, wait a minute. That's not the reason Freddy laughed.

Nathan: Frogs can't fish.

Teacher: Right. Okay, Mr. Mays says, "I don't have a frog, but if I did, I'd take it fishing," and Freddy thinks, hah, going fishing with the frog sitting down with the fishing pole?

Relationship Step

Teacher: . . . Did you know before this that fish like to eat frogs?

Group: Nooo.

Teacher: I didn't—I never heard of using frogs for bait. Do you think they really do?

Nathan: Yeah.

Teacher: You think so.

Ann: My daddy—my daddy—use bread.

Teacher: Yeah, some people use bread. What else do you use for bait?

Shirley: Fish.

Teacher: Sometimes you use smaller fishes.

From "Using the Experience-Text-Relationship Method with Minority Children," by Kathryn Hu-Pei Au, *Reading Teacher*, March 1979. Reprinted with permission of the author and the International Reading Association.

recognize and produce standard written English patterns and at the same time experience good literature. Remember, exposure to literature facilitates language growth (Chomsky, 1972).

This strategy is both a corrective and a basic language arts technique, and the teacher must know the language patterns of the children and the language patterns in the text for the strategy to be most useful in developing written standard English patterns.

Teaching strategies such as the language experience approach, sentence building activities, the experience-text-relationship method, and choral reading are examples of techniques for teaching reading and language together. These techniques, along with supportive writing activities, are useful for the corrective reading program.

Language, and ultimately literacy, is easier to learn when language (as outlined by Goodman, 1986, p. 8) is real and natural, is whole, is sensible, is interesting, is relevant, belongs to the learner, is part of a real event, has social utility, has purpose for the learner, is accessible to the learner, and is chosen by the learner to use it. Goodman (1986) and others (Davidson, 1988) advocate "whole language" approaches to literacy in contrast to the "basic skills" approaches to literacy.

Concluding Remarks

Before this chapter concludes, several more points about dialect differences and reading must be made. First, the extent to which dialect differences contribute to reading failure is not totally clear. Research studies can be cited to support or refute the position that they interfere with reading. (See reviews by Harber & Bryen, 1976; Hall & Guthrie, 1980.) Much reading failure is more related to other factors found in lower income populations, such as limited exposure to books, poor nutrition, and different cultural experiences. While dialects may not necessarily *interfere* with reading, evidence supports their *influence* in reading (Wolfram et al., 1979). As discussed earlier, teachers will notice pronunciation influences on auditory discrimination tasks, because much of the auditory discrimination of such word pairs as cot/caught, oil/erl, oil/all, and past/pass depends on the linguistic rules of the hearer (Geissal & Knafle, 1977). If these words appeared in meaningful contexts, the dialect difference would not cause a communication breakdown. Therefore, teachers need to distinguish between a dialect difference and a real auditory reading problem.

Dialects often manifest themselves in oral reading. The reader may say "pawk the caw" for "park the car," yet comprehension does not suffer. In oral reading, to aid their comprehension process, readers may "translate" a printed standard English sentence into their own native dialects, for example, they may delete a suffix or the *be* verb (Goodman & Buck, 1973). Should teachers correct children's oral reading, when dialect features are manifested? If the dialect rendition does not interfere with meaning, leave it alone, so that the child can continue to focus on meaning. If too much attention is given to correcting dialect pronunciations in oral reading lessons, *teachers may interfere* with comprehension (Goodman & Buck, 1973; Anderson et al., 1985). An exception occurs when the oral reading focuses on practicing standard patterns, as in a choral reading lesson.

Finally, teachers must respect the language and culture of minority children as the first step to facilitating or correcting reading strategies. Evidence is increasing that attitudes of teachers toward the language of the children they teach may be a major reason that minority children eventually need corrective reading instruction. Goodman and Buck (1973, p. 6) stated this point more directly:

> The only special disadvantage which speakers of low status dialects suffer in learning to read is one imposed by teachers and schools. Rejection of their dialects and educators' confusion of linguistic difference with linguistic deficiency interferes with the natural process by which reading is acquired and undermines the linguistic self-confidence of divergent speakers.

> Simply speaking, the disadvantage of the divergent speaker, Black or White, comes from linguistic discrimination. Instruction based on rejection of linguistic difference is the core of the problem.

Teacher attitude and lack of knowledge about linguistic and cultural diversity have been found to be factors when minority children do not learn to read standard English; many teachers fail to take into account language characteristics of the children they teach (Smitherman, 1985). Teachers must respect the languages and cultures of the children they teach. This is crucial to successful standard English reading instruction.

Summary

This chapter presents an introductory survey of language variation that you may find among children in your corrective reading program. Dialect or language differences do not cause reading failure, because language variation is natural. Linguistically variant children bring to your classroom a rich linguistic and cultural repertoire that can be channeled into reading growth.

You now know the importance of understanding reading in terms of a wider framework of communicative competence, which consists primarily of using language and reading "to get things done" and secondarily of using the total set of language structures. You also know that language development is intimately related to reading development. Separating the two may add to the problems of corrective readers. Many learners become disabled in their reading development because reading skills are taught in isolation, out of the meaningful context in which language and reading grows, or because teachers do not respect dialect differences.

Finally, you now know how to adapt several instructional strategies to expand the reading and language abilities of your children. May your students be linguistically rich and literate!

References

Allen, R. (1976). *Language experiences in communication.* Boston: Houghton Mifflin.

Allen, R., & Allen, C. (1976). *Language experience activities* (2nd ed.). Boston: Houghton Mifflin.

Anastasiow, N. J., Hanes, M. L. & Hanes, M. D. (1982). *Language and reading strategies for poverty children.* Baltimore: University Park Press.

Anastasiow, N. J. & Hanes, M. S. (1974). *Sentence repetition task.* Bloomington, IN: Indiana University, Institute for Child Study.

Anderson, R. C., Hiebert, E. H., Scott, J. A., & Wilkinson, A. G. (1985). *Becoming a nation of readers: The report of the commission on reading.* Washington, DC: The National Academy of Education, National Institute of Education, and the Center for the Study of Reading.

Andersson, B. V., & Barnitz, J. G. (1984). Cross-cultural schemata and reading comprehension instruction. *Journal of Reading, 28,* 102–108.

Au, K. H. (1979). Using the experience-text-relationship method with minority children. *The Reading Teacher, 32,* 677–679.

Au, K. H., & Kawakami, A. J. (1985). Research currents: Talk story and learning to read. *Language Arts, 62,* 406–411.

Barnitz, J. G. (1979). Developing sentence comprehension in reading. *Language Arts, 56,* 902–908, 958.

Barnitz, J. G. (1980). Black English and other dialects: Sociolinguistic implications for reading instruction. *The Reading Teacher, 33,* 779–786.

Barnitz, J. G. (1982). Standard and nonstandard dialects: Principles for language and reading instruction. *Reading: Exploration and Discovery, 5,* 21–32.

Barnitz, J. G. (1985). Reading development of nonnative speakers of English: Research and instruction (Monograph No. 63). Language in Education: Theory and Practice series (ERIC Clearinghouse on Languages and Linguistics) Washington, DC: Center for Applied Linguistics, and Orlando, FL: Harcourt Brace Jovanovich. Also available on microfiche, ED 256 182.

Barnitz, J. G. (1986). Toward understanding the effects of cross-cultural schemata and discourse structure on second language reading comprehension. *Journal of Reading Behavior, 18,* 95–116.

Barnitz, J. G. (1988). Sociolinguistic and cultural foundations. In P. M. Lamb and R. D. Arnold, eds., *Teaching reading: Foundations and strategies* (3rd ed.). R. C. Katonah, NY: Owen.

Burling, R. (1973). *English in black and white.* New York: Holt, Rinehart and Winston.

Carrell, P. L., Devine, J., & Eskey, D. E., (Eds.). (1988). *Interactive approaches to second language reading.* Cambridge: Cambridge University Press.

Casbergue, R. (1984). *An investigation of the cloze reading inventory as a quantitative and qualitative measure of the reading proficiency of selected suburban school children.* Unpublished doctoral dissertation, University of New Orleans.

Cazden, C. B., John, V. P., & Hymes, D. (Eds.). (1972). Functions of language in the classroom. New York: Teachers College Press.

Ching, D. C. (1976). *Reading and the bilingual child.* Newark, DE: International Reading Association.

Chomsky, C. (1972). Stages in language development and reading exposure. *Harvard Educational Review, 42,* 5–32.

Conklin, N. F., & Lourie, M. A. (1983). A *host of tongues: Language communities in the United States.* New York: Free Press.

Cowan, J. R. (1976). Reading, perceptual strategies and contrastive analysis. *Language learning, 26,* 95–109.

Davidson, J. L., (Ed.). (1988). *Counterpoint and beyond.* Urbana, IL: National Council of Teachers of English.

DeStefano, J. S. (1978). *Language, the learner and the school.* New York: Wiley.

Dixon, C. N. (1977). Language experience stories as a diagnostic tool. *Language Arts, 54,* 501–505.

Dunn, L. M., & Dunn, L. M. (1981). *Peabody picture vocabulary test* (revised). Circle Pines, MN: American Guidance Service.

Eckhoff, B. (1983). How reading affects children's writing. *Language Arts, 60,* 607–616.

Farr, M. & Daniels H. (1986). *Language diversity and writing instruction.* New York: ERIC Clearinghouse on Urban Education and Urbana, IL: ERIC Clearinghouse on Reading and Communication Skills.

Fennimore, F. (1980). Attaining sentence verve with sentence extension. In G. Stanford (Ed.), *Dealing with differences,* Urbana, IL: National Council of Teachers of English.

Ferguson, C. A., & Heath, S. B. (1981). *Language in the USA.* Cambridge: Cambridge University Press.

Geissal, M. A., & Knafle, J. D. (1977). A linguistic view of auditory discrimination tests and exercises. *The Reading Teacher, 31,* 624–644.

Goodman, K. S. (1972). Dialect barriers to reading comprehension. In D. L. Shores, *Contemporary English: Change and variation.* Philadelphia: Lippincott.

Goodman, K. (1986). *What's whole in whole language?* Portsmouth, NH: Heinemann Education Books.

Goodman, K., & Buck, S. (1973). Dialect barriers to reading comprehension revisited. *The Reading Teacher, 27,* 6–12.

Goodman, K., & Goodman, Y. (1978). *Reading of American children whose language is a stable rural dialect of English or a language other than English.* University of Arizona, Final Report, Project NIE-C-00-3-0087. (ERIC Document Reproduction Service No. ED 173754.)

Goodman, K. S., Goodman, Y. M., & Hood, W. J. (Eds.) (1989). *The whole language evaluation book.* Portsmouth, NH: Heinemann.

Goodman, Y. M. & Burke, C. L. (1972). *Reading miscue inventory manual: Procedure for diagnosis and evaluation.* New York: Macmillan.

Grognet, A. G., Pfannkuche, A., Quang, N. H., Robson, B., Convery, A., Holdzkom, D., Quynh-Hao, H. T., & Vu, T. N. (1976). A *manual for Indochinese refugee education.* Arlington, VA: The National Indochinese Clearinghouse (Center for Applied Linguistics).

Hall, M. A. (1982). Teaching reading as a language experience (3rd ed.). Columbus, OH: Merrill.

Hall, W. S., Cole, M., Reder, S., & Dowley, J. (1977). Variations in young children's use of language: Some effects of setting and dialect. In R. O. Freedle (Ed.), *Discourse production and comprehension.* Hillsdale, NJ: Ablex.

Hall, W. S., & Freedle, R. (1975). *Culture and language.* New York: Halstead Press.

Hall, W. S., & Guthrie, L. F. (1980). On the dialect question and reading. In R. Spiro, B. Bruce, & W. Brewer (Eds.), *Theoretical issues in reading comprehension.* Hillsdale, NJ: Erlbaum.

Halliday, M. A. K., & Hasan, R. (1976). *Cohesion in English.* London: Longman.

Harber, J. R., & Bryen, D. N. (1976). Black English and the task of reading. *Review of Educational Research, 40,* 387–405.

Harste, J. C., Woodward, V. A., & Burke, C. L. (1984). *Language stories and literacy lessons.* Portsmouth, NH: Heinemann Educational Books.

Heath, S. B. (1983). *Ways with words: Language, life and works in communities and classrooms.* Cambridge: Cambridge University Press.

Hudelson, S. (1984). Kan yu ret an rayt en Ingles: Children become literate in English as a second language. *TESOL Quarterly, 18,* 221–238.

Hymes, D. (1974). *Foundations in sociolinguistics: An ethnographic approach.* Philadelphia: University of Pennsylvania Press.

Kachru, B. B. (Ed.). (1982). *The other tongue: English across cultures.* Chicago: University of Illinois Press.

Kochman, T. (1972). Toward an ethnography of black American speech behavior. In T. Kochman (Ed.), *Rappin' and stylin': Communication in urban black America,* Chicago: University of Illinois Press.

Labov, W. (1975). *The study of nonstandard English.* Urbana, IL: National Council of Teachers of English.

Labov, W. (1983). Recognizing black English in the classroom. In J. Chambers (Ed.), *Black English: Educational equity and the law.* Ann Arbor, MI: Karoma.

Labov, W. (1988). *Lexical competition in the short order cuisine.* Paper presented at the American Dialect Society meeting, held in conjunction with the Linguistic Society of America annual meeting, New Orleans.

Labov, W., & Harris, W. (1983). De facto segregation of black and white vernaculars. Paper presented to the Annual Conference of New Ways of Analyzing Variation in English, Montreal.

Marcus, M. (1977). *Diagnostic teaching of the language arts.* New York: Wiley.

Norton, D. E. (1980). *The effective teaching of language arts.* Columbus, OH: Merrill.

O'Hare, F. (1973). *Sentence combining: Improving student writing without formal grammar instruction.* Urbana, IL: National Council of Teachers of English.

Reynolds, R. E., Taylor, M. A., Steffensen, M. S., Shirley, L. L., & Anderson, R. C. (1981). *Cultural schemata and reading comprehension* (Tech. Rep. No. 201). Champaign, IL: University of Illinois, Center for the Study of Reading.

Ruddell, R. B. (1965). The effects of oral and written patterns of language structure on reading comprehension. *The Reading Teacher, 18,* 270–275.

Shafer, R. E., Staab, C. & Smith, K. (1983). *Language functions and school success.* Glenview, IL: Scott, Foresman.

Shuy, R. W. (1967). *Discovering American dialects.* Urbana, IL: National Council of Teachers of English.

Shuy, R. W. (1981a). A holistic view of language. *Research in the Teaching of English, 15,* 101-111.

Shuy, R. W (1981b). Learning to talk like teachers. *Language Arts, 58,* 168-174.

Shuy, R. W. (1988). Sentence level language functions. In J. R. Staton, R. W. Shuy, J. K. Peyton, & L. Reed, (Eds.), *Dialogue Journal Communication.* Norwood, NJ: Ablex.

Silvaroli, N. J., Skinner, J. T., & Maynes, J. O., Jr. (1977). *Oral language evaluation.* St. Paul, MN: EMC Corporation.

Smitherman, G. (1985). "What go round come round: King in perspective." In C. K. Brooks (Ed.), *Tapping potential: English and language arts for the black learner.* Urbana, IL: National Council of Teachers of English.

Soule, J. C. (1964). *Never tease a weasel.* New York: Parents Magazine Press.

Staton, J., Shuy, R. W., Peyton, J. K., & Reed, L. (Eds.) (1988). *Dialogue journal communication: Classroom, linguistic, social and cognitive views.* Norwood, NJ: Ablex.

Stauffer, R. G. (1980). *The language experience approach to the teaching of reading.* New York: Harper & Row.

Steffensen, M. S. (1974). *The acquisition of black English.* Unpublished doctoral dissertation, University of Illinois at Urbana-Champaign.

Steffensen, M. S. (1978). *Bereiter and Engelman reconsidered: The evidence from children acquiring Black English Vernacular* (Tech. Rep. No. 82). Champaign, IL: University of Illinois, Center for the Study of Reading.

Steffensen, M. S., & Guthrie, L. F. (1980). *Effect of situation on the verbalization of black inner-city children* (Tech. Rep. No. 180). Champaign, IL: University of Illinois, Center for the Study of Reading.

Straker, D. Y. (1980). Situational variables in language use (Tech. Report No. 167). Champaign, IL: University of Illinois, Center for the Study of Reading.

Strickland, R. G. (1962). The language of elementary school children: Its relationship to the language of reading textbooks and the quality of reading of selected children. Indiana University, Bloomington, *Bulletin of The School of Education, 38,* 1-131.

Tatham, S. M. (1970). Reading comprehension of materials written with select oral language patterns: A study at grades two and four. *Reading Research Quarterly, 5,* 402-426.

Teale, W. H., & Sulzby, E. (Eds.). (1986). *Emergent literacy: writing and reading.* Norwood, NJ: Ablex.

Thonis, E. W. (1976). *Literacy for America's Spanish speaking children.* Newark, DE: International Reading Association.

Tompkins, G. E., and McGee, L. M. (1983). Launching nonstandard speakers into standard English. *Language Arts, 60,* 463-469.

Troike, R. C. (1972). English and the bilingual child. In D. L. Shores (Ed.), *Contemporary English: Change and variation.* Philadelphia: J. B. Lippincott.

Wangberg, E. (1982). Pattern books: an activity for beginning reading instruction. *Reading Horizons, 23,* 22-24.

Wolfram, W., & Christian, D. (1989). *Dialects and education: Issues and answers.* Englewood Cliffs, NJ: Prentice Hall Regents.

Wolfram, W., Potter, L., Yanofsky, N. M., & Shuy, R. W (1979). *Reading and dialect differences (Dialects and educational equity).* Washington, DC: Center for Applied Linguistics.

CHAPTER 12

Reading-Related Factors

Objectives

After you have read this chapter, you should be able to

1. identify three basic categories of reading-related factors associated with reading problems;
2. explain the teacher's role with regard to each of the basic categories of reading-related factors;
3. recognize symptoms of poor general health or possible visual, auditory, or neurological problems;
4. prepare objective anecdotal records;
5. suggest ways to establish a classroom environment that might help alleviate the stress for a child with mild emotional adjustment problems.

Study Outline

Important Vocabulary and Concepts

affect
attentive listening
auditory acuity
auditory blending
auditory comprehension
auditory discrimination
auditory memory
auditory perception
bibliotherapy
cognition

intelligence
listening
nonreading problems
psychomotor
reading-related factors
variables
visual acuity
visual perception
visually handicapped

Overview

For many years educators and others have been concerned because some children fail to learn to read. The list of potential causes is long and includes such factors as low intelligence, inappropriate experiences, emotional blocking, lack of motivation, poor health, hunger, inability to perceive objects and sounds, dysfunction of the central nervous system, processing problems, and poor teaching. Only one factor in this list, poor teaching, can be directly controlled and changed substantially by educators. The remaining factors (plus many others) are not directly related to teaching reading to children, but are important to a child's learning; thus they are referred to as **reading-related factors,** or **nonreading problems.**

Concerned citizens and other professionals often condemn the teaching profession for not assuming responsibility for correcting the problems presented by factors that arise and are perpetuated outside of the school setting. This condemnation is unjustified without considering the sources of the problems and assigning responsibility to others as well. Teachers are not physicians, psychologists, or sociologists; reading problems caused by noninstructional factors must be treated in concert with specialists in other disciplines. Many school systems today appropriately use interdisciplinary teams to work through these problems.

Although classroom teachers without advanced training in clinical reading are not expected to have in-depth knowledge of reading problems based outside the school and classroom, they must be aware of some important factors that contribute to reading difficulties. One purpose of this chapter is to raise the awareness level regarding contributing causes to reading problems.

With increased awareness, teachers should become more confident in identifying symptoms that suggest a reading-related factor. They can then describe behaviors and symptoms to appropriate specialists, who, in turn, can help decide whether the suspected problem actually exists. Teachers thus serve as screening agents.

Teachers in the early grades are often the first to observe these symptoms. If they refer children promptly, much can be done to alleviate contributing causes before they become the basis of severe reading problems.

Historical Background

The interest in concomitant problems associated with reading failure originated to a great extent with clinicians from other disciplines. They observed that many of their clients and patients also had reading problems. These observations motivated further study to determine if, in fact, these concomitant problems were causing reading difficulties. Many studies conducted early in the twentieth century compared good and poor readers to determine the incidence of specific problems. In general, these early studies revealed that reading-disabled children exhibited concomitant non-reading problems more frequently than good readers did. This finding held for several different types of reading-related factors.

More recently, as educational investigation has become more precise, correlational studies tend to verify the findings of earlier "head count" studies. These studies yield relatively high correlation between two factors, or **variables**—reading development and the non-reading problem being investigated. Unfortunately, many people have overinterpreted the results of these correlational studies. The proper interpretation of high correlation coefficients is that the *relationship* between reading achievement and the other problem is high. The conclusion that the non-reading problem caused the reading difficulty *cannot* be drawn from a correlational study, because an unknown factor may be influencing both the non-reading problem and poor reading.

Another research approach identifies a large group of children with a particular non-reading problem and assesses their performance in reading. Such studies often reveal a wide range of reading achievement scores, indicating that some children with the problem read satisfactorily and some do not. Those who read well somehow compensate for their problem. Therefore, it is extremely important for teachers and others to know that the presence of a specific non-reading problem is no guarantee that the child will not learn to read. It *is* reasonable to conclude, however, that a particular problem may impede reading progress. Furthermore, when a child has two or more non-reading problems, the chances for success in reading are diminished. The multiple causation hypothesis (Monroe, 1932; Robinson, 1946) must be considered seriously.

Three Basic Categories

Factors associated with reading problems can be placed in three basic categories: physical (including neurophysical), psychological, and environmental, which includes instructional factors. Teachers, by the very nature of their training and function, should be held responsible for instructional factors associated with poor reading achievement. Thus, this text focuses on helping teachers (1) identify students making poor progress in reading and (2) provide appropriate instruction for these students. The improvement of reading instruction through better informed teachers is a major goal of this text.

Physical Factors

General Health

Learning to read is a demanding task for many children. A child must be alert, attentive, and capable of working for a sustained period of time. Any physical condition that lowers the level of stamina or impairs vitality can have a deleterious effect on learning. Serious illnesses and prolonged absences from school obviously may result in learning gaps. Many conscientious parents and teachers work hard to alleviate such problems; homebound instruction is also provided by many school systems for children who are bedridden or otherwise incapacitated for extended periods of time.

More subtle forms of illness and physical problems sometimes elude parents and teachers. Chronic low-grade infections, glandular disturbances, allergies, and persistent minor illnesses such as mild respiratory problems can induce a general malaise and lower the vitality level. Insufficient sleep may inhibit learning, and malnutrition may lower ability to attend and learn.

Teachers, of course, are not physicians and cannot appropriately assume medical responsibilities. Yet, they do function as substitute parents while school is in session and must be sensitive to the general well-being of each child in their class. When teachers are concerned about possible health problems, they should seek help from the school nurse and principal. Communication with the parents should be initiated according to local school policies.

Occasionally teachers encounter parents who resist counseling efforts regarding their child's health. Little can be done to help children when this happens. If the problem is serious enough, however, legal procedures can be instigated. Usually other community agencies, such as the child welfare department, become involved in these cases.

When children are not in good health, teachers must try to accommodate their problems as much as possible. Let these children rest, put their heads on their desks, go to the nurse's office, or whatever seems reasonable for the particular problem involved.

Visual Acuity

Visual acuity is keenness of vision. Acuity problems are usually physiologically based and can be corrected by ophthalmologists or optometrists. The role of the classroom teacher is to identify children with visual acuity problems that may have gone unnoticed by parents or other teachers.

While some children learn to read in spite of visual problems, the emphasis here is not so much on the cause of reading failure as it is on comfort and efficiency. When children can deal comfortably with print at normal near-point distance (about 14 to 18 inches), the chances are quite good that they will be able to attend to a task as long as their peers. Discomforts such as headaches or burning or watery eyes diminish their chances considerably. Children who see relatively clearly work more efficiently for longer periods of time without having to direct undue energy to accommodate visual deficiencies.

Formal Assessment Techniques

Some school systems have reading or other specialists with special training to help identify children with vision problems. Even with special training, however, these people are not vision specialists, and their work should be considered as screening only. Instruments typically used for screening purposes are the *Keystone School Vision Screening Test* (Keystone View) and the *Master Ortho-Rater Visual Efficiency Test* (Bausch and Lomb). Other devices often used for the screening of vision are the *Rader Visual Acuity Screening Chart* (Modern Education Corporation), the *Snellen Chart,* and the *Spache Binocular Reading Test* (Keystone View).

Informal Assessment Techniques

Probably the most important function for classroom teachers is to observe the behavior of their students. Spache (1976) has compiled an excellent checklist, much of which is validated against professional visual examinations. Figure 12.1 is based on this checklist. The reading behaviors listed must be interpreted with caution. Sometimes these behaviors occur because the child has *reading* problems, not *visual* problems. If they occur during the reading of difficult materials but not during the reading of easy materials, chances are good that the symptoms reflect reading rather than vision problems. When in doubt, the teacher should refer the child to appropriate vision specialists, whether in or out of the school setting.

Instructional Strategies

The classroom teacher usually should not initiate correction of visual acuity problems. These problems are often resolved through the proper prescription of glasses. If the vision specialist believes a problem can be corrected through exercise, such activities typically are conducted by the parents under the doctor's supervision or by special teachers working on a one-to-one basis outside the regular classroom.

Classroom teachers should provide children with mild vision problems the best possible conditions to accommodate their weaknesses. Children with far-point problems should be able to see the chalkboard better if their desks are in front of the room. Ample light is necessary, and the children should be reminded occasionally to rest their eyes after lengthy reading assignments. Ease of reading rather than speed is emphasized for these children.

Sightsaving books printed in large type (12 to 24 point) can be requested for use in regular classrooms. Children needing this type of material are often classified as **visually handicapped.** Because Public Law 94-142 calls for mainstreaming children with special needs, these children are no longer found only in special education classes. Some visually impaired children function quite well in a regular classroom. Methods using tactile discrimination and word tracing are useful.

FIGURE 12.1 Checklist of symptoms of possible visual problems. (Adapted from George D. Spache, *Diagnosing and Correcting Reading Disabilities,* 2nd ed. Copyright 1981 by Allyn and Bacon, Boston. Used with permission.)

	Check If Present
Appearance of Eyes	
One eye turns in or out at any time	_____
Reddened eyes or lids	_____
Excessive tearing	_____
Encrusted eyelids, frequent styes	_____
Complaints from Close Work	
Headaches	_____
Burning or itching eyes	_____
Nausea or dizziness	_____
Print blurs	_____
Behavior at Desk	
Squints, closes or covers one eye	_____
Tilts head constantly in close work	_____
Excessive blinking	_____
Strains to see chalkboard	_____
Frequent errors in copying from chalkboard	_____
Consistently holds head or book in unusual position	_____
Excessive left-right head movements	_____
Behavior During Reading	
Loses place on line, needs finger or marker	_____
Skips up or down a line	_____
Writes up- or downhill despite guidelines	_____
Misaligns vertical or horizontal figures or numbers	_____
Misreads known or familiar words	_____
Avoids sustained reading	_____
Whispers to keep place	_____

Visual Perception

Visual perception skills include visual discrimination of form, visual closure, constancy, and visual memory. A student may have normal visual acuity skills but underdeveloped visual perception skills.

Visual discrimination of form, a skill commonly referred to as visual discrimination, requires recognizing similarities and differences between letters and words used in reading. For example, the student must be able to distinguish between *H* and *K* or *c, e,* and *o.*

Visual closure is the ability to identify or complete, from an incomplete presentation, an object, picture, letter, or word. The student must identify the whole even though the whole is not provided. For example, the student must be able to recognize that  needs another feature or that 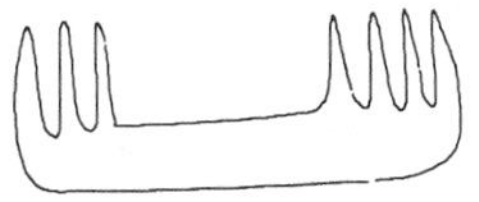 has teeth missing or that f_ _tb_ll represents the word *football.*

The concept of *constancy* is evidenced when a figure, letter, or word remains the same regardless of a change in shape, orientation, size, or color. This concept is critical for reading because many types of print are used and students must not be confused by slight changes, for example, *a* and a. Also, many letters are the same in shape but are different letters depending on their orientation, for example, *b,d; p,q;* or *n,u,* and *c.* In the world of objects, orientation has never made a difference—a chair is a chair no matter which way you turn it. However, when dealing with letters and words, orientation can make a difference.

Visual memory is the ability to remember the sequence of letters in words. This ability is most obviously reflected in spelling; however, it is also important in reading when words are encountered having the same or many similar letters but a different sequence. For example, a child deficient in visual memory may have difficulty distinguishing between *ate, eat,* and *tea.* Many mature readers have to tax their visual memory skills upon encountering *through, though,* and *thorough.*

Formal Assessment Techniques

Several of the skills just described are often called reading readiness skills. Standardized instruments assess visual discrimination, visual closure, constancy, and visual memory skills among other things. The following reading readiness tests are recommended:

- *Clymer-Barrett Prereading Battery,* Personnel Press
- *Gates-MacGinitie Readiness Skills Test,* Riverside
- *Macmillan Reading Readiness Skills Test,* Macmillan
- *Metropolitan Readiness Tests,* The Psychological Corporation
- *Murphy-Durrell Reading Readiness Analysis,* The Psychological Corporation

Informal Assessment Techniques

If a teacher knows the descriptions of the various visual perception skills, he or she can develop informal activities to assess the visual abilities. Ditto sheets can be easily prepared that request students to identify the "same letter or word" (e.g., o | c o c e; cake | coke cake coke) or the "letter or word that is different" (e.g., b b o b; bed bad bed bed).

Visual closure tasks at an early stage usually involve picture or shape completion tasks. In the following example, the student is asked to complete the second drawing so it looks like the first.

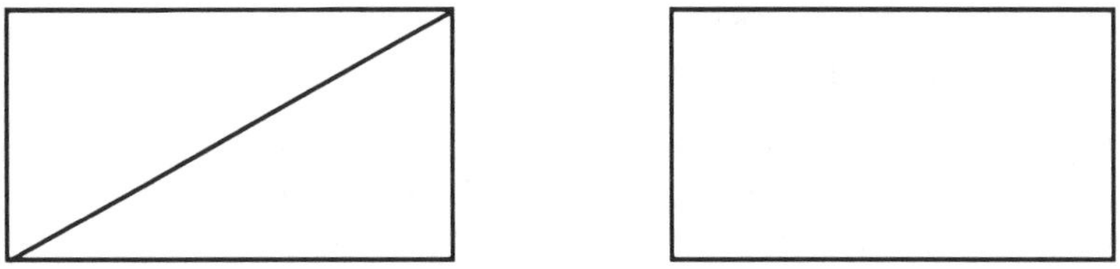

Constancy is often assessed as a specially designed visual discrimination task. Again, finding the "likes" and "differents" is the direction, for example: d | b b b d or p p q p.

Visual memory is more difficult to assess. Initially, a modification of the party game where several objects are presented on a tray for viewing, then covered, and participants are asked to write down as many as they can remember may be used. For classroom use, three or four objects may be shown. Then cover, remove one, and ask the students what was removed. Letters and words can be assessed in a similar fashion. A word or letter is shown for about two seconds. Students are then asked to locate the word or letter from a list of words or letters.

Instructional Strategies for Visual Perception

Many activities are readily available to teachers in developmental reading texts and activity books for helping children with visual perception skills. Some of the more representative exercises are provided here.

1. Have the student mark the letter that is like the one at the beginning of the row: B | E B D
2. Direct students to identify "What's Missing?" in a picture.
3. Direct the students to mark the letter or letter group that looks like the first item in each row:

ap |	pa	la	ap
bl |	lb	bl	bi
du |	du	bu	ud

4. Show the student a series of letters, remove the series, and have the student write from memory what was seen. Reshow the series if necessary until the student succeeds.

Auditory Acuity

Auditory acuity is keenness of hearing. Students obviously need to hear adequately in school. Children with high-tone hearing deficiencies have more difficulties learning to read than those with low-tone deficits. The consonants that give distinction and meaning to speech in our language are relatively high pitched (especially *s*, *l*, and *t*), whereas vowel sounds are lower in pitch. Most teachers of young children are female, and their voices are higher than those of males. Thus, it is understandable why high-tone deficits are more critical than low-tone problems when teaching children to read. Much early reading work involves oral-aural participation. Successful performance with phonics activities also requires good auditory acuity.

Hearing loss is basically a medical matter best handled by a hearing specialist or otologist. Yet the teacher can be of considerable help by identifying children suspected of having hearing problems.

Formal Assessment Techniques

Screening for auditory acuity with an audiometer is a reliable procedure. However, teachers must be specially trained in the use of this sensitive instrument and even then, results should be considered tentative. Children who do not pass the audiometric screening should be referred to a hearing specialist in the school or to other proper personnel for professional diagnosis. Reliable audiometers for school use are manufactured by Beltone, Grason-Stadler, Maico, and Zenith. Different models are available for both group and individual assessment procedures.

Informal Assessment Techniques

Classroom teachers must be sensitive to and observant of behaviors or symptoms that suggest hearing loss. The list of common symptoms in figure 12.2 (Kennedy, 1977, p. 391) will help the teacher find children who should be seen by the school nurse, speech and hearing specialist, or reading specialist. A decision can then be made whether to suggest medical assistance.

Fortunately, many schools have speech and hearing specialists. Children entering school are usually screened by the specialist, and many problems are identified early. Teachers find these services helpful, and the speech teacher is usually most eager to consult with and assist the faculty with possible problem children.

Sometimes teachers jump to conclusions about hearing problems when a child shows symptoms of loss. The symptoms may be only temporary because of congestion from colds or an ear infection. The wise teacher will observe behavior over a period of time, say three to four weeks, to determine if the problem persists. If it does, referral should be considered.

Teachers can structure some activities to help determine hearing loss.

- *Simon Says.* The teacher plays *Simon Says* with small groups. The children are told to face away and follow the directions. If a child consistently has trouble keeping up with classmates, the teacher may suspect a hearing problem.
- *Low voice or whisper test.* The teacher stands about twenty feet away from the child (first on one side, then the other). The student is then asked to repeat the words the teacher says in a normal, clear voice. A child who cannot do this task at fifteen or less feet may have a hearing problem. A variation of this procedure is to talk softly (or whisper) while standing just behind a child. If the child does not respond as his or her peers do, a hearing problem may exist.
- *Watch tick test.* The teacher holds a stopwatch or loudly ticking wristwatch about twelve inches from the child's ear, gradually extending the distance to about forty-eight inches. Normal children should hear the ticks forty to forty-eight inches from the ear (Kennedy, 1977). If the distance is less than forty inches, a weakness may exist, and the teacher should consider referring the child.

Obviously, the procedures mentioned above are informal in nature, and results of assessment vary depending on factors such as noise level of the environment, differences in teachers' voices, and loudness of watches. A good way to judge the adequacy of these factors is to "test" several students, and observe those children who differ significantly from the larger group. If a child rather consistently deviates from the peer group, more reliable assessment procedures are probably in order.

Instructional Strategies

Corrective work for children with auditory acuity problems, particularly those who are deaf or hard of hearing, is an intricate task that requires specially prepared teachers. Facilities for these children are usually provided in special schools or special

Figure 12.2 Checklist of symptoms of hearing difficulties. (Reproduced by permission of the publisher, F. E. Peacock Publishers, Inc., Itasca, Ill., from Eddie C. Kennedy, *Classroom Approaches to Remedial Reading,* 1977, p. 391.)

	Yes	No
Inclines one ear toward speaker when listening	___	___
Holds mouth open while listening	___	___
Holds head at angle when taking part in discussion	___	___
Reads in unnatural tone of voice	___	___
Uses faulty pronunciation on common words	___	___
Has indistinct enunciation	___	___
Often asks to have instructions and directions repeated	___	___
Breathes through mouth	___	___
Has discharge from ears	___	___
Frequently complains of earache or sinusitis	___	___
Has frequent head colds	___	___
Complains of buzzing noise in ears	___	___
Seems to be inattentive or indifferent	___	___
Does poorly in games with oral directions	___	___
Has trouble following trend of thought during oral discussions	___	___

education classes. However, many children with mild hearing deficiencies, or with deficits corrected by prosthetic devices (e.g., hearing aids), function quite well within the regular classroom. Special provisions need to be considered, such as seating the child close to where the teacher and others are talking. It is also helpful to face these children directly so they will have the advantage of watching lips closely if needed. Clear enunciation is essential.

Hard-of-hearing children may have difficulty when oral discussion and recitation are in progress. Listening to others read may be difficult, too. Teachers should stress silent reading and a visual approach to word analysis for these children. Phonics may be quite difficult or, for some, impossible to learn. Emphasis should be placed on visual and structural analysis techniques and context clues for training in word recognition.

Listening Skills

While most children in school have adequate auditory acuity for learning to read, additional auditory skills, classified as listening skills, are important to consider.

Listening is an area where much assumptive teaching occurs. Many teachers believe listening develops naturally and is simply a matter of either paying attention or not paying attention. Not true. After extensive study Lundsteen (1979) concludes that **listening** is "the process by which spoken language is converted to meaning in the mind."

Assessing Listening Skills

The assessment of listening skills thus covers a wide range of abilities. At a very basic level, listening does include auditory acuity, that is, the student must be able to hear noises and sounds. Unfortunately, many teachers equate the ability to hear with the ability to listen. Listening also requires **auditory perception.** This refers to the ability to discriminate, remember (auditory memory), and blend sounds together. Listening involves *attending* to the sounds and concentrating on getting the message. Because students with reading problems may also be easily distracted, **attentive listening** becomes a crucial area to assess. Listening requires **auditory comprehension**, or the ability to get meaning from the oral message. Auditory comprehension ranges from literal understanding of the message to critical evaluation of what was heard. All of these components must be considered to assess listening skills accurately.

As with visual perception, a number of skills are included in the area of auditory perception: discrimination, memory, and blending. **Auditory discrimination**, or the ability to distinguish sounds, is critical for language acquisition and phonics instruction. **Auditory memory** is the ability to remember a sequence of sounds. Reading requires that the reader associate "an auditory sequence of speech sounds with a visual sequence of letter symbols" (Dechant, 1981, p. 252). **Auditory blending** refers to the blending of phonemes to form a word. This skill is important if students are learning to read through a synthetic phonics approach.

When assessing auditory discrimination skills, students should not be facing the teacher so that lip reading becomes a factor. Some common procedures follow.

1. Pronounce word pairs (e.g., big-pig, pat-pot, some-come, rug-run). Direct the student to answer "same" if the two words sound the same, or "not the same" or "different" if the two words sound different in any way. Several examples should be given for practice, and enough word pairs to assess all positions reliably (beginning, middle, end); probably about ten pairs are adequate for each position.

2. The same concept can be modified and presented to groups of students by providing each student with a sheet of paper listing the item number followed by the words *same* and *not the same,* or *yes* and *no* (fig. 12.3). Again, word pairs are pronounced and students are to circle "yes" or "same" if the two words are the same and "no" or "not the same" or "different" if they are different.

Assessing auditory memory determines a student's ability to follow oral directions and remember information presented orally in class. Generally, assessment requires students to recall and reproduce a series of unrelated words. For example, the teacher

FIGURE 12.3 Sheet used in testing auditory acuity.

1	yes	no
2.	yes	no
	or	
3.	same	not the same
4.	same	different
	and so on	

may say, "Listen to these words and be ready to repeat them in the same order: cow . . . tie . . . bed. Now you say them." With young children, several practice items are needed. The number of words can also be increased if three appear to be too easy. Rae and Potter (1981) give additional formats (fig. 12.4).

Testing the ability to pay attention is complicated; a student may be attending to the speaker without being able to understand the speaker (Norton, 1980). Therefore, Otto and Smith (1980) suggest that procedures designed to assess attention should *not* stress the student's ability to process ideas.

According to Norton (1980), "the ability to follow oral directions explicitly demands attentive listening." Because idea processing is not being evaluated, directions must be simple. For example, a young child may be told: "Take out your blue crayon, your green crayon, and your red crayon. Pick up the red crayon and show it to me." Or for older students: "Take out a piece of paper and a pencil. Put the point of your pencil on the top center of the paper and draw a circle the size of a quarter. Draw a larger circle below the first circle. Draw a smaller circle inside the first circle." The older the student, the more complicated the oral directions might be.

Activities found later in this section (p. 334) can also be used as informal assessment instruments.

Several group standardized tests assess auditory comprehension. The *Sequential Tests of Educational Progress* (STEP) assess listening for grades four through college. These tests reportedly measure ability in identifying main ideas, remembering details and sequence, and understanding word meanings. Unfortunately, many items on the test can be answered without first listening to the oral presentation. The STEP have also been criticized because students must both listen and read to answer the questions. To assess listening comprehension accurately, the knowledge must have been gained only by listening to the test source.

Some other tests of listening comprehension, which appear to be more valid, are the *Cooperative Primary Tests*, the *Durrell Listening-Reading Series* and the *Brown-Carlsen Listening Comprehension Test*. The *Cooperative Primary Tests*, published by Educational Testing Service, Cooperative Test Division, Princeton, NJ 08540, provides two assessment forms for grades 1 through 3. In this test the teacher reads words, sentences, stories, and poems; the child marks correct pictures.

The *Durrell Listening-Reading Series* has three levels (primary, 1–2; intermediate, 3–6; advanced, 7–9) that compare reading and listening abilities for vocabulary and

Figure 12.4 Assessing auditory memory. (From G. Rae and T. Potter, *Informal Reading Diagnosis: A Practical Guide for the Classroom Teacher*, 2nd ed. © 1981, pp. 40, 41, 147. Reprinted by permission of Prentice-Hall, Inc., Englewood Cliffs, N.J.)

AUDITORY MEMORY TEST: LEVEL I

Directions to the teacher:
Level I is to be given individually. The teacher will need a small box (approximately 3 by 5 inches) with a lid, a small ball, a nail, a paper clip, and a pencil with an eraser.

An index card with a X on it is also needed. Spread items on a table in front of the child and place the index card to the child's left as a starting point.

You may repeat once if the child hesitates on the first three combinations below. Do not repeat for numbers 4 to 7.

Directions to the child:
Can you tell me the names of the things I've put on the table? Good. Now I'm going to say the names of some of the things. When I do, I want you to put them in a row on the table. I'll say only some of them and you are to put them in the same order I say them. The first one goes right under this X. (Point to card.) Be sure to wait until I say "Go" before you pick anything up. Let's try it.

1. Ball, nail. Go. (Have child return them each time)
2. Box, pencil. Go.
3. Clip, box, nail. Go
4. Ball, clip, box. Go.
5. Nail, box, clip, pencil. Go.
6. Box, nail, ball, clip. Go.
7. Pencil, ball, box, nail, clip. Go.

AUDITORY MEMORY TEST: LEVEL II

Directions to the teacher:
The various parts of this test may be given to individuals or groups. Children will have an answer sheet to mark (see p. 332). It is sometimes necessary to practice reading the material in advance to avoid mispronunciations and to avoid stressing a particular answer. You may repeat once.

Directions to the children:
Today you are going to have to be good listeners and remember what I read to you. After I read, I will ask you to put some numbers in front of pictures that tell the order in which you heard the words I said. Don't do any writing until I say "begin." Let's try sample A. Listen to the words I say: "dog, bird, cloud." Now, put a one in front of the picture of the first word I said, and a two in front of the second word. (Pause.) Listen again: dog, bird, cloud. Did you put a one in front of the picture of the dog? What did you put the two in front of? What would you put in front of the picture of the cloud? Good! (Check answers to make sure they all understand.) Let's begin now.

Sample A ___ dog, bird, cloud.

1. ___ car, house.
2. ___ boy, rabbit, dog.
3. ___ The wall is by the fence.
4. ___ The girl and the cat sat in front of the tree.
5. ___ The horse and the dog ran over the hill to the house.
6. ___ The fountain by the house has birds and butterflies on it.
7. ___ The many-colored leaves are falling from the trees and the children are raking them.
8. ___ Put your comb and brush on the table and sit in the chair by the fireplace.
9. ___ The train passed two houses, a barn, and a tree as it sped along.
10. ___ The book is about a rabbit, a dog, and a boy who lived in the forest by the hills.

(continued)

FIGURE 12.4 Assessing auditory memory *(continued).*

AUDITORY MEMORY TEST: LEVEL II

Name _____ Grade _____

PART I   SECTION A   CHILD's ANSWER SHEET

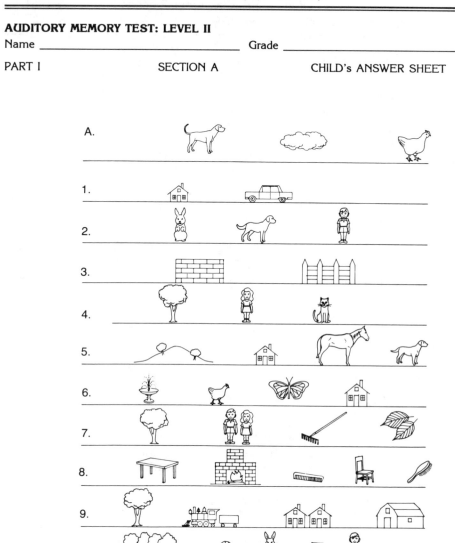

sentences. Optional responses are read to the students so they do not have to read to answer the questions.

The *Brown-Carlsen Listening Comprehension Test* is designed for grades 9 through 13, and contains five subtests: Immediate Recall, Following Directions, Recognizing Transitions, Recognizing Word Meanings, and Lecture Comprehension. Both the Durrell and Brown-Carlsen tests are available from The Psychological Corporation, 757 Third Avenue, New York, NY 10017.

Classroom teachers are likely to rely on informal listening assessments they prepare themselves. One common technique uses an individually administered informal reading inventory. Instead of the student reading the graded passages, the passages are read to the student and comprehension questions asked. The listening comprehension level is the highest level at which the student can answer at least 75 percent of the comprehension questions correctly. For more specific listening skills, such as listening for main ideas, sequence, details, and so forth, activities that are used to teach these skills can also be used as informal assessment instruments.

Instructional Strategies for Listening Skills

Students are not naturally good or poor listeners. Listening skills can, and must, be taught (Devine, 1978; Hollow, 1955; Lundsteen, 1979).

Techniques for teaching auditory perception skills to corrective readers are not essentially different from those recommended in developmental reading texts. To develop auditory discrimination skill, the teacher should begin with practice in listening for known sounds within known words. This not only provides success for the student but also a better idea of the nature of the task. The teacher must understand that "poor auditory discrimination is often accompanied by inaccurate or indistinct speech. The child who pronounces *with* as *wiv* is not likely to notice any difference between final *v* and *th* in words. It is hard for many children to discriminate among short vowel sounds because those sounds do not differ greatly. It is particularly difficult for children to discriminate between sounds that are the same in their dialect but not in standard English. For instance, a child who pronounces *pen* and *pin* alike is apt to respond that the words are the same when spoken by an examiner" (Harris & Sipay, 1980, pp. 382–383). Therefore, the teacher must make a decision as to whether instruction in auditory discrimination in such cases would be time well spent, or whether visual learning should be emphasized until articulation errors are remedied.

Useful activities for auditory discrimination skill development follow. These activities are representative of those currently found in use in classroom settings.

1. Students are asked to locate or mark pictures that begin or end with a particular sound.
2. Students are asked to listen to pairs of words and determine if they begin or end with the same sound.
3. Pictures are provided, with a choice of two letters for each picture. Students are to choose the letter that represents the beginning or ending sound of the picture.
4. Using a familiar story, or nursery rhyme, the teacher selects words to be changed to new words by altering one or two sounds. The teacher then reads the story slowly while the students listen for words that sound wrong. Students must identify the incorrect word and state what the word should sound like. The teacher then continues reading. Brown (1982) calls this activity "fractured fables" and provides an example:

> Little Bo *Beep* has lost her *shape*
> And doesn't know where to find them.
> *Leaf* them alone, and they'll come home
> Wagging their *tells* behind them. (p. 248)

Auditory memory exercises are designed to develop the ability to attend to, recognize, and recall sequences of numbers, letters, and words. The following are representative activities.

1. Give students a series of numbers to dial on a telephone or type on a typewriter or microcomputer.
2. Require students to repeat clapping patterns (e.g., clap/clap-clap/clap).
3. Require students to decide if two sound patterns are alike. Claps, taps, or toy flutes can be used (e.g., -/-/-; -/-/- -).
4. Pronounce two words for the students, then repeat one of them. Students are required to note if the repeated word was the first or second word of the pair.
5. Have students repeat a series of three to seven unrelated words in sequence, from memory.

Auditory blending was discussed in detail in chapter 6. Some additional activities for developing auditory blending skills follow.

1. Have students join beginning consonant sounds to ending phonograms (e.g., /b/ -ake, /k/ -ake, /f/ -ake, /l/ -ake, /m/ -ake).
2. Combine visuals with the auditory task given above. While pronouncing /k/ -ake, show the word card cake and continue by covering the initial consonant with the various other consonants, for example, make.
3. Provide riddles, such as, "I'm thinking of a word that starts like man, /m/, and ends like lake, ake. What is the word?"

Attentive listening is indeed a prerequisite to academic success. Wilt (1958) reports that attentive listening is required by elementary school students for as much as 60 percent of their time in school. All too commonly students ask for directions to be repeated or are scolded for not following directions. Part of the problem may be lack of clarity on the teacher's part. Otto and Smith (1980, p. 307) suggest four factors as causes of inattentiveness: "(1) poor motivation to hear the speaker's message, (2) too much teacher talk, (3) excessive noise and other distractions, and (4) lack of a mental set for anticipating the speaker's message. By careful attention to these four factors, a teacher can help students become more attentive listeners."

Specific activities and methods help students develop attentive listening. *Simon Says* involves careful listening to directions. A leader gives an oral command, and the group must do as told *if* the "magic" words "Simon says" precede the command. If the command is not preceded by "Simon says," those students who obey the command are eliminated from the game.

To encourage students to listen, give oral directions only once. When a student requests a repetition, ask other students to recall and restate the directions. Learning centers for listening can easily be developed. Listening center supplies may include commercial or teacher-made tapes, records, radios, and concrete materials.

Furness (1971) claims that it is especially appropriate for students with learning problems to number the steps of the oral directions, repeat the number of steps involved, and relate each step to its number. Otto and Smith (1980) stress teaching students with learning problems to anticipate what the speaker will say—much like in a directed reading-thinking activity but a directed listening-thinking activity instead.

Students with learning problems need help in defining the purposes for their listening. For example, to help students listen to oral directions, key words such as "first," "second," and "finally" may be stressed. Have students close their eyes and visualize themselves carrying out each step of the directions as they hear it. Then ask them to describe each step. Finally, have them physically perform the activity.

Some additional activities for developing attentive listening follow.

- Using *Pin the Tail on the Donkey,* direct the blindfolded child to move to the right, to the left, and so on.
- Using a cassette tape, provide a series of numbers *once,* such as 8-5-2-6-9. Ask which number is closest to the sum of two plus two.
- Have each student prepare a two-minute talk on "How to Make a Peanut Butter Sandwich." As the directions are spoken, ask the listeners to first visualize themselves following the directions, and next, for some volunteers to do *exactly* as the speaker directed. (This activity can be just as valuable for the speaker.)
- To help students listen attentively and also for details, play simple listening games with increasingly difficult instructions given to one student and then another. For example, "Jim, take the book and carry it to the windowsill." "Bill, you take it from the windowsill to my desk." "Janet, you take it and walk around the desk twice with it." And so forth.

An effective listener must be able to follow a sequence of ideas, perceive the organization, recognize the main ideas and important details, predict outcomes, and critically evaluate what is heard. The same can be said for an effective comprehender. Thus, many of the activities found in the comprehension chapter can be used, with only slight modifications, for instruction in auditory comprehension. In addition, the following techniques and activities are recommended.

1. *Listening for main ideas and supporting details.* The teacher selects paragraphs in which the main idea is stated (easiest) or inferred (more difficult). These paragraphs should also state several supporting details. The difficulty level of the paragraphs conform to the students' ability level. One example follows.

I have a puppy. It is little. It can run
and jump. My puppy can do tricks. The
puppy is funny.

The teacher reads the paragraph and asks the students to listen carefully for the main idea. After they have suggested a main idea, they should tell why. A request for a good title might be substituted for the term *main idea* in case students are unfamiliar with this term. In either circumstance, the students are told that the main idea, or title, can be turned into a question in order to find the supporting details. For example:

What is a puppy?
Why is the puppy funny?

After students hear the paragraph read once more, ask them to identify supporting details. The main idea question will be answered by the supporting details. In other words, of the two questions suggested, one will be answered by the supporting details.

For example:

> It is little.
> It can run and jump.
> It can do tricks.
> It is funny.

These details best answer the first question, so the first sentence, "I have a puppy," represents the main idea. If working with titles, "A Puppy" or "My Puppy" are appropriate suggestions. Descriptive paragraphs are especially helpful for this activity.

2. *Listening for details that do and do not support the main idea.* Further development of listening skills includes a "weighing of information" for its importance to the topic. The teacher may read a paragraph in which one detail does not relate to the rest of the paragraph or to the main idea. The students are then asked to state the main idea, the supporting details, and the non-supporting detail. For example:

> Bob and Mary do not know what to do. They don't
> want to watch TV. They looked for a game to play,
> but could not find one they liked. Mother went to
> visit her friend.

3. *Listening for sequence.* Activities to develop this skill first stress listening for key words that signify sequences, such as "first," "second," and "finally." Once the students have been alerted to these key words, they listen to an oral presentation that emphasizes the usefulness of such words. For example:

> I have a picture of three monkeys. The first monkey is covering his eyes. The next one is covering his ears. The third one is covering his mouth with his hands. On the bottom a sign says, "See no evil, hear no evil, speak no evil."

Point out to students how the key words signal a certain sequence. This can be demonstrated by rearranging the order of the paragraph to make less sense. Also help students discover the usefulness of the introductory statement, "I have a picture of three monkeys," and show how each of the monkeys is then identified by a signal word: "first," "next," "third." This type of activity can be easily adapted to develop understanding of paragraph structure in preparation for writing paragraphs.

Other activities include cutting up comic strips into their individual frames, whiting out the words, mixing up the frames, and then reading the original comic strip aloud while the students put the strip back into order. A flannel board provides the opportunity for students to listen to a story, hear its sequential organization, then retell it via pictures, or main idea statements, in proper sequence.

4. *Listening to predict outcomes.* The procedure is much like that with a directed reading-thinking activity (Stauffer, 1981). The title of a story is read to the students, and they are asked to write a prediction, or suggest to the teacher, what they think they will hear about in the story. The teacher discusses the reasons for these predictions with the students and then reads the story. Some stories lend themselves to breaks where repredicting can occur. This activity motivates each student to listen carefully to see if their prediction is correct. Films can also be used in this manner, or a talk or lecture can be stopped at certain points to have students predict what

the speaker will say next. The level can be very easy (predicting the next word in a sentence) or more difficult (predicting the possible content or conclusion).

5. *Listening to evaluate.* Students are aided in this area by learning to develop questions to be answered by listening or to listen for cause and effect relationships, propaganda, or persuasive statements. As for any lesson, students must be prepared, in this case by giving students something to anticipate. For example, after the topic of the talk or lecture is previewed, the students are asked to list three questions they would like to hear answered. A planned study guide helps students use what they already know and alerts them to information important for understanding what is heard. Devine (1981, pp. 24–25) suggests that an effective listening guide should include:

a. A preview of the talk to include a statement of its purpose and perhaps even an outline.

b. A list of new words and concepts.

c. Questions for students to think about as they listen.

d. Space for students to write questions *they* want answered as they listen.

e. Provision for "anticipation" (that is, some problem, question or student concern that students can look forward to learning about as they listen).

f. Questions to help the student-listener personalize what is being said, for example, "Have you ever had an experience like this?" or "In what way does this affect your own life?".

g. Space for students to write such things as main ideas and supporting details.

h. Appropriate visuals, which may be duplicated in the guide (e.g., graphs, tables).

i. Follow-up activities (e.g., possible test questions, related readings).

Activities for evaluative listening may include (1) identifying cause and effect and (2) discriminating information from propaganda.

In *identifying cause and effect,* a cause is stated, followed by the reading of a series of consequences, some of which are results of the cause and others that are not. Students are to identify any matching cause-effect relationships. For example:

Cause

It was the hottest summer that had ever been recorded.

Effects

- The greatest danger was the possibility of frostbite. *(No match)*
- The hospital reported large numbers of cases of heatstroke. *(Match)*
- After a while, a bad water shortage developed. *(Match)*
- Most people dressed carefully, wearing many layers of clothes. *(No match)*
- It was uncomfortable to leave your home to go outdoors. *(Match)*

In *discriminating information from propaganda,* television commercials provide a never-ending source of material. Tapes are prepared to be analyzed and later placed in listening centers to give practice in listening for persuasive statements. A speaker whose purpose is to persuade also provides information while trying to convince the listener of something. Listeners are constantly exposed to such situations. Examples other than the TV commercial include the campaigning politician at all levels of government, the salesperson (e.g., cars, magazines, appliances), and very often our friends. The listener must be able to distinguish statements that inform from those that are intended to persuade. The listener then examines and evaluates only the information before deciding what to do. Students are first instructed in the differences between informative and persuasive statements. For example:

Information tells you about the item being sold.
1. This bicycle comes with a headlight and a rear light.
2. This bicycle is lightweight (twenty pounds) and has hand brakes.

Persuasion tries to make you think you want to buy what is being sold.
1. This bicycle is only for people who want the best.
2. Famous stars prefer this bicycle.

A list of statements is then read to students and they determine which inform and which persuade. For example:

- These knives are made of stainless steel. *(Information)*
- Our gum contains no sugar. *(Information)*
- Why not use what the pros use? *(Persuasion)*
- The jackets come in three sizes. *(Information)*
- Just what you've been waiting for! *(Persuasion)*
- The rubber sole will keep you from slipping. *(Information)*
- This is a nonalkaline pH shampoo. *(Information)*
- This is a special gift for that special person. *(Persuasion)*
- This dish will not chip or crack. *(Information)*
- Everyone thinks _____ is the best. *(Persuasion)*

In conclusion, listening must be considered a vital prerequisite to academic success that is often overlooked. It may be mistakenly assumed that a student who hears also listens well. Instruction in listening skills must begin in the early grades to prepare the older student to take good notes and get the most from lecture material.

The lack of listening materials places even greater responsibility for the development of instructional techniques on the classroom teacher. The following questions (Burns, 1980) alert teachers to their responsibilities.

1. Do I provide a classroom environment (emotional and physical) that encourages good listening?
2. Am I a good listener and do I really listen to the pupils?
3. Do I use appropriate tone, pitch, volume, and speed in my speaking?
4. Do I vary the classroom program to provide listening experiences (films, discussions, debates, reports) which are of interest to the children?
5. Am I aware of opportunities for teaching listening throughout the day?
6. Do I help pupils see the purpose for listening in each activity?
7. Do I help children see the importance and value of being good listeners?
8. Do I build a program in which listening skills are consistently taught and practiced? (p. 113).

Other listening strategies may be found in the professional literature. One of the most complete collections is still *Listening Aids Through the Grades* (Russell &

Russell, 1979), which includes almost 200 teaching ideas ranging from general to specific and from simple to complex.

Neurological Factors

Reading requires a brain that is functioning adequately. Fortunately, most people have central nervous systems that work well enough to allow them to learn to read, and the exceptions are rare, being perhaps 20 to 30 percent of children with *severe* reading problems who show signs of neurological deficits (Denckla, 1972). Among these are a few children who have neurological disorders that interfere with learning to read and with achievement in other curriculum areas.

Considerable confusion exists concerning children who have learning problems due to neurological involvement. These children have been labeled as "learning disabled," "dyslexic," and a host of other exotic terms. Terms of this nature are avoided in this text because they are counterproductive to helping teachers teach children to read.

Harris and Sipay (1980) list five main types of children with neurological deviations:

- Those who have survived a difficult birth.
- Those with injured brain tissue resulting from a severe insult to the head or serious childhood diseases, particularly those associated with high, sustained fever such as encephalitis.
- Those with congenital, or inherited, brain defects.
- Those with irregular or slowly developing brain tissue, sometimes called developmental delay or maturational lag.
- Those with apparently normal brain structure, but with a biochemical anomaly that may interfere with nerve impulses or signal transmission.

Formal Assessment Techniques

If a defect is suspected, family physicians usually refer children to a pediatric neurologist for a complete workup. In addition to standard medical procedures, such as electroencephalograms, doctors examine children for so-called soft signs. Sometimes results are obtained from observing and recording psychological rather than physical symptoms. A diagnosis based on soft signs has been considered to have doubtful validity (Schain, 1971–1972, in Harris & Sipay, 1980, p. 283). When psychological data are used as a basis for a physiological diagnosis, that diagnosis should be considered as suggestive rather than conclusive.

Informal Assessment Techniques

Accurately assessing neurological involvement is difficult even for medical and psychological specialists. Therefore, teachers must be extremely cautious and conservative regarding informal assessment.

Two types of data can be used for informal assessment, a child's history and observed symptoms. Teachers should be aware that the symptoms listed in the checklist in figure 12.5 are tenuous and, at best, suggestive. When neurological impairment is suspected, teachers should refer the child to a specialist, using established channels provided by the school system.

FIGURE 12.5 Checklist for possible neurological factors.

	Yes	No
History		
Family history suggesting hereditary factors	____	____
Serious problems during pregnancy	____	____
Serious problems during birth	____	____
Serious problems immediately after birth	____	____
Serious medical history (e.g., high fever)	____	____
Serious blow to head	____	____
Seizures or convulsions	____	____
Behavioral symptoms		
Poor balance, awkwardness	____	____
Delayed speech development	____	____
Extreme distractibility	____	____

Psychological Factors

Psychological factors refer to processes of the mind or psyche. Because of the delicate nature of the brain, many psychological studies are necessarily indirect, abstract, and theoretical; thus, the findings are more tenuous than results of investigations in the physical sciences. Information from psychological investigations is subject to different interpretations, frequently depending on the theoretical positions of the researchers.

Three psychological areas of concern to teachers are the cognitive, the affective, and the psychomotor domains. **Cognition** can be considered roughly as thinking, while **affect** refers to feelings. The **psychomotor** domain refers to the psychological field of physical activity. What people think and what they feel often are not the same, although the two processes are frequently so interrelated that it is difficult to separate them. Teachers of reading are pimarily concerned with children's thinking, but to be truly effective they need to be concerned with feelings, too. Two important psychological factors are considered in the following section; intelligence, which is a cognitive factor, and social and emotional adjustment, which are in the affective domain.

Cognition–Intelligence

Intelligence can be conceptualized in the broad sense as reflecting a person's general ability to think, to act purposefully, and to solve problems. Intelligence is an abstract, elusive concept that has been a source of debate for years by psychologists and educators alike. Because no one has ever "seen" or experienced intelligence, it can only be talked about.

A more operational definition would be that intelligence is what tests measure. Such a definition reminds us that a child's intelligence is often judged on the basis of a test score. This score may or may not accurately reflect true capacity; an intelligence test score is only an estimate of mental capacity and reflects the rate of mental development based on a relatively small sample of specific test items.

Reading is an intellectual process, and intelligence, however it may be defined, unquestionably influences the successful acquisition of reading skills and, in later years, the rate and comprehension of what one reads. Low intelligence is probably not a direct cause of reading problems but indirectly can interfere with learning to read. Teachers must adjust the curriculum to meet the needs of children with lower intelligence. Generally, these children require a more structured reading program, more practice and repetition, and closer scrutiny than their more typical peers. An analytic approach to teaching enhances their chances of learning to read.

The major reason for considering the intelligence of children for teaching reading is to estimate a child's potential reading capacity. Reading capacity is a standard, usually based on an IQ score, which is then compared to actual reading achievement, usually based on a reading test score. Thus, the teacher compares what a child *should* be achieving in reading to what the child actually *is* achieving. If the discrepancy is significant, the child is not reading at the expected level.

Formal Assessment Techniques

Because formal assessment requires the use of intelligence test scores, several relevant issues must be considered. Schools using intelligence tests depend, for the most part, on group intelligence tests. Generally, tests used for young children in primary grades are constructed so that they do not require reading, for example, the *Pintner-Cunningham* and the *Kuhlman-Anderson Measure of Academic Potential.* Concern has been expressed (Traxler, 1939) that intelligence tests that are non-language based may not be tapping the verbal abilities needed in learning to read, because the correlation between reading and non-language intelligence tests is quite low. Group intelligence tests for older children usually require reading, and poor readers usually score poorly on these tests. When this occurs, it is difficult to separate low reading ability from low mental ability, and teacher judgment becomes extremely important. When teachers are doubtful about a child's intelligence, particularly if the child is having difficulty reading, referral to the school psychologist for further assessment is recommended.

Informal Assessment Techniques

The use of intelligence test scores in recent years has become a sensitive, political issue. Increasingly, schools are discontinuing the use of intelligence tests except under specific conditions that usually involve a trained specialist (such as a school psychologist) using either the appropriate Wechsler (e.g., WISC-R) or Stanford-Binet scale, both of which require special training for administering and interpreting. Many classroom teachers, then, must use their own judgment to estimate a child's intelligence.

An important informal procedure often used today is to determine a child's ability to understand and deal with oral language (i.e., listening comprehension). This level of development becomes the substitute for an IQ score by comparing potential achievement with actual achievement. The rationale is that, with instruction, children should be able to read and understand written language as well as they hear and understand oral language. Using and interpreting informal measures of listening capacity has been discussed in chapter 4.

Affect–Emotional and Social Adjustment Factors

How people perceive themselves and the world around them gauges their emotional and social adjustment. People who do not feel good about themselves often have problems resolving inner conflicts and relating effectively with others in their environment.

This generalization holds true with children who have trouble reading. Results of studies on the incidence of emotional maladjustment among good and poor readers, in general, suggest that more poor readers than good readers have adjustment problems (T. Harris, 1969), but the differences between the groups is not clearly evident. Some poorly adjusted children are good readers. (Studies of children attending reading clinics [Robinson, 1946; Monroe, 1932] report, rather consistently, a higher incidence of emotional involvement than poor readers in a general school population.) Studies such as these suggest that the more serious a reading problem becomes, the greater the chances are that a poor reader will develop adjustment problems.

It would be very dangerous to conclude that emotional instability *causes* reading problems. A more appropriate conclusion would be that adjustment problems are likely to *contribute* to reading problems. Behavior problems probably interact with other causes of reading failure to make learning to read even more difficult for poor readers.

Another issue to consider is the degree of maladjustment. Severe emotional dysfunction hinders progress in learning more than moderate problems. Deep-seated problems are more difficult to remedy and tend to interfere longer than milder, more transitory problems. Neville (1967) noted that a certain amount of anxiety in people apparently helps them learn more effectively.

Whether psychological problems are a cause or the result of reading problems is not clear, but the presence of these problems can be safely assumed to inhibit reading progress. Quite often, children who improve in reading also improve in terms of self-concept. Thus, the classroom teacher should make every effort to help children feel good about themselves, especially if they have problems with academic subjects such as reading.

Formal Assessment Techniques

Discussion of formal assessment techniques will be brief because most require formal training in the areas of projective techniques, interviews, and other specialized psychological procedures. One fairly reliable source for assessing self-concept is the *Piers-Harris Children's Self Concept Scale* (Piers & Harris, 1969). This instrument consists of 80 yes-no items and can be administered to groups as well as individuals. Kuder-Richardson Formula 21 reliability estimates range from .78 to .93 for the instrument.

Self-concept, as measured in the Piers-Harris instrument, is assumed to refer to a set of relatively stable self-attitudes (Wylie, 1974). The actual items are evaluative as well as descriptive. For example, consider item 2 (I am a happy person), item 5 (I am smart), and item 20 (I give up easily). Responses to these and all other items both describe the person responding and reflect an evaluation that person is making about himself or herself.

Buros's *Eighth Mental Measurements Yearbook* (1978) contains a detailed and generally favorable review of the *Piers-Harris Children's Self Concept Scale,* and the interested reader is referred to that source.

Informal Assessment Techniques

Responsible classroom teachers are concerned with the well-being of their charges, including social and emotional aspects. Occasionally teachers observe students who seem to have unusually severe problems in these areas. Teachers may have an advantage over parents in identifying social and emotional problems because they are not as close to the children and also can compare one child's behavior to many others. After teachers have taught for a few years, they have a fairly good idea of what constitutes bizarre or aberrant behavior. While teachers should not dabble in amateur psychology, they should recognize unusual behaviors in children, particularly when those behaviors are frequent and persistent.

When teachers become aware of a possible problem child, they should reflect on precisely what the child is doing to cause concern. Figure 12.6 is a checklist of some of the symptoms associated with psychosocial problems.

Many other behaviors are also possible symptoms. A checklist helps teachers organize their thoughts and prepare a case for referral to the school psychologist, counsellor, or other trained specialists. In many school systems, psychologists have a heavy workload and the waiting period after referral can be many months. A well-prepared and documented referral by a thoughtful teacher may expedite results.

Carefully prepared anecdotal records are a teacher's best tool for presenting a case for referral. Remember that behaviors should be described objectively rather than presented as tentative conclusions. Consider the following examples:

	Conclusions vs.	*Objective Description*
11/18	Jennifer had a temper tantrum.	Today, when Jennifer discovered she did not have her paper posted on the "good work" bulletin board, she ran up to the board, ripped off several papers belonging to classmates, then she began to cry.
11/20	Jennifer fought with Susan in the cafeteria line.	Susan accidentally pushed Jennifer while they were in the cafeteria line. Jennifer then began to hit and kick Susan with unusual intensity. The look of anger and hate in her face frightened both Susan and me.
4/7	Liticia refused to participate in the reading group and at other times today.	Liticia was unusually quiet today. When I asked her comprehension questions, she dropped her head and eyes. I let someone else answer. Later when I tried to reengage her in the group activity, she still would not respond. I tried several other times to communicate with her today and had no luck. She did not talk with me all day.

The incomplete sentence technique is often used to gain insights into the child's feelings about reading and self in general. Typically, a student will be asked to complete twenty to fifty sentence starters either orally or in writing. Some examples follow.

My reading group _____.
The teacher thinks I _____.
My books _____.

Information from such an instrument should be considered tentative and must be verified because students often respond as they think the teacher wants them to. This is a limitation of any self-report technique. A frequently used incomplete sentence test was developed by Boning and Boning and can be found in appendix B.

FIGURE 12.6   Checklist of symptoms associated with emotional maladjustment.

	Yes	No
General Traits or Behavior		
1. Displays signs of excessive shyness	___	___
2. Displays signs of introversion	___	___
3. Displays signs of lack of confidence	___	___
4. Gives up easily on school tasks	___	___
5. Plays alone	___	___
6. Daydreams	___	___
7. Displays signs of overdependence	___	___
8. Seeks approval excessively	___	___
9. Has numerous unexplained absences	___	___
10. Displays signs of nervousness	___	___
11. Does not work cooperatively with classmates	___	___
12. Argues and fights with classmates	___	___
13. Constantly disrupts class	___	___
Reading-Related Traits or Behavior		
14. Shows fear of the reading task	___	___
15. Refuses to read orally	___	___
16. Displays antagonism toward reading	___	___
17. Does not get along with others in reading group	___	___
18. Does not attend during reading lesson	___	___
19. Does not complete reading assignments	___	___
20. Displays fear or nervousness during recitation	___	___

Instructional Strategies

Fortunately, most severely disturbed children have already been identified and placed in special therapeutic programs before entrance in school. Most school systems today also have special classes for emotionally disturbed children. However, some children with relatively mild adjustment problems function quite well within the regular classroom. Sometimes these children do not learn well, and their response to failure and frustration from not learning academic subjects interacts negatively with their poor adjustment. This can create a negative spiral that worsens with time.

Failure may also have a devastating effect on well-adjusted people. Thus, the following suggestions are for helping students who are having unfortunate emotional reactions, whether from lack of accomplishment in reading or from other sources. They can be appropriately used with most students.

1. *Create a facilitative learning environment.* The teacher must make special efforts to establish a warm, trusting working relationship with poor readers. Teachers should listen carefully. Often children feel the need to discuss what is bothering them with a trusted adult. Teachers may be so occupied that they fail to hear the clues given. Dialogue journals can provide students and teachers with a vehicle for "talking" to each other (Staton, 1988). Teachers also must be careful not to use their own values to judge non-reading behaviors, lest they contribute negatively to the other problems. On the other hand, children often need reassurance and suggestions, particularly

regarding their troubles, whether they are academic or otherwise. The teacher must establish a free and open atmosphere, but at the same time set certain limits. The teacher should maintain those limits, being pleasant but firm when necessary. The basic purpose of establishing rapport is to create an environment in which a child's self-confidence and self-esteem are nurtured.

2. *Create opportunities for success.* The old axiom "nothing succeeds like success" is appropriate for students having trouble reading. Teachers help structure success experiences. Children should work at a difficulty level that is easy enough for them. Find something they can read easily, even if it is their own names. Increasing the difficulty level if it is too easy is healthier than decreasing it after failure.

Older students often respond negatively to "baby stuff." This problem can be avoided if teachers use materials that appear more mature than they really are. High interest-low vocabulary books and stories without pictures of younger children are recommended.

A process called **bibliotherapy** (Hafner, 1977) can provide opportunities for 'troubled' students to identify with a character or situation in a book, and experience a catharsis or perhaps gain insight into their own problems. Bibliotherapy, then, can help a child come to grips with personal problems and realize that reading can be a useful activity for personal growth.

More difficult tasks can be spaced among easier ones. Children often can work with new and difficult tasks for only a few minutes before becoming too frustrated to continue. Interspersing success experiences between such tasks often relieves undue pressure.

3. *Provide ample reward and reinforcement.* Because many poor readers have less than adequate confidence in their ability to learn to read, they often need more encouragement than usual. Praise children when they succeed or, if necessary, when they attempt a task that is difficult and threatening. Social reinforcement can be given verbally ("very good," "nice try") or nonverbally (a reassuring smile, a pat on the back).

A more structured approach using behavior modification techniques adapted to individual needs often helps children having more serious problems. Extrinsic reinforcers applied by the teacher should, in time, be integrated into the child's own personality structure. When this occurs, and the child personally feels the reward for accomplishment, the reinforcement becomes intrinsic. When children enjoy reading or when they are pleased doing a particular reading task, the reinforcement becomes the satisfaction in doing the task. One problem often overlooked by teachers is that some children need considerable practice before they can attain a sense of satisfaction. Sometimes, teachers try to push for growth too fast and change learning tasks before the child reaches the satisfaction of mastery.

4. *Encourage student participation.* Generally speaking, children who analyze, plan, and evaluate their reading are those who profit most from corrective instruction. Teachers should encourage students to understand what they need to learn to improve their reading. With teacher help, many students can verify, rather intuitively, the reality of identified learning gaps. They can also demonstrate to the teacher that they can be successful with certain tasks that the original analysis suggested was lacking. Proper, meaningful interaction between pupil and teacher leads to efficient learning routes.

When children understand their need to learn a set of reading behaviors, the goals become much clearer and their attainment is facilitated. Children like to keep track of their progress in attaining goals, and teachers should encourage them to make progress charts and otherwise keep a record of their own growth. These charts and graphs become concrete evidence that help the child maintain goal-seeking behaviors. They also become an important evaluation tool for both child and teacher.

Common psychological factors that negatively influence reading achievement have been discussed in this section. Other psychological factors that occur less frequently have not been discussed here. More detailed information can be obtained from books on remedial reading.

Environmental Factors

Much of what occurs in the environment, or surrounding world, influences, directly and indirectly, the people who live there. Environmental factors that have a strong influence on school achievement and reading progress are cultural differences (especially language-related differences, see chapter 11), unfortunate conditions within the home, and inadequate schools that provide poor instruction.

Cultural Differences

In recent years considerable evidence has demonstrated that economic differences influence school achievement. Low income and poverty have been positively correlated with low achievement (Dyer, 1968). Schools in poor areas, such as ghettos and certain rural areas, generally do not offer the same benefits to children as the more affluent systems characteristic of suburban school districts.

Children from minority groups, in particular, have lacked the benefits of a good education. The Coleman Report (1966) suggested, however, that the problems are basically due to factors outside the school and beyond school control. The culture of the poor tends to focus on survival while the culture of the middle class tends to emphasize other values, including achievement.

The language used by poor and culturally different children has received considerable attention in recent years. When the language of instruction differs from the child's native language or dialect, problems in understanding are likely. Different languages or dialects are not wrong in themselves; communication is quite complete within the community where a dialect is spoken. However, when teachers use so-called standard English and reading materials are written similarly, problems can and do arise. (Refer to chapter 11 for more detailed discussion of linguistically variant children and the corrective reading program.)

Because of environmental differences, children come to school with experiences and backgrounds that vary from their more typical middle class peers. Thus, the content of reading matter may be inappropriate for these students. Despite recent efforts of publishers to provide content suitable for all students, some children need special conceptual, experiential, and language training in school to help them through the early years when reading instruction is normally introduced.

Home Environment

The family and home have a significant role in providing the proper setting to promote school achievement. For instance, within groups labeled poor and culturally different, family values vary. Some children from poor homes are successful in school, and much of their success probably emanates from within their homes.

On the other hand, unfortunate home environments are found in every social, cultural, and economic group. When a home is unstable and the family setting does not nurture feelings of security, learning problems may arise. Factors frequently mentioned are broken homes, family conflicts, sibling rivalry, and quarreling, over-protective, dominating, or neglecting parents. No one can deny that these factors have negative effects on a child. However, many children exposed to these conditions successfully learn to read. Hence the response to problems at home is a highly individual, idiosyncratic matter.

School Environment

Schools and instructional programs are also cited as causing problems in reading. From time to time schools are attacked by special interest groups and authors (Flesch, 1955; Holt, 1964; Kozol, 1972) claiming that they do not provide good instruction. Two common responses from schools have been to increase the amount of phonics to be taught and to move toward a "back to basics" curriculum. Such responses have often led to mixed results, sometimes benefiting and sometimes hindering student learning. Recently, the National Commission on Excellence in Education, appointed in 1981 to study the nation's educational system, concluded that our nation is at risk due to mediocrity in education (*A Nation at Risk*, 1983). The report further calls for widespread action to reform our nation's educational system. Federal, state, and local governments need to join forces with parents, teachers, and students in an effort to identify and solve local educational problems and improve school curricula and student achievement.

Improved instruction can be facilitated by two groups of educators: administrators and teachers. Administrators can work to alleviate certain rigid school policies that lead to imbalanced curricula and other inappropriate outcomes. Examples of such policies are (1) requiring teachers to emphasize reading skills to the detriment of learning reading as an information gathering process, (2) overemphasis on the affective domain to the detriment of basic cognitive learnings, (3) requiring teachers to instruct children in a specific sequence at a specific time to the detriment of children needing supplementary or corrective instruction, and (4) requiring students to attain a specified level of achievement before they are promoted to the detriment of weak but achieving students. Teachers become frustrated and their efforts are hindered by such unfortunate administrative policies.

Poor teaching is frequently cited as a reason for children not learning to read well. Among the many complaints the more common are: using unsuitable teaching methods; using overly difficult reading materials; using dull or otherwise inappropriate reading methods and materials; overemphasizing skills in isolation, especially phonics; giving too much or too little emphasis to reading skills; and teaching reading without integrating it into other curricular areas. Perhaps the judicious application of an analytic approach to teaching reading will substantially alleviate many instructional inadequacies.

Instructional Strategies

Naturally, classroom teachers should be aware of environmental factors that may be interfering with a child's reading accomplishments. It is very difficult, on an individual basis, to designate a specific environmental factor as *the* cause of a child's reading problems. Rather, a factor should be considered as a possible contributor to reading difficulties. Teachers are not sociologists or social workers, and few have been trained in techniques that pinpoint contributing factors. Thus, the role of the teacher becomes one of identifying *possible* contributing factors and referring the child to appropriate specialists or agencies in accordance with school policies. School districts often have social workers, counselors, and nurses to help teachers in the decision-making process.

Many schools have special programs for so-called disadvantaged students that have been funded by the federal and state governments. Examples are bilingual language and reading programs and special remedial programs, both within and outside the school system. Many communities today have mental health clinics that deal with family adjustment problems on a sliding scale fee basis that can be afforded by those of most modest circumstances. Community welfare agencies often have child welfare departments concerned with poor children caught in untenable living conditions. Thus, a major responsibility of teachers is to be knowledgeable regarding community services available for the children they teach and for their families.

Anecdotal records should be used to document teacher observations, with care to maintain a high level of objectivity. This means the teacher must be careful to describe behaviors, rather than simply assigning labels such as "this child's father is abusive." Teachers must remember not to overlook the privacy rights of children and their families. Anecdotal records must never read like gossip.

Instructional factors, such as those discussed in this section, are usually within the control of school personnel, specifically the classroom teacher and the building principal. They should assume responsibility for instructional factors that promote rather than inhibit learning to read. To maximize instruction in the classroom, teachers must think about the children—how they learn their basic skills, how they learn to apply those skills, and how they learn the joy of reading. These topics are of major concern in analytic teaching discussed in the next chapter.

Summary

The intent of this chapter is not to study causes and correlates of reading failure but to help make teachers aware of the variety of factors that affect the reading process. Many of the factors mentioned, such as overall health, intelligence, and emotional maladjustment, affect learning in general. Other factors, including visual and auditory acuity, visual perception, and listening skills are more directly related to reading.

In many cases the teacher can only refer children with such problems to other sources. Physicians, including neurologists, and psychologists may be needed if one of the related factors is severe enough. In some cases, teachers can give specific help as, for example, with visual perception skills or auditory comprehension. In all cases, teachers should be understanding and caring and attempt to make the educational environment comfortable for children with problems.

References

Brown, D. A. (1982). *Reading diagnosis and remediation.* Englewood Cliffs, NJ: Prentice-Hall.

Burns, P. C. (1980). *Assessment and correction of language arts difficulties.* Columbus, OH: Merrill.

Buros, O. K. (1978). *The eighth mental measurements yearbook.* Highland Park, NJ: Gryphon Press.

Coleman, J. S. (1966). *Equality of educational opportunity.* Washington, DC: U.S. Government Printing Office.

Dechant, E. (1981). *Diagnosis and remediation of reading difficulties.* Englewood Cliffs, NJ: Prentice-Hall.

Denckla, M. B. (1972). Clinical syndromes in learning disabilities: The case for "splitting" vs. "lumping." *Journal of Learning Disabilities, 5,* 401–406.

Devine, T. G. (1978). Listening: What do we know after fifty years of research and theorizing? *Journal of Reading, 21,* 296–304.

Devine, T. G. (1981). *Teaching study skills: A guide for teachers.* Boston: Allyn and Bacon.

Dyer, H. S. (1968). Research issues on equality of educational opportunity: School factors. *Harvard Educational Review, 38,* 38–56.

Flesch, R. (1955). *Why Johnny can't read.* New York: Harper & Row.

Furness, E. L. (1971). Proportion, purpose, and process in listening. In S. Duker (Ed.), *Teaching listening in the elementary school.* Metuchen, NJ: Scarecrow Press.

Hafner, L. E. (1977). *Developmental reading in middle and secondary schools.* New York: Macmillan.

Harris, A. J., & Sipay, E. R. (1980). *How to increase reading ability* (7th ed.). New York: Longman.

Harris, T. (1969). Reading. In R. L. Ebel (Ed.), *Encyclopedia of educational research* (4th ed.). New York: Macmillan.

Hollow, M. K. (1955). *An experimental study of listening at the intermediate grade level.* Unpublished doctoral dissertation, Fordham University, New York.

Holt, J. (1964). *How children fail.* New York: Pitman.

Kennedy, E. C. (1977). *Classroom approaches to remedial reading* (2nd ed.). Itasca, IL: F. E. Peacock.

Kozol, J. (1972). *Free schools* (rev. ed.). New York: Bantam.

Lundsteen, S. (1979). *Listening: Its impact on reading and other language arts* (rev. ed.). Urbana, IL: National Council of Teachers of English.

Monroe, M. (1932). *Children who cannot read.* Chicago: University of Chicago Press.

National Commission on Excellence in Education (1983). *A nation at risk: The imperative for educational reform.* Washington, DC: U.S. Department of Education.

Neville, D., Pfost, P., & Dobbs, V. (1967). The relationship between text anxiety and silent reading gains. *American Educational Research Journal, 4,* 45–50.

Norton, D. E. (1980). *The effective teaching of language arts.* Columbus, OH: Merrill.

Otto, W., & Smith, R. J. (1980). *Corrective and remedial teaching* (3rd ed.). Boston: Houghton Mifflin.

Piers, E. V., & Harris, D. B. (1969). *The Piers-Harris children's self concept scale.* Los Angeles: Western Psychological Services.

Robinson, H. M. (1946). *Why pupils fail in reading.* Chicago: University of Chicago Press.

Russell, D. H., & Russell, E. (1979). *Listening aids through the grades* (2nd ed.). New York: Teachers College Press.

Schain, R. J. (1971-1972). Neurological diagnosis in children with learning disabilities. *Academic Therapy, 7,* 139-147.

Spache, G. D. (1976). *Diagnosing and correcting reading disabilities.* Boston: Allyn and Bacon.

Staton, J. (1988). Discussing problems. In J. Staton, R. W. Shuy, J. K. Peyton, & L. Reed (Eds.), *Dialogue journal communication: Classroom, linguistic, social and cognitive views* (pp. 202-244). Norwood, NJ: Ablex.

Stauffer, R. G. (1981). Strategies for reading instruction. In M. Douglas (Ed.), *45th Yearbook of the Claremont Reading Conference,* Claremont, CA.

Traxler, A. E. (1939). A study of the California Test of Mental Maturity: Advanced battery. *Journal of Educational Research, 32,* 329-335.

Wilt, M. (1958). A study of teacher awareness of listening as a factor in elementary education. *Journal of Educational Research, 43,* 626-636.

Wylie, R. C. (1974). *The self-concept.* Lincoln: University of Nebraska Press.

CHAPTER 13

Analytic Teaching: A Summary

Janet C. Richards

Objectives

After completing this chapter, you should be able to

1. define analytic teaching;
2. explain how analytic teaching provides for student reading success through individualization of instruction;
3. discuss the importance of honest student-teacher communication;
4. identify how children are unique;
5. discuss the value of ongoing observation of students;
6. explain how to document information about children in order to provide individualized reading instruction;
7. define reflective thinking;
8. discuss the role of the teacher as a reflective decision maker.

Study Outline

I. Introduction
   A. Mainstreaming
   B. Children of different cultures and dialects
   C. ESL students
   D. Unstable home environments
   E. Teacher accountability
   F. Decreases in federal funding

II. Analytic teaching: a way to teach all children
   A. Prerequisites for analytic teaching

1. Knowledge of the reading process
2. Appreciation of student differences
   a) Cognitive domain
   b) Affective domain
3. Belief in children as capable human beings

III. Functions of the analytic teacher
   A. Communication
   B. Observation
   C. Reflective thinking
   D. Decisions

Important Vocabulary and Concepts

ad hoc reading groups
analytic teaching
reflective thinking

Overview

Teachers have become increasingly aware of the necessity to individualize reading instruction. Classrooms are filled with diverse groups of students whose personalized reading needs must be met. Teachers are encouraged and required more than ever before to develop better ways of helping all children learn to read in our constantly changing world. A number of factors emphasize this need.

Mainstreaming

The mainstreaming of children with special educational needs is now a reality. Students with physical or mental handicaps are no longer isolated from the joys of participating in regular class activities. Additionally, gifted and talented students must be challenged and effectively taught in regular classrooms.

Children of Different Cultures and Dialects

Federal mandates, such as busing of children to schools outside their home districts, have produced radical shifts in many school populations. As a result, teachers have become knowledgeable about different cultures and dialects and now recognize how a child's dialectical and cultural background affects his reading success.

English as Second Language (ESL) Students

Another impetus to individualizing reading instruction is the increased immigration to the United States. Over 3.6 million children in our schools have limited English competence (Rotberg, 1982). Teachers want to help these ESL students learn to read and write English successfully. Teachers must understand how specific first language constraints influence childrens' English reading and writing competence (Hudelson, 1981).

The author wishes to thank Dr. Janet C. Richards, New Orleans Public Schools, for contributing this chapter.

Unstable Home Environments

Teachers are challenged to meet the special instructional needs of angry, depressed or frustrated children who live in unstable home environments. Siblings who abuse alcohol or drugs, parents who argue or are divorced, and frequent moves because of economic hardships may affect children's school attendance and ability to perform in school.

Teacher Accountability

Public awareness concerning teacher accountability has placed added demands upon the classroom teacher to be as effective as possible. Public pressure on schools to demonstrate their worth enforces quality teaching.

Decreases in Federal Funding

Decreases in federal funding have reduced the number of on-site school reading specialists and clinicians. Many school systems cannot afford to pay auxiliary personnel. Today's teacher must accept the responsibility for helping all children become successful readers. But, how can a classroom teacher possibly begin to meet the reading instructional needs of all children? One way is through analytic teaching.

Analytic Teaching: A Way to Teach All Children

Analytic teaching is a way of thinking about individual children and their capabilities as successful readers. Such teaching begins with the belief that each child is unique. It consists of activities that foster student-teacher communication and help students to assume responsibility for their own education.

Prerequisites for Analytic Teaching

Knowledge of the Reading Process

The first prerequisite for successful analytic teaching is knowledge of the reading process. The analytic reading teacher is a life-long student of reading. Reading conferences, courses and professional journals help expand the analytic reading teacher's repertoire of instructional strategies. The analytic reading teacher transforms basal texts, phonics supplements, language experience approach materials, and independent reading libraries into a sound, research-based reading instructional program according to his or her particular beliefs about what constitutes reading (Harste & Burke, 1977).

Many theoretical models of reading attempt to explain the reading process. The transactional psycholinguistic model (Goodman, 1985), currently supported by numerous researchers, provides insights on the ways a proficient reader anticipates and reconfirms meaning in text. Advocates of this model believe that reading is a quest after meaning; it is "tentative, selective and constructive" (Goodman, 1985, p. 827). The successful reader is one whose attention is on comprehension of text.

Teacher Appreciation of Student Differences

Good reading teachers know that children naturally differ and that no two students pass through the same developmental stages of reading in the same way (Hittleman, 1983). Student differences are evidenced both in the cognitive and affective domains.

Cognitive domain.   Cognitive domain differences include linguistic competence, which refers to how well a child understands language and communicates verbally; home language and culture, which refers to ethnic diversity; cognitive functioning or intellectual development; learning style or specific preference for processing information through kinesthetic, auditory, or visual modalities; and readiness for specific reading instruction.

Affective domain.   Affective domain differences include interest in literature, motivation to read, feelings of success, self-esteem, and belonging, and feelings of control of one's environment (Rotter, 1966).

Belief in Children as Capable Human Beings

Effective reading teachers realize that all students possess ability to learn. Successful analytic teachers believe that children are capable human beings who want to learn and are ready to learn somewhere along the reading instructional continuum. They also believe that students are capable of making some good decisions concerning their educational needs.

Student reading performance and subsequent reading instructional needs change often. Children are dynamic, with potential to thrive in a stimulating learning environment. As reading is taught, most students' reading ability dramatically improves.

If you appreciate and welcome each child's uniqueness, and believe in the desire to learn, you possess the prerequisite humanistic components necessary for successful analytic teaching.

Functions of the Analytic Teacher

Communication

Analytic teaching begins with student-teacher communication. If the teacher is willing to plan and discuss individual reading programs with children, they will strive to become willing partners in the instructional process.

Analytic teaching requires extra teacher time. Once children accept some responsibility for their reading instruction, the teacher gains the time needed to observe children, make decisions about their reading instruction, and actively teach children to read.

Daily, short morning meetings are quite effective for fostering group communication (Glasser, 1969). Meetings work best when teacher and students face one another in a seated circle. Topics for discussion include proposed individual and group reading activities, individual and group reading progress, and long-range reading instructional goals. The reasons for children's activities and goals should be provided (e.g., "Joe has really improved his language experience stories since he has learned to use a thesaurus; he would like to explain how a thesaurus works, and how it helps him discover and use more exciting vocabulary").

If feasible, a daily, short afternoon meeting is also helpful to discuss what exactly did take place that day and to provide suggestions for the following day's reading work.

Teachers *must* be honest. Did a student work exceptionally well? Compliment him in front of the group. Does a child need to try harder? Ask him what he thinks might help him to accept responsibility for his instruction. Did a reading group misunderstand some inferential reading comprehension questions? Brainstorm suggestions with the group.

When children are honestly informed about the nature of their reading strengths and difficulties and why they should work in a certain way (Rae & Potter, 1981), most wholeheartedly form a bond with the teacher that leads to reading success.

Observation

An analytic teacher constantly observes children to watch for the emergence of reading patterns (Hittleman, 1983) and to document the students' instructional needs. Teacher observation is never wasted time. Materials for reading instruction (basal texts, language experience approach supplies, library books, content area texts, study skill materials, and phonics supplements) should *not* be assembled before children's needs are determined.

How and What to Observe

During the first weeks of school, the teacher should observe the children to discover what they are capable of achieving in reading. At the same time, the teacher notices peer interaction; student interests, thinking ability, and language; and each child's self-esteem and ability to complete assignments.

Suggestions for a week of student observation include the following:

1. *Free time.* Who interacts with whom? Who are the loners? Who reads independently? Who needs structure? Who needs freedom?

2. *Reading groups* (random assignments). Who displays adequate attention span? Who becomes restless? Who enjoys discussions? Who appears to need experiential activities for text comprehension?

3. *Playground.* Who displays leadership ability? Who appears to be a follower? Who is athletically gifted? Who needs to learn to take turns?

4. *Lunchroom.* Who appears lethargic or tired? Who appears overly hungry? Who likes to talk? Who needs to learn table manners?

5. *Class meetings.* Who understands problem solving or brainstorming? Who is shy? Who becomes easily bored? Who enjoys speaking?

6. *Uninterrupted sustained silent reading.* Who chooses books on an independent reading level? Who silently mouths words? Who becomes easily distracted? Who points to words and sentences with the finger?

7. *Small groups.* Who cooperates? Who completes a task? Who works to best abilities?

8. *Art and music.* Who recognizes his or her innate creativity? Who displays immature artistic work (i.e., not on baseline level) (Lowenfeld, 1970)? Who is artistically gifted?

9. *Phonics lessons.* Who appears to have adequate auditory perception and memory? Who can generalize phonic rules? Who enjoys phonics lessons?

10. *Teacher reading.* Who listens and remembers? Who needs to develop schemata for text vocabulary and story content? Who needs to exert more self-control? Who appreciates good literature? Who understands inferential language (i.e., metaphors, similes, and idioms)?

11. *Student creative writing.* Who needs to learn how to brainstorm ideas for a story via semantic mapping? Who needs to learn the differences between expository and expressive writing? Who needs help with the mechanics of writing (e.g., spelling, punctuation)? Who is ready to learn about paragraphing? Who needs to practice penmanship skills? Who needs to concentrate on the "message" of the story? Who needs help in using reference materials?

After Observation

After initially observing students, the analytic teacher forms some general ideas about children and their reading. Some questions may now be *tentatively* answered and confirmed. The analytic teacher decides which students

1. may work best together.
2. display similar interests.
3. appear to be similar with regard to estimated reading abilities.
4. need special or extra instruction.
5. need extra attention to remain on task.
6. need to develop more self-esteem.
7. need individual help in particular reading skills.

Reflective Thinking

When teachers consciously and seriously think about how to group and teach children effectively they engage in reflective thinking. Reflective thinking enables teachers to question and solve educational problems in a thoughtful and deliberate manner (Dewey, 1933; Posner, 1989). Research increasingly confirms that reflective teachers make quality decisions about students and their instruction (Grant & Zeichner, 1984; Richards & Gipe, 1988).

Decisions

An analytic teacher must feel confident about his or her ability to formulate reading instructional plans and long range goals for both individuals and groups of students. The analytic reading teacher assumes the role and responsibility of a reflective decision maker (Cooper & Worden, 1983).

Decisions and professional judgments must be made daily. During one school day a teacher may ask the following:

1. Is this student reading as well as he or she can today? If not, why not? What reading approach or strategy could help? Will a conference help? Will peer tutoring help?

2. Should this student continue to remain in the reading group that is exploring poetry? If so, what additional instructional strategies may enable this child to grasp the necessary concepts?

3. Will a whole-class phonics lesson on consonant blends prove beneficial?

4. How can student-teacher conferences motivate students to become wide readers?

5. Should the students who need special reading instruction at this particular time remain in basal readers. Would they benefit from more instruction time? an individualized reading approach? an eclectic approach? more activities with a language experience approach?

Beginning teachers anxious to use the analytic approach to reading may find the preceding question formulation and reflective decision-making process difficult because of lack of experience, lack of a necessary understanding of the reading process, or lack of confidence in professional judgment. *Do not worry!* If you are sincere about the benefits of analytic teaching (successful readers who accept responsibility for their learning), you will want to understand the reading process. You will consider students' self-esteem, and you will become confident, and grow in your abilities as a reflective decision maker.

Flexible Reading Groups

Most teachers group children for reading instruction. Reading groups need to be flexible. Children's instructional needs change frequently. In analytic teaching, students do not automatically become locked into a particular reading track.

The analytic teacher communicates to children the reasons for reading group flexibility. Children receive direct reading instruction in what they need at a particular time. The analytic teacher thinks of individuals and their reading needs and is not bound by grade-level texts or tests.

Ad Hoc Grouping

The analytic teacher constantly thinks "who is ready to learn what now?" **Ad hoc reading groups** are easily formed and disbanded according to student interests or instructional needs.

Alternate Group Instruction

It is a good idea to alternate the order of reading group instruction so that the same children do not have to wait for their turn.

Three reading groups daily seem to be as much as a teacher can handle effectively. In analytic teaching, the first reading group is not the advanced group, nor is the third reading group the less able group. Groups are formed to expedite reading instruction according to individual children's needs.

Student Reading Group Designations

A chart may be placed adjacent to the reading group space with student designations assigned for a particular day or week. Children become accustomed to the analytic teacher deleting or inserting children's names on the chart according to their interests or reading instructional needs. For instance, if one day the basal reading story is about horses, the analytic teacher encourages students who are particularly interested to sit in on that reading group, regardless of their reading ability. Perhaps on another day a pertinent group lesson is being taught about affixes. The analytic teacher knows which children would benefit from a preview or review of this particular reading skill and groups children accordingly.

Children will accept reading group changes because the analytic teacher non-judgmentally plans necessary reading instruction with the children.

Student Sign-up Sheet

Another good idea is to place a sign-up sheet with daily or weekly reading group topics and skills listed on the sheet (fig. 13.1). With teacher approval, children may sign up for any of the three reading groups. This allows and encourages them to accept responsibility for their own education.

Student-Teacher Conferences

Children are quite capable of helping the teacher formulate plans concerning their reading instruction. The analytic teacher usually decides to conduct weekly student conferences to discuss individual student reading progress, strengths, problems, interests, and goals.

Children who feel that their efforts are appreciated and their input recognized will work to their fullest potential and capabilities. Children will welcome individual conference time if the teacher is nonjudgmental, empathic, fair, and honest.

Documentation and Record Keeping

Analytic teachers take time to keep records in order to monitor children's reading progress and reading interests. Documentation should include conference communications, teacher observations, test results, and examples of student work. Documentation can be accomplished by the following:

FIGURE 13.1 Example of a student sign-up sheet.

Group 1 Topic: Family Skills: Syllabication; locating main ideas	Group 2 Topic: Animals Skill: Sight word expansion	Group 3 Topic: Outer Space Skill: Sequence of events
1. _____	1. _____	1. _____
2. _____	2. _____	2. _____
3. _____	3. _____	3. _____
4. _____	4. _____	4. _____
5. _____	5. _____	5. _____
6. _____	6. _____	6. _____

FIGURE 13.2 Example of checklist.

Name _____ Date _____	Yes	No	Comments
Appears motivated			
Appears to work to fullest ability			
Appears interested			
Understands how to determine unfamiliar vocabulary by using surrounding words in the sentence or text (context)			
Is developing reading independence	✓		(1) has read 3 books this week (2) recognizes when vocabulary or ideas in a story are not understood (3) rereads difficult portions of text in order to improve comprehension
Needs help with reading skills	✓		pronouns, antonyms
Needs to develop reading comprehension skills	✓		main idea, drawing conclusions
Needs help with phonic analysis	✓		initial/final consonant digraphs

1. Checklists (fig. 13.2)
2. Anecdotal records (fig. 13.3, 13.4)
3. Student self-evaluations
4. Examples of students' work
5. Tape recordings
6. Photographs
7. Children's ideas about their feelings. (A happy face will succinctly convey the message in kindergarten!)

FIGURE 13.3 Example of anecdotal record.

Name: <u>Jane</u>

10/3/91 During reading group, Jane volunteered to answer a question for the first time.

11/4/91 Jane is becoming more motivated to read and appears more confident in her reading ability. She has read three books this week.

Children who have access to their own files develop awareness of their ongoing reading improvement. Student responsibility and initiative are also encouraged when they can read about their strengths and long-range goals.

Classroom Management

Effective classroom management is really a common sense way of organizing all class activities so that both students and teacher know what is expected and accept responsibility for what happens during the school day (see Glasser, 1969 for a detailed discussion).

Effective Management Gives Teachers Time

Teachers need energy and time to teach. A good classroom management system encourages student participation and frees the teacher for teaching. As Spaulding (1983) notes: "A classroom management scheme that relies on strict teacher direction deprives students of opportunities to learn self-management skills." A good classroom management system is always planned in conjunction with the children in the classroom.

Rules and Consequences

Rules concerning student behavior should be a joint decision of teacher and students. Consequences for inappropriate behavior should also be formulated through cooperative student-teacher efforts. These decisions should be as limited as possible and posted in writing in the classroom so that everyone knows what is expected. The following are examples of succinct, positively stated rules.

1. We care for and return class supplies to the proper place.
2. We speak softly.

FIGURE 13.4 Example of student/teacher conference documentation

---

Name _____   Date _____

Literature discussed   _____

Problems   _____

Success   _____

Weekly goal   _____

Long-term goal   _____

---

3. We give 100 percent effort in our academic work and in our behavior.
4. We clean up our area.
5. We listen when others speak.
6. We share.
7. We are kind to others.

Testing

After observing the students, the analytic teacher usually will want to learn more about some children through testing. Testing helps teachers determine specific student reading strategies and oral and silent reading comprehension abilities.

Although testing is only a small portion of analytic teaching, it provides information about students that can be used to plan specific reading lessons. Testing also provides concrete information about student progress. The following tests are useful.

1. Informal reading inventories
2. Teacher-constructed tests
3. Cloze or maze procedures
4. Criterion-referenced tests
5. Standardized tests

Remember that analytic teaching is much more than grouping children according to test scores (Hittleman, 1983) and identifying student failures or inadequacies. Testing is but one portion of analytic teaching. Testing only indicates what children accomplished on the particular test.

The analytic teacher uses test scores wisely and in conjunction with all other information. For instance, some students may read quite successfully within the regular classroom setting but perform quite poorly on a reading test. Other students may perform quite well on a reading test but exhibit extremely poor motivation to read. The analytic teacher makes professional decisions about children's reading instruction only after serious observation.

Evaluation

An analytic reading teacher knows that continuous evaluation of each student's reading progress is essential in order to determine future reading instruction. Student evaluation should be concerned with the following:

1. Readiness for particular reading skill instruction
2. Initiative and responsibility
3. Motivation to read
4. Growth in self-esteem
5. Development of critical reading skills
6. Development of wide reading interests

Student evaluation and feedback should be ongoing, honest, nonjudgmental, and as positively stated as possible.

Student evaluation may be accomplished through individual conference, letters or notes to children, parent-child-teacher conferences, and student self-evaluation.

Evaluation should also encompass the entire reading program, to include teacher effectiveness. Peers, administrators, and students may be asked to offer constructive criticism.

Summary

Teachers have become increasingly aware of their responsibilities in teaching large and diverse groups of children that may include ESL students, students of different cultures and dialects, students with special instructional needs including students from unstable home environments, and children with varied interests and talents. Public awareness of teacher accountability has also placed demands upon the classroom teacher to be as effective as possible. Analytic teaching allows the teacher to meet the needs of all children.

Three prerequisites for successful analytic teaching are (1) knowledge of the reading process, (2) appreciation of children's uniqueness, and (3) belief that all children can learn.

Along with a sound, research-based reading instructional program are ten critical teaching activities that assist children in becoming successful readers.

1. Student-teacher communication
2. Ongoing observation of students
3. Reflective thinking
4. Reflective decision making by the teacher
5. Flexible reading grouping and regrouping
6. Student-teacher conferences
7. Documentation of students' behaviors
8. Effective classroom management
9. Testing
10. Evaluation of students, teacher, and reading instruction

Analytic teaching helps children to become successful, motivated readers for the following reasons:

1. Children are informed about their reading ability.
2. Children are involved with planning their own reading instruction.
3. Children are not locked into one reading group.
4. Student-teacher communication is honest and nonjudgmental.

References

Cooper, J. D., & Worden, T. (1983). *The classroom reading program in the elementary school.* New York: Macmillan.

Dewey, J. (1933). *How we think: A restatement of the relation of reflective thinking to the educational process.* Boston: D. C. Heath.

Glasser, W. (1969). *Schools without failure.* New York: Harper & Row.

Goodman, K. S. (1985). Unity in reading. In H. Singer and R. B. Ruddell (Eds.), *Theoretical models and processes of reading.* Newark, DE: International Reading Association, 813–840.

Grant, C., & Zeichner, K. (1984). On becoming a reflective teacher. In C. Grant, *Preparing for reflective teaching* (pp. 11–18). Boston: Allyn and Bacon.

Harste, J., & Burke, C. (1977). A new hypothesis for reading teacher education research: Both the teaching and the learning of reading are theoretically based. In P. D. Pearson (Ed.), *Twenty-sixth yearbook of the National Reading Conference,* Clemson, SC.

Hittleman, D. (1983). *Developmental reading, K–8: Teaching from a psycholinguistic perspective* (2nd ed.). Boston: Houghton Mifflin.

Hudelson, S. (Ed.). (1981). *Learning to read in different languages.* Washington, DC: Center for Applied Linguistics.

Lowenfeld, V. (1970). *Creative and mental growth* (5th ed.). New York: Macmillan.

Posner, G. (1989). *Field experience: Methods of reflective teaching.* New York: Longman.

Rae, G., & Potter, T. (1981). *Informal reading diagnosis: A practical guide for the classroom teacher.* Englewood Cliffs, NJ: Prentice-Hall.

Richards, J. C., & Gipe, J. P. (1988, April). *Reflective thinking and the teaching abilities of prospective teachers.* Paper presented at the meeting of the American Educational Research Association, New Orleans, LA.

Rotberg, I. (1982). Some legal and research considerations in establishing federal policy in bilingual education. *Harvard Educational Review, 2,* 49–168.

Rotter, J. (1966). Generalized expectancies for internal versus external control of reinforcement. *Psychological Monographs, 80* (1), 1–28.

Spaulding, R. (1983). A systematic approach to classroom discipline, Part I. *Phi Delta Kappan, 65,* 48–51.

APPENDIXES

APPENDIX A

Text Readability

Readability refers to the difficulty level of printed material. Low readability means the material is difficult to read; however, an index for such material will be a high number often given in terms of grade level. Likewise, material with high readability (easy to read) will be reflected by a low index.

Several factors affect the readability of material: the number of difficult or new words, the length and complexity of sentences, the number of new or unfamiliar concepts, the organization and cohesion of the material, the reader's background knowledge for reading the material, and even the material's appearance.

Thus, the use of any readability index as the sole determinant of a book's appropriateness is not advised. (See IRA, NCTE statement on the use of readability formulae in *Reading Today*, 1985, p. 1) However, if the teacher uses the index in conjunction with the other factors affecting readability, determining the readability index of a material can be a valuable and valid exercise (Fry, 1989).

Several methods can be used to determine readability. You will be provided with directions for using three methods: Fry's Graph for Estimating Readability (fig. A.1), the Raygor Readability Estimate (fig. A.2), and the RIX procedure.

Fry's Graph

When using Fry's graph be aware that grade-level scores are most valid near the center line on the graph. Scores falling in the gray areas are invalid, and additional samples may be needed. Fry's estimates are considered accurate to within plus or minus one year of the true estimate of readability.

Raygor Readability Estimate

For those who have a difficult time counting syllables, the Raygor graph is often preferred. With this graph, words with six or more letters are counted as long words. The other procedures used are identical to those of Fry, except numerals are *not* counted when using Raygor.

RIX Index

The RIX index is a relatively new and easy procedure for estimating readability (Anderson, 1983). In addition, the RIX procedure produces results similar to those

Figure A.1 Fry's readability graph.

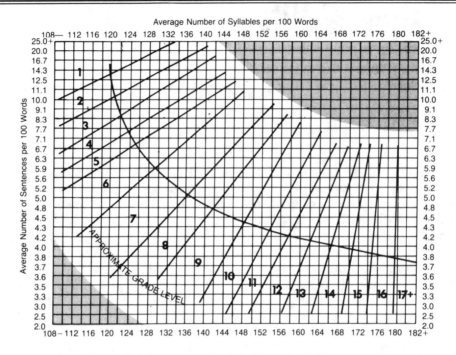

Average Number of Syllables per 100 Words

Expanded Directions for Working Readability Graph

1. Randomly select three (3) sample passages and count out exactly 100 words each, beginning with the beginning of a sentence. Do count proper nouns, initializations, and numerals.

2. Count the number of sentences in the hundred words, estimating length of the fraction of the last sentence to the nearest one-tenth.

3. Count the total number of syllables in the 100-word passage. If you don't have a hand counter available, an easy way is to simply put a mark above every syllable over one in each word; then when you get to the end of the passage, count the number of marks and add 100. Small calculators can also be used as counters by pushing numeral 1, then push the + sign for each word or syllable when counting.

4. Enter graph with *average* sentence length and *average* number of syllables: plot dot where the two lines intersect. Area where dot is plotted will give you the approximate grade level.

5. If a great deal of variability is found in syllable count or sentence count, putting more samples into the average is desirable.

6. A word is defined as a group of symbols with a space on either side: thus, *Joe, IRA, 1945,* and *&* are each one word.

7. A syllable is defined as a phonetic syllable. Generally, there are as many syllables as vowel sounds. For example, *stopped* is one syllable and *wanted* is two syllables. When counting syllables for numerals and initializations, count one syllable for each symbol. For example, *1945* is four syllables, *IRA* is three syllables, and *&* is one syllable.

Note: This "extended graph" does not outmode or render the earlier (1968) version inoperative or inaccurate; it is an extension.

FIGURE A.2 The Raygor graph.

These are the directions for using the Raygor graph:

1. Count out three 100-word passages at the beginning, middle, and end of a book. Be sure to include proper nouns in your word count, but do not count numerals.

2. Count the number of sentences in each passage, estimating to the nearest tenth.

3. Circle and count the words having six or more letters. Words having six or more letters are defined as *long* (hard) words.

4. Average the sentence length and the number of long (hard) words over the three samples, and plot the average on the graph.

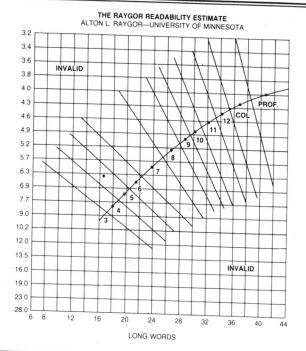

THE RAYGOR READABILITY ESTIMATE
ALTON L. RAYGOR—UNIVERSITY OF MINNESOTA

LONG WORDS

of other widely used and accepted short procedures (Fry, Raygor, and SMOG) and has been translated into a program for use with microcomputers, making it an even simpler procedure (Kretschmer, 1984). All that is required once the program has been stored on a disk is to type in the material being assessed for readability. The program listing for Apple II and Apple IIe (fig. A.3) is not copyrighted and can be copied freely. (A program listing for the TRS-80 is also available in Kretschmer's article.)

Directions for the program's use are a part of the programming and are found in lines 200 to 535. Briefly, text (at least 100 words—the longer the sample, the more accurate the index) is typed in *without* punctuation. At the end of a sentence, the operator does *not* type a period, but *does* space after the last word. Then the return key (ENTER on some machines) is pressed, signalling the computer that a sentence has ended. The subsequent output reveals one of the nicest features of the program, the sentence-by-sentence monitoring of readability. This is certainly a useful feature for assessing readability of written material, as well as material that is in the process of being written.

An example of the printout for a familiar children's story is shown in Figure A.4. The printout also demonstrates the limitations of readability formulae. *The Three Bears* is showing a 4th–5th grade readability based on sentence length and long words. However, the reader's background and the predictability and repetitiveness of the story must also be considered.

FIGURE A.3 Program listing for Apple II and Apple IIe computers to be used with the RIX index of readability. (From "Computerizing and Comparing the RIX Readability Index," by Joseph C. Kretschmer, *Journal of Reading*, March 1984. Reprinted with permission of the author and the International Reading Association, Newark, Del.)

```
]PR#0
]LIST

100  REM  RIXRATE READABILITY PROGRAM
105  HOME : PRINT : PRINT : PRINT
110  FOR X = 0 TO 39: PRINT "#";: NEXT X
115  PRINT : PRINT : PRINT : PRINT  TAB( 7)"RIXRATE READABILITY PROGRAM"
120  PRINT : PRINT : PRINT  TAB( 9)"BASED ON THE RIX FORMULA"
130  PRINT : PRINT : PRINT  TAB( 13)"BY J. ANDERSON"
140  PRINT : PRINT : PRINT  TAB( 6)"BASIC PROGRAM BY J. KRETSCHMER"
150  PRINT : PRINT : PRINT  TAB( 3)"MIAMI UNIVERSITY, OXFORD, OHIO -- 198
     3"
160  PRINT : PRINT : PRINT : FOR X = 0 TO 39: PRINT "#";: NEXT X
170  FOR P = 1 TO 3000: NEXT P
180  HOME : PRINT "DO YOU NEED INSTRUCTIONS? <Y OR N>": INPUT A$
185  IF A$ = "N" THEN 800ELSE190
190  HOME : INVERSE : PRINT "INSTRUCTIONS": NORMAL
200  PRINT : PRINT "1. YOU WILL BE ASKED TO TYPE A SHORT"
210  PRINT "   TITLE FOR THE TEXT TO BE ANALYZED BY"
220  PRINT "   RIXRATE."
230  PRINT : PRINT "2. AFTER THE TITLE IS ENTERED, A STATUS"
240  PRINT "   WINDOW WILL APPEAR AT THE TOP OF THE"
250  PRINT "   SCREEN.  RIXRATE MONITORS READABILITY"
260  PRINT "   SENTENCE BY SENTENCE.  ALL FIGURES"
270  PRINT "   WILL BE AT ZERO UNTIL A COMPLETE"
280  PRINT "   SENTENCE IS ENTERED."
290  PRINT : PRINT "3.  TYPE IN THE TEXT, SPACING AFTER EACH"
300  PRINT "   WORD AS USUAL, BUT OMIT ALL PUNCTUA-"
310  PRINT "   TION EXCEPT APOSTROPHES AND HYPHENS."
320  PRINT : PRINT "4.  SIGNAL THE END OF A SENTENCE BY "
330  PRINT "   PRESSING <RETURN>. BE SURE TO SPACE"
340  PRINT "   AFTER THE LAST WORD."
350  PRINT : PRINT "   <PRESS ANY KEY TO CONTINUE>"
360  GET A$: IF A$ = "" GOTO 360
370  HOME : PRINT "5.  DIALOGUE EXPRESSIONS SUCH AS <WHAT?"
380  PRINT "   ASKED ANN> SHOULD BE CONSIDERED ONE"
390  PRINT "   SENTENCE."
400  PRINT : PRINT "6.  USE THE BACK ARROW KEY TO CORRECT"
410  PRINT "   MISTAKES, BUT BE CAREFUL TO SPACE"
420  PRINT "   ONLY ONCE FOR EACH WORD."
430  PRINT : PRINT "7.  BE SURE TO INCLUDE ENOUGH SENTENCES"
440  PRINT "   TO CONSTITUTE AN ADEQUATE SAMPLING"
450  PRINT "   OF THE TEXT.  TAKE BLOCKS OF SEVERAL"
460  PRINT "   SENTENCES FROM THE BEGINNING, MIDDLE"
470  PRINT "   AND END OF THE TEXT."
480  PRINT : PRINT "8.  FINALLY, REMEMBER THAT READABILITY"
490  PRINT "   ESTIMATES ARE ONLY ONE FACTOR IN DE-"
500  PRINT "   TERMINING THE DIFFICULTY OF WRITTEN"
510  PRINT "   MATERIAL.  CONTENT AND OTHER FACTORS"
520  PRINT "   ARE EQUALLY IMPORTANT."
530  PRINT : PRINT "   <ANY KEY TO START--TO END PROGRAM"
535  PRINT "   PRESS CONTROL-RESET>"
540  GET A$: IF A$ = "" THEN 540
800  HOME :S = 0:SL = 0:W = 0:LW = 0:R = 0
810  INPUT "TEXT TITLE (9 LETTERS OR LESS): ";T$: GOSUB 3000
820  GET L$: IF L$ = "" THEN 820
830  PRINT L$;:R = R + 1          .
840  IF L$ =  CHR$ (8) THEN L = L - 1: GOTO 820
850  IF L$ =  CHR$ (32) THEN W = W + 1:L = 0: GOTO 820
860  IF L$ =  CHR$ (13) THEN S = S + 1:SL = W / S: GOSUB 1000: GOSUB 3000

870  L = L + 1: IF L > 6 THEN LW = LW + 1:L =  - 30
880  IF R > 600 THEN R = 0: GOSUB 3000
890  GOTO 820
1000 RX = LW / S: IF RX < .2 THEN G = 1: RETURN
1010 IF RX < .5 THEN G = 2: RETURN
1020 IF RX < .8 THEN G = 3: RETURN
1030 IF RX < 1.3 THEN G = 4: RETURN
1040 IF RX < 1.8 THEN G = 5: RETURN
1050 IF RX < 2.4 THEN G = 6: RETURN
1060 IF RX < 3.0 THEN G = 7: RETURN
1070 IF RX < 3.7 THEN G = 8: RETURN
1080 IF RX < 4.5 THEN G = 9: RETURN
1090 IF RX < 5.3 THEN G = 10: RETURN
2000 IF RX < 6.2 THEN G = 11: RETURN
2010 IF RX < 7.2 THEN G = 12: RETURN
2020 IF RX > 7.2 THEN G = 13: RETURN
3000 HOME : PRINT "TEXT: ";T$
3010 PRINT "TOTAL NO. WORDS: ";W
3020 PRINT "NO. OF SENTENCES: ";S
3030 PRINT "NO. OF LONG WORDS: ";LW
3040 PRINT "AV. SENT. LENGTH: "; INT (10 * SL + .5) / 10
3050 IF G = 13 THEN  INVERSE : PRINT "GRADE LEVEL = COLLEGE": GOTO 3070
3060 INVERSE : PRINT "GRADE LEVEL: ";G
3070 PRINT : FOR X = 0 TO 39: PRINT "#";: NEXT X: NORMAL
3080 RETURN
```

FIGURE A.4 Printout of sentence-by-sentence assessment of readabilility using the RIX program.

```
###########################################DO YOU NEED INSTRUCTIONS? <Y OR N>
?N
TEXT TITLE (9 LETTERS OR LESS): 3 BEARS
TEXT: 3 BEARS
TOTAL NO. WORDS: 0
NO. OF SENTENCES: 0
NO. OF LONG WORDS: 0
AV. SENT. LENGTH: 0
GRADE LEVEL: 0


###########################################ONCE UPON A TIME THERE WERE THREE BEARS
WHO LIVED TOGETHER IN A HOUSE OF THEIR OWN IN A WOOD
TEXT: 3 BEARS
TOTAL NO. WORDS: 20
NO. OF SENTENCES: 1
NO. OF LONG WORDS: 1
AV. SENT. LENGTH: 20
GRADE LEVEL: 4


###########################################ONE OF THEM WAS A LITTLE WEE BEAR AND ON
E WAS A MIDDLE-SIZED BEAR AND THE OTHER WAS A GREAT BIG BEAR
TEXT: 3 BEARS
TOTAL NO. WORDS: 42
NO. OF SENTENCES: 2
NO. OF LONG WORDS: 2
AV. SENT. LENGTH: 21
GRADE LEVEL: 4


###########################################THEY HAD EACH A BOWL FOR THEIR PORRIDGE
A LITTLE BOWL FOR THE LITTLE WEE BEAR AND A MIDDLE-SIZED BOWL FOR THE MIDDLE-SIZ
ED BEAR AND A GREAT BOWL FOR THE BIG BEAR
TEXT: 3 BEARS
TOTAL NO. WORDS: 74
NO. OF SENTENCES: 3
NO. OF LONG WORDS: 5
AV. SENT. LENGTH: 24.7
GRADE LEVEL: 5


###########################################AND THEY EACH HAD A CHAIR TO SIT IN A LI
TTLE CHAIR FOR THE LITTLE WEE BEAR AND A MIDDLE-SIZED CHAIR FOR THE MIDDLE-SIZED
 BEAR AND A GREAT CHAIR FOR THE GREAT BIG BEAR
TEXT: 3 BEARS
TOTAL NO. WORDS: 108
NO. OF SENTENCES: 4
NO. OF LONG WORDS: 7
AV. SENT. LENGTH: 27
GRADE LEVEL: 5
```

References

Anderson, J. (1983). Lix and Rix: Variations on a little-known readability index. *Journal of Reading, 26*, 490–496.

Cullinan, B., & Fitzgerald, S. (1984 [Dec.]–1985 [Jan.]). Background information bulletin on the use of readability formulae. *Reading Today, 2* (3), 1.

Fry, E. B. (1989). Reading formulas—maligned but valid. *Journal of Reading, 32*, 292–297.

Kretschmer, J. C. (1984). Computerizing and comparing the Rix readability index. *Journal of Reading, 27*, 490–499.

APPENDIX B

Gathering Affective Information

The corrective reading program must develop learners who read and who feel good about themselves and their reading ability. To promote positive reading attitudes, a teacher must gather information about students' attitudes and self-concepts. Efforts to change negative attitudes or reinforce positive attitudes proceed once a student's attitudes toward reading are known. A teacher gleans some of this information from observing children for such behaviors as (1) choosing to read a book during free time; (2) requesting that a book be read aloud; (3) checking out books from the library; (4) finishing books started; and (5) talking about books read. In addition, paper-and-pencil techniques provide more detailed information as well as a record of this information for interpretation.

The Incomplete Sentence Projective Test (Boning & Boning, 1957) presented here allows each student to write (or provide orally) information regarding how they feel about the item in question (fig. B.1). Responses may be more honest if the teacher tells students the information will be used to provide materials they will enjoy. Any interpretation should be modified and verified by observations over time.

Before administering the incomplete sentences, decide whether oral or written responses are most appropriate. Directions for an oral administration might be: "I will begin a sentence with a few words and then stop. When I stop, you tell me the very first thing that you think of to finish the sentence. I will write down just what you say. Let's do a practice sentence. I think pizza tastes _____. Are you ready to begin?" Directions for a written administration might be: "Finish each sentence with the first idea that comes to your mind. Let's try the first one together."

In order to interpret the results the following areas have been identified by item number.

Overall attitudes and self-concept: 1, 3, 4, 5, 8, 9, 14, 16, 19, 20, 22, 25, 27, 29, 30, 33, 35, 36, 38, 42
Family relations: 6, 11, 26, 31
School attitudes: 7, 10, 12, 18, 21, 24
Reading process: 2, 28, 32, 34, 37, 40, 41 (Boning and Boning [1957] found that the most revealing responses were to item 40.)
Reading interest: 13, 15, 17, 23 (Use item 17 to get clues for helping direct children toward increased recreational reading.)

Responses to the overall attitudes and self-concept area are very important to evaluate. They often provide insight into a child's academic problems. Some supplementary questions for the reading process and reading interest areas follow.

FIGURE B.1 Incomplete sentence projective test. (From Boning, T., and Boning, R. "I'd Rather Read Than . . ." *Reading Teacher*, April 1957, p. 196. Reprinted with permission of the International Reading Association, Newark, Del.)

1. Today I feel ....
2. When I have to read, I ....
3. I get angry when ....
4. To be grown up ....
5. My idea of a good time is ....
6. I wish my parents knew ....
7. School is ....
8. I can't understand why ....
9. I feel bad when ....
10. I wish teachers ....
11. I wish my mother ....
12. Going to college ....
13. To me, books ....
14. People think I ....
15. I like to read about ....
16. On weekends I ....
17. I'd rather read than ....
18. To me, homework ....
19. I hope I'll never ....
20. I wish people wouldn't ....
21. When I finish high school ....
22. I'm afraid ....
23. Comic books ....
24. When I take my report card home ....
25. I am at my best when ....
26. Most brothers and sisters ....
27. I don't know how ....
28. When I read math ....
29. I feel proud when ....
30. The future looks ....
31. I wish my father ....
32. I like to read when ....
33. I would like to be ....
34. For me, studying ....
35. I often worry about ....
36. I wish I could ....
37. Reading science ....
38. I look forward to ....
39. I wish ....
40. I'd read more if ....
41. When I read out loud ....
42. My only regret ....

1. *Supplementary reading process questions:*
   a. Reading is . . .
   b. I cannot read when . . .
   c. When reading new words I . . .
   d. Reading out loud . . .
   e. I read better when . . .
2. *Supplementary reading interest questions:*
   a. I like reading about . . .
   b. I don't want to read about . . .
   c. The best thing about reading . . .
   d. I laugh when I read about . . .
   e. The best book I know about . . .

Reference

Boning, T., & Boning, R. (1957). I'd rather read than. . . . *The Reading Teacher, April,* 196–200.

APPENDIX C

Stages in Spelling Development

The stages represented here should be viewed from a developmental perspective; that is, a child's spelling is likely to change over time so that it resembles the examples seen at each stage. The following stages are more fully discussed in *The Beginnings of Writing*, pp. 100–104 by C. Temple, R. Nathan, N. Burris, and F. Temple.[1]

Stage 1: Prephonemic Spelling

Forms letters accurately but there is no match between letters and phonemes in words. Letter strings *look* like writing, but are not meaningful. At least the child recognizes that in some way letters represent language.

Examples: candy SCOZ]

went ƎN º C

(strings of letters) Crtog Dok

Stage 2: Early Phonemic Spelling

The phonetic principle has been discovered; however, letters for only one or two sounds in a word are generally written down. One or two phonemes in a word are represented with the rest perhaps omitted altogether or a random string of letters supplied.

Examples: My brother was crying all night.

MBRW KLN+

I like to go to the zoo.

I LK +o G++Z

---

[1] The majority of material in this appendix was taken from C. Temple, R. Nathan, N. Burris, and F. Temple, *The Beginnings of Writing*, pp. 100–107. Copyright © 1988 by Allyn and Bacon, Boston. Reprinted with permission.

Stage 3: Letter-Name Spelling

Once the concept of word has become stabilized, the child moves quickly to letter-name spelling. The phonemes of a word are represented by letters of the alphabet. The letters used show a relationship to the sound heard in the word. This is an important stage for reading; soon after a child produces letter-name spelling he or she begins to read.

Examples:

JacKiE
I had a apel For lungsh
(I had an apple for lunch.)

bob —
a boy so The man run Awa
(A boy saw the man run away.)

Stage 4: Transitional Spelling

Once a child begins reading, spelling begins to change as the child notices differences between letter-name spelling and the spelling of the words found in texts. Transitional spelling looks more like standard spelling (e.g., silent letters, unusual letter combinations), but the child is uncertain of when to use some of the standard spelling features. Transitional spellers have not yet integrated all the features of standard spelling. With more exposure to print and more opportunities to write, transitional spellers will become correct spellers.

Examples:

Can I go see a movee wif
My fren Susi sed her mom
sed oka win we go
(Can I go see a movie with my friend Susie? She said her Mom said oK. When can we go?)

Goin To The zoo is fun I
lik The linz and The big
burdz wit blue feters

(Going to the zoo is fun. I like the lions and the big birds with blue feathers.)

Assessing Spelling Development

In order to accurately assess spelling development, children must write words they have *not* been taught, or memorized. If a child is willing to write freely, then those words can be assessed for spelling development. However, some children are unwilling to write freely because they are not confident of their spelling ability. For these children a more structured approach is needed. The following is a recommended word list for spelling assessment from *The Beginnings of Writing*, pp. 105–107. Directions, scoring and a scored example are provided.

Directions

1. Explain to students they are not expected to know how to spell all of these words. You want to know how they *think* the words should be spelled. They should do their best, but this exercise will not be graded.
2. If they are stumped by a word, they should first try the beginning of the word, then the middle, then the end.
3. Teacher will read the word, then the sentence, then read the word again, twice. (Do not exaggerate any of the parts—just say the word normally.)

Spelling List

1. late — Kathy was late to school again today.
2. wind — The wind was loud last night.
3. shed — The wind blew down our shed.
4. geese — The geese fly over Texas every fall.
5. jumped — The frog jumped into the river.
6. yell — We can yell all we want on the playground.
7. chirped — The bird chirped when she saw a worm.
8. once — Jim rode his bike into a creek once.
9. learned — I learned to count in school.
10. shove — Don't shove your neighbor when you line up.
11. trained — I trained my dog to lie down and roll over.
12. year — Next year you'll have a new teacher.
13. shock — Electricity can shock you if you aren't careful.
14. stained — The ice cream spilled and stained my shirt.
15. chick — The egg cracked open and a baby chick climbed out.
16. drive — Jim's sister is learning how to drive.

Scoring

The words are scored according to what stage of spelling they reflect. The word is scored:

    0 if it is <u>prephonemic</u>.
    1 if it is <u>early</u> <u>phonemic</u>.
    2 if it is <u>letter</u> <u>name</u>.
    3 if it is <u>transitional</u>.
    4 if it is <u>correct</u>.

For example:

1. Lat	2
2. wnd	2
3. sead	3
4. Gees	3
5. Bout	2
6. u L	2
7. cutp	2
8. L os	2
9. Zud	2
10. suf	2
11. trad	2
12. t er	2
13. S ock	3
14. sad	2
15. cek	2
16. drif	2

The mode should be determined. The mode is the single score that occurred most often. (The average can be distorted by the possibility that the child had memorized some of the spellings.) In the example above, the mode is 2, meaning that most of the child's spellings were in the letter-name stage.

A Holistic Scoring System for Writing

Note: A holistic scoring system is a subjective judgment based on the assumption that more than one judge will give the same score to a piece of writing.

Qualities	Poor	Below Average	Average	Above Average	Excellent
Meaning	1	2	3	4	5
Authority	1	2	3	4	5
Voice	1	2	3	4	5
Development	1	2	3	4	5
Design	1	2	3	4	5
Clarity	1	2	3	4	5
Holistic Judgment	1	2	3	4	5

The column labeled "Qualities" in the above table is based on Donald Murray's list of "Qualities of Good Writing" found in Temple et al. (1988), p. 241. Simply put, each of these categories is described as follows:

Meaning. The writing must have content. It must say something. This is often not discovered until the whole piece is read.

Authority. The writing is filled with specific, accurate, honest information. The reader is convinced that the writer knows the subject.

Voice. The writer's voice must come through as an individual voice.

Development. The writer satisfies the reader's need for information. All the reader's questions are answered.

Design. The writing is well-organized. It is complete. It has form, structure, order, focus, and coherence.

Clarity. The writing is concise, and has a simplicity as reflected in the use of just the right words, the most effective verbs, the clearest phrase. The reader sees through the writer directly to the subject.

CHECKLIST OF TEACHER AND STUDENT WRITING PROCESS BEHAVIORS

Teachers need to evaluate their own performance as well as their students' when it comes to the writing process. If students are not provided the appropriate opportunities to develop in composing good writing, it is not fair to evaluate them in this area. (The following lists are adapted from Temple, et al., 1988, p. 246.)

Teacher Behaviors

	Yes	No
1. Writes while students write during writing time.	——	——
2. Shares evolving drafts with class.	——	——
3. Keeps track of student's progress systematically.	——	——
4. Provides publishing opportunities for students.	——	——
5. Makes sure students share their work with others.	——	——
6. Seeks out support materials to help students write.	——	——
7. Has a literature component in the writing program.	——	——
8. Holds teacher-student writing conferences.	——	——
9. Periodically shows students their progress as writers.	——	——

Student Behaviors

Name: _____

1. Writes during designated time.

   Almost always   Sometimes   Rarely

2. Uses constructive strategies for getting drafts started (e.g., talks about topic with others, reads about the topic, brainstorms ideas, organizes ideas such as with a story map, generates outlines, generates questions, considers audience, etc).

   Almost always   Sometimes   Rarely

3. Is willing to help classmates by listening to their drafts.

   Almost always   Sometimes   Rarely

4. Realizes other students may have meaningful suggestions.

   Almost always   Sometimes   Rarely

5. Is growing in understanding of the difference between revising (e.g., uses invented spellings or leaves unknown words blank, pauses, rereads, focuses on meaning first) and editing (e.g., inserts, deletes, changes, reorganizes to clarify and improve writing, proofreads, consults peers, dictionary, thesaurus, or other resources).

   Almost always   Sometimes   Rarely

6. Uses support systems available in the classroom (e.g., personal dictionaries, spelling books, dictionaries, classroom library, thesaurus).

   Almost always   Sometimes   Rarely

7. Is learning to view revision as part of the writing process.

   Yes   No

8. Is an active participant during sharing time (e.g., makes work available for others to read by publishing it, reads a finished piece orally, exchanges written works with peers for silent reading and comments).

   Almost always   Sometimes   Rarely

APPENDIX E

Johnson's Basic Vocabulary for Beginning Readers

Johnson's First-Grade Words

a	day	I	off	table
above	days	if	old	than
across	did	I'm	one	that
after	didn't	in	open	the
again	do	into	or	then
air	don't	is	out	there
all	door	it	over	these
am	down	its		they
American		it's	past	think
and	end		play	this
are		just	point	those
art	feet		put	three
as	find	keep		time
ask	first	kind	really	to
at	five		red	today
	for	let	right	too
back	four	like	room	took
be		little	run	top
before	gave	look		two
behind	get	love	said	
big	girl		saw	under
black	give	make	school	up
book	go	making	see	
boy	God	man	seen	very
but	going	may	she	
	gone	me	short	want
came	good	men	six	wanted
can	got	miss	so	was
car		money	some	way
children	had	more	something	we
come	hand	most	soon	well
could	hard	mother	still	went
	has	Mr.		what
	have	must		when
	he	my		where
	help			which
	her	name		who
	here	never		why
	high	new		will
	him	night		with
	his	no		work
	home	not		
	house	now		year
	how			years
				yet
				you
				your

Johnson's Second-Grade Words

able	different	last	real	water
about	does	leave	road	were
almost	done	left		west
alone		light	same	while
already	each	long	say	whole
always	early		says	whose
America	enough	made	set	wife
an	even	many	should	women
another	ever	mean	show	world
any	every	might	small	would
around	eyes	morning	sometimes	
away		Mrs.	sound	
	face	much	started	
because	far	music	street	
been	feel		sure	
believe	found	need		
best	from	next	take	
better	front	nothing	tell	
between	full	number	their	
board		them		
both	great	of	thing	
bought	group	office	things	
by		on	thought	
	hands	only	through	
called	having	other	together	
change	head	our	told	
church	heard	outside	town	
city		own	turn	
close	idea			
company		part	until	
cut	knew	party	us	
	know	people	use	
		place	used	
		plan		
		present		

APPENDIX F

Useful Phonics Generalizations

1. The "c rule." When *c* comes just before *a, o,* or *u,* it usually has the *hard* sound heard in cat, cot, and cut. Otherwise, it usually has the *soft* sound heard in cent, city, and bicycle.

2. The "g rule." When *g* comes at the end of words or just before *a, o,* or *u,* it usually has the *hard* sound heard in tag, game, go, and gush. Otherwise, it usually has the *soft* sound heard in gem, giant, and gym.

3. The VC pattern. This pattern is seen in words such as *an, can, candy,* and *dinner.* As a verbal generalization it might be stated as follows: In either a word or syllable, a single vowel letter followed by a consonant letter, digraph, or blend usually represents a short vowel sound. (Note that C stands for either a letter, digraph, or blend, e.g., bat, bath, bask.)

4. The VV pattern. This pattern is seen in words such as *eat, beater, peach, see, bait, float,* and *play.* As a verbal generalization it might be stated like this: In a word or syllable containing a vowel digraph, the first letter in the digraph usually represents the long vowel sound and the second letter is usually silent. According to Clymer, this generalization is quite reliable for *ee, oa,* and *ay* (fee, coat, tray) and works about two-thirds of the time for *ea* and *ai* (seat, bait), but is not reliable for other vowel digraphs such as ei, ie, or oo, or diphthongs oi, oy, ou, and ow.

5. The VCE (final e) pattern. This pattern is seen in words such as *ice, nice, ate, plate, paste, flute, vote,* and *clothe.* As a generalization it might be stated this way: In one-syllable words containing two vowel letters, one of which is a final *e,* the first vowel letter usually represents a long vowel sound, and the *e* is silent. If the vowel is not long, try the short sound.

6. The CV pattern. This pattern is seen in one-syllable words such as *he, she, go, my, cry, hotel, going,* and *flying.* As a generalization, it might be stated this way: When there is only one vowel letter in a word or syllable and it comes at the end of the word or syllable, it usually represents the long vowel sound.

7. The "r rule." This rule applies to words like *far, fare, fair, girl, fur, her,* and *here.* As a generalization it might be stated as follows: The letter r usually modifies the short or long sound of the preceding vowel letter. (See May and Eliot's *To Help Children Read,* 1978, p. 38.)

8. There are basically three syllabication rules worth knowing. These are represented by the *VCCV, VCV,* and the *Cle* patterns. For the VCCV pattern, the rule is to divide between the two consonants. This pattern is represented in words such as *blanket, happy,* and *represent.* For the VCV pattern, the rule is to divide before, or

after the consonant. Words representing this pattern are *robot, robin, divide,* and *before.* For the last pattern, Cle, the rule is to divide before the consonant. Words representing this pattern are *Bible, uncle, table,* and *example.*

(*Note:* Phonics generalizations should be taught inductively. Known words in a meaningful context should be used to illustrate a letter-sound relationship. When teaching something new, use words familiar to children. To learn whether children can apply what has been taught, use words they cannot read. Practice phonics in context whenever possible. Once a generalization has been taught inductively, concentrate on unknown words in the context of a sentence or brief passage.)

References

Bailey, M. H. (1967). The utility of phonic generalizations in grade one through six. *The Reading Teacher, 20,* 413–418.

Burmeister, L. E. (1968). Usefulness of phonic generalizations. *The Reading Teacher, 21,* 349–356.

Clymer, T. L. (1963). The utility of phonic generalizations in the primary grades. *The Reading Teacher, 16,* 252–258.

Emans, R. (1967). The usefulness of phonic generalizations above the primary grades. *The Reading Teacher, 20,* 419–425.

Books to Build Self-Esteem in Black Children*

There is a disproportionate number of minority students, a large number of which are black Americans, who do not learn to read and write successfully (Ogbu, 1987). Additionally, an unusually high percentage of minorities are found in special education programs compared to the number of minority students in the general school population (Ross, DeYoung, & Cohen, 1977). The reasons why this is so are complex. But part of the reason involves a historical lack of role models within the cultural group who have improved their lot in life as a result of academic success (Ogbu, 1987). Schools alone cannot change this condition; however, schools can make an effort to provide proof that academic success *can* make a difference in one's life. One way of providing this proof is through literature. The following bibliography is intended for teachers of all grade levels. The books mentioned can either be read *by* students or read *to* students.

Picture Books

Adoff, Arnold. (1971). *MA n DA LA*. New York: Harper. (Also: *Black is brown is tan*, 1973)

Agard, John. (1989). *The calypso alphabet*. New York: Henry Holt & Co.

Anderson, Lonzo. (1974). *The day the hurricane happened*. New York: Scribners. (Also: *Izzard*, 1973)

Appiah, Sonia. (1988). *Amoko and Efua bear*. New York: Macmillan.

Baldwin, Anne Norris. (1972). *Sunflowers for Tina*. New York: Four Winds.

Barrett, Joyce Durham. (1989). *Willie's not the hugging kind*. New York: Harper.

Buffett, Jimmy (1988). *Jolly mon*. San Diego, CA: Harcourt.

Bunting, Eve. (1988). *How many days to America?* New York: Clarion.

Caines, Jeanette. (1980). *Window wishing*. New York: Harper. (Also: *Abby*, 1973; *Daddy*, 1977; *Just us women*, 1982)

Clifton, Lucille. (1973). *All us come cross the water*. New York: Holt. (Also: *My brother fine with me*, 1975)

---

*The bibliography contained in this appendix was prepared by Coleen C. Salley, a colleague of the author at the University of New Orleans.

Clifton, Lucille. (1977). *Amifika*. New York: Dutton. (Also: *The boy who didn't believe in spring*, 1973; *Good says Jerome*, 1973; *My friend Jacob*, 1980)

Cohen, Miriam. (1977). *When will I read?* New York: Greenwillow. (Also: *The new teacher, 1974; Lost in the museum*, 1979; *First grade takes a test*, 1983; *See you tomorrow, Charles*, 1983 and others in this series)

Craft, Ruth. (1989). *The day of the rainbow*. Minneapolis, MN: Viking.

Crews, Donald. (1978). *Freight train*. New York: Greenwillow. (Also: *Parade*, 1983; *Carousel*, 1982; *School bus*, 1984; *Bicycle race*, 1985)

Cummings, Pat. (1986). *C.L.O.U.D.S.* New York: Lothrop (Also: *Jimmy Lee did it*, 1985)

Dale, Penny. (1987). *Bet you can't*. Philadelphia, PA: Lippincott.

Desbarats, Peter. (1968). *Gabrielle & Selena*. San Diego, CA: Harcourt.

Deveaux, Alexis. (1973). *Na-ni*. New York: Harper.

Dobrin, Arnold. (1971). *Scat!* New York: Four Winds.

Dragonwagon, Crescent. (1986). *Half a moon and one whole star*. New York: Macmillan. (Also: *Home place*, 1990)

Feelings, Muriel. (1974). *Jambo means hello*. New York: Dial. (Also: *Moja means one*, 1977)

Fife, Dale. (1971). *Adam's ABC*. New York: Coward.

Flournoy, Valerie. (1980). *The twins strike back*. New York: Dial. (Also: *The patchwork quilt*, 1985)

Fraser, Kathleen, & Levy, Miriam. (1971). *Adam's World: San Francisco*. Niles, IL: Whitman.

Freeman, Don. (1968). *Corduroy*. Minneapolis, MN: Viking. (Also: *A pocket for Corduroy*, 1978)

George, Jean Craighead. (1978). *The Wentletrap trap*. New York: Dutton.

Gray, Genevieve. (1974). *Send Wendall*. New York: McGraw.

Greenberg, Polly. (1968). *Oh Lord, I wish I was a buzzard*. New York: Macmillan.

Greenfield, Eloise. (1974). *She come bringing me that little baby girl*. Philadelphia, PA: Lippincott.

Greenfield, Eloise. (1976). *First pink light*. New York: Crowell.

Greenfield, Eloise. (1980). *Grandmama's joy*. New York: Collins.

Greenfield, Eloise. (1988). *Grandpa's face*. New York: Philomel.

Grifalconi, Ann. (1987). *Darkness and the butterfly*. Boston: Little, Brown.

Hall, Carole. (1977). *I been there*. New York: Doubleday.

Hamilton, Virginia. (1980). *Jadu*. New York: Greenwillow.

Havill, Juanita. (1986). *Jamaica's find*. Boston: Houghton. (Also: *Jamaica tag-along*, 1989)

Hill, Elizabeth Starr. (1967). *Evan's corner*. New York: Holt.

Howard, Elizabeth Fitzgerald. (1989). *The train to Lulu's*. New York: Bradbury. (Also: *Chita's Christmas tree*, 1989)

Isadora, Rachel. (1979). *Ben's trumpet*. New York: Greenwillow.

Johnson, Angela. (1989). *Tell me a story, Mama*. New York: Orchard.

Johnson, Herschel. (1989). *A visit to the country*. New York: Harper.

Keats, Ezra Jack. (1969). *Goggles*. New York: Macmillan. (Also: *Snowy day*, 1962; *Hi, cat!*, 1970; *Pet show*, 1972 and others in this series)

LaFarge, Phyllis. (1973). *Joanna runs away*. New York: Holt.

Lessac, Frame. (1989). *Caribbean canvas*. Philadelphia, PA: Lippincott.

Lewin, Hugh. (1984). *Jafta-the journey*. Minneapolis, MN: Carolrhoda. (Also: *The wedding*, 1983; *Jafta's father*, 1983; *Jafta's mother*, 1983; *The journey*, 1984)

Lexau, Joan. (1964). *Benjie*. New York: Dial. (Also: *Benjie on his own*, 1970; *Me day*, 1971)

Little, Lessie Jones, & Greenfield, Eloise. (1978). *I can do it myself*. New York: Crowell.

Lyon, George Ella. (1989). *Together*. New York: Orchard.

Mayer, Mercer. (1976). *Liza Lou & the Yeller Belly Swamp*. New York: Parents.

McKissack, Patricia C. (1989). *Nettie Jo's friends*. New York: Knopf. (Also: *Mirandy and brother wind*, 1988; *Flossie and the fox*, 1987)

Mendez, Phil. (1989). *The black snowman*. New York: Scholastic.

Miles, Miska. (1965). *Mississippi possum*. Boston: Little, Brown.

Milgram, Mary. (1978). *Brothers are all the same*. New York: Dutton.

Moss, Marissa. (1990). *Regina's big mistake*. Boston: Houghton Mifflin.

Musgrove, Margaret. (1976). *Ashanti to Zulu*. New York: Dial.

Myers, Walter Dean. (1984). *Mr. Monkey and the gotcha bird*. New York: Delacorte.

Myers, Walter Dean. (1972). *The dragon takes a wife*. New York: Bobbs.

Ness, Evaline. (1963). *Josefina February*. New York: Scribner.

Ormsby, Virginia. (1971). *Twenty-one children plus ten*. Philadelphia, PA: Lippincott.

Otey, Mimi. (1990). *Daddy has a pair of striped shorts*. New York: Farrar.

Pomerantz, Charlotte. (1989). *The chalk doll*. Philadelphia, PA: Lippincott.

Prather, Ray. (1974). *No trespassing*. New York: Macmillan. (Also: *Anthony and Sabrina*, 1973)

Prather, Ray. (1975). *New neighbors*. New York: McGraw.

Price, Leontyne. (1990). *Aida*. San Diego, CA: Harcourt, Brace.

Ross, Dave. (1980). *A book of hugs*. New York: Crowell.

Samuels, Vyanne. (1988). *Carry go bring come*. New York: Four Winds.

San Souci, Robert. (1989). *The boy and the ghost*. New York: Simon and Schuster.

San Souci, Robert. (1989). *The talking eggs*. New York: Dial.

Schroeder, Alan. (1989). *Ragtime Tumpie*. Boston: Little, Brown.

Scott, Ann Herbert. (1967). *Sam*. New York: McGraw.

Seed, Jenny. (1989). *Ntombi's song*. New York: Harper.

Sleator, William. (1979). *Once, said Darlene*. New York: Dutton.

Sonneborn, Ruth. (1971). *I love Gram*. Minneapolis, MN: Viking.

Steptoe, John. (1969). *Stevie*. New York: Harper. (Also: *Train ride*, 1969; *Uptown*, 1969)

Steptoe, John. (1980). *Daddy is a monster . . . sometimes*. Philadelphia, PA: Lippincott.

Stolz, Mary. (1988). *Storm in the night*. New York: Harper.

Thomas, Ianthe. (1979). *Hi, Mrs. Mallory!* New York: Harper. (Also: *Lordy, Aunt Hattie*, 1973; *My street's a morning cool street*, 1976; *Walk home tired, Billy Jenkins*, 1974)

Tusa, Tricia. (1987). *Maebelle's suitcase*. New York: Macmillan.

Udry, Janice May. (1968). *What Mary Jo wanted*. New York: Whitman. (Also: *What Mary Jo shared*, 1966)

Walter, Mildred Pitts. (1983). *My mama needs me*. New York: Lothrop. (Also: *Brother to the wind*, 1985)

Walter, Mildred Pitts. (1980). *Ty's one-man-band*. New York: Four Winds.

Ward, Leila. (1978). *I am eyes: Ni Macho*. New York: Greenwillow.

Whiteside, Karen. (1980). *Brother Mouky and the falling sun*. New York: Harper.

Williams, Ver B. (1986). *Cherries and cherry pits*. New York: Greenwillow.

Winter, Jeanette. (1988). *Following the drinking gourd*. New York: Knopf.

Easy Fiction

Agle, Nan Hayden. (1976). *Joe Bean*. San Francisco, CA: Seabury.

Anderson, Joan. (1988). *A Williamsburg household*. New York: Clarion.

Baldwin, James. (1976). *Little man little man: A story of childhood*. New York: Dial.

Blue, Ross. (1969). *A quiet place*. New York: Watts.

Bontemps, Arna. (1970). *Mr. Kelso's lion*. Philadelphia, PA: Lippincott.

Caines, Jeanette. (1988). *I need a lunch box*. New York: Harper.

Cameron, Ann. (1981). *The stories Julian tells*. New York: Knopf. (Also: *More stories Julian tells*, 1986)

Claverie, Jean. (1990). *Little Lou*. New York: Stewart Talbori.

Clymer, Eleanor. (1971). *The house on the mountain*. New York: Dutton.

Cone, Molly. (1967). *The other side of the fence*. Boston: Houghton.

Cushman, Jerome. (1970). *Tom B. and the joyful noise*. Philadelphia, PA: Westminster.

Feelings, Muriel. (1970). *Zamani goes to market*. San Francisco, CA: Seabury.

Greenfield, Eloise. (1978). *Talk about a family*. Philadelphia, PA: Lippincott.

Grimes, Nikki. (1977). *Growin'*. New York: Dial.

Hamilton, Virginia. (1973). *Time-ago lost: More tales of Jahdu*. New York: Macmillan. (Also: *Zeely*, 1967)

Hamilton, Virginia. (1989). *The Bells of Christmas*. San Diego, CA: Harcourt, Brace.

Hegwook, Mamie. (1975). *My friend fish*. New York: Holt.

Konigsburg, E. L. (1971). *Altogether, one at a time*. New York: Atheneum.

Mathis, Sharon Bell. (1975). *The hundred penny box*. Minneapolis, MN: Viking.

Shearer, John. (1981). *Billy Jo Jive and the walkie-talkie caper*. New York: Delacorte.

Taylor, Mildred D. (1975). *Song of the trees*. New York: Dial. (Also: *The friendship*, 1987; *The gold Cadillac*, 1987)

Turner, Ann. (1987). *Nettie's trip south*. New York: Macmillan.

Walker, Alice. (1988). *To hell with dying*. San Diego, CA: Harcourt.

Fiction

Alexander, Anne. (1974). *Trouble on Treat Street*. New York: Atheneum.

Anker, Charlotte. (1975). *Last night I saw Andromeda*. New York: Walck.

Bacon, Martha. (1968). *Sophia Scrooby preserved*. Boston: Little, Brown.

Carlson, Natalie Savage. (1963). *Marchers for the dream*. New York: Harper. (Also: *The empty schoolhouse*, 1965)

Chesnutt, Charles W. (1973). *Conjure tales*. New York: Dutton.

Cohen, Barbara. (1974). *Thank you, Jackie Robinson*. New York: Lothrop.

Colea, Robert. (1972). *Saving face*. Boston: Little, Brown.

Collidge, Olivia. (1970). *Come by here*. Boston: Houghton.

Detrevino, Elizabeth Boston. (1965). *I, Juan de Pareja*. New York: Farrar.

Edwards, Pat. (1988). *Little John and Plutie*. Boston: Houghton.

Fitzhugh, Louise. (1974). *Nobody's family is going to change*. New York: Farrar.

Fox, Paula. (1973). *The slave dancer*. New York: Bradbury.

Graham, Lorenz. (1966). *I, Momolu*. New York: Crowell.

Greene, Bette. (1977). *Philip Hall likes me, I reckon maybe*. New York: Dial. (Also: *Get on out of here, Philip Hall*, 1981)

Hamilton, Virginia. (1968). *The house of Dies Drear*. New York: Macmillan.

Hamilton, Virginia. (1983). *Willie Bea and the time the Martians landed*. New York: Greenwillow.

Hamilton, Virginia. (1990). *Cousins*. New York: Putnam.

Hentoff, Nat. (1981). *Does this school have capital punishment?* New York: Delacorte.

Hobson, Sam. (1976). *The lion of Kalahari*. New York: Greenwillow.

Hopkins, Lila. (1989). *Talking turkey*. New York: Watts. (Also: *Eating crow*, 1988)

Hunt, Irene. (1977). *William*. New York: Scribners.

Killens, John. (1975). *A man ain't nothin' but a man*. Boston: Little, Brown.

Konigsburg, E. L. (1969). *Jennifer, Hecata, Macbeth, William McKinley and Me, Elizabeth*. New York: Atheneum.

Micklish, Rital. (1972). *Sugar bee*. New York: Delacorte.

Moore, Emily. (1988). *Whose side are you on?* New York: Farrar.

Myers, Walter Dean. (1980). *The black pearl and the ghost*. Minneapolis, MN: Viking. (Also: *The golden serpent*, 1980)

Myers, Walter Dean. (1983). *Tales of a dead king*. New York: Morrow.

Myers, Walter Dean. (1985). *Adventures in Grenada*. New York: Penguin. (Also: *Hidden shrine*, 1985; *Ambush in the Amazon*, 1986; *Duel in the desert*, 1986)

O'Dell, Scott. (1989). *My name is not Angelica*. Boston: Houghton.

Paterson, Katherine. (1978). *The great Gilly Hopkins*. New York: Crowell.

Raskin, Ellen. (1978). *The westing game*. New York: Dutton.

Roth, Arthur. (1976). *Two for survival*. New York: Scribners.

Schlee, Ann. (1973). *The guns of darkness*. New York: Atheneum.

Smith, K. (1989). *Skeeter*. Boston: Houghton.

Smucker, Barbara. (1977). *Runaway to freedom*. New York: Harper.

Springer, Nancy. (1989). *They're all named wildfire*. New York: Atheneum.

Stolz, Mary. (1963). *A wonderful, terrible time*. New York: Harper.

Tate, Eleanora. (1980). *Just overnight guest*. New York: Dial.

Taylor, Mildred. (1976). *Roll of thunder hear my cry*. New York: Dial. (Also: *Let the circle be unbroken*, 1981)

Taylor, Theodore. (1969). *The cay.* New York: Doubleday.

Walter, Mildred Pitts. (1985). *Trouble's child.* New York: Lothrop.

Wilson, Johnneice Marshall. (1988). *Oh, brother.* New York: Scholastic.

Yarbrough, Camille. (1989). *The shimmershine queens.* New York: Putnam.

Folktales

Aardema, Verna. (1973). *Behind the back of the mountain.* New York: Dial. (Also: *Whose in rabbit's house?* 1977; *Why mosquitos buzz in people's ears,* 1975; *Bringing the rain to Kapiti Plain,* 1981; *What's so funny, Ketu?* 1982; *Oh, Kojo! How could you?* 1984; *Princess Gorilla and a new kind of water,* 1988; *Rabbit make a monkey of lion,* 1989)

Bang, Molly Garrett. (1976). *Wiley & the hairy man.* New York: Macmillan.

Berry, James. (1989). *Spiderman Anancy.* New York: Holt.

Bryan, Ashley. (1989). *Turtle knows your name.* New York: Atheneum. (Also: *The cat's purr,* 1985; *Lion and the ostrich chicks, and other African tales,* 1986; *The dancing granny,* 1987; *Sh-Ko and his eight wicked brothers,* 1988)

Courlander, Harold. (1947). *Cow-tail switch & other West African stories.* New York: Holt.

Dayrell, Elphistone. (1968). *Why the sun & the moon live in the sky.* Boston: Houghton.

Dee, Ruby. (1988). *Two ways to count to ten.* New York: Holt.

Diop, Birago. (1981). *Mother crocodile.* New York: Delacorte.

Elkin, Benjamin. (1968). *Such is the way of the world.* New York: Parents.

Graham, Lorenz. (1946). *David he no fear.* Crowell. (Also: *Hongry catch the foolish boy,* 1946)

Grifalconi, Ann. (1986). *The village of round and square houses.* Boston: Little, Brown.

Guirma, Fredric. (1970). *Princess of the full moon.* New York: Macmillan.

Guirma, Fredric. (1971). *Tales of Mogho.* New York: Macmillan.

Haley, Gail. (1970). *A story, a story.* New York: Atheneum.

Hamilton, Virginia. (1988). *In the beginning.* San Diego, CA: Harcourt. (Also: *The dark way,* 1990)

Hamilton, Virginia. (1985). *The people could fly.* New York: Knopf.

Harris, Joel Chandler. (1986). *The adventures of Brer Rabbit.* (Adapted by Van Dyke Parks.) San Diego, CA: Harcourt. (Also: *Jump again!* 1987)

Helfman, Elizabeth. (1971). *The bushmen and their stories.* San Francisco, CA: Seabury.

Jaquith, Priscilla. (1981). *Bo Rabbit smart for true.* New York: Philomel.

Keats, Jack Ezra. (1965). *John Henry.* New York: Pantheon.

Kirn, Ann. (1968). *Beeswax catches a thief.* New York: Norton.

Korty, Carol. (1969). *Plays from African folktales.* New York: Scribners.

Lester, Julius. (1972). *The knee-high man & other tales.* New York: Dial. (Also: *The tales of Uncle Remus,* 1987; *More tales of Uncle Remus,* 1988)

Lester, Julius. (1989). *How many spots does a leopard have?* New York: Scholastic.

McDermott, Gerald. (1973). *The magic tree.* New York: Holt. (Also: *Anansi the spider,* 1972)

Prather, Ray. (1978). *The ostrich girl.* New York: Scribners.

Rose, Anne. (1976). *Akimba & the magic cow.* New York: Four Winds.

San Souci, Robert. (1989). *The talking eggs.* New York: Dial.

Seeger, Pete. (1986). *Abiyoyo*. New York: Macmillan.

Steptoe, John. (1987). *Mufaro's beautiful daughters*. New York: Dial.

Tadjo, Veronique. (1989). *Lord of the dance*. Philadelphia, PA: Lippincott.

Walker, Barbara. (1990). *The dancing palm tree: And other Nigerian folktales*. Lubbock, TX: Texas Tech University.

Walkstein, Diane. (1973). *The cool ride in the sky*. New York: Knopf.

Poetry

Adoff, Arnold. (1976). *Big sister tells me that I'm black*. New York: Holt.

Adoff, Arnold. (1974). *My black me, A beginning book of black poetry*. New York: Dutton.

Adoff, Arnold. (1978). *Where wild Willie*. New York: Harper.

Agard, John. (1989). *The Calypso alphabet*. New York: Holt.

Bontemps, Arna. (1941). *Golden slippers*. New York: Harper.

Brooks, Gwendolyn. (1956). *Bronzeville boys & girls*. New York: Harper.

Bryan, Ashley. (1974). *Walk together children*. New York: Atheneum.

Clifton, Lucille. (1970). *Some of the days of Everett Anderson*. New York: Holt. (Also: *Everett Anderson's good-bye*, 1983, and others in this series)

Feelings, Tom. (1981). *Daydreamers*. New York: Dial.

Fields, Julia. (1988). *The green lion of Zion Street*. New York: Macmillan.

Giovanni, Nikki. (1971). *Spin a soft Black song*. New York: Hill and Wang.

Greenfield, Eloise. (1978). *Honey, I love and other love poems*. New York: Crowell.

Greenfield, Eloise. (1988). *Under the Sunday tree*. (Illus. Amos Ferguson.) New York: Harper.

Grimes, Nikki. (1978). *Something on my mind*. New York: Dial.

Hopkins, Lee Bennett. (1970). *City talk*. New York: Knopf. (Also: *On our way: Poems & pride & love*, 1974)

Hopkins, Lee Bennett. (1970). *The city spreads its wings*. New York: Watts.

Hopkins, Lee Bennett. (1970). *This street's for me!* New York: Crown.

Hughes, Langston. (1969). *Don't you turn back*. New York: Knopf.

Johnson, James Weldon & J. Rosamond. (1970). *Lift every voice & sing*. Wheeling, IL: Hawthorne.

Lawrence, Jacob. (1968). *Harriet and the promised land*. New York: Simon and Schuster.

Lessac, Frame. (1989). *Caribbean canvas*. Philadelphia, PA: Lippincott.

Little, Lessie Jones. (1988). *Children of long ago*. New York: Philomel.

Mendoza, George. (1971). *And I must hurry for the sea is coming in*. Englewood Cliffs, NJ: Prentice-Hall.

Rollins, Charlemae. (1963). *Christmas Gif'*. Chicago, IL: Follett.

Tadjo, Veronique. (1989). *Lord of the dance*. Philadelphia, PA: Lippincott.

Biography

Adler, David A. (1989). *A picture book of Martin Luther King, Jr.* New York: Holiday House. (Also: *Jackie Robinson* [Illus. Robert Casilla], 1989)

Alexander, Rae Pace, and Julius Lester. (1970). *Young and Black in America.* New York: Random House.

Brenner, Barbara. (1970). *Wagon wheels.* New York: Harper.

Burchard, S. H. (1980). *Earl Campbell.* San Diego, CA: Harcourt.

Davidson, Margaret. (1986). *I have a dream: The story of Martin Luther King.* New York: Scholastic.

Feelings, Tom. (1972). *Black pilgrimage.* New York: Lothrop.

Gault, Frank & Clare. (1975). *Pelé the king of soccer.* New York: Walker.

Gibson, Althea. (1958). *I always wanted to be somebody.* New York: Harper.

Gordy, Berry, Sr. (1979). *Movin' up.* New York: Harper.

Greenfield, Eloise. (1978). *Mary McLeod Bethune.* New York: Crowell.

Greenfield, Eloise, & Little, Lessie Jones. (1979). *Childtimes.* New York: Crowell.

Hamilton, Virginia. (1972). *W. E. B. Dubois: A biography.* New York: Crowell.

Haskins, James. (1979). *Andrew Young: Man with a mission.* New York: Lothrop.

Heidish, Marcy. (1976). *A woman called Moses.* Boston: Houghton.

Jackson, Jesse. (1974). *Make a joyful noise unto the Lord!: The life of Mahalia Jackson.* New York: Crowell.

Johnston, Brenda. (1974). *Between the devil and the sea: The life of James Foster.* San Diego, CA: Harcourt.

Jones, Margaret. (1968). *Martin Luther King, Jr.* Chicago: Children's Press.

McKissack, Patricia C. (1984). *Martin Luther King, Jr.: A man to remember.* Chicago: Children's Press. (Also: *Michael Jackson: Superstar*, 1984)

McKissack, Patricia C. (1989). *Jesse Jackson.* New York: Scholastic. (Also: *Mary McLeod Bethune: A great American educator*, 1987)

Moore, Carman. (1969). *Somebody's angel child: The story of Bessie Smith.* New York: Crowell.

Northup, Solomon. (1971). *In chains to Louisiana.* New York: Dutton.

Shapiro, Milton. (1969). *Jackie Robinson of the Brooklyn Dodgers.* New York: Simon & Schuster.

Smith, Senator Margaret Chase. (1968). *Gallant Women.* New York: McGraw-Hill.

Stanley, Diane. (1988). *Shaka: King of the Zulus.* New York: Morrow.

Vass, George. (1979). *Reggie Jackson from superstar to candy bar.* Chicago: Children's Press.

White, Florence. (1975). *Malcolm X.* Champaign, IL: Garrad.

Young, B. E. (1974). *The picture story of Hank Aaron.* Englewood Cliffs, NJ: Messner.

Ziegler, Sandra. (1978). *Bill Cosby coming at you.* Chicago: Children's Press.

References

Ogbu, J. U. (1987). Opportunity structure, cultural boundaries, and literacy. In J. A. Langer (Ed.), *Language, literacy, and culture: Issues of society and schooling* (pp. 149–177). Norwood, NJ: Ablex.

Ross, S. L., DeYoung, H. G., & Cohen, J. S. (1977). Confrontation: Special education placement and the law. In R. E. Schmid, J. Moneypenny, & R. Johnston (Eds.), *Contemporary issues in special education* (pp. 26–28). New York: McGraw-Hill.

Index